SEX MONEY MURDER

SEX

MONEY

MURDER

A Story of Crack, Blood, and Betrayal

JONATHAN GREEN

W. W. NORTON & COMPANY
Independent Publishers Since 1923
New York London

For information about permission to reproduce selections from this book, write to
Permissions, W. W. Norton & Company, Inc., 500 Fifth Avenue, New York, NY 10110

For information about special discounts for bulk purchases, please contact
W. W. Norton Special Sales at specialsales@wwnorton.com or 800-233-4830

Manufacturing by LSC Communications Harrisonburg
Book design by Lovedog Studio
Production manager: Lauren Abbate

Library of Congress Cataloging-in-Publication Data

Names: Green, Jonathan (Journalist)
Title: Sex Money Murder : a story of crack, blood, and betrayal /
Jonathan Green.
Description: First edition. | New York : W.W. Norton & Company, [2018] |
Includes bibliographical references and index.
Identifiers: LCCN 2017061642 | ISBN 9780393244489 (hardcover)
Subjects: LCSH: Gangs—New York (State)—New York—Case studies. | Drug
traffic—New York (State)—New York—Case studies. | Crack (Drug)—New York
(State)—New York—Case studies. | Murder—New York (State)—New York—Case
studies. | Crime—New York (State)—New York—Case studies.
Classification: LCC HV6439.U7 N4438 2018 | DDC 364.106/609747109048—dc23
LC record available at https://lccn.loc.gov/2017061642

W. W. Norton & Company, Inc., 500 Fifth Avenue, New York, N.Y. 10110
www.wwnorton.com

W. W. Norton & Company Ltd., 15 Carlisle Street, London W1D 3BS

1 2 3 4 5 6 7 8 9 0

For K, G, and C

Contents

Act III
ULTRAVIOLENCE: THE FALL OF SEX MONEY MURDER

Any city, however small, is in fact divided into two,
one the city of the poor, the other of the rich;
these are at war with one another.

—Plato, *Commonwealth*, book IV

Author's Note

The founding members of the gang Sex Money Murder are masters of the art of deception and use violence to propel themselves to the top of a hierarchy. So there are inherent challenges for a journalist seeking to document the truth in their story. Hundreds of hours of digitally recorded interviews with all four of my main sources are bolstered by court transcripts, Freedom of Information Act (FOIA) requests, document requests from the New York City Police Department and the Bronx district attorney, and hundreds of subsidiary interviews. My methodology in re-creating scenes of dialogue or action, some of which took place twenty years ago or more, was to buttress face-to-face interviews with scores of follow-up calls or texts to my sources to learn, for example, a particular facial expression, or the music that may have been playing at the time, or any other small observations that enabled me to render these scenes with greater accuracy and detail. Notwithstanding, the human memory is inaccurate and often subjective. Wherever possible I have tried to corroborate with other gang members or police officers, and in some cases I have had the benefit of old photographs. I have had access to crime scene videos and stills and to police reports, some culled by a private investigator and a lawyer working on my behalf. Requests for medical records, juvenile criminal records, and further documents from the US attorney's office under FOIA were repeatedly denied. In some instances, I have used street names or a pseudonym to protect the identities of those in the federal witness protection program. I bear responsibility for any errors of fact in this book.

Act I

SOUNDVIEW: THE GENESIS OF VIOLENCE

THE ROOF

UP HIGH ON THE PEBBLED-TAR ROOF overlooking the projects, Suge took another hit from his blunt. He held the smoke in his lungs, welcoming the rush in his limbs, the warmth over his skin, and finally the numbing of his mind. It would help deaden his conscience for the murder he was about to commit.

When Suge allowed the purplish smoke to escape his mouth, it hung briefly like a gossamer in front of the Manhattan skyline before gusting winds snatched it away. It was Thanksgiving Day 1997. Suge gripped the heavy Colt .45 pistol in his hoodie pocket, warm now after resting in his hand for so long, its weight reassuring him. He let himself stare over the smokestacks and flat roofs of the Bronx to the skyscrapers two miles southwest in midtown, the Empire State, the chrome spine of the Chrysler Building, before turning his gaze to the Upper East Side, the most expensive real estate in the United States, a world created by rich white men and the dynasties that had built America.

Seven stories below, at 1704 Randall Avenue, where crack vials littered the ground, he could see the bleak open squares of concrete hemmed in by blank red walls and row upon row of dark, empty windows. Everyone here knew to stay away from the windows.

The kids in Soundview called the roof that Suge was on Pebble Beach. A decade earlier, when he was a boy and Manhattan felt like a faraway kingdom, Suge had brought girls up here on dates, looked out with them at the metropolis, and told them one day he would be a millionaire.

The brackish air off Long Island Sound was getting cooler. Suge's right lung ached as he held the smoke in. A scar ten inches below his armpit marked where a bullet had entered, burst his lung, and dragged him down into a coma. Now, he stamped his feet and rasped a couple of times to help his breathing.

Suge was five foot six, a lean stack of knotted muscle. His broad mouth and upper jaw revealed two front teeth with a slight gap set above a defiant, jutting chin. Hyperkinetic, never fully at rest, he passed the blunt back and forth to a tough, sinewy kid called MAC-11, who had earned his name for his skill with a submachine gun.

Outside the stairwell, someone had sprayed a familiar tag: *SMM*, short for Sex Money Murder. SMM was one of the most feared "sets"—like battalions in an army—of the United Blood Nation. Suge was a general and head of security, and this was his territory, the Soundview Houses.

To outsiders, Soundview was a jungle—gang-run, crack-blighted, its residents held prisoner by fear and violence. To Suge, it was a place of safety from the police and rival gangs, a fortress and a powerful state within a state. Randall Avenue was the only way into Soundview, and the only way out, as if urban planners had built the place with defense in mind. Inside these walls, Suge's authority was unquestioned. Soundview lived by rules laid down by him and his brethren. Beneath the grid of dark rooftops was a vast market for the crack his crew supplied.

The orders that had brought Suge to the rooftop came down from SMM's godfather and Suge's childhood friend, Pistol Pete. Where Suge was raw and forthright, Pete flashed a thousand-watt grin and then slipped behind you to shoot you in the back of the skull. He was only five-seven, but he ruled the black underworld through fear and a Robin Hood reputation that made him a hero among young dealers throughout the projects.

Pete came from an American drug dynasty. His father had worked with drug kingpin Nicky Barnes in the 1970s and then helped to establish another syndicate in the early 1980s to bring high-grade heroin to Harlem and the Bronx with the Mafia. But by the mid-1990s, Pete's crack empire had made him more powerful and respected in the underworld than his father ever was. And while the Mafia had Sinatra and the Rat Pack, Pistol Pete had New York rappers like Lord Tariq and Peter Gunz, who rhymed about his life and crimes. Pete was a celebrity, spending time in clubs with Tyra Banks, Sean Combs (Puff Daddy, later P. Diddy), and the Ralph Lauren model Tyson Beckford.

The Pistol was incarcerated on federal drug and weapons charges in the Charlotte-Mecklenburg County Central Jail in North Carolina. But he could dictate life or death in Soundview anytime. The week before, he had phoned Suge from jail and said that David "Twin" Mullins, their friend and fellow gang member, was a snitch. "Twin gots to go," Pete told him. Although it was never explicitly stated, committing the murder would give Suge OG, or Original Gangster, status. This might mean he'd get his own autonomous subset under the aegis of Sex Money Murder.

At first Suge didn't wholly believe that Twin had ratted. For a start, Twin had higher status than Suge in SMM; he was Pistol Pete's partner. He and his twin brother, Damon Mullins, were well liked in Soundview. And not only was Twin a wealthy drug dealer, but he, too, had murdered for SMM out of loyalty, killing those who had planned to murder Pete. But then Suge stopped himself. You never analyzed, fed your conscience with doubts before a murder, asking why you would kill one friend to remain loyal to another. That would almost certainly get you killed. And in Soundview, you never went back on a job like this. Faking moves got you killed, too. If Suge failed to murder him, Twin's retaliation would be swift. He would almost certainly kill Suge, and Suge asssumed they might come for his grandmother, who also lived in Soundview.

Over several weeks Pete had convinced Suge that eliminating Twin was the only way to get Pete out of prison. Twin was cooperating with prosecutors on his case, he claimed, and his evidence and testimony would put Pete away for life.

On the roof, Suge pushed away any doubts. He never evaluated the consequences—it simply wasn't in his DNA. The perfect gang member, ruthless, unquestioning to a fault. Twin had to die today.

Under his hoodie Suge wore a bulletproof vest, a Kevlar plate strapped over his chest. He had loaded the .45 with alternating hollow points and full metal jacket bullets. The hollow points would spin irregularly through the body cavity, shredding organs as they went. But if his mark wore a bulletproof vest, the solid bullets had a chance of puncturing the Kevlar without fragmenting first.

Below him, on the large patch of grass between 1704 and 1680 Randall, he could see thirty football players in bright colors warming up, getting ready for the annual Turkey Bowl between the Soundview and neighboring Castle Hill projects that had been a tradition for five years. Supposedly this was the one day when guns and animosities between rival drug dealers would be set aside or expressed only through football. Even so, many players wore bulletproof vests.

MAC-11 peered over the edge and relayed that Suge's target wore a white Dallas Cowboys jersey with the number 21 in royal blue. Suge tracked several of his SMM allies in on the murder scheme down below. Several of Twin's men, he suspected, were armed and ready to protect him, so some of the SMM men had discreetly positioned themselves directly behind them. When Suge started shooting, a man called Total Package would pass a .38 revolver under his puffy jacket to Green Eyes, another SMM gangster standing next to him. Green Eyes would kill Twin's bodyguard and any of his retinue who might attempt to shoot back. Other SMM members were armed and stationed at strategic exits from the projects, blocking anyone from escaping. The three talked easily with Twin before the game, "rocking him to sleep." This was a familiar SMM move—they lulled their victims into a false sense of security with friendliness, masking their deadly intentions, before murdering them.

On the roof, the wind clawed at Suge, and a thick scar on his head throbbed in the cold. The pain was the legacy of a pistol-whipping he had suffered seven years earlier. Pistol Pete had orchestrated the murder of the culprit who had hurt Suge, so now Suge was going to repay the favor by killing for Pete.

+ + +

ON THANKSGIVING night, a wind blew over the yard at Cayuga
Correctional Facility in upstate New York as Emilio "Pipe" Romero,
an SMM boss serving time for attempted murder, moved through his
daily workout.

An Original Gangster, Pipe was the highest-ranking Blood in the
prison and commanded a powerful and growing army of inmates. Pipe
made $1,000 a week selling other prisoners drugs that were smuggled up
from Soundview by an SMM soldier. He also smuggled in Blue Gem Star
razor blades, wrapped in electrical tape to slip past the metal-detecting
wands the guards passed over all visitors. Pipe used some blades to cut up
crack; others he sold for $25 each. Known as bangers, the blades were the
perfect jailhouse weapon for the "Buck 50" face slashings—so called for
the 150 stitches to the face that a victim required—for which the Bloods
had a reputation.

Pipe cast an eye out to the woods in the darkness beyond the wire. He
had been denied parole yet again at his latest hearing. Still, he enjoyed
Thanksgiving lunch, the energy powering his workout. When his security detail asked if he wanted to go into the dorms with the 8:45 p.m.
return, he declined.

The bars were cold to the touch as he used his arms and chest to lower
his body toward the ground, then lift it up again. He enjoyed the satisfy-
ing burn of his muscles and let his mind drift, back to the annual football game in Soundview. He had last played in 1994. Back then he was
only 120 pounds, the baby of SMM and years younger than the rest, but
he'd caught several touchdown passes. The year before, in 1993, Twin
and Pistol Pete had gone after each other relentlessly. By the next year
they were friends again and business partners, scoring at will for the Sex
Money Murder football team. No one wanted to tackle either of them
too hard.

He thought of the high times with Twin, rolling into the Tunnel
nightclub in downtown Manhattan in a fleet of black Chevrolet Subur-
bans, Mercedes coupes, and Toyota Land Cruisers. They had a phrase:

"Make It Reign." And they threw money around like confetti. They bought dozens of bottles of champagne at a time, though they weren't old enough to legally drink. One time, Twin shot dead a man who had been sent up from North Carolina to assassinate Pistol Pete as the apocalyptic bass of Biggie's "Gimme the Loot" reverberated round the club. Twin, Pipe, and Pistol Pete had carried out murders together and shared money, cars, and women. Their bond was stronger than family ties.

Now Pipe was hearing rumors that Twin was "999," cooperating with law enforcement, and that he was to be killed. In fact, Pipe's brother Ro, a young Blood looking to enhance his reputation in the neighborhood, had written to him to say that he had almost shot one of the "Doublemints"—Blood code for Twin and his identical brother.

Pipe knew Twin wasn't snitching. Sometime over the past few weeks, he had written back and ordered his brother to stand down. If Twin were cooperating, Pipe would also be up on a federal indictment—because Pete, Twin, and Pipe had committed some of their most serious crimes together. In his latest letter, Pipe had ordered his brother to stay near the phone, so that he could call and explain the situation and give orders. Yet every time he called, Ro wasn't there. Pipe called Suge repeatedly, but he, too, seemed to be ducking the calls. Pipe had heard nothing from Pistol Pete about Twin being a snitch and marked for death. Pipe tried not to dwell on it, but the feeling of powerlessness was nearly unbearable. He could only hope that his brother and the other Bloods in Soundview would follow his orders and not murder Twin, who was like a brother to him.

Pipe had become a sort of moral compass for SMM. He balked at the killing sometimes, and urged the younger members to focus more on making money than murder. He reminded them that their purpose was to rise up out of poverty, not to kill one another off.

At 9:45 p.m. Pipe headed inside. In the dorms, rows of beds were separated by light blue chest-high dividers. His red slippers were waiting for him, sitting on a red rug near a red towel. He had posted no pictures of family or friends in his cubicle, lest they become targets. Instead he put up a picture of Jonelle, an off-and-on squeeze, wearing a thong bikini and crawling on all fours. Running up her right thigh was a series of dog-paw tattoos, part of the Bloods' iconography.

He planned to call friends in the neighborhood after his shower and see who had won the game.

+ + +

AS THE YOUNGEST on the Bronx's new gang investigation squad, thirty-year-old Detective Pete Forcelli had been ordered to work Thanksgiving. He had been handpicked by the Bronx's chief of detectives to lead the squad, an indication that his reputation for ambition and drive was being recognized by the brass. For the time being, though, the unit was housed in a former closet in the Forty-Fifth Precinct. Their first target was Sex Money Murder.

All over the city the crack epidemic had birthed neighborhood crews who had made housing projects impregnable dominions. From their base in Soundview, SMM had become a multimillion-dollar enterprise that offered murder for hire and cut distribution deals for crack in a dozen cities in half a dozen states. In the Bronx they were taking over projects like Bronx River and Castle Hill. Forcelli's informants told him that there were scores of murders attributable to the group.

Forcelli didn't like to work the day shift. Most of the action took place at night, when he could jump from murder scene to murder scene, running on adrenaline and ending his shift when dawn's first light swept over the city, then making a trip to Gold's Gym. The gym was his sanctuary, a place where he could enjoy his solitude and forget about work and the pressures of supporting his family on a young detective's salary. Inspired by Sylvester Stallone in *Rambo* and *Rocky*, Forcelli could bench three hundred pounds. He had been married for only a few years, and his wife did most of the child care. She would be alone with their three-year-old daughter and eighteen-month-old son today on Thanksgiving. This, Forcelli told himself, was what it took to be a detective.

The Bronx was the center of a homicide epidemic in New York, with more than half the city's murders in the late 1980s and early 1990s. While there had been concern over the killings, which peaked in 1990 at 2,605, they had been largely ignored. Black drug dealers murdering black drug dealers was a problem no one wanted to deal with. Instead, the front pages of the *New York Post* were devoted to the feds and their elite anti-Mafia units waging war on the five familes. A recent internecine war among Colombo crime family members in Brooklyn had seen eleven killed, garnering twenty-four-hour news coverage. Yet in a three-block area in Hunts Point, over the Bronx River from Soundview, three times that number had been killed in a few months. The murders of black kids barely made the papers. Forcelli had chalked up hundreds of arrests in the southeast Bronx, where he'd seen two close colleagues shot and killed. As a housing cop, his was viewed as one of the most perilous of assignments. In 1996, those who lived in New York public housing were three times more likely to be hit by gunfire than residents in the rest of the city.

Forcelli had started as a patrolman ten years earlier, and Soundview had been his beat. He'd seen boys in the neighborhoods come of age in the early days of crack, carrying out shootings before they'd been through puberty. They reminded him of child soldiers in Africa, hardened to violence by years of exposure, eyes bloodshot from weed, and unquestioningly subservient to neighborhood gangsters who acted like rebel commanders. Forcelli had chased down kids armed with machine guns who had enough money stashed in their apartments to pay his salary for five years. Some of them were third-generation Soundview gangsters whose fathers were dead or in prison. They saw themselves carrying on a family dynasty, taking their best shot at the American Dream.

As he made his way up the steps of the Forty-Fifth Precinct building and passed through the tall, thick oak doors, Forcelli always felt inspired and at ease. The place was a bastion, left over from a time when the rule of law was respected. It reinforced his sense of purpose. In a city where the police were largely disparaged and distrusted, the Forty-Fifth held its ground.

The precinct was sleepy on Thanksgiving. Forcelli found his partner and another detective hunched over a little TV watching football. Above the noise, Forcelli sifted through the paperwork on his desk, then decided to head out on his own. He climbed into an unmarked Ford Windstar and headed west along the Bruckner Expressway toward Soundview. Today the gangsters in the neighborhood would be visiting relatives and baby mothers, all the people they might run to if they were wanted on warrants.

A few days earlier, Forcelli had spoken to John O'Malley, an investigator with the US attorney's office for the Southern District of New York and the best detective he had ever worked with. O'Malley was tall and silver-haired, a native of Soundview. He had developed a reputation in law enforcement for equanimity and fairness, and for his mastery at winning the trust of gangsters while getting them working for the prosecution. He had helped pioneer the federal takedown of street gangs in the Bronx, and he had a particular interest in Sex Money Murder because of their ultraviolent reputation and the fact that they were in his old neighborhood.

Forcelli had talked to O'Malley about a change in strategy in the Bronx: They had gotten permission to prosecute SMM and other gangs under the federal racketeering laws known as RICO (Racketeer Influenced and Corrupt Organizations Act), first developed to prosecute the Mafia. When Forcelli first made detective in 1993, he caught new murder cases every week and got only four days to work a case before moving on to the next. For years Forcelli had tried to arrest corner crack dealers and killers, only to see them released a few days later after terrified witnesses in the projects refused to help the police, let alone testify in open court. Even if a jury convicted gangsters, when they went inside they had their teeth fixed and lifted weights to get back in shape while running their operations from their cells before returning to the street, more powerful than before. Now, finally, he had the luxury of time to strategize, investigate, and build a full case against Sex Money Murder. Forcelli and his team were now backed by the authority to request the death penalty and life sentences for major offenders. It was all part of a major push by the US attorney's office to "reclaim" neighborhoods from the gangs and to break the generational cycle of sons following their fathers into prison—in Soundview and tough inner-city neighborhoods like it, a state prison term had become a rite of manhood, and even held some romance. Using RICO, just as the feds did with Mafiosos such as Salvatore "Sammy the Bull" Gravano, the authorities would offer some street gangsters the chance to cooperate. If they refused, they would go to prison in a place far away from the Bronx, beyond the reach of family, to serve life terms. This was all part of a "Weed and Seed" strategy: Once the hardcore gangsters in the neighborhood were swept up and removed, an injection of federal money for social services would help rejuvenate the area.

As Forcelli slowed and turned onto Randall Avenue, the massive shadows of the Soundview projects loomed over him. On the corner of Commonwealth Avenue and Randall, mothers tugged their children past a few recalcitrant drug dealers in hoodies waiting for passing trade at the spot known as Cozy Corner. Even the local priest from Holy Cross didn't come through here unless he was wearing his clerical collar. Cops at the precinct said you could spot a license plate here from any state of the union. Today Forcelli ignored the hustlers and instead drove in and out of parking lots, slowly and methodically pausing occasionally to write down plate numbers. He entered the horseshoe-shaped road at the center of the projects and made his way past 1710 Randall. Drawing alongside a small grassy patch between the buildings, he saw young men assembled in jerseys, warming up for a football game. He decided to get some lunch. Nothing seemed amiss. He would never have thought to look up to the top of the building, where two faces were peering down.

+ + +

SUGE SAW one of the SMM men on the field looking up at him in greeting. He snapped his head back, walking away from the roof's edge. The crowd from Castle Hill was much larger than he had anticipated, which meant that he could be more easily identified—or shot, if he bungled the killing. Suge took a last hit from his blunt to fortify himself. "You ready, Moe?" he asked. MAC-11 nodded, his eager face framed by a goatee and shoulder-length cornrows. He was ready to make a name for himself by killing for Sex Money Murder.

As they moved to the stairwell door, Suge briefly wondered if he'd ever see the Manhattan rooftops again. Then he and MAC-11 vaulted down the stairs, which always reeked of urine, and descended to the ground floor.

Outside, Suge dropped his joint and ground it out under his black sneaker. He noticed that MAC-11's face wasn't concealed. "Yo! Cover your face, Moe!" he said. But MAC-11 was too amped to take advice, focusing instead on his target.

"Fuck that," said MAC-11. "We in the hood. Ain't nobody going to say nothing."

Fool, thought Suge as he pulled his hood up and laced the drawstrings under his chin so that only part of his eyes and nose was visible. But it was too late now. Suge needed to focus on his own task. Together they walked directly across the field in the middle of a play before MAC-11 veered to the left. Halfway through, it occurred to Suge to slow his gait, to bounce in on his toes, casually, as if warming up for the game.

Twin had just made a play but was crouching over the ball, ready to snap back to the Castle Hill team. Suge walked up behind him, closing the distance, his right hand around the butt of the pistol. He went through a mental checklist: Was the gun chambered? What was the recoil like so he could be ready for subsequent shots from the blowback of the first? A Smith & Wesson 9mm was tucked into the waistband of his black track pants as a backup. He quickly traced its outline.

Just eight yards away, Twin turned from the scrum to look directly into Suge's eyes. Suge pressed on, pulling out the gun. The long barrel of the .45 got stuck in his hoodie pocket. He fumbled, extended his arm, and aimed at Twin's head. Twin gave a knowing look that would haunt Suge for the rest of his life. Suge squeezed. He didn't hear the crack of the big gun; instead, he heard the thump of the bullet going low and hitting Twin's body. He fired one more. This time he heard a sharp whip-lash report. Then the gun jammed. Panicked, he tried to rack the slide, jiggled at the trigger. Nothing.

Chaos erupted around him. MAC-11 had crossed the field to go after the other twin—hitting him in the backside—but after Suge's shots he blazed rounds indiscriminately. Ephraim "E-Man" Solar, Twin's body-guard, started to reach for a gun, but he was too late. Green Eyes shot him multiple times with the revolver Total Package had passed him according to plan, but then he ran out of bullets. Solar staggered, still alive, lunging for Green Eyes's throat. In a frenzy Green Eyes tried to pistol-whip him to death. MAC-11 gave up chasing the other twin and circled back. He shot E-Man in the head with a bullet that cleaved his skull. In the melee, two other bystanders were hit.

Now Twin had gotten up and was running. Suge's heart pounded, as if a phantom had reared up out of the ground before him. Panicked at his bungled murder attempt, and suspecting that Twin was wearing a bulletproof vest under his football jersey, Suge realized he had little time if Twin got to a gun.

"Finish him, Suge!" shouted one of the shooters working with him. In disbelief that anyone would be stupid enough to shout out his name in front of witnesses, Suge turned to shoot whoever it was. In a split second he reconsidered and focused back on Twin. Suge pulled out the 9mm and fired three shots in quick succession left-handed as they ran across the road. Twin, hit in the hand and leg, left a bloody trail. Suge contin-ued firing like a hunter running down a wounded deer. He clipped Twin two more times just before he lurched across Randall Avenue. Twin ran into a patch of lawn before collapsing next to one of the buildings under a window. Suge ran up and then abruptly slowed his walk in a way that he hoped wouldn't attract attention, as he heard distant sirens. But no one was looking. Twin lay in the grass, quivering, staring at Suge with incredulity. Suge, his arm dangling by his side, grasping the pistol loosely, moved alongside and didn't hesitate. He shot once again, the bullet rip-ping off Twin's nose, exposing white flesh.

He fired his last three remaining bullets at Twin's curled-up body.

One

LI'L GUNBUSTER

(1988)

PIPE WOKE AT 7:00 A.M. AND ADMIRED himself in the bathroom mirror. He wore a freshly laundered white T-shirt, and his skin glowed in the dreary yellow light. Only a few months ago, before he started dealing, he and his brother would sometimes trade sneakers and jeans each day before school to give the impression to other kids they had more than one pair. Today, his profits from crack afforded him a new pair of Reeboks and some skinny-leg Levi's. He glowered in the mirror, affecting seriousness. A black shadow was just coming in on his upper lip, and he had the first traces of what would become a thick, wiry beard. He was looking older, he thought—more purposeful. He was eleven.

Pipe took his name from his mother's former boyfriend, a tall, brawny man with thick biceps and square shoulders known as Leadpipe. The nickname apparently referred to his endowment. Pipe's father, Big Bimbo, a legend in the neighborhood and a onetime gang member with the Black Spades, a crew that had originated in Soundview in the 1960s before spreading to the rest of the city, did not approve of the nickname. But Big Bimbo had gone in for his second term in prison a few years earlier, and the name stuck. No one could remember Li'l Pipe being called anything else.

At around 8:00 a.m. Pipe left their seventh-floor apartment at 1715 Randall Avenue, taking the stairs by habit to avoid the police, who often waited at the ground-floor elevator door. The walls were collaged with the tags of local crews: New Born Criminals, Soundview's Most Wanted. He pushed open the door to the lobby, smoothed his

T-shirt over his chest, and bounced into the low sunlight of an early spring morning.

Like most of the neighborhood, the Soundview Houses, thirteen seven-story redbrick buildings in two T-shaped sections, had been cut off from the rest of the Bronx in the early 1970s by the construction of the Bruckner Expressway. The Houses were clustered on the western edge of the low-lying Soundview peninsula, roughly two and a half miles long at its widest point to the north, where it connects to the southeast Bronx, and demarcated by the Bruckner. To the south, the land devolves into salt marshes at Clason Point, the triangular tip jutting into the East River. By 1988, the Soundview Houses complex accommodated around 1,250 families, mainly black and Puerto Rican; 3 percent were white. Roughly 40 percent were on welfare, and only twenty families had at least two family members working.

Pipe's mother demanded that he and his siblings—Ro (Rufino), Eddie, Kawaan, Geralda, Annette, and baby Chantal—always play within sight, and run home as fast as they could when she sent them on errands. The Soundview community was fiercely tight-knit, and the mothers of his friends had free rein to discipline him and his brothers if they caught the boys straying too far.

To the east were the Castle Hill projects. Kids from the two projects saw each other as natural class enemies. In the no-man's-land between was Adlai Stevenson High School, one of the most dangerous in America. In the 1970s the Black Spades and Savage Nomad gangs walked the hallways wearing jackets that read KILL WHITEY.

Ten blocks from Soundview, on neutral ground, was the Kips Bay Boys & Girls Club. The distinctive brown-brick building was a safe midpoint where Soundview and Castle Hill kids could intermingle and play sports largely free of violence, although once Pipe's sister had a fistfight with a girl called Jennifer Lopez, who would one day make her neighborhood of Castle Hill famous.

Pipe walked east along Randall Avenue. At the end was a median strip where the kids had set up stained mattresses scavenged from Dumpsters that they used as trampolines. Just beyond, in Soundview Park, was a dumping ground called Snakeland, where a boy had had his face blown off by an abandoned gas cylinder; now it was littered with household trash and porn magazines. Pipe could force his way through to the edge of the Bronx River, a swamp dotted with small islands formed by old refrigerators, car hulks, and, according to legend, the occasional human corpse. He and his friends swam in the polluted water and wrestled horseshoe crabs out of the muck. At around four or five every afternoon, hordes of rats climbed out of the river and made their way into the neighborhoods. From the shore, the Hunts Point Terminal Market was visible across the river, a hive of belching diesel trucks and the world's largest shipping hub for produce.

Pipe passed a few commuters heading toward the elevated number 6 train at Elder Avenue, the lifeline to Manhattan. He crossed the north-south sweep of Rosedale Avenue at the crossroads with Randall Avenue: Cozy Corner. The corner drew its name from a bar that used to be there in the seventies. Along with the pizza shop, there were a couple of delis, a liquor store, the Met Foods, where Pipe worked packing bags, and a methadone clinic. A few doors down was a numbers spot run by the mob. Pipe went into Papa Yala's to pick up coffee, a bagel, and a few loosies—single cigarettes—passing a twenty to the Yemeni owner, who sat behind a counter running along the right side of the store.

Pipe's world was quickly changing, thanks largely to the drug that had arrived at Cozy Corner to take over from heroin. In the old days, men would sit on the sidewalk and play dominoes, drinking out of brown paper bags, untroubled by the pacified users, who swayed and nodded out. A couple of years before, Pipe had found his mother, Miss Annette, sitting on the blue shag toilet-seat cover in their bathroom, her sleeve rolled up, tying a rubber tourniquet around her arm. "Get the fuck out of here," she said. "Can't you see I'm busy?" He returned an hour later to find her leaning so far forward from a sitting position that he was amazed she was still upright. Pipe helped her to her room. He had learned to walk her to the check-cashing store when the welfare check came, and to take some of the money before she spent it on drugs. When he couldn't catch her in time, the family went hungry.

While the heroin trade had been largely controlled by the Mafia, who had the resources to buy kilos for $200,000 and import them to the United States, crack was far more accessible. Colombian cartels flooded Miami with cheap cocaine, and a kilo could be had for as little as $10,000 before it was smuggled up the Eastern Seaboard. No need for massive international networks and large down payments. In New York, a six- or seven-man crew could set up an operation, take over a block, and turn almost immediate profits. Law enforcement could dismantle centralized networks of heroin distributors, but the diffuse, hyperviolent crack trade was much harder to eradicate. There was no clear hierarchy, no one boss to maintain order.

Crack was sweeping through Soundview and rewriting the social contract by the day. In 1988, 150,000 people toiled in the crack business in New York. The parks in Soundview, which had been full of children even during the heroin epidemic, were now empty. The adults who worked regular jobs were captive to the encroaching violence. Many didn't leave their homes from dusk to daybreak, praying that the volleys of gunfire never got too close. Despite Soundview's population density, since crack had arrived it often looked like a ghost town.

One day at the end of 1987, Pipe went to visit his cousin Pookie on the northern lip of the projects. He found him stuffing a desiccated rocklike substance into little plastic bags. "This is the new stuff they got out here, man," Pookie said. Pipe watched as Pookie and other guys filled the bags, and when they were finished a man with burn scars on his face, known as Crackhead Bemo, shouted up from below the window, demanding bags to sell. Before he'd discovered crack, Bemo had been a young pro baseball prospect. Now he roamed the neighborhood breaking into cars for stereos and doing whatever he could to get a rock or two, while offering kids like Pipe a start in the business. He became Pipe's mentor in the game.

Pipe helped sell crack out of the pizza parlor on Cozy Corner, breaking now and then for marathon sessions with the other boys on the Out Run video game. He held vials for Pookie and other dealers on the block, storing them in a black pouch that hung inside his pants. Crackhead

Bemo steered deals his way, approaching Pipe with the money from a customer who stood a safe distance away and buying nickels—vials worth $5 each. For each deal he earned $2 from Pookie. Pipe used his profits, $20 most nights, to supplement the job at Met Foods. Pipe had a convincing scowl, a father in jail, and a gangster pedigree. He quickly earned a measure of respect.

He decided to hustle his own drugs for greater profit with D-Spot, head of a local crew called Da Lynch Mob. D-Spot blasted mix tapes from the trunk of his car, often surrounded by young women, and sold blue-stoppered crack vials on the southern side of the projects. Drug dealers took pride in their distinctive colorful stoppers, like the labels on bottles of fine wine, denoting both quality and provenance. By now Pipe knew all the crackheads—White Boy John, who worked on cars in the projects for a few dollars but now had a habit; mothers of his teenage friends. Pipe moved more product than dealers twice his age. D-Spot eventually agreed to a 60/40 split and handed Pipe a huge bag of vials. The first time out, Pipe hustled all night, selling fifty nickels. He gave $150 to D-Spot and kept $100 for himself. A day or two later Pipe brought home a bucket of chicken and a tub of banana-strawberry ice cream he'd bought for his family. He handed Miss Annette $75. She ordered him into her bedroom out of earshot while his siblings ate. "Where did you get this money from?" she demanded. "Ain't no way in hell you pack no bags and you able to buy all this food and give me seventy-five dollars." Pipe invented an excuse, and Miss Annette, whether she believed it or not, abruptly left the matter alone. For their own reasons neither of them wanted to get into a conversation about drugs, whether about using them or selling them.

By the time Pipe quit the job at the supermarket to focus on drug dealing full-time, he had noticed that even some once-respectable people, like a supervisor there, had the glassy look of a crack smoker.

By the age of eleven, Pipe was the man of the house. He wasn't sure what it meant, but that was how his mother began referring to him. He watched *The Cosby Show* on the black-and-white TV with the coat hanger as an aerial from the top bunk in his bedroom. Pipe modeled himself on Dr. Huxtable and thought he might become a doctor one day, living in a brownstone townhouse. He helped his younger siblings with their homework and made them dinner when they got home from school—sometimes mayonnaise or syrup sandwiches, or rice with margarine. This was if they hadn't blown their $65 in food stamps—which arrived in a blue-and-white book around the fifth of each month—in the Chinese restaurant on Commonwealth. On those days Pipe headed down to the Community Center on Seward Avenue, to the north of the projects, and picked up a large "welfare cheese," which he brought home and grilled to perfection.

+ + +

PIPE EASED through the apartment door backward so as not to spill the coffee. He moved past the cramped kitchen down a long, dark hallway to his mother's room. He pushed the coffee into her hand and laid the bagel on the bedside table with the cigarettes. Still in bed, with the curtain drawn, she mumbled thanks, her smile revealing dimples, a family trait. Pipe thought of dropping a couple of extra twenties beside her, but though she let Pipe buy food and cigarettes, she mostly refused his profits from dealing.

He remembered a day three years ago, when he was eight. He and his mother stood on the sidewalk as a shimmering forest green Cadillac with fins and chrome rims drifted around the corner and slowed to a halt in front of them, Leadpipe at the wheel. They headed off to the Cross County mall in Yonkers. When they arrived, Leadpipe parked outside the glass doors leading into Macy's and kept the engine running. Inside, Pipe's mother unfurled a few Macy's bags from within her coat and, after quickly scanning the aisles for security guards, began to load them with clothes, perfume, and designer goods from different departments. When they were full, she handed them to Pipe, who carried them to the waiting Cadillac.

Sometimes his mother stole to order for people in the neighborhood in return for money to get heroin; other times it was for the family or herself. Only a few weeks after Leadpipe drove them to Macy's, a security guard pounced after Miss Annette picked out a couple of suits and lingered too long in another aisle. Undeterred, she pushed the bags into Pipe's arms, told him to run, and blocked the guard. Pipe ran through the doors and launched his little body into the backseat of Leadpipe's car with the poise of an Olympic diver. In halting breaths he told Leadpipe what had happened. Pipe's mother slipped into the car an hour later, tousled and agitated, ordering Leadpipe to drive home.

Eventually she was arrested for shoplifting, leaving Pipe home to take care of the family alone. She was sentenced to six months in jail. Within days two police officers and a woman from Social Services cornered Pipe outside the apartment and marched him inside. The children were forced to get dressed, then escorted to the front of the building to await the car that would take them to foster care. Pipe and his sister Annette locked eyes and took off, heads down, little fists pumping, making a break north to Seaward Avenue, where they burst out of the projects. Pipe surged ahead, vaulting a chain-link fence. On the other side he turned his head to see Annette with the police. She screamed for her brother. Pipe looked north along the avenue to freedom, hesitated, then reluctantly scuffed back to the police officers and his sister.

Within a few days, Pipe and Ro—born nine months after Pipe—arrived at the first of several foster homes, run by a kindly woman named Mrs. Brown, who owned a two-family house with a backyard. She took the boys to church every Sunday, ensured that they did their homework, and assigned light household chores. Pipe began to excel at school, making the honor roll, and for a while he was free to be a child.

He and his siblings were returned to Soundview sometime in 1986. Elated to see his mother, Pipe was soon saddled again with all the tasks of a parent. On one hand, he was glad to be needed, and to be back with his mother. On the other, he missed the freedom of life with Mrs. Brown.

+ + +

AFTER DROPPING the coffee and cigarettes at his mother's bedside, Pipe headed off to IS 174, a windowless junior high on White Plains Road about fifteen minutes away, at around 8:30 a.m. He met a friend on the corner of Taylor Avenue, and they lit a blunt and passed it between them as they walked to school. By the time they got there Pipe was hungry. At a store opposite the school, the boys bought heroes for a dollar. Some girls arrived. Pipe grabbed a couple of them on the backside, only to receive a slap or an angry pout. At 8:45 a.m. he learned that there were no tests that day. No point in being at school. He returned to the pizza joint at Cozy Corner to try to sell his last ounce of crack.

At around noon he bumped into a cousin of his friend Pete. The girl said that Pete wanted to see him, so Pipe went home and at two o'clock set off through the projects to Pete's apartment. Pete thrived on trouble—violent fights, drug debts. Pipe's mind raced. The two had met a year before at Pipe's cousin's apartment, and despite the age gap—Pete was fourteen—they had bonded quickly. With Pete, he could relax into his eleven-year-old self and let someone else be the authority. Also, Pete didn't struggle like the Soundview kids, exuding an air of prosperity that Pipe admired. He'd been schooled privately at St. Raymond Elementary. Compared to Pipe, he enjoyed a luxurious life, with a well-heeled family that wanted for little: He always had the latest sneakers, computer games, and BMX bikes, and he liked being the center of attention. Quickly Pete was becoming the big brother that Pipe had never had.

Pipe cut northwest. A boom box pulsed gangsta rap as he caught sight of the Lafayette Boynton Houses, co-ops and rentals for lower- and middle-income earners. He was buzzed in at 875 Boynton and went to the ninth floor, where Pete met him at the door, shirtless and shoeless, in shorts. Pete was well nourished, with chipmunk cheeks, straight white teeth, and soft, buttery skin.

Pete had been teaching Pipe how to box, to put his hands up to protect his chin and temples and to snap down on punches. On the way into the apartment, Pete threw a flurry of playful punches before easing off. His motocross bike was parked on the balcony. He boasted that he had stolen it from some white kids in Soundview Park. He had shown Pipe how to sit on it, how to twist the throttle gently while easing off on the clutch. Pete had watched him blasting along the banks of the Bronx

River with the wind in his face. Pete was teaching him everything he knew. Some nights Pipe slept on the floor of Pete's room next to his bed.

Pipe had gotten into some trouble at his school after he beat up a Hispanic kid who went home and told his older cousins. The boys had waited outside the school for Pipe, who had slipped out unseen and told Pete about it. The following day, Pete and his friend B-Love showed up at the school. B-Love had broad features, bright eyes, and a wide, dopey grin. Pete and B-Love ambushed the Hispanic boys and gave them a fierce beating. For the first time in Pipe's life, someone had stood up for him.

But more than that, Pete chose Pipe over the others. In February Pipe had spotted B-Love emerging from the ground-floor bedroom window of Pete's girlfriend's apartment and reported this to Pete. Pete said that he'd come straight down in a cab and sort out the situation. When he arrived he found B-Love jumping Pipe. Pete punched B-Love in the face. "Don't you ever violate my little brother again," he said. "He's family."

Pipe still didn't know why he'd been summoned today. Pete handed him a strawberry Pop-Tart from an overstocked fridge, and the two boys collapsed on the sofa and played Sega for a while until the phone rang. When Pete hung up, he told Pipe he had a proposition. Some local kids were hustling crack in the Lafayette Houses on a spot that Pete's friend, a rival dealer, wanted to control. They were taking his customers, costing him money. Somebody needed to scare them off with a gun. The dealer was offering 250 grams of crack in payment. Pete offered 100 grams as bounty if Pipe wanted to do it.

Pipe said that he would do the job on his way home, and Pete ushered him into his makeshift bedroom. His mother, Ma Brenda, had hung a large curtain to separate his space from the living room. On a wall inside was a shrine to various Mafiosi: posters of Albert "Mad Hatter" Anastasia, who ran the brutal enforcement arm of the Mafia, Murder, Inc., so ruthlessly he became known as "Lord High Executioner"; Carmine "the Cigar" Galante, head of the Bonanno crime family; Nicky Scarfo, head of the Philadelphia mob; and Lucky Luciano, godfather of the five families in New York City.

Pete rummaged in a small plastic chest at the foot of the bed, pushing aside T-shirts and hoodies and musty old football gear. "There," he said, holding aloft a black revolver.

The first time Pipe had come to the apartment, Pete had sworn him to secrecy, then produced a sawed-off .30-30 rifle from under his mattress. He'd showed Pipe how long the bullets were, and consequently how deadly. Pete had dropped a round into the chamber, let him hold it. "Do you want to shoot it off the terrace?" he had asked with a sly grin. Pipe had declined.

Now he handed Pipe the revolver—.22 caliber, with a polished wooden handle. Pipe grasped it. The weapon belonged in his small hand. He didn't have to cock it back, Pete instructed; he just had to squeeze the trigger. Pipe would have nine shots.

Pipe wasn't listening. He wanted the gun for himself. Pete seemed to read his mind. "It's yours," he said. He suggested that Pipe change his clothes, and he pulled out some black sweatpants, a black T-shirt, and a black ball cap. They embraced briefly at the front door. Pipe slipped out into the falling dusk, heading east on a path that ran up Story Avenue. Bruckner Boulevard thrummed with commuter cars. At 875 Morrison Avenue he heard the faint tinkle of laughter and voices near the front entrance. Two blocks down, he saw the lights of the Forty-Third Precinct. A youth in on the plot with Pete caught sight of Pipe and broke away from the group. He gave Pipe a description of his targets, two brothers: one in a black T-shirt and black shorts, talking to some girls, the other in a white T-shirt nearer the lobby.

To Pipe they looked to be fifteen or so—big kids, almost men, much taller than his four-foot-something frame—as he closed on them.

He jerked the gun from his pocket. One of the girls screamed. The brothers ran. Pipe pulled the trigger, and the gun seemed to explode. He pumped off a couple more rounds at the brothers. Each bullet now felt somehow refreshing, the shots driving the stresses and the powerlessness of his life away. As a slight eleven-year-old, he always felt that the world loomed large and forbidding. He had no control over his mother's addictions, his forced stays in foster homes. But as the gun snapped in his hand, everything receded—the older kids he was shooting at, the Lafayette towers. They shrank with each gunshot, while Pipe grew to a colossus.

The boy in the white T-shirt jerked back from a round in his shoulder. Another shot or two hit his arm. He slid off a green signpost, and the brothers stumbled together around the corner.

Silence. Pipe's shooting arm fell to his side. He rammed the smoking gun back into his pocket. He heard a female voice above and looked up to see a silhouette behind the curtains of a fourth-floor window. Whoever it was knew not to stick her head out. Timidly, she asked if someone had been shot.

Pipe hesitated. "I don't know," he said flatly. "I think so."

And with that he turned toward home.

He knew from the crime movies he'd watched that when people ran from a shooting they got caught. He walked slowly and calmly across the concrete running track in the middle of Soundview Park, the barrier between Soundview and the Lafayette towers, an area everyone avoided after dark. Far behind him he saw the flickering lights of police cars and heard sirens.

As he crossed Metcalf Avenue into the Soundview project, a wave of exultant, raw power washed over him like nothing he'd ever experienced. If the police came for him here, he would know where to hide, and he knew that the community would protect him. Up on Randall he saw D-Spot standing outside his Volkswagen Rabbit. The trunk was open, music turned up. A few boys were gathered around, drinking and bouncing to the beat.

Midway to his building, Pipe ran into Everton, a hyperactive Jamaican in his early twenties.

"Wassup, little man!"

Everton commented on Pipe's black outfit before describing a confrontation he'd had with a few young kids in the neighborhood.

"Them dudes was talking trash," Everton said. "I told 'em, 'I'll get my li'l man Pipe to pop one in your ass. I'll give 'im a gun myself.'" He collapsed into laughter.

Pipe flared with rage at what he deemed disrespect. He wasn't just a kid—as of ten minutes ago, he was, in the language of the street, a gun-buster. Pulling the gun out of his pants, he held it to Everton's face. It still smelled of freshly burned gunpowder.

"You don't need to give me no gun, nigga," stormed Pipe. "I got my own. You don't know me. It ain't no game. I ain't playing."

Everton put his hands up. The silence filled with the whine of sirens. The older Jamaican placated him: "You ever need anything, man, just holler."

Pipe stalked back to his apartment. In his room he hid the gun in a plastic toy box under his bed. Ro sat looking at his brother. Pipe told him not to touch it. Ro knew not to ask questions.

Pipe went to B-Love's apartment at 1710 Randall and called Pete.

"It's a done deal."

"You good?"

"Call you tomorrow."

Pipe left the apartment and went next door to 551, the building on the corner of Randall and Rosedale where he and the others congregated most days. Inside he sat on the steps in the stairwell that led to the lobby. Six months ago, he'd seen his first dead body, lying just beyond the door of B-Love's building—the man had been blasted with a shotgun in the stomach and the side of the head. Ambulances and police swarmed the scene. Pipe ran upstairs and told his mother. She'd told him to keep walking when he saw such things, and never to get involved.

Ever since then he'd had nightmares. Sometimes he dreamed of the feet of some invisible person making footprints in the carpet near his bed. Other times, he dreamed that when he walked past the closet near his front door, an unseen hand dragged him into the darkness. No matter how he struggled, the force always overpowered him.

B-Love joined Pipe and offered him a forty. Pipe didn't like the taste of alcohol but drank the bottle of beer anyway. It tasted different now—or something was different, anyway. Now he could protect himself and his family. The gun had liberated him and empowered him to make a life of his own. It gave him control.

Two

DO NOT YIELD TO EVIL[1]

A DUSTING OF SNOW SWIRLED AROUND John O'Malley's ankles as he stamped his feet on Soundview Avenue, a woolen hat pulled low over his ears. It was December 1969, and O'Malley was seventeen. He and his friends had pooled their money and bought a few Christmas trees to sell. He set up his makeshift stand outside Holy Cross Church. Every now and then a brown-cassocked Franciscan Friar of the Holy Name dashed up the steps.

O'Malley was a commanding six feet tall, and his periwinkle eyes devoured all he saw as he stood glancing up and down the busy street lined with double-parked cars. He waited for patrons but kept a wary eye on the trees in case someone snatched one. He'd earned a few dollars so far, but things were slow.

Sometime in the early afternoon a commotion erupted across the street. Two men burst out of a bank. O'Malley heard the pop of a revolver. In the chaos, one of the men dropped a bag of money on the sidewalk, where it fell open. Pedestrians lunged at the cash blowing into the street while someone leaned over the hood of a parked car, squeezing off shots at the two men.

O'Malley ran to a phone booth, dialed, and reported a robbery. "I think there's an off-duty cop involved," he said. The police swarmed in shortly after.

With the crowd scattered, O'Malley packed up for the day and

---

[1] The Bronx borough motto is *Ne Cede Malis*.

left, walking past well-ordered single-family brick-and-frame houses, each with its own front yard and a place to park the family car, the old emblems of the American Dream in the 1950s. Even at seventeen, he says, he could feel the decline of that dream in the Bronx.

As O'Malley neared home, 47 White Plains Road, the smell of sea salt seeped into his nostrils. The two-bedroom clapboard house had been constructed in 1920, near the end of Clason Point, not far from the estuary of the East River, which ran into the Atlantic. Low-flying planes into LaGuardia made the family crockery rattle. Near the front gate was a small oak tree his father had planted when O'Malley was ten, the sapling the boy's height. It was now beginning to flourish as O'Malley grew into early manhood.

His two sisters and his father were home. His father, who worked as a clerk at the insurance giant American International Group (AIG), had a side job as a chauffeur and served as a volunteer firefighter. O'Malley told him about the bank robbery. The older man was stoic about the chaos developing around them. At one time his family had slept every night with the doors unlocked. Not anymore.

As a child, John O'Malley's only exposure to crime was through his uncle Jack, a Queens homicide detective. He remembered Jack, newly divorced, roaring up to their house in a red Ford Mustang, a cigar clenched between his teeth, his revolver in an ankle holster. He showed his eight-year-old nephew his shiny gold detective badge, number 1944. Pulling the gun from his ankle, he emptied it of ammunition and let his nephew trace his name with the lead tip of one of the bullets. John's mother never quite approved of Jack.

The boy knew he wanted to be a police officer—he admired Uncle Jack's sense of justice and resolve, and he was enamored with the guns, cars, and badges. Two of his other uncles, Barney and Tommy, were detectives, and two cousins were patrolmen. But as he grew up, crime went from a glamorous abstraction to a local reality. At ten he stood on his stoop at dusk and watched a group of black men head to the beach at the end of White Plains Road to fish. Returning with their catch, they were set upon by white kids drinking on the street, who surrounded them and beat them with baseball bats and chains. John's father called the police.

A few years later, walking the family dog one morning before school, John spotted something in the grass on the path opposite his house. When he got closer he saw a dead body—a prostitute, the police later told his father. By the time he turned thirteen, the racial makeup of the neighborhood was shifting. One day he and a friend were menaced buying firecrackers near Holy Cross School and narrowly got away on a bike. He didn't tell his father—he shouldn't have been buying firecrackers to begin with. Construction on the Soundview Houses began the same year John's father planted the oak tree outside their bungalow. The imposing hulks—which looked entirely alien to the clustered, wood-framed cottages of Clason Point—loomed over the landscape of his childhood.

✦ ✦ ✦

THE SOUNDVIEW Houses were originally erected as a symbol of hope. Groundbreaking took place at the corner of Randall and Rosedale Avenues—later known as Cozy Corner—on September 23, 1952. The police department band played in a light rain. Deputy Mayor Charles Horowitz proclaimed, "Soundview is the American way of giving low-income families a better chance—to parents, a chance to rear children in wholesome surroundings; to children, a chance to grow up as decent citizens; and to older folks, the chance to spend their declining years in comfort instead of squalor."

Among the crowd offering polite applause was the forty-year-old architect Max Urbahn, who had helped design the Jefferson Memorial in Washington, DC, and who went on to design, among other projects, prisons, military installations, and the forty-two-story Franklin D. Roosevelt Station Post Office in Manhattan. His signature achievement would be the design of NASA's Verticle (now Vehicle) Assembly Building at the Kennedy Space Center in Cape Canaveral.

An invitation had been sent to Robert Moses, arguably the most powerful man in the city, commissioner of parks and construction coordinator of the Committee on Slum Clearance. In the narrative of Moses and his effect on New York, he was seen either as a visionary, creator of New York's future, or, as argued persuasively in Robert Caro's *The Power Broker*, the racist engineer of the city's lasting inequalities. An unelected official, in 1929 he had banned buses to Long Island's Jones Beach State Park, discouraging blacks and anyone without a car from going. He built ten new swimming pools in the city but only one in the black neighborhood of Harlem. Because he believed blacks did not like cold water, he kept the others at seventy degrees but left the Harlem pool, and the one at Jones Beach, unheated.

Soundview emerged as the centerpiece of a grand plan. In March 1939 Moses had discovered a remote shadowland, sequestered from the rest of the city in the southeast Bronx, that offered sweeping views of Manhattan and Long Island Sound. He had ordered the city's garbage dumped in Soundview rather than on Rikers Island, envisioning a park built on the landfill.

Three years later President Harry Truman's Housing Act of 1949 gave Moses more power than he had dreamed of: Title I was slum clearance; Title II, authorization for Federal Housing Administration (FHA) mortgage insurance; and Title III, federal funding to build more than 800,000 public housing units. The legislation granted the state the power of eminent domain. Anything Moses chose could be condemned, and allegations of corruption ensued as favored bidders linked to the New York Democratic Party were able to buy premium real estate at rock bottom prices. Since 1946 Moses had also been commissioner of the New York City Planning Commission, which gave its approval on July 12, 1950, for a new, low-rent public housing project called the Soundview Houses. On November 25, 1952, the area was "completely cleared of all residential and commercial tenants."

Moses drew inspiration for his housing projects from the Swiss-French architect Le Corbusier, who had developed the idea of "towers in the park" in Paris—soaring vertical cities set in public parks that housed dense populations.

Completed on October 29, 1954, the Soundview Houses—seven stories high, shorter than similar complexes to avoid planes coming in and out of LaGuardia—were earmarked for tenants who lived in over-crowded apartment complexes or in substandard conditions and who would be granted free gas and electricity at a fixed rent of $42 a month. Annual income was capped between $2,700, for a family of two, and $3,672, for a family of five or more. Veterans of the Korean War were allowed to earn a few hundred dollars more per year.

Each floor was allotted to one white, one black, and one Hispanic family, with the last apartment going to any family at the discretion of the New York City Housing Authority (NYCHA). Other housing proj-ects bloomed: the James Monroe, Castle Hill, Bronx River, Bronxdale, and Sack Wern Houses.

It only took a few years for the grand plan to backfire spectacularly. Millions of families fleeing the Jim Crow South competed for space with 52,000 Puerto Ricans who had become US citizens under the Jones Act of 1917.

Moses turned his eye on the rest of the Soundview peninsula. He wanted to tear down the 245 Clason Point houses, the O'Malleys' among them, on the grounds that the area was blighted and the tidy homes "unsanitary." A major exposé published on October 31, 1959, in the *Nation* showed how corrupt the deal was and what a moneymaker it was for Democratic Party insiders. Ultimately, all of the Clason Point houses were spared.

+ + +

BY THE MID-1960S, the Soundview Houses were descending into anarchy. On January 7, 1965, Julius Friedman, chief manager of the projects, demanded more police coverage: "Last night there was a homi-cide at Clason Point and there was a forced entry by detectives into a Soundview apartment where they apprehended a tenant who had been implicated in a shooting of a corrections officer the previous night and elsewhere a number of mail boxes were broken into (not reported by our Housing Patrolmen). I also received a report this morning that on the previous two days, two adult female tenants independently of each other reported that they had been followed by a suspicious loiterer. At this very moment, the Superintendent has just come in to tell me that somebody threw a television cabinet from the top roof of the Building in 12, narrowly missing a woman and child."

By the 1970s, white families, many of them Jewish, had become a minority in the Soundview Houses. Some found themselves targeted when fires were set outside their doors. Their children were bullied in school. Most Jewish families left for Co-op City, a huge development in the Baychester section of the Bronx. The rest of the borough seemed to have been overtaken by violence, drugs, and warring gangs.

On the school bus, some girls set O'Malley's sister's hair on fire. From then on, their father drove the two sisters to school. Then came the heroin epidemic. At fourteen, O'Malley worked at the Shorehaven Beach Club. One day after work when he dropped by the Ferry Inn to pick up a soda, he saw an older neighborhood kid he recognized as Anthony slumped awkwardly at a picnic table. When O'Malley got closer he saw a syringe hanging from his arm. The boy was dead of a heroin overdose.

+ + +

O'MALLEY ATTENDED Mount Saint Michael Academy in Wakefield, a neighborhood in the North Bronx. At $35 a month, it was expensive, but his father was determined that his son get a good education. Every day the boy, dressed in his neat dark blue school uniform, with a starched blue shirt and a freshly knotted tie, took the bus to Westchester Avenue, another to Fort Apache on Simpson Street, and then the number 2 subway train. He dreaded the line because at Gun Hill Road the carriage filled with tough black and Puerto Rican kids who glared at and jostled him. O'Malley prayed for his safety over the next four stops and was relieved when he could alight at 241st Street and walk the half mile to school.

O'Malley made no secret of his desire to join the police. At graduation from Saint Michael, his classmates wrote in his yearbook: "Johnny O! Good luck with the NYPD!" But landing a job wasn't so easy.

After years of watching the changes in the neighborhood, O'Malley's family fled the Bronx in 1973, joining an ongoing white flight. His father had been offered work in New Hampshire with AIG. Between 1970 and 1980, the Bronx's population shrank from 1.472 million to 1.169 million, and its white population dropped almost 50 percent, from just over a million to 554,000. The population that left had skills, income, and influence; their departure created a vacuum and competition for resources among newly arrived communities that had little power or political acumen. At the same time, one of Robert Moses's last projects, the Bruckner Expressway, opened. It ran east-west along the top of the Soundview peninsula, cutting the area off from the rest of the Bronx.

John O'Malley stayed in the Bronx and eventually found well-paying work with Westinghouse Elevator. But on Friday evening, December 17, 1973, he got the call he had been waiting for his whole life. He was to show up at the police academy the following Monday morning.

In June 1974 O'Malley reported for duty at the Forty-Seventh Precinct, in the northernmost section of the Bronx. In his first few days he caught sight of an intimidating, ramrod-straight lieutenant who seemed to inspire fear and respect among the men. O'Malley recognized him as Lieutenant "Iron Mike" Murphy—the man who had single-handedly taken on the armed robbers coming out of the bank in Soundview five years earlier.

Following the 1970–72 Knapp Commission's probe into police corruption, Internal Affairs had set up "integrity tests" in the precinct, leaving money in the backseat of police radio cars to see which officers would take it for themselves. Rookies were drafted to inform on older cops. Every day one of O'Malley's peers was ordered to report to the lieutenant. When O'Malley's turn came, the officer asked if he wanted to be a "field associate." He explained that his job would be to keep an eye on other police officers and to report illegal or immoral activity. O'Malley refused. He was no snitch.

The heroin epidemic led to a cycle of crime and destitution, and then arson, as landlords paid teenagers as little as $3 to torch their buildings for insurance payouts—more lucrative than trying to collect rent from addicts. O'Malley helped protect fire crews as they battled blazes while they were attacked by youths. Over two weeks in August 1973, fires consumed fifty-six separate blocks around Charlotte Street. Some parts of the South Bronx lost half of their housing, a level of destruction unknown anywhere in the world outside of wartime bombing. The scorched hulks, marked with *X*'s by the fire brigade to denote they were unsafe to enter, became heroin-shooting galleries.

When O'Malley headed out on his runs, the wheels of his patrol car crunched over masonry from collapsing buildings. The summer air smelled of soot and melting aluminum. Morale in the police department continued to hover at an all-time low. The brass were so scared of allegations of corruption that they scaled back attempts to arrest street-level heroin dealers out of concern that cops would take the dealers' money and not report it. The heroin business flourished over a fifteen-year period, changing from a small-scale model, in which dealers would sell to family and friends in houses and bars, to more of a corporate system, with full-scale drug organizations run by owners who hired managers who in turn used runners, pitchers, touts, baggers, and lookouts.

O'Malley joined a dispirited department and partnered with a fifty-year-old alcoholic named Doyle. He parked outside a bar on Gun Hill Road, an arterial road crossing the borough, on a four-to-midnight shift and left O'Malley in the car with orders not to move. "Don't touch the radio," he said. A few minutes passed before the radio erupted: shots fired, burglaries . . . "Four-seven, Frank come in!" O'Malley sat moored to his seat, fighting the urge to answer. As the hours ticked by, and more desperate calls for help came and went, O'Malley panicked, thinking his career had been ruined. Eventually two other cops rolled up and pulled Doyle out of the bar. Back in the car, Doyle, drunk and furious at being disturbed, refused to answer any calls before driving himself and O'Malley back to the precinct at midnight.

Assigned to a different training officer after his night with Doyle, O'Malley began to make his mark in a city that hovered on the verge of bankruptcy. Striking sanitation workers left mounds of stinking garbage in the street.

But in the summer of 1975, civic leaders sacked 5,550 cops, O'Malley among them. Hundreds of police officers marched to city hall, blocking rush-hour traffic and hurling bottles. At Kennedy Airport and Port Authority Bus Terminal, the police union handed out "survival guide" brochures entitled "Welcome to Fear City" to tourists.

O'Malley drove a cab through the wasteland to make ends meet. In 1976, New York City housing commissioner Roger Starr, a Robert Moses acolyte, proposed a policy of "planned shrinkage." He suggested that the South Bronx be abandoned as a way to thin the population. From 1972 to 1976, as the city closed fifty essential firefighting units, almost all in densely populated black neighborhoods, it was said that fires and chaos would empty out the Bronx.

+ + +

O'MALLEY HAD a regular gig driving home a horn player at Charlie's Inn on Harding Avenue in Throgs Neck, a smoky East Bronx bastion of three-martini lunches and family dinners. There he met seventeen-year-old Annie, a nursing student who had won a scholarship from a Bronx pigeon-racing club to attend the Montefiore School of Nursing at Mount Vernon. Her father kept pigeons on the roof of their house. Annie made extra money waiting tables at Charlie's. O'Malley learned that her father was a homicide detective in the Bronx. Their first dates involved driving down to the Jersey Shore with a crate of pigeons on the backseat, detouring via the Delaware Water Gap, where they released the birds for return to Annie's roof. Annie refused an invitation to spend a weekend in the Hamptons with O'Malley, but in time he impressed her. By the time they got engaged, in August 1977, he had been rehired by the NYPD.

O'Malley was assigned to the Fortieth Precinct, in Mott Haven—a South Bronx neighborhood of empty warehouses and burned-out homes once referred to as "the worst slum in America." In the fall of 1977, President Jimmy Carter, surrounded by Secret Service agents, visited Charlotte Street and the South Bronx. Such trips, the *New York Times* editorialized, were "as crucial to an understanding of American urban life as a visit to Auschwitz is crucial to an understanding of Nazism."

O'Malley made his reputation amid the Stygian chaos. One of the city's bigger heroin markets was on East 141st Street between Willis and Brook Avenues. His patrol car slid past eight-foot-high piles of rubble, the headlights sometimes picking out darting drug addicts in the blackened windows of abandoned buildings. When he caught kids coming in from the New Jersey suburbs to buy heroin, he took their numbers and called their parents, warning them not to let them come back to the Bronx.

Mostly he arrived for his shift half an hour early and made arrest after arrest in a police force beset by cynicism and sloth. After he completed a "gun run"—a notification over the radio of a suspect with a gun—or a missing-child call, O'Malley made sure dispatchers knew of his availability. He bounced from call to call, making ten felony collars a month with his partner. Once, he and his partner spotted a man loitering with intent and followed him into a tenement building and down a hole in the floor into a room with disco lights. They heard voices through some hastily erected drywall and decided to punch their way through, emerging as ghoulish forms covered in dust with guns drawn. A group of shocked drug dealers thrust their hands in the air. A search revealed four hundred pounds of marijuana.

A few months later the lieutenant called him into his office to complain that O'Malley and his partner had the most civilian complaints in the precinct. O'Malley countered that they had the most arrests, too. Within a year, he was moved to the anti-crime squad and into plainclothes.

Not all the cops in the precinct liked O'Malley. In the locker room a cop called Freddy Sherman sneered at O'Malley as a "supercop." "We all get paid the same, so slow down," he said.

During some time off, O'Malley and his fiancée were enjoying a lunch in the beer garden at Charlie's Inn. After dessert O'Malley went to use the bathroom. Freddy Sherman barged in, taking a place next to O'Malley at the urinal, only to begin another "supercop" tirade about the rarity of O'Malley taking a day off.

After the men zipped up, they faced off. A fight exploded. Sherman swung first. O'Malley ducked and threw a whirling haymaker that broke Sherman's nose and sent him reeling into the sink, tearing it off the wall. A geyser of water jetted upward. The crash alerted others, and the fight was broken up. Sherman left the bar with a white handkerchief pressed to his bloodied nose.

Within hours O'Malley's right thumb, badly sprained, began to throb and swell. He was unable to fire his revolver, so was given a week off. On his return he found a message on the large blackboard to the right of the commanding officer's door: "O'Malley see the CO."

O'Malley entered nervously. When the CO asked how his hand was, he braced for a rebuke. Instead the CO extended his hand for O'Malley to shake. "Good job," he said.

✦ ✦ ✦

O'MALLEY AND ANNIE married in October 1979 and moved into a small apartment in Throgs Neck. The middle-class redoubt of working families, tucked away in the southeastern part of the borough, was a holdout against the social collapse across the Bronx.

Within a few years they found a small house for $71,000 a few blocks from their church, St. Benedict's, in an upper-middle-class neighborhood called Country Club. It had a pocket square of garden and seemed like a good place to start a family. The area was clean and well tended, home to senior mob bosses who ensured no criminality disrupted their neighborhood.

Annie was now a nurse, but the couple's combined income was nowhere near enough to come up with the 25 percent down payment of $17,700. She suggested they borrow from her mother. Against O'Malley's instincts—he declared, "I'd rather live in a phone booth than ask for handouts"—they did borrow the money and moved in. They paid it back within a year. Their first child, a boy, was born in July 1984.

Four months later, O'Malley made it to the Detective Bureau and took the first opening available—on Harlem's Twenty-Fifth Precinct detective squad. The murders were unremitting. O'Malley "caught" his first homicide at 130th Street and Park Avenue in East Harlem. A crumpled body lay under the giant steel expanse of the Metro-North train tracks carrying commuters to Westchester.

The catch was considered a "dump job"—the man had been murdered elsewhere—and, by seasoned detectives, a loser case, not likely to be solved. They tossed the paperwork to the new guy. That night O'Malley received a call from one of his sisters, who said that she had been looking out the window of her commuter train in East Harlem only to see a man who looked like her brother standing over a dead body. O'Malley said her eyes hadn't deceived her.

The next few days he chased down every lead. He discovered that the murdered man was nicknamed Pet Shop. He came from O'Malley's old precinct in the South Bronx. O'Malley eventually got a tip-off. Within two months he had locked up the killer.

Solving cases like this over the next two years or so was enough to get him selected, in February 1986, for the Bronx Homicide Task Force, where he'd be working murders exclusively. He reported to the Forty-Eighth Precinct. On each side of the office door ran an alleyway of filing cabinets stuffed with photographs of the Bronx's most wanted. The office was eye level with the Cross Bronx Expressway. If the heat in summer got too much in the concrete precinct house, a detective might be forced to open a window. By the end of the day, a white shirt would be black at the wrists and arms from the soot that settled on the desk and papers. At 4:00 p.m. the bureau's phones would ring as other cops called in asking what the traffic was like to the George Washington Bridge before they left for the evening commute home.

In this cramped, chaotic office, rookies swarmed around the legendary detective Vernon Geberth, a thickset man with a penetrating gaze and a ferocious intellect. He viewed solving homicides as a vocation like the priesthood. His mantra: "Remember, you are working for God."

He had long had his eye on O'Malley, who he could tell had a feeling for the streets and a compulsive work ethic, as well as a gift for earning the trust of sources. It was he who had pressed for O'Malley's promotion to the Detective Bureau, and he who had brought him back to the Bronx. His confidence in the young detective was rewarded with

O'Malley solving his first case in the new squad—a man pushed over a railing to his death—a case considered unsolvable. O'Malley focused on the man's stepson, ultimately eliciting a story of how the dead man had abused him, and finally a confession. People just seemed to want to tell O'Malley things, even when it wasn't in their best interest.

Meanwhile, Geberth took his rookie detectives to murder scenes like an exuberant science teacher taking his students on a field trip. He brought O'Malley and others to a tenement where a woman had been smashed over the head with a baseball bat, and had her throat cut and a soda bottle rammed into her eviscerated stomach. The killer had quaffed her blood in an act of "anthropophagy," said Geberth with a pedagogical flourish. The veteran pointed to slashes on her breasts and legs. Because they didn't leak blood, he pointed out, they were inflicted after the woman had died.

Geberth insisted that his detectives go to the morgue at Thirtieth Street and First Avenue in Manhattan. The first time O'Malley walked through the door, the stench overpowered him. The medical examiner got down to work, expertly taking what looked like a tile saw and slicing off the top of a man's cranium before pulling his face off. O'Malley's legs buckled, but he regained his composure. Grinning and doing everything he could to get O'Malley to fold to the floor, the medical examiner sliced open the central body cavity like a mechanic opening the transmission of a car. He reached inside and tugged out the liver, tossing it onto a scale with a moist slap. He did the same with the heart. Afterward, he chomped into a sandwich and gave O'Malley a wink.

AT HOME, O'Malley and Annie talked endlessly about the crime sweeping the Bronx, and how this would affect their young family. Would it be fair to their son, and the other children they hoped to have, to send them to Bronx public schools that were awash in drugs? Annie wanted to stay. She had family and friends here, and she and John had both been born and raised in the borough. But she knew they'd be taking a chance. O'Malley thought that they owed it to their children to get out, and once Annie got pregnant with their second, it was enough to force the decision.

In June 1986 they packed up and left Throgs Neck and drove to a leafy town in upstate New York where they had bought a new house. When they hit the Cross Bronx Expressway, Annie turned her head to look out the window onto East Tremont Avenue, where she had first pushed a stroller, and shed a tear. The Bronx they had known was gone.

Three

HIT A KILLER,
BE A KILLER

NINETEEN EIGHTY-SIX WAS THE YEAR THAT crack spread like a fever across New York. Around the Soundview projects, dilapidated houses were turned into fortresses with steel doors, policed by armed guards with walkie-talkies. Addicts blew through tens of thousands of dollars in a few short days of bingeing.

Crack caused disastrous social change that tested New York's civic structures as it unleashed a wave of addiction. Like powder cocaine, crack can increase baseline dopamine levels several times over, but crack can be smoked, and this route of administration through the lungs means it hits the brain in seconds. In addition, the maximum effects of smoking crack last about seven to ten minutes, compared to thirty for powder; the shorter high can lead to severe depression and anxiety unless an addict takes another hit. And unlike with snorted cocaine, there is virtually no limit on how much a crack smoker can absorb.

A surge of addicts overwhelmed drug treatment centers like Daytop Village in Queens, where crack addicts slept on mattresses in hallways. In other facilities, single beds were welded into bunk beds, and staff offices were converted into sleeping quarters. In August 1986, the nurseries of some New York City hospitals were overwhelmed with newborns abandoned by their crack-addicted mothers. The media seized on the story of "crack babies." While the wave of panic about a new generation of violent, drug-addled children was unfounded, doctors noted that babies born to mothers who used cocaine had an increased risk of premature delivery, tended to weigh less at birth, were shorter, and had smaller heads. From

1984 to 1985, there was a 30 percent surge in reports of neglected and abused children in the city. The increase could be attributed to parents smoking crack, according to Eric Brettschneider, the deputy administrator of the New York City Human Resources Administration, in charge of special services for children. Under the grimy supports of the Jerome Avenue El at 181st Street, condoms littered the area as scores of women, many from middle-class homes, ducked into cars and darkened stairwells and sold themselves for a few dollars to buy rocks of crack.

The drug's impact was worst in poor neighborhoods, where it changed the demographics of crime. Heroin addicts stole TVs or broke into parked cars for money, but crack addicts pushed guns into their victims' faces while snatching gold chains and clothing—down jackets, leather coats. Desperate addicts who quickly succumbed to a $300-a-day habit took anything they could. Police reported a 29.8 percent increase in murders and a 15.7 percent increase in robberies in New York City in the first five months of 1986.

The criminal justice system warped under the strain. Judges dealt with up to 180 cases a day, while one-third of new prisoners on crack cases were released because the police laboratory could not keep up with the constant drug analysis for grand jury hearings. Many prisoners were simply plea-bargained out of the overburdened criminal justice system. Meanwhile, Rikers Island, overcrowded by as many as two thousand inmates, broke out in riots in October 1986. Twelve guards and ten inmates were wounded. Schools offered "teach-ins" on crack, while in the neighborhood around Washington Square Park in Greenwich Village, which in March–October 1987 saw 175 arrests a month for crack, residents took to the streets to protest the drug dealers.

In 1986, crack was available in twenty-eight states. The University of Maryland's All-American basketball forward Len Bias died of a heart attack induced by smoking freebase cocaine in June of that year, two days after he was drafted by the Boston Celtics. Public fear went into overdrive. "Larger numbers of our citizens are suffering and dying from this threat to our national security than [from] any nuclear warfare or chemical warfare waged on the battlefield," South Carolina congressman Thomas Hartnett declared. Politicians scrambled to pass the Anti–Drug Abuse Act of 1986, and a frenzy of prison building began.

✦ ✦ ✦

ONE SUMMER evening in 1986, as a diffuse light sluiced the project buildings, Pipe and several other kids stood over a crudely chalked skellzies court on the north side of the Soundview Houses. Around the inside edge of a square with six-foot sides were boxes numbered from one to twelve. The object was to flick a top into all twelve boxes. In the center was the "skull," number thirteen. Once a player reached the center, he became a "killer" and blasted all the other tops off the court to win. It had become so popular in Soundview that the NYCHA had spray-painted grids in hopes of dictating where the kids would play.

Bodega owners found the plastic tops from milk cartons missing; kids stole them to use as skellzie tops. Others swiped the gliders off the legs of school chairs, or worked the bottoms off beer bottles by rubbing them around manhole covers to make smooth-running glass sliders.

Pipe knelt to flick his top. Out of the corner of his eye, he saw a pair of green Adidas. A top was kicked into a higher box than the one at which he was aiming. He turned away to concentrate on his move. Again. Pipe exploded to his feet. "Move your top back, nigga! You cheatin'?"

The owner of the green Adidas frowned and sneered. Shawn—who would one day be known as Suge—was a garrulous and hyperactive twelve-year-old. "You're losing, so you saying I'm cheating! Get the fuck outta here!"

Shawn had a large, bullet-shaped head and a skinny, athletic frame. He was one of the fastest sprinters in the projects. He lived with his alcoholic grandmother in a building almost directly opposite Pipe's. Because they both lived near Cozy Corner, the top of the projects, they had their own clique within Soundview. When Pipe broke off to refocus on the game, Shawn dissolved into fits of laughter, pleased to get a rise out of his normally self-controlled friend.

Shawn didn't have the gangster pedigree of a family like Pipe's, but when he hung with his friend Beanie, he jumped on other kids and beat them up for fun. He wasn't as bold on his own. About a year before, Pipe had bought a Honda Spree scooter with $100 he got for packing bags at the supermarket. Shawn and Beanie had ambushed him and stolen it. When Pipe and his brother Ro hunted them down, Shawn tried to shoot Ro with a BB gun. He missed. The beef raged for a day or two but was quickly forgotten when Pipe got the scooter back. Somehow, Shawn almost always managed to get away with whatever he did.

Even though Shawn was three years older, he looked up to Pipe. The two were different. Pipe had learned to carry himself with authority, as the man of the house, patient and imperturbable, wiser than his years. Shawn, with only his grandmother to turn to, was excitable and craved the company and acceptance of other kids. He was quick and forceful in making friends, forging alliances, and proving his loyalty in return, but he was constantly trying to earn his way into the group. Funny and disrespectful, Shawn had learned to be both manipulative and charming, always able to extract a smile from the poutiest woman in the projects. He drew comfort from the fierce sense of unity in Soundview, but he could never stop proving himself. Pipe had his mother as teacher, and the occasional safety and belonging of family; Shawn learned by watching the action in the projects. From his earliest awareness he was molded by life in the streets around Soundview.

After a while Shawn triumphed at their skellzie game, using powerful moves with his top, one he had constructed for maximum glide, like an ice hockey puck. He propelled his top in the box in the middle and positioned himself to knock others out. "Hit a killer! Be a killer!" he shouted over and over.

+ + +

A FEW DAYS later, on a cool summer evening, Shawn marched from IS 174 into neighboring Pugsley Creek Park like a boxer heading into the ring. Behind him was a procession of sixth graders. A young, chubby kid in his building, David Martinez, often derided as "soft as a napkin," had become a target. Martinez had been bullied in class all day by one of the bigger kids, and finally Shawn, David's friend, had snapped and challenged his tormentor to a fight outside. The bully looked at his diminutive contender and eagerly accepted. Shawn often took up for others, getting himself into fights out of loyalty.

In the grass the boys circled each other and limbered up. Shawn's opponent, taller and stronger, set his face in a granite scowl while his thick arms and muscled trunk strained through a school shirt. Shawn used every ounce of his spare physique, staying on the balls of his feet to send lancing jabs.

He could slip out of his joshing neighborhood-kid self and turn on the menace with a fury. The taller kid punched him in the face with a couple of hard rights and muscled the younger boy with his elbows, throwing short rabbit punches, and then caught him in the head with an overhand right. Shawn wobbled. The fight seemed one-sided, set to end in a crushing injury and ignominious defeat. To lose in front of so many people would put a bull's-eye on his back in Soundview. He'd seen other kids who gave up in fights. From then on they were picked on, robbed of their money and sneakers. Once word was out in the projects that you backed down, you were indelibly marked.

Shawn paused, gathered himself, and sprang back. This time he slipped and weaved, retaliating with a devastating uppercut that made the bigger kid grimace. His opponent moved forward. Shawn backed up on him. By the time he realized Shawn had found the inside pocket, it was too late. Shawn pivoted his right foot on his toe to gain leverage and threw a devastating right, which knocked the taller kid down. He slumped to the ground, poleaxed. Shawn had earned priceless social capital with the victory. The other kids radiated a newfound respect as they melted away.

On his way home to Randall Avenue, Shawn passed a few young men slouched outside his apartment building, the prime hustle spot for local dealers, a few hundred yards from Cozy Corner. "The lean, mean, green machine!" rapped Fat Mike, one of the neighborhood's leading drug dealers, nodding at Shawn's green Adidas. A smile stretched across Fat Mike's broad face, and a muscleman charm hung from a gold chain around his neck. His greatest skill, aside from hustling crack, was his spontaneous flow of rhymes.

To Shawn, the five-foot-seven, 250-pound hustler in his early twenties was an older brother. Fat Mike was everything Shawn yearned to be. He was magnetic, with a quick wit and an ease with women. Shawn was impressed by his lifestyle and the small crew he commanded. Fat Mike's sidekick was Darrick Coleman, known for his smooth good looks and pomaded hair.

Fat Mike gave Shawn a few dollars from time to time and bought him slices of pizza. He looked out for him, seeming to take an interest in helping Shawn grow up and establish himself. When he found Shawn playing up near Castle Hill, he chided the boy and told him to get his ass home or risk a beating. Other dealers told the kids to get out of the area when they were selling just because they might get in the way of business. But Fat Mike never showed drugs to the kids and only sent them away when they were in danger.

Shawn noticed that Fat Mike had started driving a Jeep Wrangler with the spare tire on the back enclosed in a custom-made Gucci cover. He and his crew bragged about their nights out at Roof Top Roller Skating and Disco, at West 155th Street and Eighth Avenue in Harlem, showing Shawn pictures of themselves inside the club's deep interior, chatting on gold phones. Fat Mike wore a bomber jacket and a black fedora just like the members of the group Run-D.M.C.

Once, a few months before, Fat Mike had asked Shawn to go and pick up a brown paper bag lying four cars away from the front of their building. It looked like garbage. Inside, Shawn saw small glass bottles with red and black stoppers containing beige, rocklike lumps. "This shit is the new era," Fat Mike declared. "Make money with this but never use it." He tossed Shawn two dollar bills.

Shawn lowered his head as he walked into his building's cramped lobby, littered with old beer cans and empty bags. The stairwell reeked of urine, especially in the summer months when children playing outside couldn't be bothered to interrupt their play to make it all the way upstairs. In the dim hallway on the fourth floor, Shawn walked past apartments that had an odor like musty almonds, the sign of a cockroach infestation. Finally, he straightened his shirt and entered the apartment he shared with his grandmother.

Miss Julia, a gruff, diminutive woman with bowlegs and a pigeon-toed stance, stirred a stew on the kitchen stove. Despite the chaos and deterioration around them, her home remained an oasis. For thirty years she had worked in the mental health department of Bronx State Hospital.

As they cleared away the plates from dinner, Miss Julia put on a cassette: Al Green's "Tired of Being Alone." She pulled out a bottle of Johnnie Walker Red from the bottom of a cabinet and took a swig. Sometimes, as she became inebriated, she offered Shawn tidbits of his history.

A picture on the cabinet showed Miss Julia in her twenties, standing with Shawn's grandfather Maurice, who had a gray streak running through his thick black hair. She confided to Shawn that he had beaten her more than once. "He was a mean motherfucker." Shawn's family could be traced back to the Bight of Benin and the Slave Coast. The majority of slaves from Benin worked the cotton and rice plantations in South Carolina, where Miss Julia had been born. After slavery was outlawed, the family became sharecroppers. Miss Julia headed to New York City, where black women lined up early in the morning in front of Woolworth's on Jerome Avenue at East 170th Street: White housewives could pick them to work for ten to fifteen cents an hour.

Shawn was born during the Bronx fires in February 1974 to one of Miss Julia's nine children. A week after his birth, Shawn's mother asked Miss Julia to look after her son, and Miss Julia agreed. She preferred boys. Ever since, Shawn had had an uneasy and distant relationship with his mother. They sometimes went years without speaking.

Sometime after she took Shawn in, Miss Julia's house burned to the ground. In later years a rumor circulated in the family that Shawn, age two and playing with matches, had caused the blaze. They moved to Soundview after the fire.

As he grew, Miss Julia always told Shawn that the Soundview projects were a bad place, built on an Indian burial ground. Shawn discovered through a local history book at school that there were sixty food pits or underground larders around Lacombe and Leland Avenues that contained human remains. The Siwanoy Indians had once lived near the east bank of what was later named the Bronx River. From then on Shawn sometimes saw the Soundview inhabitants as the new Indian tribe, and himself as a young brave. Miss Julia did not see the enchantment in this history: "The spirits ain't right here," she told him.

On Friday nights Miss Julia drank hard and grew ornery. She yelled and cursed at Shawn before passing out with her cigarette still burning in the ashtray. With his grandmother blacked out, Shawn tore through the house, sometimes taking her whisky and cigarettes outside to offer to friends.

Other times, Miss Julia believed in strong discipline. When Shawn broke the living room lightbulb, she called him into her room, whirled an electrical cord like a bullwhip around her head, and cracked him in the neck. Once, when he'd snuck into another project against the rules, he came home to find Julia inviting him to relax and take a bath. He assumed he'd gotten away with his transgression. When he stepped out of the bath, dripping wet, she beat him with such ferocity he struggled to walk afterward.

Her swings from rage to benevolence ceased to surprise him. He woke once to find her at the kitchen table treating a cut on Crackhead Bemo's head. After patching him up, she made him a meal. When Bemo left, Miss Julia told Shawn: "Don't ever judge no one for smoking drugs."

She struggled to raise him as a God-fearing child. She took him to a local Baptist church, dressing him in a fawn-colored tweed sport coat with a white shirt, a brown tie, and black slacks. At thirteen he began to resent the weekly drag to church. "Mama, what's the difference between God and Jesus? How come they one person?" Shawn didn't accept her lucid disquisition about the Trinity. He'd rather be in the street than jammed up in church in his Sunday best. "I don't want to go to church no more," he finally told her. Miss Julia sighed and relented.

✦ ✦ ✦

THERE WAS a knock on Miss Julia's door. She opened the three locks on it to reveal Fat Mike. After that first fight outside school to protect his friend, Shawn's combat rating as a scrapper got Fat Mike's attention. Shortly after, he had set Shawn up against a younger Hispanic kid. Shawn knocked the kid out as well. Fat Mike gave him a dollar bill and some change, and Shawn felt thrilled to have been able to offer something to someone he regarded as hero and mentor. Now, Shawn came to his grandmother's elbow. "What's good?" said Fat Mike. "Wanna help me with something?"

Outside, Fat Mike threw a leg over his red scooter, and Shawn clambered on behind. Other children looked on with envy as they rode along, Shawn frowning intently but inwardly thrilled. When they reached the end of the block, Fat Mike ordered Shawn off. A couple of defiant Hispanic kids his age stood there. "These little motherfuckers cursed me out," said Fat Mike. Shawn slipped into his boxing stance and moved to the oldest-looking one. With one or two well-targeted punches he knocked the child to the ground. "See," said Fat Mike to the boy. "Done told you my little man fuck you up."

From then on, anytime Fat Mike got disrespected by neighborhood kids too young for him to lay hands on personally, he called on Shawn. Sometimes Shawn lost the fight, but he never gave up, and if he did win, and the other boy didn't want to fight anymore, he relented. He was learning that violence brought loyalty. And loyalty and friendship, in turn, brought the best chance of security. Over time, Shawn stopped seeing fistfights as violent. He saw them as a way of mediating disputes, a form of politics that preceded real violence, which involved guns, something the older kids used.

After the mission with Fat Mike, Shawn returned to the apartment and sat in his room under posters of dirt bikes and the rapper Big Daddy Kane. As Miss Julia bustled around the kitchen, he examined the five dollar bills in his bloodied hand.

✦ ✦ ✦

SHAWN PLAYED for the Young Devils, a local recreational football team. Over the course of the 1986 season, he had grown close with his teammate Peter Rollock. Shawn and Pete worked together to score touchdowns as running backs: Pete pushed his bulk through the line, creating a hole for

Shawn, who sprinted through into the open field. Pete grandiosely named the play P38, despite the fact that it was a relatively common way to score.

Shawn had first met Pete a couple of years before in front of Pete's grandmother's three-story row house. Their two worlds—the long shadows of public housing and the private houses with their big white garage doors—were separated by Rosedale Avenue. Forbidden to leave his grandmother's property, Pete stood, dressed in the latest sneakers, under a red awning, calmly watching every move: the hustling drug dealers, the stickup kids on Cozy Corner who robbed them. He was sequestered from one of the most violent ghettoes in New York City by a four-foot-high black wrought-iron fence. Eventually Shawn convinced Pete to leave his grandmother's property and go with him into the projects, where he introduced him to other kids. But by 8:00 p.m. Pete was always back home, while Shawn and the others stayed out.

From the beginning, Miss Julia took a dislike to Pete. She didn't trust his radiant grin. He always stood on her threshold politely, with his wrists crossed in front of his stomach, never entering unless invited. "Here's your friend Pete with that shit-eating grin," she grumbled, announcing his arrival to Shawn.

A surprise visitor appeared one day when they were standing outside Pete's building. A glistening black car slid around the corner on Story Avenue before it slowed to a halt, like a spaceship landing in a primitive world. A tall man with a boxer's physique and a heavy forehead stepped out. He scouted around and then beckoned Pete over. Shawn stood watching, his arms at his sides, football gear in hand. The man moved to the rear of the car, popped the trunk, and pulled out a new motorized scooter, which he set on the sidewalk in front of Pete. A few days later, Pete told Shawn that that was his dad, a gangster with connections to the mob. Shawn didn't know his own father, and his admiration for Pete at that moment was mixed with an almost unbearable jealousy.

✦ ✦ ✦

PETE STARTED getting everyone in trouble, luring them into fights. On a fall day in 1987, Shawn walked over to meet him near Lacombe

Avenue, in an area they called "white-boy territory." They sometimes stole the Italian kids' bicycles, left propped up against the fences outside low redbrick houses. It seemed that in every house was a middle-aged man in a white tank top who would come storming down to the gate, yelling, "Get the fuck outta here, you little niggers!" Shawn and the boys would sprint back home, laughing. Today Shawn went to the Castle Hill housing projects, where he was meeting Pete to play basketball. A local kid wanted to fight Pete. Pete refused, saying his clothes were new. Shawn's friend Beanie tore off his shirt and stepped in for him.

Quickly, the Soundview boy beat the challenger. But at that point Pete jumped in, followed by Shawn. Unbeknownst to the boys, the kid was backed by a small tribe of older brothers and cousins. When they showed up to even the fight, Shawn, Pete, and the others took off back to Soundview. Pete declared afterward that there would be no more "one-on-ones." All fights would be undertaken as a crew. Pete saw the power of unifying and fighting in numbers.

A few months later, Pete cornered Shawn near the lockers at 174. He had gotten into an altercation with a kid they called "Gay René." He wasn't gay but wore tight pants and T-shirts, and the name had stuck. Pete was going to fight him after school, and he wanted Shawn and others there.

After school, Shawn, a friend named PO, and B-Love—the same boy who had beaten up Pipe before Pete stepped in—all trailed out to a bus stop on White Plains Road. As Gay René tried to talk, Pete surprised him with a single straight shot that felled the boy with a broken nose. The others jumped in to support their man. Shawn brought the heel of his foot down on René's chest. Then police and truancy officers arrived. The cops got PO. Somehow Pete and the others managed to slip away.

PO gave up Shawn and B-Love, but kept Pete's name out of it from fear. The police came for Shawn at his grandmother's apartment. "You out there hurting boys!" she yelled at Shawn, as the two were led to a police car.

The Bronx County Family Court prosecutor threatened them with Spofford, a detention center over the Bronx River in Hunts Point that acted as a way station in the sprawling juvenile justice system. PO broke down in tears, begging not to be sent to a place where it was well known boys were raped. His mother howled in court, pleading for the authorities not to take her son. Miss Julia sat staring quietly ahead. She told Shawn, now thirteen, that a spell in jail might straighten him out. She half meant it. She was proud that he was willing to fight. Where she came from, a man had to stick up for himself. She even bragged to others in the projects about why she allowed him to hang out so late. "He can whup anyone," she declared. "I know his little black ass can take care of hisself." She had always supported his right to fight in the street. "If they lay a hand on you, whup they ass!" she'd told him. And yet she didn't want him to embarrass her or cause trouble when he was caught. When he did, she disavowed him and left him in the hands of the state. It was confusing to Shawn.

B-Love's mother agreed with Miss Julia. "Take 'em if you want," she told the court. Sentenced to six months' probation, Shawn escaped Spofford for the time being.

+ + +

IN JANUARY 1988, two inches of downy snow covered the projects, deadening footfalls. Hustlers pitched from the lobbies, avoiding the cold wind sweeping in from Long Island Sound. Shawn gazed out his window and took in the eerie quiet on a Sunday morning.

Two of his friends came over with an envelope of vanilla marijuana. With his grandmother out at church, they smoked in her room, languishing on her bed. After finishing their blunts, they went downstairs.

From the front steps they could see the approaching lights of a squad car. Darrick Coleman's cousin came up, sobbing. Something bad had happened at 1680, she said. The boys went over to the building, at the end of the horseshoe, facing out onto Soundview Park. The place was crawling with police and crime scene technicians in white coveralls. Ambulances pulled up.

Shawn raced upstairs to the top floor, following the cops. A resident told him that at 3:00 a.m. three armed men had burst into a neighboring apartment on the floor. Shortly thereafter, there was a thirty-second storm of gunfire. The neighbor said that Fat Mike, Darrick Coleman, and a friend of theirs had been murdered. Just the day before, Shawn had been strutting with a new Caesar haircut when Fat Mike had jumped out and annoyed him by mussing it. Now he felt a twinge of guilt that his last words to Fat Mike had been ones of irritation.

A TV crew stepped off the elevator. They jammed a camera in Shawn's face. "How do you feel?" the newswoman asked the thirteen-year-old. Shawn pouted angrily. "I ain't got nothing to say." He knew not to break the projects' code of silence.

At around 2:00 p.m. the medical examiner brought out three black body bags. Shawn convinced himself that Fat Mike had not been involved, but the last bag out of the apartment contained a huge round form. Fat Mike was dead at eighteen years old, and so was Shawn's childhood. He broke down in tears.

Sobbing in the hallway, he would not have noticed the skinny, mustached cop pushing past him with the wide-eyed look of a rookie trying to survive in the projects.

✦ ✦ ✦

A FEW HOURS earlier, Officer Pete Forcelli had pressed his way through a scrum of grieving women to the dirty-blue door of apartment 7C. It was open, but Forcelli paused, taking a deep breath, before he went in. "Keep your hands in your pockets," barked a detective inside the door. "Don't touch anything."

A filthy brown carpet was matted with dirt, blood, and shards of broken crack vials. Someone had plastered over punch holes in the walls without repainting. Stepping gingerly, Forcelli followed a trail of blood left by someone who had crawled toward the front door.

Forcelli passed a bedroom where a porn magazine lay on the floor, displaying the image of a thin black woman naked and spread-eagle. Razor blades lay on bedside tables. In the center of the living room was an upturned drawer standing on its end, with a pile of red- and black-topped crack vials and three or four more razor blades. At the end of the hall, two bedrooms: On the right door someone had daubed Do Not Disturb in white paint. In the doorway of the bedroom on the left he saw one spent 12-gauge shotgun casing, an indication of what lay beyond.

In the bedroom he came upon a horrifying scene, all of it reflected in a wall-sized mirror. The metallic scent of blood—like a bucket of rusty nails that had sat rain-drenched for days—hung in the air. The floor was a giant slick almost half an inch deep. A hundred and seventeen red and black crack vials floated in the blood. The bodies of three men, two completely nude, lay to the right of a bed against a wall sprayed with graffiti. The first victim, a 250-pound black male, lay facedown, wearing only a T-shirt, slumped against the exterior wall as if his last moments were spent trying to claw through it. There was a three-by-three-inch hole in the rear right side of his skull. The blast had been delivered at close range, maybe three feet away. Fragments of skull were embedded in the brain. Forcelli recognized the lifeless man from the neighborhood, and knew him as Fat Mike. Near his head was his pristine red scooter, propped against the wall.

The second victim had been a handsome young man with elaborate pomaded hair. He lay naked, his penis exposed. A shotgun round had been fired downward through the man's right shoulder, tearing a path through the man's internal organs. The force of the blast had spun him around, at which point a second round—a slug—had been fired into the right side of his back. A detective said his name was Darrick Coleman.

The third man, his blue underpants resting on his shoulder, lay under a table, where he had crawled to draw his last breath next to the bed. He had been shot in the torso with a shotgun and twice with a .380, once in the neck and once in the thigh.

At least fifteen detectives filled the room. Forcelli felt he was seeing the destruction of this so-called crack epidemic firsthand. It was his first crack-related triple homicide, but it would not be his last. Raised in a tough neighborhood in Yonkers, he'd seen his share of shootings and stabbings, but this, he thought, looked like true evil. Beyond that he just took it all in, a rookie learning the ropes.

A senior officer ordered him to stand outside and hold back the tenants crowding for a look. At around 2:00 p.m. the corpses were put into body bags. When Fat Mike was lifted by medical examiners, one of them noticed a weight in his sock. He had made a last desperate attempt to hide his jewelry. Inside were three gold rings, two gold chains, a yellow bracelet, and a gold muscleman charm.

The crime scene technicians and detectives drove off with a heavy-limbed weariness. Yellow tape was rolled across the door. Outside, a dozen police cars, ambulances, and crime scene vehicles lined up on both sides of the road. Forcelli and his partner got back in their car, a Plymouth Gran Fury that marked him as a housing cop, and crawled off around the horseshoe. It was almost four in the afternoon, the end of their shift. Forcelli, behind the wheel, turned to his partner as he nosed past Cozy Corner, empty of drug dealers for the first time since he'd been working Soundview. "Why do people live like this?"

It could be a bright, joyful day, the sun high in a clear sky, and yet he always felt gloom in Soundview. Some cops in the precinct assumed that the NYCHA deliberately placed all those with criminal records in this particular development. The culture of violence made it different from other projects. *People here don't care,* Forcelli thought, *or they are afraid of those who don't care.*

+ + +

FORCELLI'S FAMILY had been one of only three white families in a predominately black area of South Yonkers comprising Section 8 buildings. Sometimes they ate breakfast cereal for dinner when his father, a construction worker, wasn't able to find work and money was short. At age seven, he had seen an undercover police officer shoot a suspect across the street. As a teenager, he was a scrapper and was often picked on for being the only white kid in the area. He lounged in the parks drinking beer with his friends, blasting Led Zeppelin on a radio, and tried marijuana a couple of times. He even ran from the cops, who had once smashed the radio in frustration when they couldn't catch them. But for as long as he could remember he'd wanted to be a police officer, taking inspiration from *Starsky and Hutch* and *Kojak*.

Forcelli, patrolman 2307, was barely twenty years old on his first day in uniform, in July 1987. He wasn't a naturally imposing presence. When he went for his preemployment medical he weighed only 129 pounds. The nurse had to verify that there was no stipulation about being underweight. He had such a narrow waist, just twenty-six inches, that his duty belt didn't have enough space to accommodate his department-issued pen and pencil, as was required by the NYPD *Patrol Guide*.

New York City's 180 housing projects were patrolled by fifteen Public Service Areas (PSAs). PSA 8 covered around twenty-five square miles, or roughly half the Bronx. In it were twenty housing projects in seven police precincts containing thousands of the poorest New Yorkers. The housing cops had a motto, "Second to None," but the joke among them was that they were, in fact, second to the NYPD, the preeminent law enforcement organization, which looked down on them. (The third arm was the transit police.)

He learned in his first days that most cops in the projects were bound by the law of the street, and that this law would determine whether they would be respected. A veteran black cop gave Forcelli some advice. "Look, you're a young-looking kid," he said. "You're a white kid . . . so, in the projects, they are going to test you. If you cave in, they will fuck with you every time they see you as long as you're in this precinct. So if somebody gets in your face you need to lay them out."

On one of his first patrols, Forcelli was dropped off in the middle of the Monroe Houses, three blocks northeast of Soundview. At around dusk a local thug named KK took in the rookie cop in his oversized uniform and shiny new leather belt, standing outside 877 Taylor Avenue, a notorious crack spot. KK started spewing obscenities, jeered at him, and threatened to beat him up.

Without hesitation, remembering the old cop's words of advice, Forcelli pulled his nightstick and swung full force into the man's shins. KK collapsed to the ground, and Forcelli slapped on handcuffs. Word got around quickly. Rarely was he tested again in the Monroe projects.

Lately Forcelli had been bulking up at the gym, three to four hours every night. Sometimes after working out, he drove to Lanzetta Pastry on Allerton Avenue and ordered a dozen cannoli and a quart of milk, devouring them in the patrol car between radio calls. He was up to 140 pounds and and had grown a mustache to make himself look older.

+ + +

IN THE SUMMER of 1988, Forcelli stood on the roof of a four-story apartment building on Boynton Avenue, peering through binoculars. Housing cops would periodically work surveillance details from the roofs. Below he could see the street, swarming with children, and in among them a line of people, twenty or more at a time, waiting to buy heroin. In a sea of crack, this was a holdout area where heroin was still popular, and a growing number of addicts had developed HIV/AIDS. Every half hour or so, a hooded figure appeared to do a few transactions before disappearing inside a building. Another line would form and out he would come.

As he looked down at the scurrying figures and the endless supply and demand, he felt disgust. There would be no murders or gunfire if people stopped buying drugs. But here they were, driving the cycle of violence in their own homes. Forcelli thought of other cops in the precinct who dismissed the entire Soundview or Bronx River Houses as lost areas where the community supported criminals. "As long as they just kill each other off," one cop or another would say, "who cares?"

Through the binoculars, Forcelli saw two children jabbing at each other as if they were playing tag. Each of them held a needle picked up from a bag on the ground nearby. They risked infection with HIV or hepatitis if their game wasn't stopped. He radioed patrol.

On a Friday night, a few days after the rooftop heroin operation, Forcelli joined some other cops who liked to unwind at three bars—Riddlers, People's, and PC's—referred to by the cops as the Herpes Triangle. On Fridays, PC's, a long, dark bar lined with mirrors, was jammed with young Latinas in figure-hugging miniskirts and big hair looking to pick up cops.

As Forcelli squeezed in at the bar, he caught sight of a light-skinned Hispanic man with a gold crown on his head surrounded by three body-guards. Around his neck was a solid gold medallion that must have weighed at least two pounds. It was Chicky Rosario, self-styled Emperor of the Bronx. He was the street enforcer for the Bonanno crime family, one of the five families flooding the city with heroin. Rosario controlled the heroin on Boynton and Watson Avenues, an area equidistant between the Soundview, Bronx River, and Bronxdale housing projects. His crew used the Quick Stop Deli in Hunts Point, a few blocks from the Bronx River and across from the abandoned buildings, to sell heroin under the brand name Beef and cocaine under the brand Two Star. He also imported cocaine from either the Virgin Islands or Puerto Rico through Kennedy Airport. It was likely that the needles the children had been playing with were in some way connected with Rosario's trade. And yet here he was drinking in a bar full of cops, not only untouchable but wearing a crown, as if holding court in his own fiefdom, revered as a king while poisoning his own community.

Forcelli sipped his beer, frustrated at his ineffectiveness at taking down the bad guys. "It's like shoveling shit into the tide," he said to someone. For example, a few months earlier, he'd been tipped off by a cabdriver about a swaying drunk brandishing a shotgun near some stores in Castle Hill. When Forcelli screeched up in the police car and arrested him, he caught the drunk pushing the gun under a car. It seemed an obvious case. Forcelli testified in court, but the man's lawyer pressed Forcelli over why he hadn't written down the name of the cabdriver who'd given him the tip, something Forcelli knew wasn't that important. The lawyer went on to falsely claim that Forcelli had planted the shotgun on his client, who was the nearest black man. Forcelli lost his temper at the racist insinuation, which cost him the sympathy of the jury. The accused was acquitted, and yet again another guilty man escaped justice.

Around November 1988, Forcelli was doing a vertical foot patrol in the same building Fat Mike had been killed in. As he moved up and down the claustrophobic and darkened stairwells, where dealers had smashed out the lights, he never knew if he might run into a drug deal going down or a guy with a gun, and find himself cornered and unprepared in the maze. The other week he'd passed a palsied young woman in a raggedy dress slumped in her own excrement, a needle hanging from her tracked arms as she murmured in the half-light, scratching her arms and body. Forcelli had resolved not to slip into the us-versus-them mentality he saw all around him. He knew better. But as he stared at the Emperor across the bar, roaring with laughter at something one of his female companions had said, Forcelli felt he was losing the battle.

Four

THE LEDGER OF DEATH

PROFITS FROM CRACK COCAINE PUSHED UP homicides across the Bronx in 1988 and would play a role in at least 38 percent of all murders in New York City that year. O'Malley worked on one of three five-man teams at Bronx Homicide.

For every new murder, O'Malley cracked a new sand-colored steno pad. Soon the long, thin notebooks covered his desk in a pile several inches deep. It was impossible to spend more than a day or so on each homicide. If there were no significant leads, he'd move to the next. Often, the drug dealers would have their revenge faster than O'Malley could solve the first murder. He would identify one perpetrator only to find him murdered a few weeks later.

At Bronx Homicide a detective on the verge of retirement recorded the murders in a ledger of death, a large, frayed pale blue volume. The detective had begun the ledger on October 9, 1987, and would have to start another on December 13, 1993. In unusually neat handwriting, he wrote the name and address of the victim, the place and date of his demise, and the murder weapon.

O'Malley would come in on a Monday morning and ask, "How many bodies did we catch over the weekend?" The three days beginning Friday, July 7, were typical. At 11:30 a.m., Mighty Carvett was found shot dead at 624 East 169th Street in a dispute over crack—the 217th murder victim in the Bronx that year. At 7:30 p.m., Alberto Rodriguez was found stabbed to death opposite 321 East 153rd Street. On Saturday, at 12:15 a.m., Jose Garcia was gunned down at the Kentucky Fried Chicken at

321 East Kingsbridge. Two hours later, over at 1246 Wheeler Avenue in Soundview, Loretta Mason and Diane Clark were stabbed to death in their home. Then, at 3:00 a.m., Pedro Cruz was shot to death at 136th Street and Brook Avenue in the Fortieth Precinct. At 4:00 a.m., Manuel Figueroa was murdered with a gun on Boston Road. And in the Fortieth Precinct, Ismael Quiles was shot at 7:54 p.m. at 730 Brook Avenue. Finally, less than an hour before midnight, Vernon Braithwaite, shot dead in front of 1679 Vyse Avenue, became the seventh murder victim in just twenty-four hours. Five more murders on Sunday brought the weekend total to twelve, the last being Theodore Burgess, shot in his home in a dispute over drugs, the 232nd murder victim that year in the Bronx. Of the 430 Bronx murders in 1988, roughly half went unsolved.

O'Malley worked thirty-hour shifts when the murders backed up, falling asleep at his Underwood typewriter, one letter repeated across the page as he filled out DD5 forms. A senior cop called Shoefly appeared unannounced at every precinct house and handed out command discipline to napping cops.

After his shift, O'Malley climbed into his broken-down Dodge Dart. Sometimes his battery had been stolen or someone had put a couple of bullets in a door. Other times, he'd head home and fall asleep behind the wheel on the Palisades Parkway, jolting back to consciousness to find tree trunks suddenly looming in the windshield as he squealed back into a straight line. To stay awake he'd slap himself or drive with his hand out the window in the frigid winter air. When Annie heard him coming, she'd head out the door on her way to work at the hospital; he'd take the baby from her, change his diaper or give him a bottle.

Then it was back in again on the next shift. O'Malley and the other detectives had to set priorities within the first forty-eight hours after a homicide. Few in the community would help the police, certainly not when drug dealers were killing other drug dealers. So those cases were often passed over for cases the detectives had a chance of solving—or for the killers of children. In February 1988, O'Malley was called to a double homicide in a Morris Heights apartment. Selena Cooper and her nine-year-old daughter, Joi Little, had both been savagely raped and strangled to death, discovered by the girl's aunt on a bloodstained bed, hogtied next to one another. He found no signs of a robbery but discovered after speaking with the grandmother that Selena Cooper was a crack addict and mixing with drug dealers. O'Malley normally shielded his wife from the realities of his work, but the murder scene was so horrifying that that night he shared what he had seen with her.

The squad suffered from a lack of resources. While the FBI had deep coffers to pay informants, O'Malley and the other officers had to reach into their own pockets if they needed information. Sometimes O'Malley would get a lead from a drug addict or a prostitute, giving the informant $20 from his own pay—with the offer of more—if he thought it would help catch the killer.

Murder hung in the air like a viral mist. In 1988, the number of killings in New York City would soar by 10.4 percent over the previous year. Nationally, while young American men of all races killed each other at the rate of 21.9 per 100,000 in 1987, young black males were murdered at almost four times that rate, at 85.6 per 100,000.

It was frustrating and thankless work. Distrust between the police and the Bronx communities had broken down into outright animus. Two years earlier, in 1986, a Bronx drug dealer named Larry Davies, wanted for seven murders, shot six of O'Malley's colleagues from Bronx Homicide as they tried to arrest him at an apartment on Fulton Avenue. He escaped. O'Malley joined the manhunt, but after Davies was captured he was found not guilty of killing the drug dealers by a Bronx jury. Then, in a second trial, a jury acquitted him of the attempted murder of the police officers because he had "acted in self-defense." "Bronx jury" came to mean an impossible conviction.

One bitterly cold night O'Malley followed up at a murder scene on short notice as a favor to a colleague, dressed only in a suit jacket. He canvassed the area, shivering, as he handed out tip cards to people in a bid to get witnesses. Back at the precinct he received a phone call from the family of the victim. They demanded to talk to the detective handling the case. O'Malley introduced himself and briefly ran the names of two suspects past the family. He'd barely started on the second name when the caller blurted, "Instead of interrogating me, why don't you get off your fat ass and get out on the street and do your job?" O'Malley snapped. "Why don't you and your drug-dealing family go fuck yourself?" He slammed down the receiver.

Two hours later a family arrived at the precinct holding a tape recording of the conversation. "Who is the detective we got on tape telling us to go fuck ourselves?" O'Malley drove home certain he'd be fired. For a week, he barely slept. The complaint eventually petered out because the family didn't want to invite police scrutiny. But it was the first time he'd buckled under pressure in the job, and he knew it was a mistake he could never repeat. Years later, he told young cops the story to illustrate how you could never let your guard down. You were always accountable.

✦ ✦ ✦

THE HOUSING cops, Forcelli among them, were the front line in the growing war between the police and the dealers. One morning in April 1989, showers turned the Bronx streets into slick obsidian, and Forcelli—behind the wheel of a GMC twelve-seater after dropping cops off on foot patrol—rear-ended a sedan.

Back at PSA 8, Forcelli reported the accident, and three weeks later he was judged to have been driving with "excessive speed for the weather conditions" and handed a "command discipline" along with a thirty-day ban on driving. Worse, as punishment, he would have to work foot patrol in the Throgs Neck Houses, a mundane sentence of nugatory callouts, offering little of the action of going after dealers on which he thrived.

The project lay to the southwest of the Cross Bronx Expressway, thirty-two acres of three-story buildings on the approach to the Throgs Neck Bridge, which crossed from the Bronx to Queens. Forcelli fought his geographical prejudices. If you lived in the projects, some cops argued, then you were "an animal" and too lazy to work. You depended on welfare and easy money from drugs. Being a cop, it was all about survival and backing up your partner. Softening toward street thugs put everyone at risk. As one cop said, "There are two kinds of people in this world: cops and assholes."

Once, Forcelli and a partner had been chasing a man who had assaulted a child. Running after him, they shouted into their radios: "Man in blue T-shirt running." As the man rounded a corner someone tossed a black T-shirt down to him, and he changed while sprinting. Forcelli was discovering that people would do anything to protect their own—even those accused of assaulting children. The police, on the other hand, were seen as venal, corrupt, and untrustworthy. Each day Forcelli had to avoid "airmail"—chicken bones or D batteries thrown off the roofs at him. In Soundview, a twenty-seven-inch TV hurled from the roof had missed him by inches as it exploded on the sidewalk.

Yet in the first few days of walking around the Throgs Neck Houses, Forcelli found something different. Many of the residents held regular jobs, and an eight-hour-workday mentality prevailed. Of course, there was some crime; Forcelli noticed an informal auto repair business in the shadow of the Cross Bronx Expressway where enterprising kids disabled visitors' cars and then offered to "fix" them for a small fee once the owner returned. And there was an illegal barbershop on the first floor of 471 Swinton Avenue. Still, aside from the everyday hustles, tenants were out in the sunshine, something he never saw in Soundview. He was startled when one or two residents even nodded at him on his first days on patrol.

As he walked, he might have realized that he was going back to the roots of the Housing Authority Police Department (HAPD) and its community mandate in the 1950s as a dedicated community police force for Robert Moses's newly erected housing projects. There were crucial differences between them and their NYPD brethren. Almost half of the HAPD officers were nonwhite, mirroring the racial and ethnic makeup of the projects. The nearly all-white NYPD came roaring in to arrest people and left again. They were despised. The housing police, conversely, played ball with kids, stood on the corner when people returned from work, and listened patiently when residents voiced their concerns. The NYPD derided the HAPD as Keystone Kops, but there was no denying their value.

But the 1969–70 recession changed the HAPD's relationship with the residents. Factories padlocked their gates, and small stores struggled and closed, while low-income jobs, the lifeblood for the urban poor in the projects, dried up. Welfare payments could not keep up with inflation, and food stamps were worth a third less. Residents turned to the underground economy. Women offered informal daycare and cooked for restaurants, or even raised chickens, in their apartments. All of this was in breach of NYCHA laws and could result in eviction. Residents did not want the police in their business anymore, creating a rift between them.

✢ ✢ ✢

A FEW WEEKS into his foot patrol, Forcelli was called to investigate a decomposing body in a third-floor apartment, the type of mundane call all cops dread. The elderly could be dead for weeks before the police arrived. Forcelli, covering his mouth and donning latex gloves, forced the door to find a festering female corpse. A sergeant arrived, and Forcelli bent to the unenviable task of searching the body.

Afterward, he waited alone for the medical examiner, which could take hours. The overpowering stench drove him out into the hallway. Within minutes he could see a Hispanic man struggling to heave a big reclining chair out of his apartment. Forcelli, ever wary, thought that he recognized him as a crack fiend. Eventually the man, heaving and puffing, pushed the chair all the way up to Forcelli. "Officer," he said, "it's not good to stand. You should sit."

Awkwardly, Forcelli mumbled thanks, saying it wasn't necessary, and carried on standing, only to see the offense his refusal caused. "Okay," he said, sinking into the armchair in the middle of the hallway. The man left, and his mother came out of the apartment with a fresh mug of coffee for Forcelli.

As the hours ticked by, Forcelli sat in the dark hallway. He realized something about his role in these communities. He'd arrived at the Throgs Neck Houses with a hostile, confrontational attitude. That prejudice was impossible to maintain here.

On foot patrol, he chatted with residents. One or two confided to him that they were saving to get out or go to college. They paid the consequences when the drug dealers moved in. Forcelli began to understand that most were good, honest folks who'd been dealt a rough hand and were capable of kindness and generosity. His cynicism seemed to melt away as he sat outside this apartment.

Residents began to seek him out. Even a man who worked as a black-market mechanic in the project car lot, against NYCHA rules, asked Forcelli to talk to his sixteen-year-old boys, who were getting into trouble on the streets. Forcelli went to their apartment and tried to show them that a better life could be had without drugs and crime. The boys at least listened to what Forcelli had to say.

Still, the code of the street ruled. Around June, Forcelli got into a confrontation with a drug dealer who cruised around every day in a black Nissan Maxima. Forcelli had seen this before: A new drug dealer arrived, opening a portal to heavier crews who were able to deliver kilos rather than ounces, but consequently they also brought more substantial firepower, along with a willingness to use it. Slowly the cycle of violence would begin as the drug dealer attempted to ruthlessly eliminate rival dealers. Now, as the sun brought the residents out to soak up the rays, this new drug dealer turned up again outside an apartment that doubled as a crack house for a notorious local dealer called Frederick. People gathered, and Forcelli had to act. To back down in front of everyone could cost him his reputation, making his job impossible, if not dangerous. He'd been called before to assist cops who'd been mugged and had their guns and badges stolen. After that happened, it was too dangerous for them to walk the projects, so they spent their days in the basement records room. Forcelli sprang into action, slapping the dealer across the face before spinning him around and handcuffing him, arresting him for trespassing and disorderly conduct. As Forcelli led him away, a loud cheer and a smattering of applause arose from the residents.

A short while later Forcelli chased down a man who fired six shots right outside the precinct, sprinting three blocks to tackle him to the pavement. After that, kids in the project joked he was the fastest white guy they'd ever seen. The residents nicknamed him "Pac-Man," after the 1988 movie *Colors*, in which Sean Penn plays a Los Angeles cop fighting gang violence. A street name indicated that he had won respect. A few mothers joked that they wanted the twenty-year-old Pac-Man to marry their daughters. A father invited Forcelli to his sixteen-year-old daughter's birthday party. Forcelli politely demurred.

Empowered by some of his successes, Forcelli wanted more than ever to liberate the residents of Throgs Neck from the drug dealers. An anti-crime unit had been tasked with shutting down Frederick's crack house, but most of the cops seemed more interested in claiming overtime on arrests than in setting up long-term surveillance during regular hours. Just one arrest could generate at least twenty-four hours of overtime in the court system. And there was always the problem of the dealers' immunity from eviction.

Forcelli's partner, Pat Kelly, had been mentoring him in the language of the street. He'd taught Forcelli how felons recently released from prison shone with health after three square meals and a weightlifting regimen, while those on the street were often skinny from fast food and drugs, alcohol, and cigarettes. Wearing plainclothes, they began watching Frederick's apartment. After ten days they spotted a random buyer leaving with crack in his hand and swooped in. Back at PSA 8 they told the man he might be able to reach a deal with the DA if he cooperated. Based on his testimony, Forcelli got a search warrant to hit the apartment, arresting Frederick.

Forcelli continued to discover ways in which the system worked against him and the tenants, protecting drug dealers who held the community in fear. He tried to get Frederick evicted, but his NYCHA hearing resulted only in probation. The gangs seemed an impossible cancer to eradicate.

+ + +

WHILE FORCELLI evolved as a street cop, over at Bronx Homicide O'Malley's crime-fighting skills grew. He was learning how to detect a lie, build confidence, and bluff when he had to. Slowly he was solving murders.

Toward the end of August 1989, an armored car was robbed of

$500,000 in the South Bronx; one of the drivers was shot and killed on his first day of work. O'Malley partnered with a local precinct detective, Stanley Schiffman, who had earned fame for once getting a killer to confess by saying that his victim had a miniature camera in his eye and had recorded the image of his murderer just before he died. (Despite the confession, a Bronx jury acquitted him.) O'Malley and Schiffman interviewed the surviving driver, twenty-six-year-old Wycliff Warner, in the "box"—the interview room at the Forty-Seventh Precinct. Warner gave an emotional blow-by-blow account, saying that a car had rammed the back of the truck, and his partner, Billy Hackworth, had opened the door and been shot.

Parts of the story weren't adding up. For one, armored car drivers were instructed never to open the doors. "This guy's full of shit," said O'Malley outside the interview room. "He's hinky about something." Schiffman agreed. They could angrily confront him over his lies, but O'Malley had seen detectives explode doing this, with the accused clamming up and asking for a lawyer. And the brass was pressuring them to solve quickly. "We'll play along with it for now," said O'Malley, after securing permission from his lieutenant for a gentler approach.

They returned to the interview room. "It's terrible about your partner," said Schiffman empathetically. After a few hours they let him go home. Picking him up in the morning, they drove to Hunts Point to look at the murder scene outside the Marine Midland Savings Bank and then stopped for lunch. They saw how Warner couldn't keep his story straight, and his defensive posture was a giveaway. But as they ate pizza together, chatting about the Bronx, their families, the bond deepened. Warner warmed to the detectives. "Help us figure this out," appealed O'Malley, knowing Warner was shading the truth yet still hoping to reason with him.

After a couple of days O'Malley and Schiffman were no nearer to a confession, so they came up with a ruse. "Look, they're busting our balls downtown about this," O'Malley told Warner. "They want you to take a polygraph, so let's just get it out of the way. Nothing to be alarmed about." In truth, any lie detector results were not admissible under state law. Warner took the test and failed miserably.

Commiserating with Warner, they took him back to the Forty-Seventh Precinct, where O'Malley looked him in the eye, appealing to his decency. Warner regarded the detectives and crumbled. He admitted that he had set his partner up and shot him in the head while an accomplice, Cuthbert Joseph, bagged the money. A weight seemed to lift off his shoulders as he spoke. O'Malley arrested Joseph, who told the detectives that he had stashed the money in an apartment on Vyse Avenue. From a hallway closet, O'Malley and Schiffman extracted a duffel bag containing more money than they had ever seen. It took all night to count it: $498,940. The following day showed O'Malley and Schiffman leading the suspects on a perp walk in front of TV cameras.

Though the case added to O'Malley's reputation, these were small successes, tiny victories in a city where murders were getting out of control when they peaked in 1990, at 2,262. The greatest number of these per capita, 54 per 100,000, were in the Bronx. Next came Manhattan with 33.8, Brooklyn with 33.3, Queens with 16, and Staten Island with 7.7. Detectives competed with one another over which precinct would reach one hundred homicide cases first. Beyond the Bronx, the Thirty-Fourth Precinct, in Washington Heights, competed with the Seventy-Fifth, in Brooklyn, with its eight public housing complexes. It became an NYPD tradition among homicide squads for detectives to pay all funeral expenses for the 100th murder victim every year.

In 1990, a fifteen-year-old black male in Harlem had a 37 percent chance of reaching the age of sixty-five. New York City was divided into areas where violence was commonplace and where inhabitants were largely shielded. If you lived on the Upper West Side you were safe until you went north and crossed Eighty-Sixth Street, where your chance of being the victim of a major crime doubled. Those living in the Nineteenth Precinct, the Upper East Side, lived in one of the safest in the city. But if you lived in the Thirty-Second Precinct, you were thirty-one times more likely to be murdered than someone living in Bayside, Queens. In short, the odds that an urban black male in America would be murdered with a gun were greater than they had been that a US soldier would be killed in Vietnam.

O'Malley and other Bronx cops like Forcelli despaired at the stark difference between how the city handled the Bronx's soaring black homicide rate and how it handled the murder or rape of wealthy white residents, or tourists, in Manhattan. Brian Watkins was a twenty-two-year-old high school tennis star from Idaho attending the US Open with his family in New York. He was fatally stabbed in the subway station at Fifty-Third and Seventh Avenue while protecting his father from a Queens gang who'd slashed his pants to get at his wallet. The city went into overdrive. A scrum of reporters besieged the NYPD, demanding to know the identity of the culprits. Within two hours of the murder, at around ten o'clock on a Sunday night, Manhattan cops were rounding up suspects. By Tuesday the family was being led into the precinct at Forty-Second Street, jostling with TV cameras and photographers to view fifty-four men for nine lineups. Eight teenagers from Queens were charged as a swarm of well-funded Manhattan detectives, some looking for kudos for solving the case, gave statements on the arrests to the media.

While some of the Manhattan detectives wore form-fitting suits, pompadours, and pinkie rings, in the Bronx, O'Malley and other detectives dressed in polo shirts and jeans, because they knew they'd never be interviewed about their cases. Few people were interested in young black kids caught in a steady and unremitting cavalcade of death.

Meanwhile, Forcelli had returned to car patrol duty in Soundview. When he asked at the precinct what perpetrators he should be looking out for, he was told one name: Peter Rollock.

Five

THE KIDS FROM COZY CORNER

AS PETE ROLLOCK SAW IT, he was born to be a Mafia godfather. His father enjoyed prestige in the underworld after having made a name for himself working with the heroin baron Nicky Barnes in the 1970s. Pete had gangster bona fides, and he wore them with honor. As Pete and Pipe walked up to Cozy Corner, the old-time gangsters offered a reverent "Hey! What up, little Petey!" Pete saw himself as the scion of an American dynasty. He moved like an heir apparent, and, perhaps unsurprisingly, he was infatuated with living up to his father's reputation.

"My pops and Nicky Barnes, yo," Pete once told Pipe proudly. "The only niggas to be with the five families." He liked to show off a well-thumbed newspaper article that linked the Lucchese family and Nicky Barnes with his dad. Barnes was said to have a heroin business worth $72 million a year. Only the Italians, his business partners, had the connections to bring product from the poppy fields of Asia and the cash to pay $220,000 a kilo while using Barnes's organization to distribute through inner-city neighborhoods. "My pops could go anywhere in the city, black neighborhoods and Italian neighborhoods," he bragged.

Leonard "Petey" Rollock, a.k.a. "the Boxer," was a lower-level distributor busted in a DEA sting after selling heroin to an undercover agent in the Bronx in November 1976. Barnes got life without parole, and Leonard Rollock got fifteen years. On his release, Rollock and James Jackson, Barnes's nephew, formed the Jackson organization, running their operation out of a Harlem hotel on 116th Street while procuring high-grade heroin through a connection to Gambino boss John Gotti. Barnes resented the success of his erstwhile business partners, and eventually cooperated and helped indict forty-four traffickers. In a final sweep, Jackson and Rollock were arrested in February 1987. Jackson, like Barnes, cooperated and by September turned on Pete's father. Leonard Rollock would be sentenced in the Southern District of New York to fifty years for racketeering in 1992. Because he refused to flip, Rollock commanded respect in prison as a strongman, true to his gangster creed. "Nicky Barnes snitched," Pete said, when he heard of his father's indictment in the summer of 1988. "Motherfucker is putting my pops away."

+ + +

PETE AND PIPE came to a halt on Cozy Corner and looked up at the giant 30' × 15' mural on the wall next to the supermarket. It had been six months since the slaying of Fat Mike and his crew and the triple murder that had rocked Soundview, establishing a new benchmark for violence. The mural said, in large blue letters, KIDS FROM COZY CORNER. To the left of the inscription was a man with a snarling face, twisted with venom, as he blazed with a flame-spewing semiautomatic pistol. The *o* in "Cozy" was an exploding orange bullet. To the left was an ersatz biblical scroll; on it, in a bluish-black stylized copperplate, "RIP" was written above three names: Baldie, Darrick, and Mike. There were still vague traces of a makeshift shrine—a cardboard box cut open front and top, containing pictures of Fat Mike along with candles, prayers, and mementos in his honor. At school, relatives of the murdered men sobbed in class. Pipe saw the community pull together, a tight-knit family ruptured by grief. The killing—a triple homicide of ordinary and well-liked young men by their peers—demonstrated to everyone in Soundview how far so-called friends in the drug game were willing to go to protect their own profits. On the street, the code was changing. Hustlers were saying that they would have to kill to make a name and to protect themselves. Families, it was rumored, would now be targeted to get revenge. There were no boundaries anymore.

Sometime in the past few weeks they had run into a neighborhood hustler they knew called Stymie. He had survived the triple homicide in January. He gave little away, but the story eventually emerged. Some of the men were sniffing cocaine as they bagged up crack. Around 3:30 a.m., they heard a knock on the door. When they opened it they saw Kirk Johnson, whom they'd all known since childhood. Kirk blocked the door, raised a sawed-off shotgun, and called to four other men, all armed, down the hall.

The assailants had been ordered not to sell crack on Cozy Corner by the crew that controlled the southern side of the projects, who took orders from a man named Lester. Johnson and the other four worked for ET Larry, the other dominant dealer in the area, who controlled the crack trade in the Sack Wern Houses with his green-topped vials but was looking to expand into Soundview. He'd earned the nickname because some of the kids in the neighborhood thought his long neck and large features made him resemble E.T. in the Spielberg movie. The men marched Fat Mike and the others into the back bedroom, where they were ordered to strip before their jewelry was taken. Fat Mike, perched on the end of the bed next to Stymie, refused to remove his T-shirt. Waverly, known as Baldie in the neighborhood, a low-key street hustler, begged for his life, pleading that his young daughter had just been born. "Why are you doing this?" he implored. "It's not necessary." Hull, the owner of the apartment, also begged for his life: "I don't have anything to do with this . . . Why don't you let me go?"

One of the gunmen, Nelson Burgos, cut them off. "Fuck, they all going to die tonight," he said. Kicking one of them in the face, he raised a .380 and shot at Stymie, who lifted his right arm in defense. The bullet dug into his elbow. Burgos shot him in the chest. The third time, Burgos sent a bullet crashing through Stymie's groin, ripping off one of his testicles.

Stymie, still alive, squinted as the killing unfolded. Johnson stood on the bed with a 12-gauge shotgun and blasted Fat Mike in the side of the head point-blank. Stymie saw running feet leaving the room.

Hull, who also survived, got up, fell down again, and managed to crawl down the hall before collapsing. Stymie staggered to the living room to call 911. Two officers arrived, saw the carnage and the men clinging to life, and backed out. They shouted from the hallway, asking the wounded if everyone had left while taking cover on either side of the front door as they waited for backup. An ambulance arrived, and Stymie was taken to the hospital. From his bedside, he told the police everything he knew. Kirk Johnson was quickly identified as the shooter. He bolted to Seattle, and his family fled the projects. He and his men made just $300 for the murders. NYPD detectives finally caught up with Johnson, and under enormous pressure from the community, Stymie eventually testified against him. It was an unprecedented move: the community urging a gangster to snitch.

Pete and Pipe looked at the mural and understood its poignancy. Everyone loved Fat Mike, but beyond that, the murders made it clear that seemingly ordinary kids like Kirk Johnson could become treacherous, mortal enemies overnight. Up to this point the allure of the gangster life, romanticized in the pictures of Mafiosos on the walls in Pete's bedroom, had been a game, mostly posturing. Even Pipe's own shooting had been a warning rather than an attempt to kill. But the triple killing gave some indication that they were unprepared for the violence. Suddenly things had gotten serious. D-Spot, for example, had a gun that Pipe had seen, but he'd never had to use it. It was for show. Now people started carrying guns intending to use them. No one wanted to end up like Fat Mike.

Indeed, Pipe stood before the mural with a fully loaded TEC-9 semi-automatic pistol in his book bag. Inscribed with thick silver writing on the bag was the name of its owner: Peter Rollock. Pete had enlisted Pipe as his gun bearer. Most days Pipe slipped into the back of Pete's classes with him at Stevenson High School, baseball hat pulled low over his eyes, three years too young for tenth grade, always ready to hand the gun over if Pete needed it. Recently, outside the front gates of Stevenson as they were leaving school, Pipe had spotted the two kids he had shot. One had a plaster cast on his arm. Privately, he was relieved he hadn't killed them, and even more so that he hadn't been recognized as the shooter.

Pete was talking about taking the crack business to another level. He was still a small-time supplier and didn't hustle, considering it beneath him, unlike Pipe, who sold on the corner. Pete had been buying from Da Lynch Mob, but he said he had a new drug connection in Manhattan who could give him the break he needed with significantly more "weight"—slang for multiple kilos. His father had supplied heroin, but Pete would dominate the crack trade. He had heard users describe that first velvet high as a ride on a high-speed elevator where you soared to the top. The next ride was never quite as high, and so users would always be seeking to get back to that original feeling. It was a limitless and clamoring market.

Hustlers couldn't re-up fast enough in Washington Heights, the epicenter of New York's rapidly growing Dominican community. The steeply wooded enclave at the north end of Manhattan had become a terminus for drug dealers all over the city. While the cocaine came from Colombia, the Dominicans had the street-level contacts to distribute the drug in poor neighborhoods. Street lore has it that a Dominican, Santiago Luis Polanco-Rodriguez, or Yayo, as he was known, was the marketing genius who brought the drug, wholesale, to New Yorkers. The King of Crack forged links with African American and Hispanic communities in poor neighborhoods from the seat of his gray Mercedes convertible. Pete had several connections in Washington Heights and began distributing to hustlers in Soundview in larger quantities.

As Pete's drug operation flourished, he enlisted a growing crew of resolute kids from the Soundview projects, like Pipe, willing to commit violence in his name.

The murder of Fat Mike had changed the entire drug landscape in Soundview. ET Larry had quickly filled the vacuum his gunman Johnson had left by taking out Lester's crew. Lester had vanished. Green crack vials started to turn up on Cozy Corner, indicating ET Larry was taking over. But when ET Larry heard that Stymie was talking to the police, he, too, left town in a hurry. All this offered an opportunity for Pete, Pipe, and the crew to expand and to take over Soundview. They formed an easy alliance with D-Spot and Da Lynch Mob.

Pete and Pipe knew that they would have to kill ET Larry and his men if they returned. Pipe told himself that he couldn't be scared of dying, or his weakness would be his undoing. In fact, he was afraid, though he told no one. To Pete and everyone else, he appeared impassive.

Pete talked all the time about the money they would make. "I want to be just like my pops," he said. "Just without the jail time bit."

✛ ✛ ✛

IN THE FALL of 1988, twelve-year-old Pipe stood at 551 Randall Avenue, on the corner of Rosedale, his regular hustle spot overlooking Cozy Corner. He kept the .22 Pete had given him either in a broken mailbox inside the lobby or under the steps near a back entrance.

Standing on the block was an art form: It was either the center of the universe or the most boring place on earth. Competition was intense at Cozy Corner, and Pipe had seen soft hustlers get chased off the block at gunpoint. "Niggas is trying to eat out here, man," the attacker would say, snatching the drugs and chasing the weaker one off into the night. Sometimes one or two cops came and robbed the dealers of their money or planted drugs on them. At 11:00 p.m., just when their tour was over, some of the cops who wanted extra overtime raced up to Cozy Corner in their car to snatch the slowest runner, leading to a night of paperwork and time and a half. The dealers learned to use a decoy to lead the cops on a chase before giving up and submitting to a search, which, of course, revealed no drugs or weapons.

A figure came up: "Gimme two, li'l man." Pipe took the dirty bills and folded them into a hard-packed rosette of money in his back pocket before he dropped the crack vials into a grasping hand.

Half an hour later, as Pipe slouched on the corner, a shoeless woman approached him, her filthy underpants and smudged bra visible through a torn dress. Her eyes looked ready to pop out of their sockets. Her mouth, caked in a white substance, showed loose teeth in blackened gums. When she came close to him, Pipe recognized her as Janet, once one of the sharpest older women in the neighborhood and an aunt of one of Pipe's friends.

"Yo, Janet, that you?" asked Pipe in disbelief. Before becoming a crack addict, she wore colorful flowing dresses, exuded a powerful femininity, and cared for her two children, the first only a couple of years younger than Pipe. "You know what it's like when you got that monkey on your back," she said. Janet pleaded with Pipe for crack on credit. Pipe gave her a couple of dime bottles—two $10 servings.

The drug was moving closer to home. Pipe's mother had switched from heroin to crack for the occasional binge. The drug caused her to launch into paranoid and deranged tirades. She claimed that her children were talking about her and once tried to choke one of Pipe's sisters.

As her addiction to crack progressed, she lost her grip on motherhood and her ability to protect her children. Once when Pipe came back late from a trip to the store she swung clumsily at him with a hammer, shouting that he was out on the block talking about her. Pipe ran away but just as darkness came, with nowhere else to go, crept back into the building and made his way up the dark, musty stairwell, to the top where the door led to the roof. The eleven-year-old pulled his arms inside his T-shirt and attempted to sleep, shivering on the cold and filthy concrete, praying he wouldn't be harmed in the night by addicts, rival dealers, or a nervous cop with his finger on the trigger during a vertical patrol. Before crack his mother would have punished him for staying out at night, and certainly for doing something as dangerous as sleeping in the stairwells. At dawn his brothers and sisters woke him with the news that his mother was sober and it was safe to return: "Momma say come back in the house." In the doorway she apologized profusely, gravely upset at what she had done. Pipe knew that his mother still loved him, and he never stopped loving her. By now he always knew that when the drugs wore off, she'd be her old self again. He learned to look past the moment and to wait patiently for her to return. What could he do? He had to feed the family. He vowed he'd never take crack himself, but the accumulation of money became the ultimate goal, no matter the cost.

When he'd turned twelve, his mother had organized a surprise for him. "I seen the way you run after those dirty li'l-ass girls," she said. With her son in the full flush of puberty, and knowing that kids in the projects had sex early, she was worried about the new plague sweeping the beleaguered Bronx. First they'd been besieged by heroin and fire, then crack and homicide; now it was HIV/AIDS.

So his mother set the virginal Pipe up with his first meaningful sexual encounter, focusing on safety. A nineteen-year-old female friend of the family who owed Miss Annette a favor agreed to show Pipe how love-making worked. While his mother sat next door in her room and the rest of his siblings were outside playing, the young woman undressed in Pipe's bedroom. She ordered Pipe to undo his pants and drop them to the floor. Then she lay back on his bunk bed and ordered him to start with oral sex. The twelve-year-old balked shortly after he began. "I ain't putting my face down there," he protested loudly. His mother burst into the room. "No, you ain't gotta show him all that," she said. "Show him everything else."

"See," Pipe pouted. "My moms say I ain't gotta do that." Miss Annette left the room, and his initiation resumed. Pipe stopped abruptly when he felt a powerful urge to urinate. The young woman said that the sensation was normal. Shortly thereafter he took one more step toward manhood.

Out on the street, the heady promiscuity of crack offered too many chances for an adolescent to resist. Pipe and the other teenage boys had long lusted after an unattainable twenty-year-old, a young woman in the projects who wore tight skirts, her hair always perfectly done. She had looked at them disdainfully until she started buying crack. Now, when she ran out of money, she offered sexual favors to teenage hustlers. Pipe took her to the roof they called Pebble Beach and he and another dealer had sex with her. Sometimes she removed her teeth for blow jobs.

By the spring of 1989, Pipe needed more product. Pete's promised connection in Washington Heights had come through, and he was sup-plying as many hustlers as he could. He gave Pipe all the cocaine he had, but Pipe was selling out all the time. When he complained to Crackhead Bemo, the old mentor promised Pipe a conduit to the purest crack the projects had ever seen. One night they lockstepped to a meeting near the projects' basketball court. Bemo had been impressed over the past few months, seeing Pipe outsell many of the other kids on the block. He pointed out a Silver Honda Accord. A man in his early thirties dressed in a gray suit sat at the wheel. It looked as though he had just left his office. Crackhead Bemo introduced them: "This is my li'l man Pipe. He's a good hustler." The man introduced himself as Ed. Pipe climbed into the front passenger seat and Bemo returned to the projects.

Ed offered Pipe fourteen grams of crack on consignment. Pipe promised to give him $400 in return in around a week's time. The boy stuffed the drugs into his pocket. He bought some small green bags at a bodega and bagged up the crack—potent and unadulterated—in his bedroom. Proudly, he took to the block with his own crack, marked up in the distinctive green bags. Soon he had lines forming. Pipe made the $400 easily, put it aside, made another $400 to re-up for a second batch. He kept $400 profit for himself.

He had reached a whole new level of financial success on his own. He lavished riches on his family. They ate Chinese takeout every night. His siblings could have McDonald's whenever they wished. Pipe opened a line of credit at a store on Cozy Corner so his siblings could always get candy. He generally kept his new wealth hidden under the sole of his sneakers. Sometimes, when he slept, his siblings crept in and snatched $100 bills.

The drug that was destroying his mother was also the family's financial salvation. Yet his mother had been deeply involved in the drug game. He remembered one day back when he was eight, before he had begun selling crack. He had cut school to take care of his sisters. His mother left them at around 8:30 a.m., muttering something about her food stamps being terminated and needing to hustle up some money. As a rule she forbade them from watching cartoons until three. At around eleven that morning there was a knock on the door. Pipe tiptoed up to look through the peephole. He suspected a truancy officer. Instead he saw the magnified, disheveled form of his mother slumped against the door. She clung to the walls as she staggered in, her face a bloody mess. "Don't cry," she whispered, seeing Pipe's face. She said she had been hustling heroin on the block when a rival crew abducted her. They took her to an apartment nearby, tied her up with duct tape, and demanded to know where her stash was. She refused to tell them. They pistol-whipped her, threatened to kill her, and then smashed her kneecaps with claw hammers. Still she refused to yield. The men dragged her outside with the intention of taking her to the waste ground behind the projects and killing her. As they struggled to get her out the front door, her drug connection showed up and opened fire with a revolver. The men fired back. They dropped Pipe's mother and ran.

Now, she told him never to do business with anyone who would not look him in the eye. You could see into a man's soul through his eyes, she said. If he ever had doubts in the middle of a deal, or even later, he should trust his instincts and "close the door," she told him. Thereafter he nursed a healthy distrust of everyone he met. But still she refused to take any money from him. Pipe tried a different approach. He asked her to hold the money for him. She accepted, and eventually she dipped in, always apologizing when she did so. Pipe never asked for the money back.

There were other avenues to get easy money and to test his growing power in the neighborhood. Pipe's .22 was an untapped conduit for cash. He and B-Love decided to stick up one of the fourteen-year-old kids from the Monroe projects who had gotten jobs through the Summer Youth Employment Program. There was a check-cashing store near the Monroe projects that the Summer Youth kids used. B-Love and Pipe waited on a corner and then jumped one of them, revealing the .22 revolver in Pipe's waistband. "Please don't shoot me," pleaded the boy. "I'll give you the money." He handed over his paycheck—$600 or $700—and ran home, too frightened to go to the police. Pipe was thrilled with what felt like a fortune. He didn't feel sorry for the victim, but he did feel his power increasing.

+ + +

BY THE EARLY months of 1990, Pete and Pipe were together all the time. One day Pete stopped by, only to be intercepted by Pipe's mom. "Listen, my son got a lot of love for you," she told him. "And I hope you're the same with him." Pete declared that as far as he was concerned Pipe was his brother. Pipe's mother launched into an inquisition. She elic-

ited everything there was to know about Pete and what sort of boy he
was. Only when she had finished did she call Pipe to announce Pete's
arrival. When they got out on the street Pete told his friend it felt like his
mother had just put him on trial.

A day or so later Miss Annette called Pipe into her room and told him
that she had spoken to Pete. She said that she trusted Pete—that likely
he would be the first one to kill for Pipe. But, she predicted, he was all
about himself. Sure, he wanted Pipe to get rich with him, but, she added
sternly, Pete would never want Pipe to make more than him. Pipe filed
the information before heading out the door.

A few weeks later Pete came striding up to 551 in a satin Sacra-
mento Kings jacket, a purple baseball cap pulled low over his eyes. He
had bought the new gear with the money he was generating from his
Dominican contacts. He gathered everyone around him. "Yo, listen, we
doing our own thing now," he said. "We ain't selling no blue tops with
Da Lynch Mob no more. We dealing our own work. We enterprising our
own little clique. We need a name that supports the team."

Pete felt they needed an alliance—not so much a gang but a cabal
dedicated to mutual economic advancement and self-protection. "We
are KINGS," he said. "It stands for 'Killing Innocent Niggas Gangsta
Style.'" Within a week Pipe had a purple satin jacket like Pete's.

When the summer of 1990 rolled around, the KINGS had earned no
small degree of infamy, mostly from fistfights in the neighborhood. They
cultivated their own myth. Pete shot a kid in the leg near the Stevenson Commons projects. He became known for carrying small-caliber
pistols. One or two of the older gangsters on Cozy Corner called him
"Pistol Pete," and the name stuck.

Pete and Pipe started hearing their stories told back to them. Pipe
was at a party when some kids told him that they knew the reason he
was called "Pipe" was because he had snuck up on someone and split
open his skull with a lead pipe. He was more dangerous than even Pistol Pete, they said. Thirteen-year-old Pipe chuckled to Pete: "We're
blowing up, Moe!"

"Moe" had become a generic name for each other among the group.

The name originated from the hoary street wisdom of Crackhead Bemo. Like a medieval soothsayer using crack vials as runes, he flitted in the shadows of the neighborhood imparting his hard-won wisdom. Every hustler in the projects, from Fat Mike to Pipe, owed some of his success to Bemo's tutelage and connections. When he saw the KINGS jackets, he beckoned to Pipe from a vestibule. "Come and talk to Moe," he rasped. Soon they all called each other "Moe." As their enterprise flourished they didn't want to use "government names" or even street names, so "Moe" was perfect. In time it would be so distinctive that they could be in Brooklyn or Queens and its use would indicate Bronx heritage.

Crackhead Bemo observed the daily goings-on in the neighborhood like an anthropologist. One day he made a prophecy. In grave tones he declared that Pete would eventually become a killer. "But he won't last long on the streets," Bemo predicted.

✦ ✦ ✦

ON A BALMY summer evening in 1990, the KINGS strutted into the Monroe projects for a block party. The sound system pulsed with MobStyle's "Gangster Shit," a confection of piano breaks and breakbeats over an homage to TEC-9s, hollow points, and the high life of a drug dealer. The stabbing lines were delivered by an ex-dealer, Azie Faison, who, together with Rich Porter and Alpo Martinez from East Harlem, was once part of the most notorious cocaine triumvirate in New York City. Word of their exploits and wealth spread through the underground and the Bronx and Harlem projects while their legends as benevolent revolutionaries taking on a white overclass grew. Azie Faison had survived a shooting in 1987, and Rich Porter was murdered by Martinez. An early influence on New York gangsta rap, Azie's urgent lyrics were meant to warn of the dangers of the game, but they were interpreted as glorifying them.

On their way out, one of the KINGS, Jasmine "Total Package" Mansell, known as TP, was taunted. "Well! Hello, Jasmine!" a Monroe youth teased with a lisp and a limp wrist. Pete ordered TP to stand up for himself by hurling an empty soda bottle. Another bottle came back in answer. One of the Monroe kids advanced. Then another bottle crashed near them, but this one sent shards of glass over Pipe's feet. Pipe caught Pete's smirk. "Let him have it, Moe."

Pipe was already withdrawing the .22. He blasted at the boy not five feet away. The youth dived to the ground, panicked, and rolled over in a vain effort to dodge the shots. Bullets ricocheted off the ground, hitting his arms and legs. He yowled in pain.

Pete and Pipe ran south to Soundview with one of the Monroe kids, armed, in pursuit. They split up to throw him off. Pipe, still running, heard shots from somewhere in the night. Immediately he feared Pete had been hit, and cursed himself for leaving him when only he had a gun and could have defended his friend if they'd stuck together. Pipe bumped into a kid in Soundview hit by a stray bullet, blood dripping from his hand, who said Pete was waiting for him at the Pink Circle, so called because of the pink picnic tables arranged around an eight-foot box ball court. Normally teeming with shouting kids, it was now eerily quiet. They stood beneath overhead lights around the swing set, and relief washed over Pipe when he saw Pete was unscathed. Pipe caught Pete looking at him with new respect. He gave Pipe a nod. The baby of the group, Pipe had passed an unofficial test. He had protected the crew. Pipe felt himself settling into his role, proud and secure.

✦ ✦ ✦

BUT AT HOME Pipe drifted into the dark side of his new character. One day at around 1:00 a.m., bored after a day hustling, Pipe and Ro were watching a movie. Ro drowsed, and Pipe's attention drifted until he saw a scene of some men playing Russian roulette with a revolver. Pipe woke his brother and asked if he wanted to play a game. "Sure," said Ro, "what's it called?"

"Russian roulette."

Ro looked uneasy. Pipe pulled out his .22 and explained further. "It's easy," he said, before offering a variation on the game. "I put one bullet in and I spin it. I try to shoot you and see if there's a bullet there, and then you try to shoot me."

Ro recoiled. "I ain't gonna play that."

Pipe ignored him.

"I'll go first." Pipe slid a bullet into the chamber and spun the cylinder. Ro backed up to his bunk bed in horror. Without thinking, Pipe put the gun against his temple. Jerked the trigger. A metallic click as the hammer hit an empty cylinder.

Pipe sensed himself waking as if out of a trance. *What had he just done?*

Ro burst into tears. "You crazy!"

Pipe looked down at him, the revolver at his side, and fought a growing wave of revulsion. "I ain't crazy, nigga," he thundered. "You can't be scared to die. Know why? Because when you scared, that's when you die." He put the revolver away and climbed into bed but lay awake a long time, trembling. It felt like he'd been momentarily possessed.

Pipe found himself brooding on his own mortality whenever he was alone. He had concluded that, one way or another, he was going to be murdered. If he washed up dead, he realized, no one would care. He'd just be another dead black kid in the projects, and life would go back to normal for everyone. So, he reasoned, if he couldn't allow himself the luxury of being scared of dying, he had to go in the other direction. He had to laugh in the face of death.

Six

THE BIRTH OF SUGAR SHAFT

THE WHITE STONE FACADE OF THE Spofford Juvenile Center filled the windshield of the prison bus. Shawn and other youths, shackled in one of the rear seats, passed under gates topped with barbed wire, which at night were bathed in the glow from powerful spotlights. The eight-story prison sat on top of a small hill in Hunts Point, surrounded by auto shops and collapsing wooden buildings. In the breeze, plastic bags snagged and slowly ripped to tendrils on the barbed-wire-topped fences that hemmed in the prison. Built in 1957, Spofford was established to turn recalcitrant teenagers straight. Shawn knew it as a place where young men got raped. He balled up his fists, put on his fiercest scowl, and declared to himself that if any motherfucker laid a hand on him he was going to kill him.

Shawn was fifteen. He had dropped out of school to jump into the burgeoning crack business. Soon after that, he had developed a crush on Shakira, the girlfriend of the dealer Lester, who had returned a year or two after the furor over Fat Mike's murder had died down. Lester and Shakira supplied him with crack. A stunning "redbone," light-skinned and mixed-race, Shakira had watched Shawn beat up kids from her building at the behest of Fat Mike. She flirted with him, bought him sneakers sometimes. "Your little ass going to be a problem when you older," she told Shawn, smiling and wagging a finger. Despite his toughness, Shawn had a little-boy-lost vulnerability about him that women found irresistible. Shakira took advantage of his belligerence to punish a kid who hadn't made good on some crack she wanted him to sell on consignment. Shawn caught the boy outside the Sack Wern Houses, knocked him down, stomped on him, and left. Afterward, Shakira bought him his first beeper—the totem of a successful dealer. Once, he went back to re-up from her and ended up staying the night. He was slumbering when he caught sight of her naked in her bedroom, her door slightly ajar. He crept closer and watched from the shadows as her dealer boyfriend made vigorous love to her. His arousal quickly subsided to a deep and angry covetousness.

But at 6:30 p.m. on a July evening in 1988, after a successful day selling on Cozy Corner, half a dozen plainclothes police officers pounced, slamming him against a wall. At the Forty-Third Precinct on Fteley Avenue, Shawn's first thoughts focused on the certain wrath of Miss Julia. A few months earlier she had found crack vials in his closet and flushed them down the toilet. When she arrived at the precinct, she stood over Shawn, shackled to the bench in the general waiting area. "I should leave you here," she said, pacing up and down in front of him, her gold jewelry glinting in the drab precinct house. Shawn lowered his head. A couple of the other drug dealers snickered at the sight of the little old lady humbling a boisterous hustler. Shortly thereafter Shawn admitted his guilt and was sentenced to eighteen months in Spofford.

The children's prison smelled like a mausoleum. Jewelry was not allowed officially, but once he joined the general population Shawn discovered that the rules didn't apply to the tougher kids, the ones in for murder. They flaunted their gold fronts—teeth encased in gold. Some of the guards were from the same neighborhoods as the inmates and knew not to mess with the kids who had connections outside. Behind the military-style structure at Spofford, it was turmoil. Children were discovered dead after assaults. Staff sometimes escorted kids to different parts of the prison to fight other kids. Female prisoners were sexually abused by counselors while shackled. Roaches ran amok in the kitchens. More than fifty children tried to commit suicide in a single year.

Inmates organized themselves by neighborhood into warring tribes.

Children from only fifteen of New York City's fifty-nine districts—the poorest neighborhoods in the city—made up half the admissions, with Soundview heavily represented. Shawn quickly aligned himself with his brethren. Up on the top tiers, from certain wings you could see all the way east, across the Bronx River and the park to the tops of the Soundview Houses, and home.

After several weeks the prison transport took him to the Tryon School for Boys, in a lush valley northwest of Albany. Shawn was placed in Barkwood, just one of a scattering of one-story cottages with sylvan names that housed kids from all over New York City, most from inner-city housing projects. Many suffered from mental illness.

When one of the counselors invested special care in him and took him fishing, which Shawn loved, all he could do was scan the river and the roads for a possible escape route back to the Bronx. He yearned for the Soundview community. Without his tribe in Soundview he felt naked, alone, and vulnerable.

After a year or so Shawn was placed in a group home near East 233rd Street in the Bronx, a transition point back into society. Miss Julia gave him money to buy boots, pants, and a new sweatshirt. Instead, he blew all the money on a New York Jets Starter jacket. He had it for a few weeks before a gang from the Edenwald Houses beat him to the ground and stole it. One weekend leave he came home to Miss Julia and decided not to return to the group home: A few days later, there was a loud knock on the door. Group home supervisors and a federal marshal entered the apartment, and before Shawn could move he was on the floor, face pressed into the carpet in his room as handcuffs bit into his wrists. Marched into the living room, he berated Miss Julia: "Why you open the door to them, Mama?" Miss Julia, flustered in the commotion, said, "I ain't know who these motherfuckers was." Shawn returned to Spofford for thirty days of further punishment.

The brutality of his confinement hardened him, inculcating a deeper understanding of the power and worth of violence, and a hunger for money from the drug game.

+ + +

SHAWN RETURNED to Soundview in mid-1990, proud to have graduated from Spofford in the same way a boastful young man in his twenties might brag about a degree from Yale. Pipe saw Shawn on the block and noted that his friend had a stiffer posture, a rougher manner, and a more defiant look now. Shawn asked for money to get started in the game again, and Pipe lent it to him.

The neighborhood had turned more violent since Shawn had been away. E40, Shawn and Pete's unofficial boxing coach, had been shot and killed during Shawn's absence. The boys were shaken by the loss. Everywhere, the shootings between dealers intensified. Shawn was playing skellzies when Lester was shot in the backside and Pipe's dad, home from a prison stretch, ran in and carried him to safety. Out on the block, there were so many kids selling crack it seemed impossible to make money.

Soon after his release, Shawn bumped into Baby Jay, a round-faced older boy with soft, expressive eyes who had lost his mother in 1985. Baby had lived with Shawn and Miss Julia for a few months after her death. He wasn't a scrapper or a gunbuster, but he was part of the Boobies, a semiofficial crew that counted Shawn among its affiliates. The Boobies had a reputation for using cocaine as well as selling it. Baby was savvy. When Shawn complained that it had been hard to make money on Cozy Corner since his release, Baby suggested that he accompany him to Springfield, Massachusetts, where the business was just getting started. He'd written to Shawn in Spofford about how much money he was making in New England. But he'd been robbed a couple of times, beaten up, and needed protection. He knew Shawn was drawn to the role of protector and enforcer.

A couple of days after their reunion, Shawn stood outside his building, his hair glistening in a newly styled Afro, as Baby circled the block in a black Volkswagen Corrado. Baby had dressed all in black to match his car. Together they slipped onto the Bruckner Expressway and then onto I-95, speeding all the way. The industrial-gray topography of the Bronx soon gave way to a New England fall of exploding auburns and russets. I-95 was a road paved with gold for drug traffickers. The farther north you went, the more contraband was worth. From New Haven they swung directly north up I-91 along the Connecticut River. Spofford and Tryon disappeared from Shawn's mind, and he was free to listen to Mary J. Blige on the car radio and imagine his riches. Shawn had just $20 in his pocket, and they had just an ounce of crack in the glove compartment to get them started, but it was enough.

"I'd die for you two times, Baby Jay," Shawn shouted over the music. "You my heart! No one messes with you now. You got me to hold you down!" He turned to Baby Jay and whooped that he was going to get rich rich: "I'ma blow up!"

+ + +

THREE HOURS later, the black Volkswagen rolled through the center of a New England city decimated by industrial decline. Springfield once prospered as the "industrial beehive," home to companies such as Indian Motorcycles and other manufacturers who drew workers from all over the country, even Puerto Rico. But by the early 1980s, factory bosses were moving their operations to the nonunionized South or outsourcing overseas. The legions of unemployed meant it was fertile ground for a crack operation. Baby pulled up outside 85 College Street, a three-story colonial. He introduced Shawn to a seventy-nine-year-old Italian grandmother who sold crack from a threadbare couch. She took an immediate dislike to Shawn but grudgingly let him stay. Afterward, in a back room, Baby wasted no time slicing crack into $20 hunks with a razor blade on an old plate, putting the rocks into bags. When he finished there were two hundred small bags. He gave Shawn fifty and said that they would share it 60/40. Baby took Shawn a couple of blocks over to Cambridge Street. Within fifteen minutes Shawn sold all of it and made $120. In New York it would've taken him half a day. Over the next few weeks Shawn met the local hustlers who admired Shawn's Pelle Pelle jacket and his New York swagger and asked if he had met any of the famous rappers like Nas. Shawn preened. "I might have," he lied, the embodiment of the urban dealer. Shawn noticed that the local Springfield hustlers wore tattered sneakers and old Patrick Ewing streetwear, gear that would have been scorned in Soundview—the mark of a chump who didn't know how to make money. Here, free of the fierce competition and out from under the shadows of powerful dealers in Soundview, where he was just another nondescript teenage hustler at their beck and call, Shawn began to like the backwater city more and more. He sensed he might stand out here, in a place where he could be special.

By early 1991, Shawn and Baby were counting out tens of thousands of dollars, money for re-ups as well as profit from the past six months. To celebrate Shawn's seventeenth birthday in February and his own eighteenth in March, Baby paid cash for a brand-new silver Isuzu Rodeo SUV. He spent another $8,000 on leather seats and a sound system. Baby gave his Volkswagen to Shawn as a "low" company car—one that would not attract suspicion—partially as a birthday present for his enforcer's personal use, but really so Suge could transport drugs for him. Suge read this as pure generosity.

When his mother died, Baby used her life insurance money to buy drugs, and now he was quickly doubling it.

Sometime in spring 1991, they drove to Soundview to re-up. Shawn had $4,000 in his back pocket; Baby, ten times that. They spent the weekend lavishing money and affection on girls in Soundview before returning to Massachusetts with two kilos of cocaine in the SUV.

"I need to give you a nickname, man," said Baby as they sped through Connecticut. "We can't be out there using our government names, everybody calling you Shawn and all that." Shawn, chomping on a candy bar, acknowledged the idea. He had spent the weekend smoking weed and was ravenous. Chocolate had become a staple of his diet since he started making money. "I'm going to call you Sugar Shaft." Shawn absorbed his new moniker. "Sugar 'cause you always hyper and eating candy," said Jay. "And Shaft because you always wants to fight or do something to somebody. You a gangster."

Shawn's transformation to gangster enforcer was complete. He had been reborn. He mouthed the words looking out the window, the first greenery of spring flashing past. Sugar Shaft, Sugar Shaft . . .

✦ ✦ ✦

WHEN THE GRANDMOTHER was arrested, Baby left Suge (as Sugar Shaft became known, pronounced "shoog") in charge of the house, which now swarmed with crack addicts every day. Baby removed himself out of harm's way to a quiet, well-appointed condo. Suge wasted no time in filling the rooms with friends from Soundview who brought up guns and swelled the crew, taking over the entire block, while helping to pitch crack in the area. Suge served crack-heads from his bedroom window until Baby told him not to. He shot guns in the air from the backyard until Baby again begged him not to draw attention to the house.

In the summer of 1991, the group of dealers went to Six Flags New England, a giant amusement park near the Connecticut border. They drove to Atlantic City and blew their money in casinos. They sunned themselves at Virginia Beach.

Suge returned to Soundview like a victorious crusader. He ran into Pipe and flaunted his new gangster alter ego. When Pipe called him Shawn, he corrected him irritably: "I'm Sugar Shaft now. Yo, so call me Suge." Pipe had never seen such a transformation. At first Pipe thought Shawn was bullshitting. Before he left, he'd just been a slightly rough neighborhood kid who begged for money and borrowed Pipe's clothes to impress the girls. Now, here he was in a blazing white outfit, wearing brand-new Nikes and with a completely different swagger. He pimp-rolled like a gangster now. He threw Pipe $150 as a gift. "Plenty where that came from," he bragged. And when Lester demanded the money from the crack he had given him on consignment, Suge rounded on him, smoldering with defiance. Lester pulled back, seeing something altogether darker in Suge's eyes.

For his part, Suge came to the realization that money brought respect, and his possession or lack of it became linked with his self-esteem. He had a dazzling gold ring embossed with a large *J* made for Miss Julia's birthday in May. She grudgingly accepted it but once again refused money. Suge discovered that when she went to the numbers spot near

Cozy Corner she took cash with her. He would follow her in, stuffing money into her pockets while she played. She pretended not to notice.

Returning to Springfield in late July, they learned that they'd become targets; their growing affluence and Suge's conspicuous and wayward nature had drawn the attention of local crews. One of the Bronxites in the house got pistol-whipped before thieves made off with drugs and money. Suge exploded: "If it's these Springfield niggas, I'm going to start shooting every one of them."

But if all their newfound wealth was drawing the attention of gangs in Springfield, it was also certainly drawing the attention of vengeful Bronx gangsters, who resented these triumphalist teenagers flashing money in Soundview.

✦ ✦ ✦

IN SEPTEMBER 1991, Suge was back in Soundview, speeding around the neighborhood on a lime green Kawasaki dirt bike. He whipped around the Soundview horseshoe one more time before blasting into Soundview Park. Life in that moment was perfect. He'd bought the bike for cash. He had $1,200 jammed in the back pocket of his brand-new pants, and he wore a new Yankees baseball cap. He had left his .45 at his grandmother's, because Jay had told him not to ride around with it.

Suge popped a wheelie, grabbed the clutch, and with the front brake engaged, spinning the bike in ever faster circles, burned a smoking circle with his rear wheel on the pavement. With that, he took off down Randall toward the Bronxdale Houses to Baby's grandmother's apartment. Feathering the clutch and the throttle, he popped another wheelie as he flew past the Monroe Houses. "Suckas!" he yelled at some kids on the corner.

He didn't notice a white car trailing him. At the Bronxdale Houses, he cut the motor and glided to a stop, resting the bike against the wall. He bounded up two steps before he felt a heavy hand on his shoulder. He turned to see Kiron Little.

"What up, Kiron?" said Suge amicably. He and his grandmother had known him for years.

"What do you mean, what up?" Kiron said, sneering. Suge saw a fist cloud his vision before he was knocked back. When he regained his balance and eyesight he saw another man producing a machine gun. He jammed the muzzle into Suge's back. Now Kiron pulled a semiautomatic pistol out of the front of his pants and aimed it at Suge.

Slowly, ET Larry alighted from a car parked in front. His pit bull panted heavily in the passenger seat. "Get in," he ordered.

Eight

KIDNAPPED:
BLOOD BEGETS BLOOD

SUGE'S LEGS BUCKLED. AS HE TRIED to regain his balance he touched his hand to the crown of his head and brought it down to see his fingers were covered in blood. Moisture began seeping from the wound, soaking his scalp and running into his eyes. He'd been hit with the heavy milled steel of a pistol butt.

After an interrogation in ET Larry's car, the men had marched Suge up a concrete ramp outside the Bronxdale Houses, through the lobby, and into the cramped elevator, where they had smashed him over the head. Surrounded by the most feared gangsters in Soundview, he had four gun barrels trained on him. His assailant, Lance, was rippling with muscle after his recent release from prison. Facing him was ET Larry himself, a tall man with skin the color of buttery caramel and an oddly squeaky voice that didn't match his formidable presence. Kiron and another man, Guidry, were jammed in, too.

Suge dropped somewhere between a cower and a crouch, protecting his head from another pistol-whipping. "What the fuck you doin', yo?" he implored.

"Shut up," thundered Kiron. "What floor Jay live on? We know he got money. That's your man. Where his money at?"

Suge shook his head and played dumb. "What you talking about?" He dropped his hands in supplication, spreading his palms. The move left his head unprotected. Kiron hit him with a gun. Blinded by the pain, Suge made a commotion in a futile attempt to draw attention.

He realized that they were probably going to kill him. He remembered Fat Mike, and the black body bags coming out after the robbery.

Suge fell to his knees, crying. He begged them to stop. "Kiron, man, what's wrong?" he implored. "Kiron, please, please. What did I do?"

Lance yanked Suge to his feet and pinioned his arms behind his back. The men stabbed at elevator buttons, ignoring his cries for mercy. Jay lived on the fourth floor. They moved past it.

"It's here," lied Suge, indicating the fifth floor. The men stopped the elevator. They dragged him into a dimly lit hallway. The gangsters demanded to know which apartment was Baby's.

Suge indicated the first door that he saw. "Five-D." Lance released him before shoving him in the back as the others encircled him from behind, pushing him up to the door as they raised their guns. Anyone inside would only see Suge through the peephole, not the gun-wielding gangsters.

Suge knocked weakly a few times. The men pushed forward on either side of him, ready to fire. Suge knew he'd be hit in the crossfire once they opened the door. In a split second he realized he had one slim chance of escape. He edged back toward the elevator and bolted, hurtling toward the stairwell at the end of the corridor. He exploded out the landing door and found himself in the stairwell. Leaping down each flight, his feet barely touched the steps. Outside, he ran for his life, weaving, sprinting back to Soundview, his face a mask of blood.

At some point he stopped and paged Baby Jay. Baby didn't page back. Suge felt the need to pray to God, something he hadn't done since he had been to church with Miss Julia. He swore that he would never get involved in drugs again if God could help him out of this mess. *Please, God, spare my life. I don't want the drug game anymore. If you'll let me live, I'll never sell drugs again.*

He slowed down his stride. Beyond God, there was one person he could turn to in crisis: Pistol Pete, whose home was about a mile and a half away. Suge broke right on Story Avenue and surged toward Boynton Avenue. Gasping for air, he fell onto the intercom at 875, smearing it with blood as he jabbed at Pete's apartment number. Suge could barely muster the breath to say his name before Pete clicked the buzzer. He burst inside and seconds later collapsed on Pete's floor.

In deep, halting breaths he got the story out. Pete led Suge to the sofa, where he examined the head wound. As Suge looked up through a veil of blood, he saw Pete's eyes moisten before hardening again. He ordered his girlfriend to get gauze, peroxide, and some of his mother's painkillers. She mopped up the blood and applied the gauze. Pete soothed his friend. "I love you, Moe," he said. "You my man . . . ain't nothing going to happen to you."

Pete disappeared and returned with his TEC-9 and two loaded magazines. "Ain't no one ever going to do this to you again," he said, racking the slide for full effect. "What do you want to do?"

Suge didn't hesitate: "I want to kill every single one of those motherfuckers." Pete sat down next to Suge and handed him a 9mm Luger with a complicated safety. "I can give you this," he said. Suge looked at the 9mm bullets. He thought about it for a while. "Ain't you got nothing bigger?" Pete left and returned with a .30-30 sawed-off lever-action rifle he had christened Betsy, the same one he had once offered Pipe the chance to shoot. The .30-30 rounds were three times as big. "I want that," Suge said.

+ + +

ET LARRY and his men were considerably older than Pete and the boys. They had a sizable arsenal and, crucially, money; they could pay others to kill on their behalf. As Pete understood it, ET Larry was looking to take over the entire drug trade in the projects. If Pete countered with more violence than ET Larry, the fiefdom of Soundview would be theirs. Suge saw only Pete's loyalty to him, giving little consideration to the bigger picture.

With its dense clusters of projects, the South Bronx was heating up. Dealers saw the money that could be made not just by controlling their own buildings but by taking over others. Cops like Forcelli ran from one project to another trying to deal with what seemed like a tidal wave of shootings. In the Edenwald Houses the authorities installed a permanent office to deal with the escalating violence.

Pete telephoned every gunbuster he knew in the hope of forming a small army. Baby arrived from Springfield, assessing the situation. He and Pete loathed each other, but the seriousness of events demanded they be allies. He left to get more guns. As they waited for friends to show, Pete changed his mind and opted for surprise: sudden and vicious retaliation. "We ain't got to wait for nobody, man," he said, pacing up and down. "Let's go shoot them in the face right now." He strapped on a bulletproof vest and pulled on an olive green army jacket with a hood over it. He threw Suge a similar jacket but had no more bulletproof vests.

They headed to the block to meet two friends. One of them, Dust Can, had been riding Suge's dirt bike earlier in the day. Suge told the story. He pulled down his hood to reveal the gash and gauze. Suge and the other boys all knew Kiron. Suge handed one of the men $300 from a roll in his pocket. "Keep an eye on us," he said. "We're going to kill them." It was an unnecessary gesture, but the youth pocketed the money anyway.

As they were talking to Dust Can, Suge did a double take when Lance, the man who had held his arms behind his back and hit him, appeared across the projects only forty feet away. "That's fuckin' Lance right there," Suge exclaimed, eyes wide. Pete barely turned his head.

"Let's kill him!" Suge said, bouncing his weight from foot to foot. Pete resisted. "Nah, chill." He had worked out the odds of reaching Lance before Lance spotted them and returned fire. He figured that their best chance lay in catching Lance inside, where he could be cornered. Suge couldn't wait—couldn't stand to see Lance walking away. "Yo, fuck this! What you mean wait?"

He set out after Lance at a mad run, wrestling the .30-30 from his pants leg. Behind, he heard muffled shouts from Pete: "Wait!" Suge jumped a small chain-link fence. Lance turned and saw his flailing pursuer and broke into a sprint. Pete gave up trying to dissuade Suge and simply followed him.

Suge bore down—in his peripheral vision he saw a few mothers pulling their children away or shielding them, people pulling their heads back into windows—and then he squeezed the trigger. He was about thirty feet away. The sound of the big gun echoed around the buildings. He missed. He flicked the lever forward and reloaded, fired again, and missed again.

Pete came from behind, cutting off Lance's retreat into a building entrance, and opened up with the TEC-9, firing from a moving crouch as he and Suge pincered in on Lance. Staccato riffs from the machine gun echoed off the red brick.

Suge shot all five rounds from the .30-30. Lance—grazed by one of Pete's bullets—slipped and fell, trying to dodge follow-up shots as Pete moved up to finish him off. Just as he neared, police sirens wailed. Flashing blue lights reflected off the project windows. The boys paused, which gave Lance the opportunity to tear into his building. Pete and Suge fought the urge to run as the police converged in the distance. They turned calmly back and walked past two boys who had been trading rhymes and had witnessed the shooting. "'Sup," Pete said. "Anyone seen us?"

"Nah, Petey, we ain't seen nothing."

But the police had spotted them. They split up. Suge raced toward Cozy Corner while Pete ducked back though the labyrinthine buildings, his familiarity with them giving him an edge over the pursuing cops as he jetted through one building and out the back door into another.

As Pete remembers it, he emerged on the northern edge of the projects opposite PS 107 and into the waiting arms of two police officers with their revolvers trained on him. He pointed the TEC-9 at them. "Drop your gun!" they shouted. Pete looked at their old revolvers and held fast. "No! You drop yours!"

The police hesitated, which gave him a split second to dodge back into the building. He ducked into the stairwell and ran up to the roof. Atop every apartment block was a rectangular housing that contained the winches for the elevator. He deposited two magazines on top of the housing, climbed down, and hurled the gun off the edge of the building, where it landed in some bushes below.

Coming back down the stairs he paused and saw an open apartment door on one of the floors and charged inside. The kid living there recognized him. Pete explained the situation, and the kid gave him a new shirt and a baseball cap. They left the apartment together and waited for a full elevator before descending to the lobby amid the scrum of other residents.

The police were waiting. They warned everyone that there was a man with a gun in the building and that residents should evacuate until the situation was resolved. Pistol Pete, unrecognized, filed out of the building with everyone else. The scene played out like an escape in one of the gangster movies Pete had spent so many afternoons watching.

+ + +

PIPE WAS circling the area on a bicycle, drawn by the sound of gunshots. About an hour later he caught sight of Pete sitting outside the garage at his grandmother's house on a plastic chair, gazing into the projects.

Pete was proud of his escape. He asked Pipe to take his bike and locate the gun he threw off the roof. Pipe cycled down. He found the gun and the magazines and returned to Pete's, triumphant.

They went to the roof of 551, just above their hustle spot, where Pete gave the gun a short burst to test it. The bullets flew toward the horizon over Manhattan. The lineaments of Pete's face tautened when he told Pipe about Suge's kidnapping and how he was going to retaliate. He waxed about his childhood with Suge, their time on the Young Devils team. Suge may have been selling drugs, but he was not known as a gangster in Soundview. Pete was not doing this for Baby Jay. The two had long nursed a distrust of each other. Pete was doing it for Suge, but even Pipe knew he was doing it, above all, for himself.

Pipe looked down into the redbrick canyons of Soundview. In the darkness, high above the rooftops, he watched his old friend happily imagining the battle that might soon take place below.

+ + +

THE FOLLOWING day, Pete and a few others bought new guns from some Dominicans in Manhattan, rejecting an offer of some hand grenades. Returning to Soundview, they attempted to ambush ET Larry, but Baby Jay stumbled into the path of B-Love, and while blocking him was unable to fire his gun for some reason, and they had to pull back. Pete ordered that Baby stay away from the next attempt.

Twenty-four hours later Pete, B-Love, and Pipe congregated outside 551 with a few others. ET Larry and his men huddled near the entrance of 1725, their headquarters, which was also the building where Suge lived with his grandmother. Because he could no longer return to his apartment safely, Suge holed up with Baby in Manhattan, returning only to carry out shootings with Pete and the others.

The two sides kept an unwavering eye on each other like World War I soldiers facing off across the trenches at Ypres, the central median a no-man's-land. Pete and his men controlled the way into the Soundview Houses at 551 on the southern side of the horseshoe, while ET Larry and the others at 1725 controlled the way out. Sometime in the afternoon an emissary came over and told Pete that ET Larry wanted to meet. Pete, Pipe, and eight or nine others chambered their guns before walking over. When they got closer they could see that their enemies were armed, too.

ET Larry spoke first. "We ain't got no beef with you," he said to Pete. Pete was unmoved. He knew they were scared of his father and his uncle and the forces he could muster. "Suge is my li'l man," he said. "You got a beef with him, you got a beef with me."

"It ain't got nothing to do with you," ET Larry said before adding that he considered Pete a friend of sorts. "You is peoples. It's Baby Jay and them." Pete shook his head. They headed back toward 551. Pipe made sure not to turn his back fully on ET Larry and his men.

+ + +

"DID YOU hear what they did to poor little Shawn?" Pipe's aunt asked one of the neighbors as word of the dispute spread around the project.

According to Suge, the projects were siding with Pete's crew. Pete's apartment became the unofficial HQ for the war. Pete, Suge, and B-Love whiled away the rest of the daylight hours, curtains drawn, watching *Scarface*, munching on chips, and checking their guns. Pete scorned Suge's impulsiveness, deriding him as a loose cannon for blowing their one chance at Lance by attacking before they were ready.

Suge spent most of his time on the balcony, smoking weed. The smoke blew back into the apartment. Pete hated it. "How you niggers gonna get money when you give all your money to the weed man?" he scolded. Pete regarded drinking and smoking weed as signs of weakness. His only vice was apple-flavored bubble gum.

As dusk fell beyond the curtains, Pete's phone rang. The caller said that ET Larry and the others were standing under Pete's window. Pete suggested to them all that they attack from the side, not from the direction of 551. ET Larry and his men would be expecting that. Suge would be with him, while B-Love would come up from the south, cutting off their escape. Suge nodded, though he didn't like taking orders. He tried to focus on the prospect of killing the men who had held him captive. Dressed in army jackets and dark clothes, they made their way out of Pete's apartment like a nighttime platoon.

There was the occasional clink of metal in the darkness as a gun hit a belt buckle or a fastener as they crept through a parking lot and then slipped up to 551, where Pipe and the others were keeping watch. Pipe, smoking a blunt, didn't notice the shrouded figures moving up on his position and pouncing out of the night.

"You slippin', Moe," Pete snapped hotly, throwing his hood back. "If we was one of them, you be dead."

Pete told Pipe the plan. Pipe suggested that if ET Larry and the others escaped south toward 551, then he and his boys would cut them down. In the past few months Pipe had amassed a sizable arsenal, and he had stored most of the guns at 639 Rosedale Avenue, where his mother now lived. Her building stood behind 1725, ET Larry's HQ.

Pipe headed off, discreetly circling 1725. While the others waited downstairs, Pipe and two associates let themselves into his mother's apartment. He unlocked the door to his room and got down on the floor to reach under the bunk beds for the duffel bag. He climbed to his feet and turned to find his mother standing over him. "What you got in the bag?"

"Nothing."

"I can't have you bringing no guns in my house," she said.

Pipe mumbled something about removing them all now.

"You know I can't tell you what to do," she said, giving him a hard stare. "You're going to do what you're going to do, but it's a dangerous game. You seen what happened to me."

Back then, he thought, when he'd first seen his mother bloody and broken, he might have stepped away from this life. But not now. Suge and Pete needed him.

She added contemplatively, "You my son, my firstborn. I love you." The words mollified Pipe. "I would hate to see anything happen to you. And I would hate to see you locked up for the rest of your life." Pipe stood with his arms by his sides. The bag of guns suddenly grew impossibly heavy. He saw the resignation in her face.

His mother sighed. She knew that where there was drug money, violence would follow. She could offer him lofty morals or she could be practical. She chose the latter. "If this is what you choose to do," she said, "then make sure you do it to the best of your ability. Because if you go in half-stepping, then ain't nothing gonna come of it. You gonna end up hurt or going to jail. If you're gonna go in, then make sure you go in all the way. Know the consequences of it." She paused, and softened. "Look, I'd rather see you in jail than dead." She asked if he understood what she had meant, but she didn't have to. "If you're going to be shooting people, then make sure you kill them so they can't come back and kill you. Know what I'm sayin'?"

Pipe nodded. "All right, Ma," he said. "I hear you." He made his way out the front door, stuffing a revolver in his pants.

He was halfway across the median, his head down, thinking about what his mother had said, when he slipped under a couple of trees and drew level with the bodega on the corner. He hadn't noticed the figures looming in front of him, one brandishing a Glock, the other a small machine gun. Lance and Kiron blocked his route. Caught unawares, Pipe was unable to reach his gun.

"You like shooting people, little nigga?" said Kiron, gesturing with his gun in Pipe's face. Lance had survived Pete's attack the previous night; he was enraged. Pipe looked for a car to take cover behind—anything, even a tree. His mouth turned dry; he couldn't form words. A pang of dread spiraled up his spine.

The men watched him. They knew who Pipe's father was, that he held sway in the projects. And gunning down a fourteen-year-old was a risky move. "I ain't gonna kill you now," Kiron said. "I'm gonna kill you later." They paused after the warning and then moved off.

Pipe bolted to 551 and breathlessly spilled out what had happened. He could see in the darkness Pete's silhouette bracing with fury. When he finished, Pete silently pulled on a bulletproof vest, racked the slide on his gun, and set off with Suge and B-Love. They crept north, hugging the buildings. Up ahead, Pete spotted ET Larry and the others. "Yo, let's get 'em," he whispered, pulling the TEC-9 from his book bag. Suge stole a glance. ET Larry and the others were smoking less than a hundred feet away.

Pete, the only one protected by a bulletproof vest, urged them to move in for the attack, to run and gun. "Yo, Pete," Suge whispered. "How come you the only one with the vest on? Why don't you run up and shoot them in the face? We'll hold you down!"

"So I gots to do everything, then?" Pete said irritably. "Like, you know what? Y'all leave and I'll do everything." Suge didn't want to argue. It was his beef; Pete was doing this for him, and he had no real right to protest. Pete and Suge would lead the charge as they were the fastest runners. B-Love would provide covering fire.

Pete and Suge walked two abreast. Their targets weren't paying attention. "Guess what," shouted Pete. They turned, agape. From ten feet away Pete swung the gun up, squeezed the trigger. Nothing. Just an oily click. At Pete's house another boy in the crew, Nugent, had taken the bullet out of the chamber and not replaced it. Without the first round in the chamber it would not fire or feed rounds. The silence resounded around them. Pete retreated, struggling with the gun's mechanism. "Oh, shit, my gun's jammed," he said over and over.

Suge sprayed fire with the MAC-10 he'd been given, saving Pete and forcing ET Larry and his men to the ground for cover. He struggled to contain the recoil. Behind him, B-Love opened up with the .30-30. Pete loaded the TEC-9. Now he, too, let loose a barrage.

The men got to their feet, but Kiron flailed and fell back to the ground. He pulled out a gun and shot back. A couple of rounds whined past Suge's ear. "Yo, Petey, we need to fall back!" shouted Suge over the racket. Pete refused. "No, we gonna get them!" More bullets flew their way. They ran in retreat, Pete and Suge taking cover behind a corner. Pete had second thoughts. "What the fuck we running for?" he spat. "We got guns."

But their hesitation emboldened ET Larry and Kiron, who pressed the attack, though they carried only revolvers.

Within a few minutes a fleet of police cars lit up the projects. The cops inside hunkered down behind the windows. Rather than racing to the scene they crawled into Randall Avenue and slowed to a stop. The guns continued to blaze. And then silence. The police waited a further ten minutes before getting out.

✛ ✛ ✛

THE NEXT MORNING, Pipe took up position on the corner. Word filtered back that no one had been killed. As Pipe waited, he saw a familiar figure ambling toward him—Kevin "Bemo" Aller, Crackhead Bemo's son, wearing baggy camouflage pants, a black hoodie, and matching chukkas. Bemo always carried a thick wad of money in his back pocket. He had grown up with his grandmother in poverty, dealing with his father's addictions. Despite hailing from the enemy territory of Castle Hill, he had been adopted as a Soundview son. Pipe's father and Bemo's father had even done some business back in the day.

Powerfully built under all his baggy layers, Bemo approached them outside 551. He knew about the war with ET Larry, he said in his husky monotone, explaining how he had been out selling his crack in black-topped vials when he'd also been warned off the block by Larry and his crew. Bemo and a friend had ambushed Lance and shot him twice in the legs, but the gun had jammed when they put it to his head. Kiron had tried to run him over in his car, then chased him with a gun. Bemo said he had come to stand with Pistol Pete.

In the daylight, Pete, Pipe, and Suge saw the pocks that their bullets had left in the buildings the previous night. The beef had now lasted ten days. They went to the roof of 551, and Pete saw ET Larry and his men entering a store. "These niggas think it's a game," he said, disgusted at their arrogance.

Pete figured that they wouldn't expect a daylight attack. The boys had become vampires, largely appearing at night to hunt down their foes while they watched *Menace II Society* and films like it during the day. This time Pete ripped an idea from *Boyz 'n the Hood*. "We need to get an auto and air them niggas out right now."

Suge and Pipe volunteered that they knew Julio, a Puerto Rican kid who specialized in stealing cars. In fact, a little while ago Pipe and the kid had crept into White Plains and stolen vehicles, driving them in demolition derbies around Soundview Park's running track. Once he stole a 5-liter Pontiac, shredding the tires before someone else took a turn and sparks from the rims set the vehicle alight. The next day a sooty hulk sat on the running track.

Pete refused to ride in a stolen car. It was beneath him, and besides, they could be arrested just for being in it, let alone carrying guns. This time Pete would sit it out. He gave Pipe his TEC-9. Bemo offered to ride shotgun.

Julio was delighted to be asked to aid the war effort against ET Larry. He picked out a Buick Century in a parking lot south of the projects. The four doors would enable them to get in and out in an emergency, and the old-timer image of the car might disguise them until they attacked. The boys kept a lookout while Julio jimmied the door, snapped the lock on the steering column, and forced a screwdriver into the ignition. The car coughed to life. Suge was designated driver, because Baby had gotten him a Massachusetts license from a corrupt DMV connection. Bemo, riding up front, took Suge's MAC-10. Pipe clambered into the backseat behind Bemo, carrying Pete's TEC-9. Suge eased the car out as they circled the block. They cruised Cozy Corner, keeping an eye out for police.

They drove around Academy Gardens, eight six-story buildings that took up a whole city block facing the Soundview projects. It had once offered lower-middle-class families a home, but now most had fled the crack epidemic, although it was still considered a step above Soundview. The boys circled five times before they spotted Lance and Kiron near an entrance facing Cozy Corner. Suge made a U-turn and accelerated slightly, bearing down on Lance. They wound down the windows as Pipe and Bemo readied their guns like an eighteenth-century frigate readying cannons for a broadside.

As they approached, Kiron passed through the security gate. Bemo's gun erupted. Pipe, too, opened fire, only to have the TEC-9 misfeed. Lance tumbled to the pavement, hit in the legs. Bemo kept shooting. The percussive thumps of the rounds echoed around the body of the car. Kiron dove for cover on the ground between the two gates. His gun skittered across the pavement, out of reach.

Suge slowed the car alongside. Bemo leveled his gun at Lance on the ground. But then in his peripheral vision he saw a young girl turn the corner, pushing a stroller. She panicked when she heard the gunshots, but couldn't place where they were coming from. In her confusion, she lurched toward the entrance of Academy Gardens, scuttling while bent double, to apparent safety. Instead, she was pushing her baby through the line of fire. Bemo paused, not wanting to hit her.

As the woman fled, Pipe and Bemo opened the doors to jump out and finish the job. Lance was helpless on the ground. But just as Bemo swiveled out of the seat, Suge screamed, "Get in!" Panicked, he made a split-second decision based on his fear of getting caught. Stomping the accelerator, he fishtailed away.

✛ ✛ ✛

THE WIND in the open windows dispersed the astringent odor of gun-powder as they swooped toward the Bruckner Expressway. The plan was to drive to Harlem, where Baby would pick them up after they ditched the car. As they drove, Pipe and Bemo snapped on Suge. "Why you drive off like that?" said Bemo. "You scared or something?" Suge shot back, "The block was hot, Moe. We can't shoot with all those people there."

It was 4:00 p.m. as Suge nosed the car along the Bruckner. They rolled up to a traffic light near the number 6 train at the Hunts Point Avenue stop. Pipe, with the MAC in his lap, squirmed in his seat, checking for police.

Then, abruptly, silence. The engine died. Suge pumped the accelerator while he worked at the mangled ignition, now just a mass of wires. The light ahead turned green. Drivers began blasting their horns and hurling obscenities at them.

There was nothing to do but abandon the car. The three boys climbed out, awkwardly concealing their guns. They left the doors open and scrambled away between the cars. Moving single file, they crossed the Willis Avenue Bridge over the Harlem River. An hour or so later, they found a pay phone and called a relative back in Soundview. Lance had been hit but had survived. The police were still there, marking out bullet casings and trying to interview residents, who, predictably, were saying nothing. They traipsed to the assigned meeting place near a public housing project on 135th Street. Baby wasn't there. Waiting on the corner, they grew paranoid, repeatedly calling Baby's pager. "DTs," warned Pipe, street code for detectives, as he pointed out an unmarked police car trolling past, two white guys inside, checking the boys out. When the circling detective car disappeared, they lit up a couple of joints and decided to keep moving.

After several hours they called home again. The police cars at the scene of the shooting had dispersed. It was safe to return. Blistered and sore, they cut over the Madison Avenue Bridge and into the Bronx. They walked solemnly now, the machine guns under their coats weighing heavily. They noticed another car trailing them. Suge glanced back several times. "If it comes past again I'ma Swiss cheese it up," he said. The car came close enough for the boys to discern what appeared to be two white detectives inside. They put their heads down and kept walking. "Shit, good thing we ain't shoot," said Suge.

Finally, beyond a pedestrian bridge spanning the Bruckner, they neared Soundview. Midway across the bridge they relaxed. Suge asked if he could check Pipe's malfunctioning gun. A spent, crumpled casing had lodged in the receiver. Suge tugged the slide back forcefully to eject the round. When they reached the middle of the bridge he held the gun aloft and fired a short burst. A police car passed beneath them. They ran, and didn't stop until they reached Pete's apartment. Suge, bad-tempered after the hike, smoked a spliff on Pete's balcony. Everyone bickered about the failed drive-by, the group eventually turning on Suge.

The next day, Pipe was at Pete's when Miss Brenda found Pete's stash of weapons. "You get all those guns out of here," she shouted. "I don't want no guns in my house."

Pete lost his temper. "Yo, stop going through my shit," he said. "I'm a grown fucking man. That's how people get hurt. From being nosy."

Two days after the drive-by, ET Larry asked for a meeting. Pete and Pipe faced him once more in front of 1725. "Y'all ain't got no morals," Larry told them. "You come through the block in daylight shooting with a hundred witnesses! You don't care."

Pete and the boys were rewriting the old street codes with a no-limits ferocity that the old-timers—men in their early twenties—could not contend with. ET Larry had underestimated them as just kids. A major generational shift had occurred between men born just a few years apart. Pete and the boys were nihilistic, respected nobody, and scorned ET Larry's seniority. The cliques that consolidated power on the streets of New York in 1991 would set a new benchmark for violence.

In the Bronx, the street gangs had often stood apart from drug dealers as separate entities, but crack had fused them as one. Now Pete and the

KINGS were morphing from a street gang into a growing drug organization looking to aggressively take over a new market. It represented a major change in the underworld.

ET Larry understood the ruthlessness of the new generation. He knew they would end his life without a second thought unless he capitulated. He had to bow down to the new prince or he would die.

"Y'all can have the projects," he said, throwing up his hands.

An uneasy peace fell on the Soundview Houses amid a heavier police presence. The guns fell silent. The hustlers who had stayed away from Cozy Corner drifted back. Pete and the boys waited for retaliation, disbelieving ET Larry would be true to his word. Meanwhile, Suge and Baby returned to Springfield.

✦ ✦ ✦

BEMO WASN'T at the meeting when ET Larry conceded, so he didn't know that a truce had been reached. Two days later, November 3, 1991, he and the others hustled as usual outside 551. When Pipe decided to get some smokes from the Academy Superette on Cozy Corner, Pete got protective and offered to go along. Pipe refused. "At least take the TEC," said Pete. Eventually Bemo said he would go instead, armed with a sixteen-shot Ruger 9mm.

At the store, Bemo was reaching into his pocket to pay when he heard a voice from behind. "You like shooting guns, little nigga?" Bemo turned to see a contemptuous Kiron—the target of their drive-by— dressed in blue jeans, a black flight jacket, and an Orlando Magic hat. He filled the entrance to the store. "Wassup now, li'l nigga?" Kiron indicated the gun in the waistband of his blue jeans. "I should kill your little ass now."

"I don't want no problems, Kiron," Bemo said, putting his hands up. Satisfied that he had intimidated the sixteen-year-old, Kiron turned to leave. "Yeah, you a little bitch-ass nigga," he said. "Next time I'ma kill you."

Kiron reached for a Phillie in his pocket. Bemo thought he was going for his gun. He had no idea of the truce that had been negotiated and sensed he finally had an opportunity to strike back for Kiron's attack. Bemo pulled the Ruger. "Oh, you a bitch now," he said.

Kiron turned to run. Bemo's first shot struck him in the back. "I'm hit!" he said as he stumbled out the door, falling to his knees. He toppled onto the sidewalk next to a poster of Humphrey Bogart advertising cigarettes. His fifteen-year-old girlfriend, Nefertiti Martin, was sitting on a car outside the store with a couple of friends. Kiron had gone to get her a drink, and there had been talk of heading that evening to the Fever on Jerome Avenue as a treat for her birthday. She screamed as her friends pulled her back from the body. She flailed wildly, kicking and punching, desperately trying to reach Kiron on the ground. She broke loose, but more people arrived and forced her into the guard booth in Academy Gardens for her own safety. She heard more gunshots.

Bemo pumped four more bullets into Kiron. Three tore into his back, one into his hand, and one ripped behind his right ear and through his brain, exiting to the left of his nose, killing him.

Nefertiti slipped past bystanders trying to restrain her from going to Kiron, who lay prone on the sidewalk.

Bemo stood over the corpse, his smoking gun by his side. He regarded the gathering crowd. "Ain't nobody seen shit," he said. "Ain't nobody know nothing!" Then he vanished.

Pipe, standing outside 551, heard the gunshots. He raced over to see Kiron lying on his face. Pipe noticed that a single spot of blood had landed and spread on the clean white toe of Kiron's Nikes.

Act II

THE RISE OF SEX MONEY MURDER

We are witnessing a breakdown of the social mechanisms that once kept crime in check and gave direction and support to police authority. The small town environments, rural or urban, which once framed and enforced their own moral codes, have virtually disappeared. We have become strangers sharing the largest collective habitats in human history. Because of the size and density of our newly evolving urban megalopolis, we have become more dependent on each other and more vulnerable to aberrant behavior than we have ever been before.

—Oscar Newman, *Defensible Space*, 1972

The police? We didn't have to worry about them niggas. We was chilling. Going wherever we wanted to go, fucking whomever we wanted to fuck, killing whomever we wanted to kill, making money wherever we wanted to make it.

—Pipe, August 2013

One

GOLD SHIELD #1944

AT THE END OF A GOLD-FRINGED October day in 1991, O'Malley arrived home to greet his family. Pleasantly fatigued from a police charity golf game, where he'd shot in the high eighties, he walked into the kitchen, where he met his wife.

"Your sister just called," she stammered. "It's Uncle Jack. He's been murdered."

O'Malley didn't believe it at first. His invincible Uncle Jack? The Queens Homicide detective who had set O'Malley on course to becoming a cop back when he was eight?

But at 3:00 a.m. that day, after picking up Chinese food for a late dinner and closing up at the Garden Grill in Woodside, the restaurant where he'd tended bar since his retirement, Jack had walked a female customer to her car. They were confronted by a five-foot-five drug-addled gunman who jabbed a pistol in their faces and demanded money. Jack, unarmed, stepped forward and swung the bag of Chinese food at the robber. Their assailant took a step back and fired a single shot to the head, killing Jack instantly.

O'Malley was tempted to get involved in the investigation, but he stepped back to let the detectives at the 114th Precinct handle it. Two weeks later they arrested the murderer, thirty-three-year-old Kevin Kennedy, a heroin addict.

In disbelief that a street punk had taken his uncle's life, O'Malley took action to preserve his uncle's legacy. He called Jack's daughter Judy, who worked for the police commissioner, and asked for his uncle's shield number so that he might request it. He learned that shield 1944 was in use by Pat Neary, a detective with the Forty-Sixth Precinct. Coincidentally, Neary had played golf with O'Malley the day he learned of Jack's murder, and when O'Malley called him Neary agreed to give him the shield. Every day since, O'Malley had carried it in his pocket; 1944 became his lucky number.

Uncle Jack's murder was just one in a city polarized by a homicide epidemic. Gypsy cabs made a healthy trade taking passengers into neighborhoods where yellow cabs refused to go. In early 1992, Mayor David Dinkins was scheduled to visit Thomas Jefferson High School in Brooklyn to urge the children to reject violence; an hour before his arrival, two teenagers, seventeen and sixteen, were shot dead in the hallway, fifteen feet from two policemen. The government funded studies on violence, probing the biological and genetic factors, while the Department of Health and Human Services declared that it would begin a five-year campaign to eradicate violence in America in the same way it would treat a smallpox epidemic, by using public health techniques. Studies showed that across the country there had been a 217 percent rise in the number of fifteen-year-olds arrested for murder between 1985 and 1991.

By 1992, New York City's drug gangs had established their neighborhood turfs. The previous two years, the bloodiest on record, had seen small neighborhood crews battling it out for territory, but now the winners controlled whole public housing projects, or crucial crossroads that were the locus of the drug trade in discrete areas. Now neighborhoods surrendered to sophisticated drug syndicates that sometimes reached across state lines, as drug traffickers made ever larger sums of money in an ocean of lawlessness. They enjoyed their growing power, drawn from the fear they inspired in their neighborhoods and the legions of boys and military-age men who flocked to the new syndicates run by a new era of warlords.

+ + +

O'MALLEY MIGHT not have involved himself in Uncle Jack's case, but his work at Bronx Homicide would become significant in how New

York would fight back against drug gangs: he learned how to go federal. Back on April 18, 1991, at 10:50 p.m., O'Malley had arrived outside 1260 Webster Avenue, behind the twenty-one-story Webster Houses—a vast landscape of redbrick housing towers in the Forty-Second Precinct. A large black man lay dead beside the blown-out driver's door of a white Nissan Stanza, shot thirteen times, his brains blasted all over the blue velour of the car's interior. At first glance it was another anonymous black male murdered in the projects, likely connected to the drug trade.

The familiar squadron of beige-raincoat-clad detectives stood around the murder scene, sharing a gallows joke or two. Howard "Howie the Hump" Denton, a legendary NYPD detective who was never without a fedora and a cigar, greeted O'Malley. His two sergeants began canvassing the projects. At around 12:35 a.m. the Bronx DA's videographer began to film the murder scene. O'Malley asked him to discreetly pan the crowd: a woman in a sequined jacket, a twentyish man in Adidas powder blue. O'Malley had learned that some killers came back to see their handiwork.

In the days following, O'Malley established that the murdered man was Steven "Pooh" Palmer and this was more than just another random murder. Detective Sergeant Vic Cruz of Bronx Homicide convened a meeting where he said that since early 1990, rumors had been circulating in the Bronx underworld about a gang of well-muscled white men dressed as cops, called the Cowboys, who were kidnapping drug dealers and murdering them if their demands were not met. Witnesses said that the Cowboys had partnered with "the Crew," black residents of the South Bronx (many of them drug dealers themselves) who knew and worked with all the wealthy drug traffickers in their neighborhoods. The Crew were setting them up to be "arrested" and kidnapped for ransom by the Cowboys.

A street informant gave the names of three of the Cowboys; all lived in New Jersey. One of the men, David "Heavy D" Cleary, was already wiretapped and under surveillance for steroid distribution. As information started to flow from New Jersey law enforcement, the names of leading drug dealers in the Bronx cropped up. Word was that the Crew had turned on each other over money. A treacherous killing cycle had started. Palmer, the main link with the Cowboys, was the first victim.

On April 23, Operation Hercules was established, so called because of the Cowboys' physiques. O'Malley and a team of detectives began to piece together the murders. O'Malley scanned arrest reports and found Albert Van Dyke, a member of the Crew who was being held for his involvement in the botched kidnapping of an underworld banker in Queens.

Out of options, Van Dyke flipped to O'Malley and the detectives, confirming the conspiracy between the Cowboys and the Crew. Palmer, Van Dyke told him, was a drug dealer from Harlem who had teamed up with Louis Ruggiero, a six-foot-eight New Jersey resident with an uncle who was a Genovese crime family capo in the Bronx. Palmer had suggested to him that there was a fortune to be made abducting drug dealers.

They had drawn up a list of ten victims, which resulted in seven kidnappings. The first ended in disaster. Derrick Augustine, one of Palmer's men, identified the Harlem dealer Otmar Delaney, who ran a thriving drug ring from his garage. Ruggiero and an accomplice followed him to his home in Yonkers and then "arrested" him before tossing him in the trunk of their car and driving him to a motel in New Jersey. There they handcuffed him to a chair and took a staple gun to his penis. Ruggiero used a cell phone to demand payment of $750,000 from Delaney's half brother. But Delaney, who had been left alone in the room, broke out and jumped behind the wheel of an idling truck outside and drove off, his hand still cuffed to the chair, before crashing. The police arrived, but Ruggiero and his accomplice escaped.

Next the Cowboys kidnapped Alvin Goings, whom Augustine also sold narcotics for, on a highway access road. They flashed badges and then handcuffed him before putting him in a bogus police car. The ransom was dropped at a gas station on the Palisades Parkway in New Jersey, a mile north of the George Washington Bridge. After the pickup, the Crew felt Palmer hadn't split the money evenly. Rumors circulated in the neighborhood that he had picked up as much as $1 million, but he claimed it was only $400,000. After this the Crew started to turn on each other, and Palmer was eventually killed.

Still, on Easter Sunday, March 31, 1991, they kidnapped the Bronx restaurateur and drug dealer David Crumpler, marching into his establishment with fake badges and guns. They took him to New Jersey and tortured him; when his family wouldn't pay the $750,000 ransom, the Crew shot him dead. His body was found in an empty lot in the Bronx.

With the information from Van Dyke, the detectives organized a meeting with Bronx ADA William Flack in a bid to convince him to prosecute the Cowboys and the Crew. Primed as if for a sales meeting, O'Malley's partner Joe Marrero, a Puerto Rican cop from Soundview, used flowcharts, diagrams, and notes from informants and Van Dyke's confession to engage the DA.

The DA and the NYPD had a history of arguing. Prosecutors often said that witnesses secured by detectives weren't credible, after the detectives faced an almost impossible task of getting witnesses to testify because they were so scared of retribution. After their pitch, the ADA rejected the case, saying that one witness wasn't enough. Moreover, he said he couldn't prosecute because the case crossed borough and state lines.

Back at the precinct the dejected detectives regrouped. Sergeant Vic Cruz said he had a connection with feds at the Southern District. But to bypass the Bronx DA and take a case federal could, it was rumored, end a detective's career, because going over the prosecutor's head to a federal agency was seen as the ultimate slight.

Regardless, in February 1992 the detectives packed up their flowcharts and drove to Lower Manhattan. In the midst of the august federal complex at 500 Pearl Street, the building at 1 St. Andrew's Plaza was sedate and purposeful. The ninth floor was like a library in contrast to the zoolike Forty-Second Precinct, with its clattering Selectric typewriters and cursing, its broken furniture, and an endless tide of unwashed humanity shuffling through.

The detectives were ushered into the office of thirty-four-year-old prosecutor Paul Gardephe. An awkward silence descended.

Sergeant Cruz began his pitch. Gardephe remained motionless. O'Malley looked at Joe Marrero. *We should put a fuckin' mirror under the guy's mouth to see if he's still breathing.* Marrero shrugged. One or two mild, seemingly disinterested questions from Gardephe. How did you get that? How do you know that piece? Then another long, pregnant silence. Cruz broke it. "So whaddya think? Is this something you'd be interested in?"

Silence. Again. Suddenly:

"That's a great case," said Gardephe.

O'Malley and Cruz edged forward in disbelief. "You gonna take it?"

"Yeah," he said. "We're going to take it."

The detectives made their way out of the building. "Holy shit!" exclaimed Marrero. "We're going federal!" At first no one really knew what that meant. But quickly they discovered that it would be quite unlike working with the Bronx DA, who was often assigned only when an investigation was completed. With the feds, they began to field daily requests from the Southern District for ballistics reports and meticulously collated evidence.

Within the first week O'Malley went in and met with Liz Glazer, one of the prosecutors on the case. O'Malley thought she looked more like a liberal social worker than a federal prosecutor, but her appearance belied a steadfast commitment to rooting out violent gangsters. She'd grown up on the Upper West Side, the daughter of a Harvard academic, and remembered the protests against the tyranny of Robert Moses and his plan to pave over a sledding hill at West 103rd Street and Riverside Park, which led to demonstrations in the neighborhood when she was a child. She had worked in refugee camps in Indonesia interviewing Vietnamese and Cambodian refugees for immigration cases as part of the American Council for Nationalities Service's mission, and she saw strong parallels between the wickedness of the genocidal regime of Pol Pot and the Mafia families who destroyed New York with corrupt construction deals, contract killings, and endless heroin.

Glazer had learned her craft helping the FBI and other agencies go after the Mafia with the RICO Act—which could tie an entire criminal enterprise together and get the top dons as well as the junior soliders, breaking the powerful code of omertà when they got men inside to flip. The case O'Malley and the other Bronx cops laid out against the Harlem and Bronx drug dealers—the Crew—struck Glazer for the insight it offered. As she listened to O'Malley she saw there was no glamour to the killings, no one with cool names like the Mafia guys, but these street crews were a major source of the sanguinary violence plaguing the city.

Two weeks later Glazer turned up at the Forty-Second Precinct to strategize. The detectives were dumbfounded. The Bronx DA never paid them a personal visit. O'Malley reversed his opinion of Glazer as a soft, anti-police do-gooder when he saw how fierce and hands-on she was. She saw a prosecutor's role as investigative, much like a detective's. She asked O'Malley to take her to the filthy New Jersey motel just outside the Lincoln Tunnel where Ruggiero had tied up Delaney, a place prostitutes took their clients. As they stood in the darkened squalor, O'Malley, now comfortable with Glazer, muttered under his breath, "Man, I couldn't even get a hard-on in here." It was the sort of coarse humor a homicide detective used to blunt the daily horror of the work, but possibly not appropriate in front of a federal prosecutor, especially a female one. Glazer was unfazed as they continued talking about the case.

They spoke on the phone every day, going over what they had and what they needed. The Bronx detectives saw that the feds had seemingly bottomless resources and that they could call in any help they needed at the FBI, the ATF, and other federal agencies. This meant money to pay informants, undercover cars with out-of-state plates, and so on. The NYPD, by contrast, seemed broke. For as long as O'Malley could remember, cars had been like gold dust in the NYPD. When Hercules started, their task force didn't have access to a working vehicle to call their own; they constantly had to borrow them. Glazer got them a vehicle from the US attorney's pool and leased them another.

O'Malley saw how easy it was to request evidence-building material, including wiretaps. Normally, when Bronx detectives tried to order wiretaps, the Bronx ADAs would reject their requests, saying the detectives lacked probable cause. But the feds had significantly more leverage: Subpoenas were issued for the Bronx detectives whenever they asked.

Wiretaps were how the detectives discovered that Cleary and Ruggiero, overheard on May 13, 1991, had an inkling that Van Dyke was cooperating. There was now no time to waste as O'Malley and Marrero traced murder scenes and plumbed other places where kidnappings and money drops had occurred, looking for clues and leads.

In September 1992, a fifty-count indictment was handed down against the Cowboys and the Crew for racketeering and other charges.

Shortly after the indictment, a gangster named Barry Shawn, incarcerated on Rikers Island, wanted to talk. He'd heard that others were flipping, and he didn't want to be the one unable to cut a deal.

Shawn was moved to the Metropolitan Correctional Center (MCC) in downtown Manhattan, where O'Malley and the other detectives got to work alongside Liz Glazer. O'Malley learned that in the federal system the debriefing of a cooperating witness was called a "proffer." Unlike many of the Mafiosos, street gangsters didn't understand RICO laws. Their lawyers assumed that they would find the same ways out for their clients that they could in the state system. But Glazer told Shawn that in order for him to be considered for a deal, he'd have to tell them every criminal act he had ever committed, and even then there would be no guarantee he would escape charges. Shawn shaded the truth and outright lied; soon the detectives suspected he was a psychopath.

Glazer watched how O'Malley and the other detectives who knew the Bronx so well could spot immediately when he was lying. They were nothing like the book-smart FBI agents from the Midwest, men and women who didn't have the instincts or experience for ferreting out deception face-to-face, and lacked the guile needed to navigate the Bronx streets. Slowly O'Malley and the others drew out from Shawn all the murders the Crew had committed. Eventually, as the detectives pushed and called out his lies, Shawn admitted having murdered Crumpler.

A few weeks after the indictment, O'Malley, working with the FBI, came crashing through David Cleary's door while he was in bed with Ruggiero's sister. Cleary asked calmly if he might be granted time to put his pants on, thereby earning the distinction of being the politest man O'Malley had ever arrested. He shivered in the cold when they took him to the cellblocks, so O'Malley gave him his blue Nike windbreaker.

Next, Bronx homicide detectives, with O'Malley's partner, Marrero, arrested Ruggiero in a Queens parking lot next to a court where he was summoned for a hearing. Finally, they captured Derrick Augustine, who had gone on the lam when police began to arrest members of both groups in the Bronx. He flipped and admitted to O'Malley that he had killed Palmer. Amazed that Augustine was admitting everything under federal pressure, one question nagged O'Malley. "Why'd you shoot him thirteen times?" he asked.

"I only had thirteen bullets in the gun."

Augustine confided that he and others felt that Palmer had not only identified them all but screwed them out of money. Originally the triggerman was to be James "Justice" Brown, whom Augustine described as a cold-blooded hit man working for Chicky Rosario, among others. Palmer suspected that Justice would be the one to kill him. So instead the soft Augustine, whom he didn't suspect, set him up.

As the proffers continued, Glazer watched O'Malley work, building the trust of the gangsters who had flipped, known as cooperators, with a combination of patience, gritty warmth, and resolve. She saw how he maintained a direct link to the criminals under investigation. He spoke to people, not at them, like other agents. And he didn't bang on the table or threaten. He never raised his voice.

As many of these murders had been committed years earlier, it took proffer sessions to persuade gangsters to talk; in these cases, wiretaps often didn't exist. O'Malley was awestruck at the effectiveness of the proffers. For years they'd struggled in the Bronx, because witnesses were too terrified to speak out. But here, with men right inside the crews who had a powerful incentive to cooperate, they found a complete archaeological map to scores of unsolved murder cases. To charge someone with a crime, they needed two cooperating witnesses to corroborate the story. In some cases they could use only one witness—as long as they also had another piece of strong evidence, like a gun that matched a ballistics report of the crime. Crucially, Glazer showed him how he could use hearsay from cooperators rather than having to present witnesses who were often too scared to talk, as detectives were required to do in the state system—which could cost them the case. The federal system made it much easier to get indictments.

But then, even more significantly, the Cowboy case split into two when another gangster they arrested, a six-foot-five Dominican named Ito, fingered a violent drug boss, Bartolome Moya, and his hit man, Andre Paige—another dangerous syndicate that was killing indiscriminately and robbing other drug dealers while dressed as DEA agents. O'Malley and his partner Joe Marrero arrested Paige in a daring daylight take-down. The task force solved three more old, anonymous murders in the Webster projects—a triple homicide carried out by Paige—as that case got under way.

Using additional evidence provided by cooperating gangsters, Glazer showed O'Malley how to add new counts and obtain a superseding indictment. The September 1992 indictment was followed, in April 1993, by a fifty-nine-count superseding indictment against the Cowboys, which meant their chance of escaping conviction was even less likely.

Cleary and Ruggiero would eventually be sentenced to life in prison.

O'MALLEY ATTENDED the September 1992 trial of his uncle's killer, Kevin Kennedy, in a Queens courtroom, accompanied by his family. The case had run concurrently with the Cowboys case. Kennedy was convicted of second-degree murder and sentenced to life with a minimum of thirty-seven years. Afterward, O'Malley felt the experience had sharpened his resolve to get closure for murder victims' families.

The heedless killing of his uncle had its roots in the drug trade, and the connections between the two cases could not be ignored. O'Malley had come to realize that the feds and RICO would be the only path to breaking up the gangs behind most of the murders in the Bronx.

Two

SEX MONEY MURDER

EVERYTHING CHANGED IN SOUNDVIEW following Kiron's murder. Pete and the crew were seen as a liberating army, exiling the tyrant ET Larry to Seattle while scores of drug dealers paid homage to the new overlord. For some time, ET Larry had been forcing Pipe's original connections, D-Spot and Da Lynch Mob, to sell his "work"—slang for crack—and not their own. Now everyone came to Pete and his crew to get their cocaine, in effect honoring the new czar of Soundview, but also to ensure that they were on the right side of might in the neighborhood. "We want to make sure paper keeps coming back to home base," one hustler told Pipe. Pete and the crew were treated with deference and fear. They were true gangsters now, their contract written in Kiron's blood. The killing had endowed them with power, security, and economic leverage, and they were now at the top of the food chain. Soundview was Pete's dominion.

A month or so after the murder, they sat in Pete's apartment rehashing Kiron's murder as Pipe sprawled on the sofa intermittently playing video games. "You gotta give it to Bem," said Nugent. "He's the first to catch a body out of all of us." Pete couldn't conceal his irritation that it wasn't he who had committed the group's first murder. He censured Bemo for shattering the truce he had made with ET Larry. Still, even though he resented having his authority undermined by Bemo's freelance killing, he recognized that the consequences fell mostly to his advantage. Several times Pete asked Bemo to repeat his story of the killing. Bemo said the bullets made Kiron's head inflate like a pumpkin. Pipe described how the medical examiner had poked his fingers into holes in Kiron's face.

A few hours later Suge arrived fresh off the bus from Springfield with a cast on his arm. He and Baby had returned to Springfield a few days after the drive-by shooting. Suge was serving a Jamaican from Brooklyn with crack when the man tried to rob him at gunpoint. In the tussle Suge, unarmed, had called to Darnell, "Get the joint, Donny!" Darnell fetched a pistol but blundered and shot Suge in the arm instead. When Suge awoke in the hospital, two detectives at his bedside charged him with assault with intent to kill the Jamaican and possession of an illegal firearm, among other charges. The Jamaican had cooperated with the police. "These bum-ass country dudes are snitches," Suge raged to Baby on a jail visit. Shortly after, Baby paid Suge's bail and the fee for a lawyer who got all charges dropped. Since then, Suge made sure he was always armed. But he failed to understand that the code of silence, which functioned so well in Soundview, didn't work in Springfield, a fact Baby had constantly tried to impress upon him. "Don't never trust these out-of-town dudes," Baby said. "We not from out here and can't never forget that. We just come out here to make money and break out."

Back in the redoubt of Soundview, where he was safe, Suge was eager to hear the news of Kiron's murder. He thanked Bemo for killing his tormentor. Bemo smiled. "You ain't got to worry about it no more."

"Good lookin'," said Suge. "We help each other."

Suge had been both kidnapped and shot in the past few weeks, and the feeling of being surrounded by true allies overwhelmed him for a moment. His old friend had driven away his enemies, avenging him. Suge took Pete's actions as loyalty. He failed to see just how much Pete had to gain by taking ET Larry out of the game because he wanted to believe that Pete loved him above all else.

+ + +

WITHIN A few days the celebratory mood was quelled when news reached them that the police were onto Kiron's murderer. Bemo's aunt, who worked at the precinct, told her nephew that detectives were looking for him. The crew knew that only one witness, Kiron's girlfriend, Nefertiti, would identify Bemo as his killer.

The next few days Pete, Pipe, and Bemo drove around looking for her. When they spotted Nefertiti leaving Stevenson High School, they ordered her into the car at gunpoint. Bemo and Pete made it clear what would happen if she cooperated with the police: "Listen, if you open your mouth we gonna kill you, your sister, your moms, your brothers . . . everybody." She nodded to signify she understood, and left for Virginia the next day.

After that Bemo suggested an even bolder move. He decided to turn himself in. "What the fuck you wanna do that for?" Pete said, incredulous. Bemo explained that while the police were looking for him he had no income, because he couldn't hustle on Cozy Corner. "If I turn myself in I know they ain't got no witnesses—the only witness they got can't be found. They can't make a case, then I can go back on the block."

About a month after the shooting Bemo walked up to the big wooden counter at the Forty-Third. "I heard y'all was looking for me," he said. As predicted, lacking witnesses, the frustrated detectives had no choice but to free him. Within days Bemo was back at Cozy Corner.

With Soundview under control, Pete made moves to consolidate the crack trade in the Bronx projects. He put aside some petty beefs that had developed over a Stevenson High School girl to make peace with two of Castle Hill's most feared men: the twin brothers David and Damon Mullins. The elder, David, known as Twin, largely controlled the Castle Hill projects and frustrated detectives at the Forty-Third because he and his identical brother would give each other alibis anytime they were arrested. An alliance with Twin would mean that Pete could supply drugs to both Castle Hill and Soundview. Pipe accompanied Pete on their first meetings with the twins.

Neither Twin nor Pete smoked or drank, and both nursed ambitions to be successful gangsters. Twin, a fitness fanatic, worked out in the lee of the Castle Hill towers, among weed-cracked lots and tarmacked basketball courts hemmed in with rust-tinged twelve-foot-high mesh fences. He pumped weights and did chin-ups in the fresh air, tanking up on chocolate Yoo-hoo after his sessions.

Twin introduced Pete to some of the most dangerous players in Castle Hill. In turn, Pete introduced him to Pipe and the crew. Twin invited Pipe to his apartment, on the nineteenth floor of 535 Havemeyer Avenue, greeting him in the living room with an M16 and boasting that he had a hookup in the military. They went to the roof of the building and fired the gun into the night sky, the 5.56mm rounds tearing toward the stars with a blistering fizz.

Bemo resented the new partnership, feeling that he should be the point man for Pete in his own neighborhood, particulary after killing Kiron. Bemo's status had risen after the killing, but he was a loner, unlike Twin, who was smooth, affable, and could command loyalty. Twin had cocaine connections and was already moving multiple kilos on his own. On a hot summer night, tensions reached a crescendo outside a deli in Castle Hill where Twin's crew stored their guns. Pipe, Pete, and Suge were standing next door, outside a pizza shop, when Twin and Bemo bumped into each other.

"You a pussy like your brother," snapped Bemo.

Twin punched him in the face. Bemo, not bothering to fight, pulled out a gun and aimed it at Twin's chest. Twin taunted him, and before Bemo could flex his finger on the trigger, Pete jumped between them. "You ain't gonna shoot him, you understand?"

Bemo now had the gun pointing at Pete's chest. "We all peoples here!" Pete shouted. Bemo lowered the weapon.

PIPE, STILL just fourteen, standing four foot eight and at 135 pounds, was now a member of one of New York's most violent crews. Four days after a bountiful Christmas with his family, he and a friend were walking up the ramp of 551 at around 8:00 p.m. when a twenty-two-year-old woman passed them. "These motherfuckers out here ain't no good," she said, looking down at the mess of tobacco and wrappers the local kids had left in the lobby. "I can't wait until I move the fuck up out of here."

Pipe felt his gorge rise. "Well, bitch, I can't wait for you to move out of here, too."

She spun to face him, looking at the kid swaddled in thick layers of clothing. "You got something smart to say?" she said. "What if I smack you?"

Pipe made a show of looking around. "This bitch can't be talking to me," he said to his friend. "Who you talking to?" he said with mock surprise. "Me?" The woman nodded. "Bitch," he said. "You put your hands on me I will smack fire out of you. Are you fucking crazy?"

The woman raised her hand to punch him in the face. As Pipe remembers it, he reflexively lunged with his right hand to block her, only to realize he still held the gun. He ended up slapping her in the face with the butt of the revolver. The gun went off.

"He tried to kill me!"

"Get the fuck outta here," Pipe retorted, inwardly cursing himself. "If I tried to kill you, you would be dead." The woman huffed back into 551.

Shortly afterward her brother and father appeared. The father restrained his son, who threatened Pipe. "Let me go, Dad!"

"Listen, you little coward," Pipe taunted him, "if you really wanted to get away from your father you would. He is only holding you with one hand and you're two times bigger than him."

Still, Pipe decided to leave before the police came. He repaired to the back of the projects, where he gathered with the crew and Ro. He handed the gun off to his brother, who hid it. Then Pipe, his brother, and a few others returned to the pizza shop to get a slice. After about ten minutes the door opened and the woman came in, flanked by police officers.

Pipe was hauled away and charged with attempted murder in the second degree, criminal possession of a weapon, criminal use of a firearm, reckless endangerment, and menacing in the third degree. After processing, he was driven through the electric gate at Spofford, the same journey Suge had made a year or so before, to await trial. Pipe felt satisfied in some sense to get his first prison term out of the way and to earn the badge of courage it conferred. In the gym playing basketball one day, Pipe blocked a kid sporting gold fronts who bragged he had carried out a double murder with his stepmother, and punched him in the stomach.

Following the assault, Pipe was moved to a facility in Brooklyn and then to another in the Bronx. It was times like these that he counted on the steadfast support of his mother. She visited him at the juvenile detention facility on Beach Avenue—a place the inmates called "the Beach House"—which stood a few blocks from Soundview. She was holding a brand-new pair of sneakers as a gift. As they spoke in the visiting room, she offered solace and some degree of contrition, lamenting that because of the environment Pipe had been raised in, prison was an inevitable outcome. She offered him advice on how to conduct himself, told him not to let anyone disrespect him, and declared she was there for him. She warned him again to leave the drug game behind. "It's dirty. No good will come of it." She told him that she was disappointed that he had handed the gun off to Ro at the scene, thereby potentially incriminating him, too, but that she understood why he'd done it. After winding his way through the juvenile justice system, Pipe pleaded guilty to the assault and was given eighteen months' probation.

He returned home but never went to see his probation officer. Soundview was full of stash pads and crack houses where the authorities would never find a fourteen-year-old. But, with the police searching for him, he quickly discovered he had no way to make money hustling on the street—he'd be arrested if they saw him—and he couldn't sign up for welfare. Suge's success in Springfield had shown him that real money could be made out of town. A friend kept returning to Soundview from Buffalo with large sums of money stashed in sports duffel bags. He said that Buffalo was the new frontier for a young hustler to get rich.

If he ran into problems, he could always fall back on Soundview, safe under Pete's control. Pipe had developed a relationship with his first real girlfriend, who worked as a cashier at a supermarket and whose older brother was a rapper. When Pipe told her that he was going out of town to sell crack she begged him to stay, offering her entire paycheck to him. He refused, saying it wasn't enough. A week after his release from the Beach House, he took a seat on a Greyhound at New York's Port Authority.

For the entrepreneurial crack dealer, the legions of unemployed in Buffalo and a local distrust of the police created a rich opportunity. Pipe would open another line from Soundview to the north.

The drug crews had even taken over some civic duties. A local dealer, Frankie Johnson, was selling $120,000 of marijuana a week and had become a city benefactor. He repaired the sidewalks on his street when the city refused to, earning the gratitude of residents. He alerted potential buyers by handing out flyers near schools to advertise his drug houses, which were painted a distinctive blue.

Pipe had been invited to the city by Ladu, one of his uncle's friends, who had brought up more men from Soundview as his operation expanded after a year of making a small fortune. Ladu had perfected a pipeline from the Bronx by using young women who worked as dental assistants and nurses and were happy to traffic in drugs for extra money. They drove down to New York, picked up "work," and drove it up concealed in household products like shaving foam canisters with false bottoms. The drugs arrived at a nondescript, well-tended house in a virtually crime-free white, middle-class neighborhood near Buffalo State University where they were stockpiled, along with guns. Ladu had chosen the location so it would not arouse police suspicion. The guns and drugs were then disbursed to a stash house and a crack house in drug neighborhoods also controlled by Ladu, as well as other areas as needed.

Winter temperatures could plummet in the wind-whipped city on the banks of Lake Erie. The first few weeks Pipe and a friend bought stolen Eddie Bauer parkas and got to work hustling in an area frequented by rural drug addicts in pickup trucks who came into town to get high. Pipe, with a beeper on his belt to alert him to customers, would stand on a corner wearing just a T-shirt under his coat, the hood cinched up tight like a periscope, as he ranged back and forth exchanging crack for cash.

In time Pipe began to work out of a stash house on the corner of Sycamore and Loepere that had fallen under Ladu's control after two other men came up from Soundview and took over some blocks. Declaring that the New Yorkers were "taking food out of their mouths" by muscling in on their drug market, a local gang started to drive past the house displaying AK-47s. Pipe and the others hung out the top-floor windows showing their guns. A meeting was called between Ladu and the locals. He told them that he and his crew could kill them and return home with minimal fuss, but since this was the locals' home turf, a feud would only draw the police, and they had nowhere to run. "But if y'all want to make some money, we can work together," said Ladu. The Buffalo crews were murderous, known for robbing crack houses and kidnapping rivals, but the plea for common cause worked. The Buffalo men saw the benefit of a drug connection that could bring weight from New York.

Each day Pipe's product was bagged at the house on Loepere before Pipe sometimes cycled it over to a house on Sobieski Street that had been converted into a crack house. The 1,600-square-foot clapboard home, built during the city's ascendance, had became a small fortress where Pipe and the crew could withstand a SWAT raid or an armed attack by rival dealers.

Pipe learned how to bag heroin. Every now and then he ducked into a local McDonald's, ordered a Big Mac, and then stuffed his pockets with plastic coffee spoons, perfect for scooping up heroin and putting it into glassine bags. He mixed the heroin with quinine, which increased the intensity of the rush, crushing it all with a card before emptying two scoops into each bag. They stamped the bags with their brand name: DOA, dead on arrival. In New York, the bags would sell for $10. In Buffalo they were worth $20.

Each morning he set out across the city, running the numbers through his head like a mathematician. Pipe was paid a basic salary, like the others, of $1,000 a week. To make extra money, he sold in the crack house. He got an ounce from Ladu "on consignment"—meaning it was free up front but its value had to be paid back once it was sold. He broke it down into 280 dime bags. At the end of a day or two he'd net $2,800, give Ladu back $1,400, and pocket $1,400 himself.

Pipe was walking out of a crack house one day when two policemen stopped him on the sidewalk. This time he had nothing on him. But, to his horror, they pulled two small Ziploc bags of crack from his pocket. "You didn't get that off me," he protested. He got out on bail the next morning.

The following day he went on a spending spree in the Walden Galleria mall in Cheektowaga, a few miles away. He splurged on American Eagle jeans, rugby shirts, button-downs from Aéropostale and Banana Republic. Afterward he returned to Soundview on the Greyhound bus with a Nike duffel bag containing $24,000.

Back in the Bronx, he went shopping for a new car with two friends, Sean "Nut" Carr and Andre "Bear" Brown, at an auction on Zerega Avenue. Bear, at six-seven and three hundred pounds, used to dangle Pipe by his ankles when they were growing up. Like Pete, he had been Pipe's protector. When Pipe's mother threw him out of the house, Bear took him in and let him sleep on his couch. In 1991, he had saved Pipe's life when some boys visiting from Harlem exchanged caustic words with Pete, Pipe, and Bear. The Harlem boys started shooting, and Pipe, nearest them, was caught in the line of fire. Bear picked him up and threw him into the lobby of the building, taking a bullet in his leg for the trouble. Pipe felt he owed him.

The only cars Pipe had driven had been stolen, so it was high time he had some respectable wheels. Still under five feet tall, he could see over the steering wheel of only one or two models, and then just barely. He bought himself a burgundy Honda Prelude with black leather seats for $7,400 and two other cars for Nut and Bear. The salesman was taken aback at the diminutive fourteen-year-old who rummaged in a duffel bag almost as big as himself and handed over bundles of cash to pay for the three cars. Nut was the only one who had a license, so they filled out the paperwork in his name.

They headed to the block in convoy. Pipe led in the Honda, crawling around the horseshoe. Kids came out of the buildings to watch. "Check out my new whip, Moe!" he shouted from the driver's seat.

Pipe may have been Pete's little brother, the baby of the crew, but now he was also becoming a man in his own right. He relished being able to provide Bear with a car after he had taken a bullet for him. Pipe saw the way other kids he had grown up with looked at him now—with envy and awe.

+ + +

PIPE'S STATUS would continue to be challenged. In March 1992, he was hustling crack outside 551. The group was harassing B-Love for getting the joint they were sharing soggy. "You put your big wet-ass lips all over this, nigga?" joked Pipe, eliciting laughter from everyone.

Suddenly B-Love turned serious. "Who's that big dude with your moms?"

Pipe turned and saw his father, with his mother at his elbow, making his way toward them. Pipe's father had returned from prison, back on work release after yet another stint upstate. "Wassup?" he said as he and Pipe greeted each other. Big Bimbo stood around five foot nine but was muscled and imposing. When Pipe tried to make small talk, his father humiliated him with a lecture, overheard by B-Love and other friends standing nearby. "Your mother wrote me a lot of letters," he scolded. "You out here selling drugs and shooting people." Before Pipe had a chance to respond, his father slapped him in the face. Humiliated and enraged, Pipe could only stand there as Big Bimbo went on demeaning him. His father said that he was sorry he hadn't been around earlier to discipline his son but that he was home now and things were going to change. "Get your ass upstairs and don't leave until I get there."

Pipe fought tears. "What you crying for?" Bimbo demanded. "I thought you was the big man now, selling drugs, huh?" Pipe was silent. His parents went to get food at White Castle, and Pipe began the long walk to his apartment. With each step, he felt more and more hatred for his father.

+ + +

PIPE'S GRANDFATHER had been a gangster-hustler who sold heroin. Bimbo took up the family business.

But after a while he found he could make more money committing robberies than hustling drugs. He and some friends stuck up bus drivers at the rate of three or four a day. Some weeks he returned to his mother's house, in the Kingsbridge section of the Bronx, with $4,000 or $5,000 from robberies and selling drugs.

His run was short-lived. One of the crew did a robbery on his own, got arrested, and ended up ratting on everyone. Nineteen years old, Bimbo went to prison on May 30, 1972, to serve a four-year sentence. His elder brother got five years. In the prison yard he fell in love with weightlifting. He was released in December 1975.

Back on the street, a lot had changed in the Bronx. Many youngsters flocked to the brotherhood of street gangs. Seventy percent of all gang members in the Bronx were Puerto Rican; the rest were mostly black. Big Bimbo's old neighborhood, Kingsbridge, now posed dangers for black families. Bimbo and Vincent Coll—later known as "Mad Dog"—joined the Black Spades. Some wore sleeveless, greasy denim jackets in a fashion known as "flying cut sleeves." Their backs were emblazoned with gang crests, like a coat of arms: the Black Spades, the Savage Skulls, the Young Lords. They were a ragtag collection that mixed the ideology of the Black Panthers with the countercultural attitudes of the Hells Angels.

But the gangs became more violent and sold the same drugs they meant to shield their communities from.

Bimbo realized he could make more money, with less risk of arrest, from loan-sharking. He kept it simple. For every $100 he lent, he demanded $200 back. "There ain't a problem if you don't give it back," he would say. "You're just going to get killed."

Bimbo paid off the cops on occasion, and they left him alone. His oldest brother became a police officer and once got him out of jail. But when Bimbo got into trouble again with another sibling, the eldest brother abandoned them. Bimbo turned back to drugs and started shooting heroin.

He met Pipe's mother and declared that he wanted to have thirteen children. They began with Pipe, but as they added more siblings for him in the following years, Bimbo went to jail for possession of a controlled substance in 1984 for two to four years, and then served more time for violation of parole, a never-ending cycle of prison and release. Pipe's mother stuck with him and gave Pipe more brothers and sisters. On visits back to Soundview, Miss Annette and Big Bimbo nursed a tempestuous but loving relationship. When he once came home drunk and she discovered a letter from another woman in his pocket, she stabbed him in the back with a butcher knife, collapsing his lung. Rushed to the hospital for treatment, he quickly reconciled with her when she came to visit.

Here he was again, finally home after another long stretch; and he was determined to straighten out his wayward son.

+ + +

PIPE CHARGED into the bedroom he shared with his brother, tears streaming down his face. He went to the lockbox under his bed that contained his gun.

"What ya doin'?" asked Ro.

"I'ma gonna kill this nigga."

"You're gonna kill Daddy?"

Pipe pulled out the gun, flipped open the cylinder, satisfied himself it was loaded, and regarded Ro. "Yes," he said.

Pipe had nursed his sisters, put money on the table, helped his mom while his father was away in prison. Who was Bimbo, a stranger to him, to come home and slap him upside the head on the block where he had a reputation to maintain?

The brothers argued as Ro tried to talk him out of it.

"I ain't got no father," Pipe said.

Fifteen minutes later he heard the latch on the door. Pipe caught his father coming through the door first, ahead of his mother, and raised the gun, aiming it at his father's chest. "If you ever hit me again I'll kill you," said Pipe.

Pipe's mom jumped in front of her husband, begging him to put the gun down.

"Don't protect him!" blustered Pipe. "I'll fuckin' kill him." He faced down his father. "Don't you ever put your hands on me. You ain't no fucking father to me." Turning to his appalled mother, he demanded, "How he gonna come home after all these years and discipline me?" Back to his father: "You crazy? You better ask somebody about me. I kill you where you stand, man!"

Then Pipe, satisfied his point had been made, fled.

Out on the block, B-Love and a few others saw that Pipe was shaking when he rejoined the group. They tried to soothe him. As he was explaining what had happened, he caught their eyes shifting to a spot behind him. B-Love and some of the others reached for their guns. Pipe turned to see his father walking up behind them. Pipe told the crew to stand down. He commanded, "That's still my pops. I can shoot him. You can't."

Bimbo asked if he could talk to his son alone. The other boys examined their feet. Pipe said that there was nothing to discuss.

Bimbo apologized. Pipe refused to listen. Bimbo continued. "I started talking to your mother . . . You know, I haven't been here all these years to watch you grow up, to show you how to be a man. You had to learn on your own. So for me to just come and discipline you wasn't right. You don't know me as a father. So I want to apologize and I want to . . ." His voice trailed off. Pipe felt his eyes begin to prick with tears.

Bimbo finished: "Hopefully we can try to be friends and try to work and build that father-and-son relationship."

"Whatever." Pipe pouted. But his anger subsided. He had almost completely cut himself off from sorrow or regret, but his father's repentance reached him.

"Wanna smoke a blunt with me?" said Big Bimbo.

Pipe cracked up. "I ain't smoking with you. You trying to go back to jail?"

Bimbo offered a conciliatory smile. "I'm just trying to be your friend."

IN THE summer of 1992, Pete went in search of an intellectual framework for their way of life. Stacks of books appeared on the floor of his room, including Sun Tzu's *Art of War* and Niccolò Machiavelli's *The Prince*, a sixteenth-century treatise on the cultivation of power, a book Pete carried with him and urged Pipe and the others to read. Pete saw his own life as a work of art—a blank sheet—on which he created a flowing narrative. Everything had symbolism and relevance; every experience was absorbed and interpreted to create his nascent gang manifesto.

Pete referenced a Machiavelli passage: "By arming your subjects you arm yourself; those who were suspect become loyal, and those who were loyal not only remain so but are changed from being merely your subjects to being your partisans." Pipe noticed Pistol Pete's growing notoriety for weapons and his emphasis on handing them out to anyone in his inner circle.

There were long screeds on the power of deception, the art of feinting to mask one's true intentions. He found a keynote passage in chapter 17, "Cruelty and Compassion," on whether it is better to be loved than feared, or the reverse. "For love is secured by a bond of gratitude which men, wretched creatures that they are, break when it is their advantage to do so; but fear is strengthened by a dread of punishment which is always effective."

Soon Pete's plans for all of them were revealed. The past few summers, Pete's cousin Loaf had visited from Los Angeles. This year, 1992, Loaf was dressed all in blue and told Pete that he had become a Crip gang member in LA. Pete teased Loaf about his blue uniform, but Loaf said LA's gangs wore gang colors and held territory, in contrast to the Pete and his crew in the Bronx, who drew their inspiration from debonair Mafia dons, and whose main focus was generating large sums of cash while cavalierly attempting to bed as many women as they could. Loaf parried: "Anyway, all you dudes care about is sex and money and murder."

Later, standing outside 551, Pete explained to Pipe that the three words perfectly encapsulated their mission. "Sex, money, murder," he said. "Look, you think about it, we get sex because we get money. And we murder anyone who fucks with our money." As Pete saw it, any murders they committed were for economic liberation in a struggle against an unjust system. Pete argued that the US government routinely killed for economic advantage, so what was different about killing to get money in the projects? Pipe, who'd never thought of things in that way, agreed. Pete said the invasion of Iraq in 1991 was about killing to get oil and therefore money. It was part of life, Pete reasoned, how empires were built. Wasn't that how America was founded? The early settlers and the founding fathers established America with brutality, racketeering, and cold-blooded speculation, while slaughtering anyone who thwarted their commercial interests.

"We're Sex Money Murder now," Pete told them. It was the American Dream inverted, a new equivalent of "life, liberty and the pursuit of happiness." In the modern gold rush that crack offered, Pete and Pipe were prospectors, gunslingers in the urban ravines of New York City, where growing infamy amid whining bullets meant that tomorrow could bring sudden outrageous riches or, just as easily, a swift violent demise.

Pipe ordered some baseball caps with *SMM* stitched on the back and designed black-and-gray varsity jackets with *SMM* emblazoned over the right breast—a small nod to a West Coast gang uniform. Pete developed a slogan. "Sex: I need it. Money: I got to have it. Murder: It's always on my mind." They belted the refrain. Pete added another line: "East Side all the time, Sex Money gonna shine." East Side denoted the East Coast. When they assembled on the block, they bellowed out in unison, in what they now termed "a roll call" like soldiers in an army platoon. Sex Money Murder had been born.

Three

COMA

IN MARCH 1992, SUGE, ON AN AIRPLANE for the first time, grasped his seat's armrest with both hands, a gold ring encrusted with diamonds and a single word, "Sugar," adorning a finger on his right. Baby had bought Suge the ring two months earlier, for his nineteenth birthday. Baby had also just turned nineteen, and he and a few others from Soundview, all wearing black Ray-Bans, were flying to Daytona, Florida, for a few days of celebration. Springfield had been six months of pure profit. Baby and Suge had fat rolls of bills in their pockets. Suge's new life was opening up opportunities he had never known existed.

Suge was indebted to Baby for taking him on at his lowest point after his release from Spofford. He had had just $20 in his pocket, but Baby had set him on the path to riches. In return, Suge laid his life on the line for Baby almost every week. Anytime anyone owed Baby money the pair would drive up and Suge would get out and lay down a salvo of bullets before they peeled off. Suge never knew if he hit his targets, and he didn't much care. It was quick, easy work like the beatdowns he did for Fat Mike in Soundview, except with guns. Baby threw him a few bills each time.

While Pete and Pipe were establishing Sex Money Murder in Soundview, Suge had veered off to become part of a loose-knit organization known as Baby Jay's crew, quite different from what was happening in the Bronx. It suited Suge, who, out from under Pete's fame, could indulge his ego and a largely unchallenged outlaw reputation in the small city of Springfield. Pete and Baby considered themselves rivals, each too proud to accommodate the other. But Baby was scared of Pete and rarely showed his face in Soundview unless he was with Suge. "How the fuck you represent the 'View and you scared to even come back in your own neighborhood?" Pete said scornfully to Pipe.

Meanwhile, Suge had found himself a girlfriend in Springfield. On Halloween, he was throwing eggs at neighborhood kids from the stash house at 85 College Street when he noticed a light-skinned Puerto Rican girl amid the ghouls. She had a sullen allure and bright green eyes.

She paused, pouting in anger, as she caught him with an egg in his hand, an impish grin on his face. He froze as their eyes met. "Mama, I ain't throwing eggs at you," he joked, issuing peals of hoarse laughter. "You're cute."

Suge teased a reluctant smile from her. She said her name was Gina. Over the months that followed, Suge spent $200 a week on her and her infant son. Unlike the mostly impoverished native boys in Springfield, he was ostentatious and profligate. His charm and bantering wit were infectious. At night, when he finished "grinding"—selling crack—they snuggled up and watched movies. Some nights, though, she noticed that he couldn't sleep. He'd break out in sweats, thrash and pant. In the morning he'd mention something about a kidnapping in New York. She didn't probe further. Instead, she touched the puckered scar on his scalp and the bullet wounds on his right forearm, and felt the metal fragments inside his flesh.

+ + +

SUGE ARRIVED back in Springfield from his Florida vacation rejuvenated and ready for action. Dressed in calf-length baggy shorts, a .380 in his back pocket, he pulled into a gas station. As he headed in to pay cash before he pumped, a large Puerto Rican man bumped into him. "Yo, papi," snarled Suge. "Excuse me!"

"I'm not your papi," said the man, returning to his car. Suge felt he might have been going for a gun, so he shot him in the leg before driving off.

Suge was growing increasingly volatile and reckless, and because of that he was drawing undue attention. Baby kicked him out of the College Street house, and Suge moved in with Gina and her family on Nursery Street at a small complex called the Liberty Hill Townhouses. The area was perfect for drug dealing because of its proximity to I-291, ideal for white addicts who yearned for the fizz of a cheap cocaine high but didn't want to linger in a dangerous and remote area to get it. Baby used Suge to open a new market there.

To Suge, the little housing development was a miniature Soundview, with the same maze of dark alleyways and cut-throughs that offered a drug dealer escape if rivals or the police came. Black men were not especially welcome, but Suge spoke fluent Spanish, and the towering Puerto Rican who controlled Gina's block, a man named Muscles, realized that it was to his benefit to have Suge and his connections around.

It had become routine for Baby to re-up every week in New York. Sometimes Suge rode shotgun. The three-hour drive each way was the only time he could ever relax. With Baby at the wheel, he tilted the seat back and slept more deeply than he ever could in New York or Springfield.

Suge's volcanic temper continued to worsen. He didn't consider the consequences of gun violence and committed himself to any conflict his friends got into, as he had in Soundview—laying the foundation for the killer he would become.

Unlike Pipe, who had set out in the drug game with certain personal rules, certainly with respect to bloodshed, Suge prided himself on having no limits. He could always find some reason, no matter how inconsequential, to justify violence. And he was happy to share inside knowledge of the trade.

He was out making drug deliveries when he passed a man from a rival crew who had fought Suge's drug associate and friend BO in a street brawl. BO was a local tough with a reputation for fistfighting who had fallen in with Suge hustling crack. Suge mentored him in the ruthless ways of the Bronx, and the previous New Year's Eve he had taken him into Magazine Park with a few others and put a firearm in his hand for the first time. He showed him how to shoot a gun into the air, and since then BO had forsaken his fists to settle disputes, instead using the revolver he now carried. Suge chased their rival, running several stop signs and red lights and even streaming past the police station on Pearl Street. Shortly afterward, the man split his tire on the curb and came to a stop. Suge jumped out and tried to shoot him in the face. The slide on his gun jammed, so he repeatedly smashed the weapon into the man's face. The man's girlfriend screamed from the car for him to stop. Back on Franklin Street, near the Liberty Hill Townhouses where Suge and other dealers hustled, Suge realized that his shirt was soaked with blood. "I did him dirty, man," he later bragged to BO.

Suge's assault ignited a major conflict between the two dominant groups of drug dealers in the area. The black gang near Eastern Avenue controlled the turf near where BO and his mother lived, and shot up their house one night, as they dove to the floor amid shattering glass and splintering wood.

By turns euphoric, depressed, and angry, Suge continued to act out. Baby now had to keep reminding him—as he fixated more on trying to murder late-payers than simply spraying bullets near them as he had in the past—that his job was only to frighten people into making good on their debts. "Just scare 'em up," said Baby. "Don't kill them." Suge took Gina on a drug delivery and shot at a man on a scooter who didn't get out of their way fast enough.

When Suge was arrested on drug distribution charges, the crew passed around a brown paper bag for donations to a legal fund. Suge had been taken to the "big house" on York Street—the site, in 1898, of the last public hanging in Massachusetts. When Gina visited, the crew sat outside on the road blasting rap from the car so that the bass streamed through the walls and doorways. Suge would tap his feet in the cell as he listened to the rallying call of the street.

On his release, Gina urged him to go back to school, to invest in a laundromat or a car wash like other drug dealers who made the transition into legitimate business. He didn't listen. He blew his money on clothes, nights out and cars. When he crashed one, he abandoned it and bought a new one. And when he had no wheels he borrowed cars from crack addicts.

When he and Gina had first met, he'd been a tough kid, but he'd had a tenderness, a wounded look, that had drawn her to him. She could see the vulnerability of a young boy still frightened by his world, fighting back fear with all the violence and bravado he could muster. Now he was on a rampage. He wore a sneering expression all the time and drew satisfaction from scaring and hurting people. He and Gina watched *Scarface* over and over again until the video was riddled with flecks from overuse. Gina watched his eyes glaze over when the advertising blimp rose in the sky with the immortal line: THE WORLD IS YOURS.

Gina suspected that Suge was doing drugs because he'd sometimes get sudden nosebleeds. At night he rarely slept, though he might doze three or four hours in the day. Once, while she was in the shower, Suge was cleaning his gun without having checked to make sure it was empty. A bullet tore through the wall, missing her head by inches.

Sometimes he returned to New York to rejuvenate. The only place he felt really safe was behind the ramparts of Soundview. Sex Money Murder was fully in control there now, bringing order to the block and protection for any ally of Pistol Pete's. Suge took Gina down to Manhattan, where he bought her a $900 purple leather-and-suede jacket. Miss Julia bustled around her, cooking her favorite food while suggesting that she get out of Springfield, leave Suge behind, and come live with her in the Bronx.

Suge grew increasingly possessive of Gina. He ripped apart her outfits in fits of jealous rage so that she couldn't go out to clubs. She learned to buy three of everything so when he destroyed one outfit she had another to wear.

Eventually Gina broke up with him; they got back together briefly when Suge persisted and chased her down, but she knew he was a "ticking time bomb." When Gina ended it again, she heard a rumor that Suge had offered another girl $20 to beat her up. Then he came to her house, and when she refused to let him in, he shot up the door. She ran away to Florida to escape.

Suge began to date a young woman with a son from a previous relationship, and before long she was pregnant with his child. The news didn't slow him down a bit.

+ + +

THE SUMMER of 1992 saw unparalleled gun violence in Springfield. When he first arrived in the city, Suge had grown accustomed to firing potshots, mostly for effect. Now, though, his victims shot back.

The Jamaican crew from Brooklyn, who had already shot Suge once, were making bigger moves all over the city, stealing the local drug dealers' women, while sensing an uptapped market on the corner of the interstates, and hoping to use the murder of one or two local dealers as an example of their growing power, much the way Sex Money Murder had done in Soundview.

Sometime around September 1992, Suge and BO went up their block to investigate sounds of a scuffle. Suge found a Jamaican hustling out of one of the crack houses, arguing with some local Puerto Ricans. When Suge approached, the Jamaican stood his ground, unfazed by the short New Yorker with the sharp tongue. "Y'all can't tell me how to hustle," he said.

"Yo, son, you can't be out here," Suge answered. "Have we got a problem?" Suge turned to AntLive, a drug trafficker from Yonkers. "Yo, why don't you punch him in the face?" The Jamaican demanded to know who Suge was. "Sugar Shaft, and this is our block." AntLive threw a quick punch, hitting the Jamaican, who backed up out of reach, pulled out a gun, and fired. Suge felt a sharp thump in his chest. His lungs caught fire.

Suge pulled the .380 and squeezed. Silence. The gun was jammed or empty. Terrified, he threw it down and ran for his life. He made it down a small incline and felt another bullet rip into his right side, just above his kidney.

Then his body began to shut down. All of his sensations grew fainter, and he felt himself slipping away. He tumbled to the pavement, struggling for every breath. A neighborhood kid skidded his car to a stop. He hauled Suge into the backseat. Suge felt a stabbing pain in his chest, and then the red light of the Mercy Medical Center loomed above him.

Hospital staff heaved him onto a gurney. Suge prayed, panicked, and at some point he shit himself. Doctors swarmed around him. His baby mother appeared at some point, looked at the bullet holes in his chest, and burst into tears.

Suddenly a mask was clamped over his face. Hands secured something around his legs, and a doctor asked him to count backward from fifty. At forty-eight his consciousness began to slip, and within minutes he floated into complete darkness.

Four

PIPELINES OF THE GAME

JOY FLOODED PIPE'S APARTMENT WHEN his mother returned from the hospital with a new baby. The arrival of Pipe's youngest sister made everyone feel like a family again for the first time in years. Big Bimbo spent his days playing with his new daughter and helping around the house.

Both of Pipe's parents had forsworn drugs, and for three months, life was as normal and as happy as he could remember. He hustled a little but largely spent his days playing skellzies and computer games, and enjoying the mood at home. And when a man abandoned two pit bull puppies on Cozy Corner, leaving them tied to a lamppost, Pipe took them in. He named them Red and Yayo. Pipe taught them to snarl at the police. He spent his afternoons at the local roller-skating rink, where he was free to be a normal teenager. Then one day, after an afternoon on skates flirting with girls, he returned to the block and learned that his mother had been taken to the hospital.

She had collapsed after developing a breathing problem. Most of the family had asthma—asthma rates in the Bronx were three times the national average—but Pipe and his mother had it worst. Smoking crack worsened the condition of her lungs.

As he waited for news, Pipe quickly took over the family chores. He packed an overnight bag in case he was called to the hospital. Big Bimbo, who had accompanied his mother there, returned home distraught. They sat waiting for news.

Sometime in the afternoon the following day, Pipe's father spotted a couple of uniformed police officers heading to the apartment. At first they thought they might be a warrant squad looking to arrest Pipe for his parole violation. Reflexively Pipe made for the stairs and the roof, but Big Bimbo told him to wait. Cops seeking parole violators were dressed in plainclothes, but these men in uniform, he reasoned, were not coming to arrest Pipe.

Pipe stood behind his father at the front door when they knocked. The policeman asked if he was Annette's husband. When he said that he was, they gave him the news. Annette had passed away in the hospital from cardiac arrest. Big Bimbo collapsed. He refused to accept it. The policemen requested he go to the hospital to identify the body when he could. Pipe sat in silence in the apartment, lacerated by grief. His mother was his anchor, the only person who really understood him and, indeed, the only person he could ever really trust. He had no one now. After an hour or so he grabbed his gun, stormed out of the apartment past his grieving father, leapt down the stairs, and ran out into the projects.

He spotted an associate named Jasper selling on the block, in breach of Sex Money Murder rules. Pipe marched up to him with the gun in his hand. "Who you hustling for?" Jasper gave him the name of some guy Pipe didn't know. Pipe demanded all his money, and Jasper complied.

The next few days Pipe felt like he was living underwater. He turned to Pete. He would allow only Pete to see just how weak and helpless he felt. Any others might see the softness and exploit it. When Pete heard that Pipe didn't have enough money to pay for funeral expenses and clothes for his mother to be buried in, he handed Pipe $1,200.

The wake was at a funeral home on East 153rd Street and Courtlandt Avenue, near the Melrose projects. Pipe waited in line with his siblings, but in the end, he saw his mother in repose, her face an etiolated mask that couldn't reflect her joy, humor, and indefatigable spirit and her special bond with Pipe. Her dimples were gone. He wanted to kiss her goodbye, but he couldn't bring himself to because he refused to accept that this was her and that her soul had moved on.

One of Pipe's cousins, a Baptist preacher, got up to deliver an address. As he spoke about Miss Annette's life, Pipe rose, turned on his heel, and stormed outside. Ro and the others went to the burial out in New Jersey. They didn't have the money for a tombstone.

+ + +

WITH HIS MOTHER gone, Pipe decided not to return to Buffalo. But there was another reason. A few months earlier, he had been forced to retreat from the city. A local crew had sent a female decoy posing as a customer, then rushed in behind her and ransacked his crack house at gunpoint. They beat Pipe up badly, knocking him out and leaving him in a pool of his own blood after smashing him over the head with the marble base of a sports trophy—before they made off with all the drugs. "Niggas gonna run up in the crib busting their joints?" Pipe had complained as one of Ladu's drug mules, who also worked as a nurse, stitched up his scalp.

In the days following, Pipe looked at photos of local gang leaders that a friend of Ladu's, a pimp, had produced in the hope Pipe might identify his assailant. A week later Pipe ambushed the man leaving a club at 1:00 a.m. "'Sup up, player?" spat Pipe, emerging from the shadows raising a gun. "You remember me, right?" Pipe shot several rounds at his chest, and the man collapsed on the ground. But hours later they heard he had survived and the bullets had either missed or were deflected by a bulletproof vest. Pipe knew a revenge cycle would start, disrupting his money flow, so he decided to return to Soundview and to look for other opportunities.

Back home, he once again took over caring for the family. He made dinner for everyone before he swaddled three-month-old Ashley, fed her a bottle, and lulled her to sleep with his heartbeat as she lay on his chest. Once she was down, he headed to Cozy Corner. The family needed money to survive, and Pipe had no idea how to negotiate a welfare claim. Since the money in Buffalo had dried up, he had no choice but to start at the bottom of the game in Soundview again. He was still seen as the baby of Sex Money Murder, and as such, he had to make his own way. He borrowed all the money he could from friends, invested in a major crack consignment, and often sold from 7:00 p.m. until sunrise. He paid his creditors and pocketed whatever he made, which went back into providing for the family.

His mother's best friend, Psyche, had an apartment at 1725 Randall Avenue that Pipe called the dungeon because she kept it completely dark with blackout drapes. Pipe rented the apartment as a place to store his stash and keep his pit bulls. One day he returned to find Psyche complaining that one of the dogs had gone berserk, smashing itself against the walls and the door. Pipe found Yayo laid out beneath posters of *Scarface* and Tupac, barely breathing. To Pipe's dismay, the dog had eaten seven grams of pure cocaine, his entire stash. Hours later Yayo came to, suffering withdrawal, but alive.

✦ ✦ ✦

WHEN PETE turned eighteen in October 1992, he arrived in Soundview sporting a Rolex, which he showed off to Pipe. He told him that his father had left him the watch, a fur coat, and around $250,000 as a coming-of-age gift that his uncle George "G-Dub" Wallace had now turned over to him. A year and a half earlier, in May 1991, Pete's mother had moved her seventeen-year-old son out of her apartment to live with Wallace in Queens. She hoped that an older man might straighten him out. But it became obvious to Pipe that rather than straightening him out, Wallace had been acting as a mentor to his nephew in the drug game. Wallace was a suave and soft-spoken gangster from the old school who never raised his voice and had, as rumor went, been mentored by Pete's dad. Always perfectly attired, he was chiseled from the gym and eschewed drinking, smoking and red meat—dietary restrictions that Pete had started to live by, too. Pete told Pipe of his plans to quadruple the $250,000 to a million. "We're going to be flipping bricks," he said, indicating that he now had a down payment on several kilos of cocaine that could be turned to profit.

Pete and Pipe continued to search for cities where they could open crack franchises. They ventured down to Baltimore and made just two hand-to-hand sales on Pulaski before a rival dealer spotted them on his turf and pulled a .45. During a scuffle over the weapon Pete ran off and abandoned Pipe, only to think twice and return with a pistol, before the man escaped. They shot the man's car up that night, but decided to return to Soundview to continue the search for softer cities easier to conquer.

Bemo had established Sex Money Murder in Kingston, New York, where there had been no resistance. He'd recruited youngsters with free bicycles and candy while intimidating any rivals with violence. Kingston had quickly earned a reputation as a place for hustlers to flip a small stake, an ounce or so, and double their money. Pete and Pipe arrived and found an easy place to prosper and sold out quickly.

Pipe had been amassing a supply of Pete's crack at home so he could re-up as needed. He called Ro at the apartment, where $500 worth sat secured in a lockbox, telling him to hand it to an associate who would courier it up to Kingston for him. Ro called back to say that the drugs were missing.

Pipe panicked as he and Pete drove back to Soundview, but he kept quiet, brooding in the passenger seat, keeping the news to himself lest he incur Pete's rage. Pipe knew exactly who the culprit was.

Big Bimbo could not recover from Annette's death. Pipe had noticed his father slowly unraveling as they both labored to keep the family together. He bought groceries with the money Pipe gave him, but more and more often Pipe noticed that he came up short with change. And now he was developing the loose-limbed swagger and rheumy-eyed look of someone who had been on crack.

Pipe confronted him on his return. Big Bimbo confessed. He offered to repay his son when he got his welfare check, but Pipe knew he couldn't afford to. Pipe peeled off some bills from the Kingston profits to pay for groceries. Then he headed out the door to work. Before he left, he told his father, "And when I get back I'll get you something to get high with." Pipe figured it was absurd for his father to be buying crack from his competitors and lining the pockets of enemies.

A few weeks later Pipe and some friends, along with two young Hispanic women he had designs on, were playing music and lying low in an apartment in Soundview they used to store drugs. They heard a knock. One of the girls went to the door and returned to tell Pipe that his father wanted to discuss something with his son. Pipe found him on the threshold, overtaken by tremors.

Pipe went to a back room and weighed out five grams—$200 worth— of some of the smoothest crack he had yet made. He came back to the door and handed it to his father. "Thank you, baby boy!" said Big Bimbo, who grinned and withdrew.

✦ ✦ ✦

SEX MONEY MURDER secured allegiance in the projects by demonstrating their generosity and by giving the appearance of community involvement. Sometimes they helped carry groceries for old people. They tossed a few dollars to kids on Cozy Corner.

Rumors reached Pete and Pipe that a couple of crackheads were robbing the elderly. The boys found a bedraggled couple in their late thirties holed up in a first-floor apartment. The owner leased the space to crackheads for a little product herself. Pipe struck the man over the head with his revolver before loading a single bullet and enacting another game of Russian roulette. He asked the couple if one of them wanted to play. Spinning the cylinder, he put the gun to the man's head and pulled the trigger. The hammer came down on an empty chamber. Then he put the gun to his own temple and did the same. The gun clicked empty a second time.

"See, you can't be scared to die," he said to the crackheads. The next chamber had a live round in it. "Don't play games with me, man! I don't have it. I'm not all right up here, you know what I'm saying? The streets done took over my mind!" The outburst left him exhausted.

They left the apartment. Pete was horrified. "What the fuck?" he said. "Are you fucking crazy?"

Pipe trudged forward glumly. His mother's death had caused him to think about mortality on a deeper level. He found himself attempting to quash any sentimentality as a way to fortify himself. Once he'd dreamed of a middle-class future. Now he was in a life where moral limits were a vulnerability that got you killed.

✦ ✦ ✦

OTHER RESIDENTS of the Soundview community tried to fight back against drug dealers. The Rev. Michael Tyson, of Holy Cross Church, had begun calling attention to the epidemic's devastation. Father Tyson had spent several years in the barrios of Puerto Rico, but nothing could have prepared him for Soundview. The day he arrived, he found that the priest he was taking over from was cleaning blood off the sidewalk from the previous night's dance at Holy Cross School. One man had been caught dancing with another man's wife, and the night had ended in gunfire. Another priest in the rectory had been beaten and robbed answering a sick call.

Father Tyson and a youth group organized a march against the dealers, despite police warnings. Death threats were called in to the rectory. The police suggested that Father Tyson cancel. He refused. The commander of the Forty-Third Precinct lent him a bulletproof vest. Cops were stationed on the roofs of the Soundview Houses. The priest and the parishioners marched around the horseshoe as drug dealers kept to the shadows or in the buildings' lobbies. They held an afternoon vigil outside a crack house at Commonwealth and Soundview, praying for the afflicted inside and for "the darkness to go away."

In early November, the youth group planned another march. This time the drug dealers exacted their revenge. They broke into the sacristy and smashed a hundred-year-old statue of the Blessed Virgin. Then they set four separate fires in the church. The fires were contained. Father Tyson and the youth group marched in defiance.

✦ ✦ ✦

ALONE IN the hospital room when he came to, Suge found that he was able to move an arm, point his toes, and feel the soft restraint of sheets. His eyes opened and the darkness dissolved. And then panic came on. He couldn't breathe. He reached up to discover a long plastic pipe down his throat. His hand went down to his penis, where he felt a catheter.

A nurse appeared at his bedside. He'd been in the intensive care unit for five days, she told him. She returned with a sedative injection. A doctor told him that the gunshots had severely damaged a lung and that he would have to walk with a cane for a few weeks. He had barely digested the news when a pair of detectives visited. Suge refused to answer any questions. They said they were working up warrants for his arrest on a litany of charges. He discharged himself as soon as as he could and returned to Soundview for a few months. Pipe and everyone else warned him against going back to Springfield. Pete told him that he was being used by Baby Jay—that he would continue to be exploited while his partner sat back and counted his money. But nothing could convince him to stay away. Lured by the cash and the friends he had made, he was back in Springfield by December 1992.

Shortly after his return, he and Baby counted out so many bills in one of Baby's houses that their hands turned black with grime. After an hour or so they had tens of thousands of dollars in neat oblong stacks. Suge had never seen so much money. Baby thanked him for his work in protecting him. Grandly, he peeled off $10,000 and handed it to him. Suge fought the urge to say that it didn't seem like much for what he had done for Baby: He'd been shot twice protecting Baby's territory.

Baby had sold over sixty kilos, netting more than $200,000, in the two years or so since he'd arrived in the city. But he'd been arrested early in 1992 with twelve grams of cocaine. He skipped bail and fled Springfield. Occasionally, he returned to bring kilos to Suge or other dealers, but his visits grew rarer. This last time counting money with Suge marked his final visit to the city. He urged Suge to come with him to a new place he had in Virginia. Suge refused. Instead he blew the money on women and partying.

A few weeks later, Suge was arrested on possession of a firearm. The authorities prosecuted him with full force. In January 1993, he found himself in court facing a host of weapons and drug distribution charges. He pleaded guilty on April 16 and was sentenced to a maximum term of four to seven years at the Massachusetts Correctional Institution–Cedar Junction, a prison southwest of Boston that had housed everyone from terrorists to Boston gangsters.

Suge complained that he was being snatched off the street just as the real money was beginning to flow. Processed and led to the block, Suge saw other inmates he recognized as rivals from Springfield. "Hey, Shaft," one of the prisoners said to him. "There ain't no guns in here. What you going to do now, huh?"

Five

MONEY BATH

BY EARLY 1993, PETE HAD BECOME OBSESSED with turning Sex Money Murder from a neighborhood crew into a syndicate capable of generating millions of dollars from crack, quite unlike the other local drug-dealing gangs. Sex Money Murder dominated Soundview, while across the Bronx gangs proliferated: to the southwest over the Bronx River in Hunts Point were the Bryant Boys and Nasty Boys; to the east in the Throgs Neck Projects was the Dewey Avenue Crew; to the north were the Albanian Boys in Morris Park, and the Edenwald Boys from the notoriously dangerous Edenwald Houses. Pete's ambition for Sex Money Murder would require major connections to supply them with kilos and expanding markets, the conquest of drug markets in other cities and states, and the establishment of pipelines. So far, his lack of knowledge of large-scale trafficking had frustrated these audacious moves.

In the first few months of 1993, Sex Money Murder consisted of little more than eight main players, in a loose pyramidal structure on which Pete sat atop, with Twin as his chief lieutenant. At fifteen, Pipe was the youngest of the group, one tier lower. Under them were one or two other neighborhood gangsters, whose expertise ran to violence or making money from selling crack, the two primary methods of advancing in the organization. Anthony "Big Ant" Hardy acted as Pete's bodyguard, and Andre "Dula" Martin, a Sex Money Murder associate from Castle Hill, played a supporting role. There was a growing band of associates who hustled product or eyed promotion through "putting in work"—slang for acts of violence.

Pete drove around in his Volkswagen Golf supplying Pipe and others with the odd kilo of cocaine. Pipe took the kilo up to the seventh floor of 1715 Randall, where it was cooked up. Next he went to a bodega on Southern Boulevard and bought miniature blue Ziploc bags, known as 12 × 12s. Together a few members of the crew bagged it all up into nickels and passed it out to half a dozen hustlers who sold around the projects. Pipe worked a 60/40 split in his favor; the total from a kilo generally yielded $15,000, of which he took around $9,000.

Pipe sold exclusively in Soundview. Another young dealer linked with the crew sold in Stevenson Commons. Twin controlled one of the Castle Hill towers, at 535 Havemeyer Avenue, but was looking to dominate all of the projects there. The product also made its way up into Kingston, largely controlled by Bemo, Twin, and Pipe's brother Ro, now a member of the crew. A small setback occurred when Pete was arrested in Kingston, on April 15, at 81 Prospect Street, the hub of Sex Money Murder's activities, and charged with possession. His sentence was thirty days in the Ulster County jail. Once freed, he never returned to Kingston; instead, he delegated his operations in the city to Twin and decided to refocus his energies on New York City.

The kilos Pete sold to Pipe came through connections he made through his uncle George Wallace, but they came sporadically, sometimes only every two weeks and sometimes separated by as much as two months. Pipe sometimes had to go to Washington Heights to buy more on his own.

But in the summer of 1993, Sex Money Murder experienced a quantum leap in productivity with the appearance of Savon Codd, a trafficker with a long, thin, doleful face and a dead-eyed stare. Some called him "Big Head." He came from the Sack Wern Houses and had pioneered a pipeline into Pittsburgh that was netting him a small fortune. Earlier, he had allied with Baby Jay to make money in Springfield, but the two had fallen out. Codd had a growing reputation in Soundview as a rainmaker who could set you back up in the drug business when you were penniless on release from prison.

Codd, whose mother had been held at gunpoint in her house while

$40,000 of his money was stolen, needed protection, and a gunbuster like Pete. And Pete, for his part, needed more product. The two were made for each each other.

Pete began to accompany Codd to Pittsburgh on drug runs around May or June. He was paid $3,000 to $5,000 just to ride shotgun on deliveries of eight to ten kilos. Shortly thereafter, Pete brought Codd into Sex Money Murder as a ranking lieutenant.

Codd showed Pete how a multistate drug-trafficking organization worked. He bought a kilo in New York for $18,000 but sold it in Pittsburgh for $46,000, a quick profit of $28,000. Key to Codd's operation was his sophistication in moving large amounts of drugs in a fleet of cars. In Pittsburgh, he leased vehicles at Three Rivers Leasing, paying cash for them at inflated prices. They came with paperwork that Codd could show to the police, who might be curious why eighteen-year-olds were driving around in extravagant cars. None of the drug dealers' names were on the papers. Codd even suggested incorporating so that they could lease cars in the name of a corporate entity.

Codd's cunning was felt immediately on the block. He arranged for Pipe to get a driver's license through a corrupt connection in New Jersey. For $500, Codd had a man take the driving test using Pipe's name. Afterward Pipe went into the DMV with the paperwork and had his picture taken for the new license.

And when Pete pulled up on the block in an old two-door Cutlass Ciera, Pipe saw a modification to the car that illustrated Codd's sophistication. "Watch this," Pete said. He pressed buttons on the dashboard, and the glove compartment popped open to reveal a secret box containing a .38 revolver. "That's a stash box," he declared proudly. Others called the hiding places "traps." "Police ain't know nothin' about that."

Codd maintained an apartment on Jerome Avenue in the Bronx, a street known to the DEA as a place Dominican crews, master craftsmen of stash boxes, plied their trade.

The bond between Codd and Pete evolved. Secure now that he was under the aegis of Pistol Pete and Sex Money Murder, Codd flaunted gold jewelry and a Glock pistol. He brought in new members who were flashy and moneyed, driving expensive cars. NSX Mike was so called because he took Pete out for a ride in his new Honda NSX, crashed it, and returned the next day with a brand-new one.

Crucially, Codd made a key introduction that would fuel Sex Money Murder's ascent. John Castro, a Dominican who had links to Colombian drug cartels through friends in Washington Heights, gave Pete access to multiple kilos whenever he needed them. Tall, brawny, and debonair, Castro was dark enough to pass as both Hispanic and African American. He had been educated at an all-male Catholic school and served in the air force before working as a corrections officer in the Bronx House of Detention. Now he ran a clothing store on 145th Street, while also supplying drugs to Sex Money Murder and other crews across the city. He practiced Santeria, and as his business partnership with Pete strengthened, he lured Pete into the religion. Pete viewed Castro as a role model; women clung to him, and he made the drug trade look fashionable.

Castro sold Pete kilos, and Pete in turn suppplied Pipe with two to three kilos anytime he requested them, while also supplying out-of-town operations. The profits grew into the tens of thousands. Pete set himself up in an apartment in the upper-middle-class neighborhood of Riverdale in the Bronx, about nine miles northwest of Soundview. He now had a Rolodex of drug connections like no other Bronx gang leader.

✦ ✦ ✦

ONE EVENING Pipe was standing on the block with Pete when he made out a row of multicolored beads laced around Pete's neck, softly agleam in the dusky light thrown by a streetlamp. Pete explained that the beads had been blessed and that it was bad luck for anyone to touch them. Green symbolized the orisha Ogun, a warrior deity who granted victory to his devotees. Inspired by Pete's messianic status, young hustlers and Sex Money Murder wannabes began wearing Santeria beads.

As Santeria spread through the growing Hispanic communities of Harlem and the Bronx following its arrival in the city in the 1940s, police began to notice carcasses of headless goats and chickens at the foot of makeshift altars, dripping with wax candles, in places like Pelham Bay

Park. The religion was born among Yoruba slaves, largely from Nigeria, brought to work in the sugar plantations in Cuba; forbidden to practice their traditional religions, they concealed their faith amid the trappings of Roman Catholicism. For example, they prayed to St. Barbara, who represented Shango, the god of thunder and lightning, whose father was struck by lightning when he beheaded her.

One evening Pete took Pipe for a ride up to a Santeria botanica near Fort Apache. The small storefront offered few clues that it was a center for Santeria practitioners, but as Pipe followed Pete inside, the peppery aroma of angelica herbs settled on his skin and clothes. Pipe shivered as demonic-looking faces hovered in the half-light. Pete spoke with easy familiarity to Raoul, a white-haired man who stood behind the counter dressed in a Hawaiian shirt. "You ready?" he asked Pete. "It's all set up in the back."

He led Pete and Pipe through heavy velvet curtains to a back room, where Raoul's sixteen-year-old niece greeted them. An old Victorian bathtub, full of dollar bills, sat on steel legs in the middle of the room. Chickens clucked in a small cage against a back wall. Pipe thought about making a break for it. "Hell no!" he blurted to Pete. "This is some hoo-doo shit, man."

Pete was calm. "I think I'ma do it."

"You going to do what?"

"I'ma take the money bath."

"I don't know about that shit, Moe."

"What about your friend?" asked Raoul. "Is he going to do it, too?"

Pete didn't pause. "Yeah, that's my little brother. He's doing it. But I'm going first."

The man told the boys to strip down to their boxers. Pete undressed, handing Pipe his gun.

Pete stepped into the tub and reclined. Raoul lit candles and some incense and then launched into deep-throated incantations in Spanish. He wafted smoke over Pete's body. Next he broke an egg over him, and Pipe saw that the yolk was filled with blood. Raoul trailed the bloody liquid over Pete's chest.

Next Raoul gestured to his niece, who took a chicken out of a cage. The bird squawked and struggled before Raoul expertly sliced its neck. He dribbled the blood up and down Pete's body.

Throughout, Pete lay still, as if he were soaking in the bathtub before a Saturday night out. The man produced another egg, which he broke over Pete. This time the egg was bloodless. The raw yolk dribbled down the side of his face.

Five minutes later the ritual came to a close when Raoul told Pete to get to his feet. He declared that whatever Pete was trying to do, he would accomplish it. "You're going to get money," he said. "And all the things you want. But there are going to be consequences. Either of two things will happen: You're going to get killed, or you're going to jail for the rest of your life." Pete showed no emotion.

Pipe, his pulse hammering a tattoo, handed the guns to Pete and climbed into the bath, settling amid the blood-soaked bills. When Raoul wafted smoke over him, Pipe flinched. Pete, sprawled on a nearby chair, burst into giggles. "You supposed to be a gangster! And you all nervous!" Pete told him to relax. "What you scared of?"

Pipe declared with as much bluster as he could that he wasn't frightened. He screwed his eyes shut and thought of something else, anything, to take his mind off this. He thought of piles of money. The cold, viscous yolk of an egg rolled down his face. He started to shake.

Minutes later he heard the loose canvaslike slap of beating feathers, a muffled caw, and then silence, followed by what he knew was the warm blood of the chicken trickling over his eyelids.

Afterward, Raoul showed them to a small shower next door. Pete cleaned up first, but before he did so he peeled off a few hundreds from the $10,000 roll in his pocket. Pipe offered to help pay. "Don't worry about it," Pete said. "I'm gonna get it back ten times."

+ + +

AT TEN O'CLOCK on a Sunday night in the summer of 1993, Pete and the crew rolled over potholes and pulled up next to the fractured sidewalks outside 551 in a fleet of buffed new cars, music blaring as they readied to head into Manhattan. Pete drove Codd's Toyota Supra. B-Love sat at the wheel of a K5 Blazer. Sex Money Murder swooped across the Bronx in this shimmering convoy and entered Manhattan by the George Washington Bridge, then sped down the West Side Highway, on their way to a club in Chelsea.

The crew drove to the fabled Tunnel nightclub on Twelfth Avenue. On most nights the club was given over to a fin-de-siècle hedonism where androgynous club kids and transgender disco queens filled the dance floors; almost the whole crowd was white. The Tunnel's owner, Peter Gatien, saw Sunday as a dead, loss-leading night, but he also saw that rap was going mainstream, so he had given the night over to hip-hop, a night he called Mecca. Within months thousands of black kids descended on the club, backing up the blocks in every direction.

Barricades lined the sides of the big Chelsea warehouses; the Manhattan club scene had rigorous protocols on who was in and who was out. Pete had been courting Puff Daddy, who in 1993 founded the label Bad Boy Records. The promoter had put Pete and his crew on the VIP list.

They waited a few minutes before a gamine woman bounded down the steps of the club. She leaned over the rail and hugged Pete. She had been raised in Soundview and had a job as a "searcher," looking for weapons before clubgoers were granted entry. Pete handed her a gift bag. It contained five loaded handguns, which she took inside.

Sex Money Murder swept through, pausing to be lightly searched in a vestibule before following Pete into the packed heart of the club. The long, vaulted ceiling of the main room ran over railroad tracks sunken into the dance floor. Rap boomed around the brick walls of the former freight depot. Housing projects from all five boroughs were represented, and young men, some on Ecstasy, scanned the room for rival crews. Scantily clad young women, glistening with sweat and sexuality, ground and bumped to the beat.

Pete led his vanguard through the throng, past the bar, and up the stairs to unisex bathrooms near the VIP room. The girl from Soundview arrived with the Christmas bag Pete had given her and handed it over in a bathroom stall. "Don't start any trouble," she said. Pete distributed the weapons.

They moved back downstairs to the "picture section," where part-iers could have themselves photographed. There they sloughed off their leather jackets like boxers about to enter the ring, revealing coils of gold chains. The rap thumping out of the club's sound system offered a nar-rative that glorified them. Pipe, now fully grown, stood only five foot seven. Pete and the others were not that much taller.

Pipe slid off his jacket to reveal a diamond-encrusted globe suspended from a gold chain inscribed with the legend THE WORLD IS YOURS from *Scarface*. Pete had given it to Pipe after a trip to G&G's jewelry store on Southern Boulevard, a staple of ascendant Bronx gangsters. One day he was having diamonds installed in his Rolex when he decided to buy Twin the $15,000 chain. Twin, unlike Pete, disliked gaudy jewelry and refused the gift. Pete offered it to Pipe instead.

Pipe headed for the bar. It had become a preclub ritual for Pete to dictate how many $90 bottles of Cristal champagne each of them had to buy. Pipe was ordered to buy ten. Twin had to buy twenty because he was making more money. B-Love and the others had to get fifteen each. Earlier that night Pete had pulled out $5,000 and distributed the money to anyone who needed it. Pipe handed over a stack of bills, and the cham-pagne came back on busboy trays.

Amid the pop of champagne corks Pete poured himself a glass, but not a drop would pass his lips. He disdained alcohol. Many of the boys were still too young to drink and, in private, preferred the taste of soda. They shifted their weight from foot to foot, pouring champagne for a pool of stunning young women.

As Pipe remembers it, Pete had caught sight of Puff Daddy in the VIP section. He dispatched Pipe as emissary. Pushing upstairs, Pipe slipped through the velvet ropes and made to approach Puff before he was stopped by a giant bodyguard. This was Anthony "Wolf" Johnson, an old friend of Pete's father. Two years before, in 1991, he had been con-victed of the attempted murder of a New York cop, and had recently been released from prison upstate. "Easy," said Wolf. Puff Daddy ordered him to back off: "He's family." Pipe strode up to Puff, who was seated like an emperor among his entourage. "Yo, what up, Puff?" said Pipe. "Pete over there. He wants to see you." Puff Daddy stood up and followed. Puff's deference to Pete was affirmation that Sex Money Murder had arrived.

In the picture section, Puff strode over and gave Pete a hug and a slap on the back. The two men exchanged a few words. Then Pete added in mild admonishment, "Yo, and this is my family." Puff didn't skip a beat. He gave each of the crew a pound on the back, too, before he returned to the VIP room.

By 1:30 a.m., the partiers who worked regular jobs had left the club, and hardcore drug dealers and rappers, with some of the most gorgeous women Pipe had ever seen, took over. After a few hours Pipe returned to the bar for more champagne. The dance floor behind them heaved like a roiling sea. Pipe bumped up against a diminutive member of Sex Money Murder, weighed down with gold jewelry, who in turn pressed up against an imperious man in his midtwenties with doe eyes and a mustache. The man turned around angrily and made a few threats. Pipe clutched a half-empty champagne bottle. When he made another remark Pipe swung the bottle down on his head. He staggered. Pipe and the crew member scurried back to the others seated in the picture section.

About twenty minutes later the man, flanked by several giant bouncers, fanned out across the room asking questions. Someone, they said, had hit Nas, one of the biggest emerging hip-hop stars, over the head with a bottle. "Oh shit," Pipe said to Twin, "I ain't know who he was."

Minutes later Nas appeared, with the bouncers, clutching a bloodied towel to his head. He moved up to where Pipe was sitting, huddled with Sex Money Murder. He took in the glowering crew, braced for a fight, and gazed at Pipe with contempt. Pete leaned forward. Nas locked eyes with Pipe. And then, abruptly, Nas averted his gaze. The bouncers asked him something, and, still looking at Pipe, he shook his head. He later identified another man, who was immediately ejected. The scene, according to Pipe, demonstrated Sex Money Murder's growing power.

They closed out the club at 4:00 a.m. Outside, the block was thronged with Range Rovers and Mercedeses, trunk-fitted with bass speakers that rumbled and made the streets vibrate. Soon Sex Money Murder joined the honking gridlock of polished luxury and headed wearily home.

+ + +

IN 1993, New York City polarized as the number of homicides dropped in the wealthy enclaves of Manhattan but rose in poorer neighborhoods, including the Bronx public housing projects.

The city had seventy-five precincts at the time, and 43.6 percent of New York's killings took place in just twelve of them. As Sex Money Murder grew in power, Soundview and the Forty-Third Precinct became one of the deadliest parts of the city, with a high of sixty-nine murders.

Forcelli drove to work avoiding certain exits on the Major Deegan because of the army of squeegee men who hassled drivers and who could drag him into a confrontation before his shift had even started.

Early in the evening of June 3, 1993, Forcelli, who had been working undercover dressed in a sanitation worker's uniform, raced to 535 Havemeyer Avenue. A running gun battle between rival drug dealers had scattered spent 9mm and .380 casings across a pathway leading to the building's back entrance. At 7:09 p.m., a hooded man had emerged from the back entrance of 535, blazing at another man who returned fire as he fell. Seven-year-old Joseph Washington, playing nearby with Edwin Stuart, a friend of the same age, tumbled to the ground. With an outstretched arm, he beseeched Edwin for help. But seconds later Edwin screamed as bullets ripped into his back.

Edwin's thirty-three-year-old father heard gunshots and ran to the playground to find his son had been hit in the spine. When ambulances failed to arrive, a police officer rushed them to Jacobi Hospital.

Joseph lost so much blood from wounds to his esophagus and aorta that he died shortly after arrival. The intended victim of the shooting, a rival dealer, died on the operating table with four gunshot wounds.

Edwin Stuart was swept into emergency surgery. A bullet was removed from his spine. For years to come, he would suffer the loss of bowel control and endure nightmares from which he awoke screaming. Both boys were linked to police families.

Forcelli, still dressed in the sanitation uniform, slipped into the crowd of residents. Repeatedly, he heard the word "*veneno*," Spanish for poison.

Forcelli knew that a fearsome local drug supplier, Raphael "Poison" Agosto, was closely tied to the Mullins twins and Sex Money Murder.

With daylight dwindling, Forcelli drove to the parking lot behind 535 Havemeyer. Conspicuously parked among the older, broken-down cars was a luxury green Jaguar, Poison's car. Forcelli slashed the Jag's tires before reversing his car and parking it on the street.

He and other officers entered 535 and worked their way down from the top through every single one of the building's 157 apartments. Many residents were hostile, while others simply refused to answer the door. When they reached the bottom, the officers noted the numbers of apartments from which there was no answer. Forcelli checked out these apartments a second time, getting down on his hands and knees to look under their doors. In 3H he saw feet pacing back and forth and heard voices speaking in urgent, hushed tones. He suspected he had his man. Poison, it turned out, was locked inside with his mother and the twins.

The situation escalated into a barricade; the suspects refused to come out. A SWAT team and hostage negotiators worked through the night as Forcelli waited in the stairwell. Agosto's mother called her boss, a Bronx councilwoman, and asked her to contact the police, demanding that they stop harassing her innocent son. The councilwoman called the police brass and Bronx borough president Fernando Ferrer.

Eventually the three men gave themselves up. By 3:40 p.m. the following day they had been taken to the Forty-Third Precinct. Poison was charged with the murder of Abraham Smith, the man who had returned fire, and Joseph Washington, along with assault in the first degree on his playmate, Edwin Stuart. After the shooting, detectives canvassed two thousand homes in Castle Hill for witnesses, but few would volunteer information. A 911 call from the projects identified the shooter as Puerto Rican, but the caller would not identify herself. "It needs to stop. My mother is outside with my three little nieces," said the anonymous source. Finally a few women, devout churchgoers who initially refused to bear witness because of perceived threats against them, were forced to swear on the Bible to what they had seen. Finally they tendered the truth before agreeing to testify. Another, Nancy Rosa, was ordered to testify due to a material witness order, a tort that compels anyone with information to testify. Before the trial she and her entire family were relocated from the Castle Hill projects because her acting as a prosecution witness might cost them their lives. Agosto would get fifty years, and Forcelli was promoted to detective for his part in the case.

Out on patrol, the single "Cop Killer," from Body Count, led by the rapper Ice-T, or N.W.A.'s "Fuck tha Police," seeped out of the open windows of the projects and drifted from powerful stereos in cars like the Suzuki Samurai that Forcelli often saw in Edenwald. A couple of years earlier Forcelli had answered an urgent call in Eastchester Heights, where he found Hector Fontanez, a twenty-six-year-old police officer, dying as he was lifted up by other cops, his bulletproof vest torn to ribbons and dripping with blood. He had been shot in the back and stomach by a twenty-one-year-old with a .357 Magnum. Sometimes kids would shout out the lyrics of "Cop Killer" at Forcelli from across the street. If he ignored them, it got worse the next time he passed, so invariably he confronted them and let them know he was watching them.

AS THE SUMMER of 1993 unfolded, Pete's bond with Twin intensified. They were pushing cocaine out through their networks. Twin bought wholesale from Pete to distribute in Castle Hill and Kingston. They split the profits evenly. While Twin was making his own moves, Pete developed his Pittsburgh connection with Codd. By 1994, when the first Manhattan Starbucks opened on the Upper West Side, the drug business had already similarly shifted from a monolithic corporate model— too easily targeted by police—to a franchise model. Twin and Pete were both making money from various out-of-town arrangements, sometimes with each other and sometimes independently.

In their downtime, the two spent hours in strip clubs in Hunts Point and brought the strippers back to Soundview for orgies. One morning in mid-August they went to Harlem Week, a celebration of black culture. The sidewalks teemed with sizzling food, music pounded out of hastily erected stages, and souped-up cars prowled with aspiring gangsters at the wheel.

Twin sat down on some old crates to play dice with a local stickup kid, Keenyon "Kato" Jenkins, on the corner of West 126th Street and Seventh Avenue. Pete sat idly in his car, half watching the dice game but more interested in the women walking by.

At around 11:00 a.m. Twin and Kato got into a heated discussion about money owed on a dice roll. Kato pulled up his shirt to reveal a handgun in his waistband. Pete, who knew that Twin was unarmed, got out of the car, circling around behind Kato undetected. He flashed a grin at Twin and calmly delivered a point-blank shot to the back of Kato's head, killing him instantly. He and Twin got in the car and drove back to Soundview.

A few days later, outside 551, Pete explained the murder to Pipe. "Nigga tried to front on Twin," he said. "I had to pop the nigga's head off." He paused. "I took a body to protect my man." Because of Kato's carelessness it was easy to shoot him, Pete indicated, and therefore, Kato had invited his own destruction because he should have known better. "I caught that nigga slipping," said Pete.

For Pipe, there was no demonstration of greater love than killing another man to protect your friend. Pete, though, rather than keeping the murder secret, advertised it to burnish his reputation. Most people in the neighborhood assumed that he had already "caught a body," so Pete didn't mention that this was his first.

On the street, the murder of Kato signaled a small vassal state switching to a war footing. Pete grew paranoid and insisted that everyone carry a gun at all times in case there was retaliation from Harlem. He ditched his .38 revolver for a .45 semiautomatic. He started advising everyone to shoot to the head.

Only Pipe and those closest to Pete noticed a change in their old friend after the killing. Pete would still joke like a teenager about kids on the block with smelly feet or poor personal hygiene. He still filled the role of the dashing playboy. But Pipe could see that he was transformed. The murder had made him afraid, and in his fear he became preoccupied with strategy and violence. It now took little for him to lose his temper.

One day Pipe heard a commotion on the block—shouting and what sounded like a dog barking and growling. He ran toward the sound and saw Ro restraining a three-year-old fawn-colored pit bull that pawed at the ground, gnashing its teeth and lunging at Pete. Ro egged the dog on, laughing as Pete jumped back in horror. Ro rescued pit bulls that were abandoned by dog-fighting rings in Soundview Park. He kept three dogs in his apartment. Pete disliked the breed, swearing that they couldn't be trusted.

Ro continued to taunt Pete. "Ya, get him, boy!" The dog reared again. This time Pete lost his temper, warning that if Ro didn't stop he would shoot the dog. Ro carried on. A single pop split the air. When the dog had kept coming at him, Pete had shot it in the head. Ro crouched over the dead animal's form and, distraught, broke down in tears. When a neighborhood kid came up and started to laugh at the toughened gangster's vulnerability, Ro jumped up and stabbed him twice in the belly.

+ + +

AS NEWS of Pete's murder of Kato spread, other reports circulated that a gangster in the Monroe projects was snitching on him for the killing. On a hazy September evening, Pete, Twin, and Pipe pedaled BMX bikes around the projects to relax, hoodies laced up around their faces.

At around 11:00 p.m., opposite the Monroe projects, they saw the man who had supposedly snitched alighting from a double-parked blue Honda Acura. Music blared from the car's interior as he headed to a pay phone. The boys took cover behind a corner. "I'ma rock him right here," said Pete. Twin argued that he should be the one to do it, as Pete had shot Kato on his behalf. The two squabbled for several minutes.

They decided that Twin would sneak up on foot while Pete shadowed him on the bicycle. Pete got close enough to raise his gun to the man's head, but the gun jammed. The man took off, and Pete followed on the bike, firing a .45 one-handed as he rode.

Some armed drug dealers standing out front thought that the attack was against them. They had recently robbed some Colombians of their cocaine and were jittery, expecting retaliation. Their first shot blew Pete's baseball hat off, and the second flung him from the saddle of the bicycle and into the road. His bulletproof vest saved him. He clambered back on and rode into the darkness.

Pipe stole the suspected snitch's Acura and sped around the projects in search of him. Twin ran into the building, following Pete. A few minutes later Pipe, hunched behind the wheel, saw a figure cycling away, clearly injured. It was Pete fleeing for the safety of Soundview.

Pete turned, recognized the car, and assumed that he was being run down by his victim. He aimed the gun at the car. "Yo, it's me!" shouted Pipe out the window, ducking as he pulled alongside.

"I'm hit," Pete said over and over, his breathing labored. Pipe saw two jagged holes in the fabric of his hoodie.

They hobbled back to 551. Pete winced as he pulled off the bulletproof vest. Two bruises on his chest mushroomed into yellow badges. The old santero had told him that jail or death would come for him. Pete saw surviving the shooting as a sign of his invincibility.

✦ ✦ ✦

BY AUTUMN, Soundview had evolved into a fortress. The police rarely went in on foot patrol, leaving Sex Money Murder with absolute dominion. A few weeks after the shooting in the Monroe projects, Pete and Pipe were on the eastern side of the projects, near Cozy Corner. Both were armed, as was now customary. At 1:00 a.m., they were startled by an unmarked blue van pulling up alongside them. Inside were plainclothes detectives clearly visible through untinted glass. "Those motherfuckers," said Pete. He pulled out the TEC-9 and pointed it at the van. The cops ducked, giving Pete and Pipe time to sprint off into the night. Pipe was angry at Pete for putting them needlessly at risk. "I wasn't going to shoot them niggas, man," Pete reasoned. "I just wanted to scare 'em up."

Three days later, Whitey, a neighborhood kid who had became a loose affiliate, was sent across the road from 551 to the bodega to buy a cigar. He was stopped by undercover detectives, who rolled up on him in an unmarked police car and caught him with drugs. "Yo, fuck it," said Pete as they watched the police surround him. "We can't let them get away with that." Pete, Pipe, and a few others piled into the elevator, sprinted across the roof to the edge, pulling out their guns as they ran. "On the count of three," said Pete. They looked down like mountain partisans ambushing a convoy of soldiers in a ravine. Pipe inhaled and pointed his gun to the sky and fired. In the shower of bullets, Pipe saw that Pete was the only one actually shooting at the police. "What the fuck," shouted Pipe over the shooting. "You is crazy, a lunatic, man!"

Down below, the police scattered. Some dropped their guns; radios skidded across the sidewalk. The boys sprinted down the steps of 551 and up the stairwell at 541 to Stymie's apartment. (Stymie was the man who was nearly murdered with Fat Mike.) After scrubbing their hands with alcohol and orange juice, which they'd heard might remove the smell of gunpowder, they left their weapons and congregated outside 1710, B-Love's building.

Twenty police officers with guns drawn spread over the area. A few officers searched the roof, examining spent bullet casings. Others moved up on Pete, Pipe, and their friends, demanding IDs. They obliged, show-ing their fake licenses, and the police moved on.

✦   ✦   ✦

WHEN PETE turned nineteen, Codd bought him a brand-new jet black Mazda RX-7 worth around $50,000. Pete brought it to Pipe to show off the modifications: a stash box and a rear windscreen with a bank of high-intensity halogen lights that could momentarily blind pursuers—and, in homage to James Bond, a revolving license plate.

Though Pete had been warned that narcotics detectives had started slipping into Mecca to listen in on the deals there, he was intent on going into the city for a meeting with Puff Daddy. Pete was determined to press Puff to sign two Soundview rappers, Lord Tariq and Peter Gunz, to the Bad Boy label, and Puff had agreed to discuss it. According to Pipe, knowing better than to refuse a request from Pistol Pete, Puff was on the verge of agreeing, and unbeknownst to Puff, Pete left the meeting with a plan to launder money through the record business.

They drove north back to the Bronx at around 4:30 a.m. On the

Bruckner Expressway, another driver kept boxing them into their lane. Pete told Pipe to roll down the passenger window.

Pete pulled a 9mm from the stash box while guiding the car in behind. Pipe, petrified, tilted his seat back, gripping the sides and moving his head to one side. Pete tried to get a shot off as the gun traced erratic circles in front of Pipe's nose, but the driver in front continued to block them in as the two cars weaved all over the road. Pete slid open the sunroof. When the man pulled in front of him, Pete stuck his hand up through the sunroof and laid down a haphazard volley of shots at the back of the car, emptying a fifteen-round magazine. The bullets tore into the back of the vehicle before it fishtailed and caromed off a concrete wall.

Pete sped on without looking back. The blue lights of a patrol car flashed behind them in the distance. Codd had outfitted the car with another modification: a switch that killed the brake lights so the police couldn't judge when Pete was accelerating or decelerating. He slowed for a red light and was clipped by another car, lost control, ground to a halt, and then smashed the car into reverse before speeding off again, this time to a house in Queens.

✦ ✦ ✦

IN NOVEMBER, Twin suggested a football game between rival projects, a chance for them to set down their guns and compete as athletes. And so, in the fall of 1993, the Turkey Bowl was born. On the field, egos came to the fore. Pete was nimble and flashy, while Twin was more of a bruiser. Pipe ended up on Twin's team that first year, despite his affiliation with Soundview. Pipe, weighing only a little over a hundred pounds, was flattened by Pete repeatedly. But that was nothing compared to when Bear, well over two hundred pounds and six foot five, went airborne and crushed Pipe like a paper bag under the wheel of a truck. Bleeding and bruised, Pipe took it all in good cheer. When the game started to favor Castle Hill, he was switched back to the Soundview team. Stymie became the focus of everyone's tackles and was slammed to the ground repeatedly. No one could forget that he had testified in the triple homicide case involving Fat Mike. People started to call him "the Black Cat" because those associated with him either ended up dead or in prison.

When Soundview pulled ahead, Twin cursed his team. "You niggas suck dick, man. I'm doing all the work out here!" Soundview won, 28 to 21.

Afterward, they all drove to Red Lobster. Sixteen-year-old Pipe looked around the table at his friends' bruised and scraped faces, happier than he'd ever seen them. They vowed to make the game a tradition.

Six

JUSTICE

AFTER THE COWBOYS CASE, O'MALLEY RETURNED to his post at Bronx Homicide, but there was one unresolved piece of the case that continued to irk him. In countless proffers, he'd heard about the underworld hit man Justice Brown, a key member of the Crew, yet he was still evading O'Malley and on the run. O'Malley asked his lieutenant for permission to pursue Justice when he wasn't working on other cases. He went on NBC's *Prime Suspect* with Mike Hegedus, seeking information on his whereabouts. And at night he visited every Manhattan precinct, asking them to put up wanted posters of Justice near the cells. Eventually he got a break—a call came from the Thirty-Second Precinct. A defendant facing serious time on a gun charge, and hoping to cut a deal, told O'Malley that a man fitting Justice's description had appeared at his brother's house in Brooklyn.

A few days later in November 1993, O'Malley and Detective Hector Beauchamp, then his partner, parked outside 2132A Fulton Street, a nondescript three-story brick house. A man whose face was obscured by a tightly cinched hoodie and steel-rimmed glasses emerged early in the afternoon. If they jumped the wrong person, he'd raise the alarm and Justice would slip the net once again. "Fuck it," said O'Malley. "We gotta take him." Beauchamp raced up the street past the suspect, made a U-turn, and then crashed up on the sidewalk as if they were going to run him down. O'Malley jumped out, gun drawn. He bluffed that he was looking for Tyrone Green, a randomly chosen name, using it as a ruse to calm Justice into thinking he would be released at the precinct. They took him to the Eighty-Third. In the cell, he removed his hoodie, and O'Malley realized that he had collared the right man. Beneath a wiry beard, a smile played on Justice's lips. "You guys were good," he said. "But you know if I was strapping, one of us wouldn't be here today." During booking, he learned that he was to be taken to the Metropolitan Correctional Center to face federal charges. He turned to O'Malley. "I guess I'm going to meet Ms. Glazer, aren't I?"

Glazer had become the scourge of Bronx gangs, her reputation spreading across interconnected crews in the city. Two weeks after Justice's arrest she called O'Malley with the extraordinary news that Justice was willing to flip. At first they thought he'd be of little use, but ultimately he confessed to five murders. In some of the killings he had fired the same gun that Derrick Augustine had used to kill Steven Palmer, and he admitted to the murder of David Torres back on March 9, 1991, another cold case.

Glazer watched O'Malley develop a relationship with Justice. She saw how he was able to extract a narrative that revealed the complex dynamics of overlapping street crews—the estrangements, the retaliation cycles, and the politics of the street. It was difficult work, requiring a feel for street life and the ability to spot a lie in the same way a conductor could hear an off note from an orchestra. In March 1994, O'Malley fed a single sheet of paper into his typewriter at Bronx Homicide and listed a staggering thirty-one murders that had finally been solved with the closure of the Cowboys-Crew case along with Justice's proffers. Glazer and O'Malley were amazed.

As Glazer had listened to O'Malley and Justice work, she saw a whole new landscape of crime, one she recognized as more destructive and more insidious than the Mafia: the street crews driving New York's homicide rates. Glazer was dismayed at the resources being poured into the war against the Mafia when the real reason behind New York's murder rate was the street killings by neighborhood crews. Meanwhile, the feds focused on the glory of Mafia cases, something she derided as "boy food." The Eastern District of New York, whose jurisdiction encompassed Queens and Brooklyn, took on the Mafia on their home turf, but they did few street gang cases because their prosecutors were fed cases by an FBI largely obsessed with Italian organized crime. The Manhattan office of the FBI had also won abundant resources to tackle the five families. In 1991, Glazer noted, the Colombo crime family had been tearing itself apart; ten people were murdered over a one-year period, garnering lurid headlines and countless articles. During that same time in the Bronx, however, three times that number were killed in a three-block area in Hunts Point, the corner of Seneca and Bryant Avenues, controlled by three warring crack gangs who sold drugs from a hole-in-the-wall. Not one of those killings received significant media coverage.

The success she enjoyed with O'Malley had shown Glazer that they could reduce the bloodshed in New York if they could apply RICO to street crews. The Justice Department was reluctant to use RICO laws for what some staffers called "Bronx mutts." Was it a dangerous precedent to set? If they used RICO laws on street crews, could they be applied to stockbrokers, for example? Senior officials were skeptical that the drug crews were "enterprises" like the Mafia.

RICO had been deployed against the drug crews in Harlem in the 1980s, but Glazer's pivot would be to use the statutes to also go after murder and violence, rarely prosecuted in federal courts.

Meanwhile, O'Malley built his skills through trial and error. Two months into the proffer sessions with Justice, the hitman got word to Glazer and O'Malley that his conscience troubled him. "I lied," he admitted flatly. Earlier, he had told them about a Baltimore murder he had been involved in, claiming he had been the getaway driver.

"Chicky ordered the hit," he said, and admitted that he had been the actual shooter. "What did we tell you about telling the truth?" scolded Glazer. The office was divided as to whether to keep using him. The standard in a case like this when a source had lied was to tear up the cooperation agreement and have him face down a judge with all of his guilty pleas. Justice realized the seriousness of his position. Ultimately, Glazer made him plead to the murder and perjury. O'Malley used the experience to press cooperators more deeply when he suspected the slightest trace of untruthfulness in proffer sessions.

They continued to use Justice to solve more cases. Most importantly—and this O'Malley never expected—he began to talk about Chicky Rosario. Rosario had been captured in 1989 after a shootout with police on the Harlem River Drive. His driver had agreed to give testimony before a grand jury. Three months later the driver turned up dead, with five bullets in the back of his head. Another crew member flipped and told a story of how Rosario got hit by a stray bullet on 145th Street and declared to one of his lieutenants, "This is the Emperor—no one shoots the Emperor!" Rosario found the names of his assailants, and he and another man went and shot them dead at a roller rink in the Bronx. He was given forty years and sent to the Great Meadow Correctional Facility; before long he was controlling it from the inside. The Southern District had decided to prosecute him federally, largely because he was still too powerful, even inside prison. As the investigation got under way, O'Malley visited Chicky's wife in the Bronx. While there he was handed the telephone. On the other end was Chicky, calling from a cell phone in prison: "Get the fuck out of my house."

When the federal indictment was unsealed, O'Malley drove to Great Meadow with Detective Billy Ralat. Rosario, shuffling out in shackles, looked at the two officers and said, "You're O'Malley, homicide, and you're Ralat, narcotics." On the drive down, the two detectives chatted with the Emperor and tested his potential to flip now that he faced life in the federal system. On that suggestion Chicky's manner abruptly changed. "Go fuck yourself," he said. He later went to trial, and O'Malley's star cooperator, Justice, helped send him away for life.

✦ ✦ ✦

AFTER HER experience with O'Malley, Glazer saw building a relationship with the NYPD—not solely the FBI—as the key to her new initiative. After a ship called the *Golden Venture* ran aground in Rockaway Beach, Queens, with 286 illegal immigrants from China aboard, she began building a RICO case with the NYPD against the Chinese smugglers. The FBI's New York director was furious that the agency was circumvented, but Glazer saw the value of the NYPD's expertise.

As more potential cases came in, Glazer realized not only that the NYPD could provide crucial help but also that every precinct had detectives who knew the names of all the major players in the neighborhood and understood the hierarchies and their interrelationships; they simply didn't have the power to stop them. Glazer needed these detectives to feed her with RICO cases to begin chipping away at the murder rate. She'd be circumventing the FBI again, which could cause some damaged egos, but she felt it was worth the risk.

She set up a meeting at One Police Plaza with all the borough commanders. The detectives sat stone-faced as she tried to convince them to use her prosecutors and the RICO laws to attack the drug crews. The more hard-bitten cops saw federal prosecutors as spoiled Ivy League brats who just wanted to play tough for a few years before going into securities enforcement and then a sinecure in a Wall Street firm. The feds stole their cases, took all the glory for themselves, and refused to give them information in return. And most cops knew that circumventing the Bronx DA could get them fired. Glazer later called the meeting a disaster.

Still, she pressed on with her agenda. Back in October 1993, a few weeks before she and O'Malley had arrested Justice, the newspapers announced the indictment of a Mott Haven gang called C & C. Gang bosses George Calderon and Angel Padilla had control of the area, setting up headquarters at 550 East 139th Street, a five-story tenement at a busy intersection. They turned the basement into a dungeon, where they raped a girl on a workbench before murdering her, and cut the ears off a drug dealer with a hacksaw before shooting him in the head and leaving him at the Harlem River Rail Yards. They rented out squares of sidewalk to neighborhood hustlers, at $800 per week to those selling crack. Heroin dealers were charged $500 per week—on the condition that they sell Calderon and Padilla's brand.

NYPD detective Bobby Addolorato helped build the case on the suspicion that at least eighty murders could be attributed to C & C. After Padilla was arrested in September 1992, the homicide rate in Mott Haven, one of the poorest areas in the nation, dropped to zero that

month, according to statistics from Addolorato and Glazer. Even better, Addolorato had managed to flip a cousin of one of the main crew
members, who had given up the whole enterprise. But ultimately, as in
the Cowboys case, the Bronx DA told Addolorato that they could not
prosecute because they could not use the uncorroborated testimony of a
single witness. The Bronx couldn't protect a witness while he or she gave
evidence, either; it would require armed guards at Bronx hotels for up to
a year. It looked like the gang would escape prosecution.

Glazer heard that the Bronx DA had turned down the case, and she
felt it was perfectly suited to her agenda. She called Addolorato and
offered to take it federal using RICO. A federal racketeering indictment
charged seventeen members of C & C, many of whom flipped, some giving up as many as eight homicides. Within a month the Willis Avenue
Lynch Mob filled the vacuum left by C & C, so Addolorato and Glazer
indicted them federally, too. Afterward, no murders took place during
the months of September and November 1994.

The success of the RICO laws with the C & C crew drew national
attention and a front-page story in the *New York Times*. The detectives
in the Fortieth Precinct were delighted. "The FBI was involved with the
mob, but no one wanted to do anything with drug gangs because they
were centered in poor communities," Lieutenant Michael Bramble told
the *Times*. "You're not talking about Damon Runyon characters dressed
in $1,000 suits and driving limousines. You're talking about homegrown
thugs preying on their own neighbors."

It was a triumph for Glazer, and reinforced her conviction that she
would need someone working alongside the feds who could navigate the
insular world of the NYPD. She needed someone who could flip cooperators and retain the trust of notoriously suspicious and cliquish detectives in the Bronx precincts. Glazer needed John O'Malley. He could
move easily in the precincts; detectives might come to him with their
cases because they trusted him, and she knew that she could trust him,
too. She called him and made the offer.

O'Malley was hesitant. He loved the NYPD and didn't see himself
leaving after twenty years with the department. He had hoped to make

it to thirty-five years on the job, retire, and open a hot dog stand in his hometown to be called Diggity Dog. Glazer said he'd work nine to five and get a federal car and an increase in salary. O'Malley said he'd think about it. The last thing on O'Malley's mind was joining the feds.

On summer Saturdays O'Malley and his two young sons swam at the town pool and barbecued, but at 2:30 p.m. sharp, O'Malley kissed them good-bye to head to work, usually to murder scenes and the frantic pace of Bronx Homicide. He was beginning to miss all their Little League games. If he took Glazer's offer, he'd get weekends off to spend with his family, but at the same time he'd be the one guy in the feds working these cases. The sober world of federal law enforcement in the Southern District would be quite different from Bronx Homicide. Glazer wanted him to take on the gangs in the Bronx and stop the killing.

Seven

THE MURDER GAME

SEX MONEY MURDER'S RISE CAME AT THE COST of Pete's increasing volatility. He took any challenge personally. Pipe, as loyal as ever to his adoptive family, had the words No Fear tattooed on his right bicep above a Grim Reaper holding back a rearing pit bull on a leash.

Sometime on an early spring evening in 1994, the crew headed to the Skate Key, a roller disco on Allerton Avenue with color-flecked carpets, mirror balls, and a history of fights. The venue was thronged with kids skating to Donna Summer and Chic's "Le Freak." Pete caught sight of a lofty character of 6 feet 5 he had played basketball with at Stevenson High. Karlton Hines, twenty-three years old, stood draped in a fur coat surrounded by fifteen members of his gang and a group of adoring girls. Pete went over to him, Pipe and the others following. "Remember me?" he asked Karlton. "We used to play basketball together?"

Hines frowned down at him. "Who the fuck are you?"

They exchanged words, Pete punched Karlton in the mouth, and others jumped in. Pipe found himself jostling with one of Karlton's crew. Then Twin and Bear joined the melee and the bouncers descended, ejecting the four members of Sex Money Murder. Pete and the others went to their cars and pulled guns from the stash boxes, but stowed them when police cars showed up. A beef had just ignited between two of the biggest drug-dealing crews in the Bronx.

+ + +

HINES WAS a basketball star who ruled the hardscrabble courts in the South Bronx. His cracked front tooth, from a tumble taken on a court in the projects, was unmistakable. For his signature dunk, he'd rocket from the floor, dwarfing the basket before he slammed the ball through the hoop. It earned him a sobriquet that became legend across the Bronx: Dunkin' Hines.

Ever since he was in the eighth grade, newspapers had written stories about the boy in a man's body from the tough Melrose Houses, said to be NBA material. Coaches from thirty-five colleges around the nation risked a foray into the Bronx projects to cultivate Karlton. Often he begged his mother to tell them that he wasn't home. Karlton dreamed of playing for Syracuse, so when he was offered a year at the Maine Central Institute (MCI) to get his grades up so he'd be eligible for a Syracuse scholarship, he took it. But Karlton loathed the solitude of Maine, a world away from the vibrant street life of the Bronx. He wrote his mother a letter and drew a frowning face. "NOT MAD, NOT HAPPY," he scrawled in the margin.

He fell in with Tim Lavin, raised in rural Maine, the son of a wealthy industrial titan. Tim was fascinated with the pounding urgency of the inner city, black life, and emergent rap—all personified by the raffish and towering figure of Karlton.

Tim's dad took his son and his new friend to a lobster lunch and then back to the family home. Karlton's jaw dropped in amazement at the swimming pool, the Jaguar, the collection of hunting rifles. Tim sensed that Karlton drew a parallel between his dad's entrepreneurial trappings and those of a Bronx drug dealer.

A few weeks later Karlton schooled Tim in how the gangsta creed worked when they were walking to the store together and some white kids harassed them. One of them, an MCI kitchen worker, shouted "nigger" at Karlton. Immediately Tim suggested that they go over and "deal with it," but Karlton demurred, pointing out that he and Tim had no idea if the kids had knives. Instead, he memorized the MCI employee's face and stormed back to the dorm in a rage. The next day at lunch Karlton strolled over to the kitchen worker and said, "Remember me?" Karlton punched him so hard that he lifted him off his feet and knocked him out. The entire school rose in the commotion as Tim rushed between them and kitchen staff helped the employee up. But instead of going back to the dorms, as Tim assumed, Karlton entered the kitchen from the loading dock and once more moved up on the injured man, who was holding an ice pack to his face while four other workers held him up. Karlton smashed him in the face again. "Don't you ever," he sneered, "call me a nigger again."

When Tim was dumped by his girlfriend and Karlton came upon him sobbing to the strains of U2's "Where the Streets Have No Name," Tim hurriedly turned off the song in embarrassment, not wanting to look weak in front of his friend. Karlton sat beside him, told him to turn it on again, and offered comfort through Tim's tears.

When Tim stayed with Karlton in the Bronx, he found a clamorous and intoxicating reality—the opposite of rural Maine. Karlton acted as Tim's protector, a giant sentinel in a raw and dangerous world. They hung out on the streets all night, drinking malt liquor and throwing the bottles in the air, watching them explode into shards in the middle of Courtlandt Avenue before falling asleep on car hoods. Once they stole a BMW 735i from a parking garage, and Tim found himself offering to drive it up to Maine, where it could be stashed, because no one would suspect a white boy.

Tim grew close to Karlton's mom, Miss Faye, who called him her "white son." Somehow she managed to care for her five sons on the meager income of a cafeteria worker at St. Luke's Hospital, sleeping on the sofa in the family's Melrose apartment while the young men took the bedrooms.

Back in Maine, Karlton's basketball coach sensed that he was uneasy; the emotional and psychological distance between the two worlds was too great. One night, in defiance of dorm rules, Karlton spent hours on the telephone home to the Bronx after lights-out. He was disciplined, and the housemaster told him to leave if he could not abide by the regulations. He took his cue and raced back to New York in his Jeep, never to return. He was expelled shortly thereafter. Tim and his family wanted him to come back; Mr. Lavin said he'd put in a good word for him and even offered to pay his tuition. And they said Aisha, the mother of Karlton's daughter, could live in their mansion in Bangor to be near Karlton while he finished school.

Karlton thanked them but rejected their offer. Back in New York, he took to playing basketball in Rucker Park, in Harlem, where the courts were concealed in a small arbor of trees overshadowed by the Polo Grounds projects and bounded by Frederick Douglass Boulevard and the Harlem River Drive.

In the late 1980s, neighborhoods all over the five boroughs fielded basketball teams comprised of local talent that were often either coached or economically supported by drug dealers and rappers. They paid local hotshots $5,000 or so a game but bet tens of thousands, often more, with rival dealers on the outcome of prearranged match-ups. Away from Maine, Karlton was king once more amid these competing teams.

Through the Rucker games Karlton became familiar with every major drug dealer in the city. As his connections developed, he asked them for cocaine, which he sold sitting on a crate from 7:00 a.m. until 1:00 p.m. He got a new name, C-Town, to go with his new drug-dealing status. He drafted other kids in the neighborhood to his crew. A friend named Tony became Trigger Tone.

When Tim visited his old friend in the summer of 1989, he found him deep in the drug game, working with his two brothers. One morning at around nine, pandemonium broke out after Karlton killed a former boxer, Tweety, with a broken bottle. The killing grew out of an argument over a drug debt. Karlton ordered his brothers to hustle Tim out of town, stuffing a fistful of money into his friend's hand, telling him he feared Tweety's allies might go after the white kid always by his side. He went on the run for eleven days, holing up at the Concourse Plaza Hotel before turning himself in. A grand jury heard testimony and refused to indict, ruling that Karlton had killed in self-defense.

With his first "body" bestowing a more powerful reputation, Karlton upped his commitment to the drug game. He got a Range Rover and put it in his mother's name, which she discovered when a court summons arrived for unpaid parking tickets. Frustrated at Karlton's deceit, and dismayed at his dealing, she found a shoe box of money in his closet and started to march to the police station with it. Karlton chased her through the projects. "Ma, you'll get everyone killed if you hand that in," he said, intercepting her. "It's not my money." She lectured him sternly but returned it.

In 1991, Tim, now stationed with the army in Iraq fighting in Operation Desert Storm, began receiving letters from Karlton. While Tim wore a bulletproof vest and toted an M16 in the desert, Karlton donned a bulletproof vest and carried a weapon for his drug business in the highrises of the Bronx. Karlton said he sat on the block smoking weed and hustling while listening to the Notorious B.I.G.; his friend, reading his letters in army camp, fretted that Karlton was getting fat and out of shape, basketball a long-distant memory.

When Tim got out of the military he went to see Karlton in New York and found that his old friend surrounded himself with an armed crew in bulletproof vests all the time. Karlton kept Tim away from the drug business in an attempt to build a space for their friendship, but the difference between them was stark. Tim was a reminder of his old life and promise, and what he might have been.

By 1993, Karlton controlled all corners of the Melrose projects, which netted him $40,000 a day from both heroin and crack. As his connections in the drug world explanded, he befriended one of Sex Money Murder's major suppliers, John Castro. The Dominican trafficker took a liking to the enterprising young basketball-star-turned-drug-dealer and planned to one day bring him into the rapidly expanding Sex Money Murder crew.

Deep down Karlton missed basketball. When he returned to play a game for the Gauchos, a South Bronx team, friends from the neighborhood filled the gym as Karlton electrified them once more. He mulled a return to basketball, but he was a gangster now and needed to project an image of menace to keep himself safe. He was stuck until a coach said he'd be paid $1 million a year by the West Stallions, who were holding tryouts April 12, 1994. He began to get back in shape for his comeback and a chance to leave the drug game behind.

And then he ran into Sex Money Murder at the roller rink.

✦ ✦ ✦

PETE WAS INTENT on killing Hines. The man had disrespected him and had to die. He felt that killing a high-profile dealer would boost his fame. Pipe didn't think the murder was worth the trouble. Everyone knew that Dunkin' Hines was a star basketball player, but he'd never, in Pipe's eyes, made a reputation as a serious gangster. Maybe Pete wanted to take over the Melrose projects? But to him the whole thing seemed somewhat arbitrary and futile. Mixed messages came through from Melrose. On one hand, Pipe heard that Karlton wasn't afraid and would do what was necessary to defend himself. Another source said he wanted it known that he apologized, that he hadn't realized he was talking to Pistol Pete.

Pete dispatched Pipe to scout Melrose. He discovered, through cousins who lived in the projects, that Hines and his crew hung out in a barbershop between East 155th and East 156th Streets. Pete drove there and spotted Karlton, but the basketball star evaded him. A few weeks later Pete was on a date at the Bay Plaza multiplex when he saw Hines, also on a date. Pete told Pipe that he had pursued Hines through the complex with an Uzi, but that once more Hines had eluded him.

Hours afterward, Hines appeared at his mother's apartment deeply spooked. He tore through closets while she looked on, demanding to know what he needed so urgently. Finally, he produced a bulletproof vest from the back of a bedroom closet. His mother begged him to remove himself from whatever he was involved in; she began praying for her son at church. At one point Karlton broke down and sobbed to his brother: "When is this shit gonna be over with?"

Around the same time, he called his old friend Tim, now living in Texas and running his own web design company. He told Tim about the beef with Pistol Pete and Sex Money Murder and said he needed to get out of town immediately. "Karlton, you tell me what you want me to do and I'm there," said Tim. "You want me to drive up there and get you, I'll do it. If you want me to fly out, I'll pick you up. You name it." Tim said that they could work out together, get Karlton back in shape, just like the old days. The call seemed to give new life to their friendship. Karlton said he'd think about it. "The drug game ain't fun anymore," he said, shortly before hanging up.

A few weeks later, at around 1:30 p.m. on April 4, 1994, Mrs. Hines straightened her hair in the mirror and applied lipstick before heading to work. She caught sight of Karlton outside their building, dressed in unlaced Timberland boots, a silver-and-black belt, and a T-shirt with a giant marijuana leaf that bore the legend DR. DRE: THE CHRONIC. He wore a diamond-encrusted Rolex. She called down to him. "Hey, you can't come up here to say hi to your favorite girl?" He was busy, so she got her boyfriend to drive her to work.

Karlton had other things on his mind. The crew was throwing a block party for two members, Trigger Tone and Samuel "BO" Barnes. Karlton and three of the crew—Tone, Carlos, and Rick—drove to a car detailing shop at 2811 Boston Road, where Karlton had dropped off his Lexus to have chrome rims installed. The garage sat a mile or two east of the Bronx Zoo on a long, monotonous arterial road leading northeast to New Rochelle.

When they heard that the car wasn't ready, Rick, a slightly built man with a flattop fade, urged them to leave. Waiting around in the open could invite scrutiny, and as the dispute with Sex Money Murder escalated, they weren't sure who might come after them next. Just as they were about to leave, though, a salesman suddenly went into a sales pitch for a car alarm. Karlton went back in to have a look.

PETE WAS slap boxing with Pipe on the block in front of the crew, his hands quickly overwhelming Pipe before the younger boy retaliated with one or two slaps of his own. "Skippy got you, Moe!" someone laughed, as Pete absorbed the stinging slaps. At that Pete grappled Pipe into a crushing headlock that had him huffing, his face red with exertion, as six or seven others whooped at the horseplay. Suddenly Pete's beeper went off with a message from Codd. Pete went to a phone and called back; Codd told him that he had received a call from an associate who worked at a garage on Boston Road. "Tell Smiley that his man is here" was the message Codd's contact passed on to Pete, meaning Hines was at the garage. "Stall him," said Codd to the man in the garage. "Keep him there as long as you can." In response the man had come up with the car alarm pitch. Minutes later Codd pulled up outside 551 in his Toyota Land Cruiser. Pete's mood abruptly changed from juvenile to mortally serious as he climbed into the passenger seat and slipped into a black-and-yellow hoodie that bore the name Grambling State, and tugged on a Pittsburgh Steelers baseball hat. Then he pulled on some some black leather gloves.

✛   ✛   ✛

TONE AND CARLOS showed their frustration as Karlton went back in with the salesman. Rick moved off to look at a BMW he liked, while Carlos accompanied Karlton. Suddenly, Carlos found himself facing a gunman who appeared out of thin air with a pistol pointed at the back of Karlton's head. "Karlton, watch your back!" Carlos shouted as he tried to push his friend out of the line of fire.

A series of shots from a 9mm handgun rang out. Karlton tumbled to the ground. Then the killer turned the gun on Carlos. He hit him in the leg, but the next two rounds missed as he made his escape. The gunman returned his attention briefly to Hines, pumping more bullets into him, before vanishing like an apparition. Tone raced over and struggled vainly to lift Hines's two-hundred-pound body into their car. "Let's snatch this nigga up and get him to the hospital!" he screamed. But then he saw that Karlton's left eye was half closed, his right fully open, gazing upward at a world he no longer belonged to. Karlton was gone. Tone burst into sobs. Rick stood there slack-jawed. Tone, realizing it was useless, broke down in tears. Police sirens wailed in the distance. They took off in the car, leaving Karlton's body faceup, head nearest the road, runnels of blood flowing the few feet to the gutter.

✛ ✛ ✛

PETE RETURNED to the block about twenty minutes later. He smirked when he encountered Pipe. "I took care of that situation," he said. "Your man C-Town ain't frontin' no more." He paused. "You're going to hear about it." It took less than an hour for the first calls to start coming through. Pipe's cousins phoned. "Your man Pete killed Karlton Hines!" they shouted. "Reporters and TV crews are all over the block."

To celebrate, Pete took Pipe and a few others to Red Lobster at Bay Plaza. He gave a detailed account of sneaking up on Hines "like a ninja." He claimed that he shot Hines in the face five times. Another kid ran; Pete tried to kill him, too, he said, but ended up shooting the kid in the leg. Pete bragged that crews in every neighborhood in the five boroughs would hear about the power of Pistol Pete and Sex Money Murder.

Pipe felt uneasy at being tugged further into the Sex Money Murder centrifuge. In his mind, when he'd started in the drug game, he'd adopted certain rules of engagement. Violence was a tool to control territory, to modify the behavior of his crew and his opponents, but he had told himself that he had limits, unlike some of the others. He would never kill for the sake of it or to move up in Sex Money Murder.

✛ ✛ ✛

MISS FAYE was at work when her aunt called to say she needed to return home immediately. As she neared her apartment building, she saw neighbors clustered outside; some were crying. Her son Keith spotted her in the cab and led her upstairs before anyone could tell her. "They killed Karlton," he told her behind the closed door of their apartment.

Miss Faye locked herself in the bathroom, unable to control her stomach. A few hours later she went to identify Karlton at Jacobi Hospital. As they drove, she told Keith that she was fighting an image in her mind that Karlton had been decapitated. When they reached the morgue she screwed her eyes shut and was led back. "It's okay," Keith said. "It's not what you think."

Karlton lay in repose, his face a mask of death but otherwise intact.

Bullets had torn up his giant hands, the ones once used to power his dunks but in his final moments to shield his face. He'd been hit in the torso, and his spine had been severed.

About a week later, not having heard back from Karlton about coming to Texas, Tim called Miss Faye. "Haven't you heard?" said one of his brothers. "Karlton's gone." Tim's knees buckled. He felt as if a weight had been placed on his chest.

The name of Karlton's killer became an open secret on the streets of the Bronx. Miss Faye nursed thoughts of vengeance against Pete Rollock's mother. She had grown up with Pete's father and knew his grandmother, who lived in the Melrose projects.

Even so, the live-or-die code prevailed. And Miss Faye knew how that went. Instead, she turned up at the police station every month, asking how the investigation into her son's murder was progressing. The police treated her with disdain; they knew that Karlton was a notorious drug dealer. Once when she asked if they were any nearer to arresting her son's killers, one of the detectives handling the case simply said, "I don't have to tell you shit." On another visit, a policewoman took Miss Faye to a side room. "Mrs. Hines, I want to ask you something," she said. "Who was his connect?" Miss Faye walked home, alone and bewildered, trapped between two cultures, neither of which could help her.

IN THE DAYS following the killing, local New York networks made the most of the tragic narrative: the quasi-famous young kid from the projects, NBA material, whose life was cut short by a bullet. "Another Sad Ending," ran the headline in *Newsday*. Pete and SMM devoured the coverage, until they came to a feature-length piece by Stephen A. Smith in the *Daily News* on Sunday, April 24, headlined "Street Struck." Carlos Mestre had given the reporter a detailed account in which he stated that he had been "face to face with the shooter." He gave a full description, explaining that the shooter wore a yellow-and-black Grambling hoodie and a Steelers cap. In the language of the street, he was "dry-snitching."

Pete looked at Pipe. "That motherfuckin' snitch gotta go."

✛ ✛ ✛

IF 1993 had been about money for Pete, 1994 was about murder. Killing had become essential to his identity. He even began taking credit for murders he hadn't committed.

After John Castro had been ripped off in a cocaine deal by a man named Domingo "Totito" Osiro, Pete shot him near the Bronx River projects, but he escaped. Totito was eventually killed in Manhattan later that summer by someone entirely unrelated to SMM. Pete took full credit for the murder. John Castro gave him $5,000 for the job.

And then Pipe was standing on the block one day in June when Pete pulled up. "This nigga tried to rob my uncle," he shouted from the driver's seat of a run-down Lincoln. "I got a body in the trunk, Moe." Pete drove the car up onto the sidewalk and popped the trunk. Lying in the back, wrapped in black garbage bags, was a six-foot corpse. Pipe would learn later that it was the body of Anthony Dunkley, a suave and high-flying drug dealer who mingled with celebrities. "I'm trying to think where to dump it," said Pete. "Maybe the landfill?"

✛ ✛ ✛

A WEEK earlier, things had been going well for Mike Dunkley, Anthony's younger brother. He rode the bus back home to Brooklyn after successfully selling his car in New Jersey. The news that day was dominated by former football star O. J. Simpson, who had allegedly killed his wife and was now leading police on a chase down a Los Angeles highway in a white Bronco. Mike, eager to get home to catch up on the story, answered his cell phone. It was his mother, flustered that Anthony's Colombian girlfriend, Maria, had come to the house in a panic looking for him. She had some wild story about men from a drug cartel who were threatening to kill her daughter back in Colombia. Mike, who knew that his brother was a drug dealer, said that as soon as he got home he would look for him.

He idolized his big brother, seven years his senior. The family had moved to Brooklyn in 1973 to join the swelling Jamaican community in Bedford-Stuyvesant. Their middle-class parents made the best of the tough neighborhood, and Anthony protected his little brother fiercely.

Anthony had become a Rasta, but his father had ordered that he either leave home or join the marines. After a three-year commitment he returned home a different man. He led a double life, driving a 1973 Oldsmobile Cutlass Supreme and working at a computer company by day. At night he stepped into his Mercedes and headed out to spin records at a couple of Manhattan nightclubs like Danceteria, where Madonna gave some of her first public shows, while dealing cocaine to an expanding pool of celebrities.

By 1988, Anthony had moved to Florida, where clubs based on the New York scene were being replicated in South Beach. Mike flew down. This time Tony met him in a red Ferrari, his shirt open to his stomach. He had linked up with the music producer David Hyatt, then mentoring R. Kelly. In the club one night Mike danced with a young Hispanic woman from the Bronx. By the second song he realized that he was dancing with Saundra Santiago, Detective Gina Calabrese on *Miami Vice*.

Mike suspected that Anthony was too deep into serious drug trafficking. He wasn't just giving celebrities a quick bump anymore. He was now a middleman between Colombian drug cartels and ultraviolent crews in New York. Anthony hung out with Haitian Jack from their Bedford-Stuyvesant neighborhood, who ran a crew that held up drug dealers. Jack had befriended rapper Biggie Smalls and Tupac. Jack offered Tupac protection and marijuana, while Tupac brought Jack to clubs like Nell's, where he met Dunkley. Dunkley and Jack opened a barbershop in Queens called Celebrity Status.

Anthony and Mike bounced back and forth between New York and Miami. Finally, sometime in mid-1994, Mike got tired of being broke and living in his brother's shadow, and declared he wanted to move back to New York to find a career. Anthony scoffed, "You just want to make small money?" He had Mike do one last favor and drive a large consignment of cocaine up to New York; it was rejected as a bad batch, and he had to drive it all the way back to Miami again. The brothers had a big fight about the drug business. Anthony admitted to feeling pressure from the cartels and the Bronx crews, and declared that he had one last big thirty-kilo consignment and then he was done. The deal was brokered by one of his old friends, George Wallace, who said he knew a crew in the Bronx who had the money to pay for such a large consignment. He didn't use their name, but it was Sex Money Murder. After this, Anthony told Mike, he was finished. Would Mike take it up for him? Mike refused any more drug trips and stormed back to New York without the cocaine.

But now, a few weeks later, Mike got off the bus from selling his car in New Jersey and set out to find his brother. He called Haitian Jack, who said that Anthony was in Europe. When he called George Wallace, he said that he had last seen him in New York on Thursday with a young woman, and that he had given him $50,000.

Mike drove around the city for days, hitting every spot he knew. He and his family weren't the only people looking for Anthony. His parents began to get menacing calls and then death threats from men in a Colombian cartel. As they saw it, Anthony had disappeared with thirty kilos of their high-grade cocaine.

Mike went to the police station and filed a missing persons report. The cops sent the report to a connection who transmitted it to the Colombian cartel as proof that Anthony had disappeared. The calls to his parents stopped. But then the trail went cold.

PETE SUGGESTED that Twin might know where to dump Dunkley's body, so he and Pipe drove over to Castle Hill. Pete told Pipe that he, Codd, and George Wallace had killed Dunkley over a disputed thirty kilos of cocaine that Dunkley had brought in from Colombia. A few days before the deal was to be made, at Wallace's house in Queens, Pete's uncle had spotted Haitian Jack driving past. Aware of his reputation for robbing dealers, Wallace began to suspect that Dunkley might be setting them up.

When Dunkley arrived at Wallace's house and sat down at the kitchen table, Pete came up from behind and shot him in the head.

Wallace was furious; they hadn't planned to kill him, and certainly not in his own home. Blood drenched the hardwood kitchen floor and leaked down to the floor below. Furthermore, Pete had brought along Codd, a witness to the murder. Wallace later urged Pete to kill Codd, too. Pete, who now had thirty kilos of free cocaine, didn't listen. He would come to regret it.

✛ ✛ ✛

THE BOYS rode down in the elevator from Twin's apartment in Castle Hill. "I'm going to let you know ahead of time," said Pipe matter-of-factly to Twin, "that we have a body in the trunk." Outside in the hot sun, Pete threw open the back of the car once more. "Yo, what the fuck," said Twin, recoiling. "You riding around here with that?" He screwed up his face in disgust. "You ain't dump it yet?" Pete said he was still trying to work out an appropriate spot. Maybe Atlantic City? Twin suggested that they search the body for money. Pete pulled out about $2,000 in bloodstained bills. He gave a few hundred to Twin and some to Pipe and pocketed the rest. Pete and Twin decided to head to Atlantic City, leaving Pipe behind.

The following day, Pete paged Pipe. He and Twin had returned from Atlantic City in the early hours and dumped the body in Soundview Park. Pete wanted Pipe to go back there. He had forgotten to remove Dunkley's pager, which would show Pete's number as the last one Dunkley had called. The body, Pete said, had been dumped behind the basketball court. "You'll smell it," he said. "Call me when you got it."

In the summer afternoon haze, Pipe reluctantly pushed through dense clumps of mugwort. A thick cloud of buzzing flies hovered near a clump of garlic mustard. Pipe burst through and almost gagged when he saw the necrotic body, the smell of decomposition hanging in the air. Pete had made a halfhearted attempt to cover the corpse with weeds.

Dunkley's white T-shirt and blue jeans were caked in blood. His eyes, dulled by death, were wide open. Pipe knelt beside the body and put his hands in the pockets. The jeans were stiff. Pipe winced. He couldn't find anything. Just then his phone rang, making him jump.

"My bad," Pete said into the phone. "I have the beeper here. Sorry. I love you, Moe."

Pipe climbed to his feet angrily and dumped the weeds back on the body.

+ + +

SOMETIME LATER, police found Dunkley's badly decomposed body. Detectives had no inkling who he was or how he had died. At Bronx Homicide, he was catalogued as John Doe.

Weeks later, though, Dunkley's body was identified through finger-prints. Mike was devastated when he heard that Anthony's body had been recovered in a remote Bronx park. Wallace put up some money for the funeral and offered his condolences to the family on the death of his old friend. He offered no clue that he had been involved in the murder.

+ + +

BY JUNE 1994 a procession of tinted minivans from Karlton Hines's crew periodically cruised around the Soundview horseshoe, windows down, the occupants ready to shoot. Samuel "BO" Barnes, one of Karl-ton Hines's major drug connections, was rumored to be hunting for revenge. Hines's murder had disrupted his money flow.

Pete was now after two of Hines's men: Barnes and Carlos Mestre, the man who had given a description of Rollock to the *Daily News*.

Meanwhile, Sex Money Murder continued to flourish. And they now bankrolled a neighborhood basketball team. Pipe had some red-and-black uniforms made up that bore the gang name on their jerseys. One of their star prospects, Jasmine "Total Package" Mansell, got a schol-arship to Fresno State, but his passion for weed and life in the projects caused the offer to fall through, so he joined Sex Money Murder. Pipe coached the team. He delighted in putting the kids through their paces on the courts near the projects.

The team played in the Rucker games for big-money bets. One day they arrived at the courts in Harlem wearing bulletproof vests under their hood-ies. Some had shotguns; Pete carried an Uzi. The road around the park was clogged with expensive cars, and dealers mingled on the sidewalks. NYPD cruisers were parked on every corner, and knots of cops stood around in the summer heat, talking into radios while leaning on the park railings.

Pete and the others had taken up a position just outside the park when a kid from Soundview ran up to say that he had seen Barnes in a burgundy Lincoln Continental down the block. Pete turned, saw the car, and broke into a half run.

Pipe tried to stop him. If Pete opened up, they'd all be arrested. Pete ran toward the car, leveling the gun, but before he could squeeze the trigger, Barnes spotted him and peeled off.

Pete returned to Pipe and the others, who blended into the crowd. But as he sauntered up, grinning at his bravado and Barnes's narrow escape, he didn't spot the small Hispanic man on crutches moving up behind him. Pipe spotted Carlos Mestre first, hobbling up and reaching for a weapon. Pipe backed up and pulled out a sawed-off shotgun. Twin, B-Love, and one or two others drew their weapons. A friend of Mestre's tugged his elbow. "Not now," he warned. Mestre gave them all a look and turned around.

Pete was furious at himself: He'd been "slipping," and caught unawares.

+ + +

A FEW WEEKS later, in July, three months after Hines's murder, Pipe and Pete drove out to Wallace's place in Queens. Every time they went to his house, Pete changed the route—making sharp dogleg turns, cutting through side streets. Pipe sat in the passenger seat as the city rolled by. They were listening to an early bootleg version of Tupac's "How Long Will They Mourn Me?," a requiem to his murdered friend Kato. Pete believed, and regularly told others, that Tupac was referring to the same Kato he had murdered in Harlem. The Kato in the song, though, actually referred to a friend of Big Syke, a rapper and Tupac collaborator who appears on Tupac's *Thug Life* album, released in October 1994.

Pete and Pipe rolled up to Wallace's house and parked in the driveway behind, next to Pete's new Mercedes and Wallace's Range Rover. Wallace had continued to mentor Pete by driving him down to Texas on a drug run, saving a reputed $150,000 in trafficking fees by taking the risk of transporting several kilos of cocaine from the border. Wallace planned to retire from the drug game, leaving Pete with his connections.

The next day, a balmy Sunday, Codd called at around one, and Pete suggested that they drive to the store they called Jew Man's, on Southern Boulevard, to buy shoes. The two-floor emporium was full of leather jackets, designer apparel, and the latest footwear.

"You got like ten million pairs of sneakers," said Pipe, puzzled. "You want more?"

"So?" said Pete.

Pete wasn't after sneakers. They raced up to the store on the corner of 167th Street, a block away from the old Forty-First Precinct, known as Fort Apache. A white Nissan Maxima was parked outside—the reason Codd had called.

Abruptly, Pete's playfulness evaporated as he pulled out his Grambling State hoodie, tugging it on in the cramped space behind the steering wheel. It had become a trademark of his deadly intentions. As soon as Pipe saw the sweatshirt he knew someone was going to die.

Pete pulled on his black leather gloves and took a look in the mirror before he put the A/C on high and hit a button on the steering wheel. A stash box slid open where the passenger-side air bag should have been. He pulled out a 9mm pistol and chambered a round.

At the same time, Pipe caught sight of Carlos Mestre stepping out of the store, his arms full of bags. He was opening the trunk as the hooded shadow moved toward him over the pavement. Mestre slammed the trunk closed, moved to the driver's side. Pipe watched as Pete took a couple of steps, loomed up behind Carlos, and shot him three times.

Pete strolled back to the car, and they raced away under the subway tracks, running red lights. Moments later a car came through the intersection and sideswiped them. Pete paused, put the car in reverse, and pulled around the other driver. Pipe grabbed the interior handle above the door with both hands and hung on, scared. He told himself that Pete had killed Mestre not only because he was a snitch but to prevent others from being killed.

Within ten minutes they had reached I-278 and were racing over Randalls Island and back into Queens.

Pete stepped out at his uncle's and assessed the damage. "Man, they gonna be looking for this fucking car," he said. "We need to lie low for a while." They left it behind the house and climbed into Pete's Mercedes to drive back to Soundview. Back on the block they joined the crew outside 551. B-Love had some news. "Y'all wanna ride over to Jew Man to see what's going on?" he asked. "Carlos just got rocked outside!"

Pete feigned surprise, struggling to keep a straight face. "Get the fuck out of here." But then he could barely suppress a smirk.

"Yo, was that you?" exclaimed B-Love, watching Pete's changing expression. "Oh man, you is dangerous!"

It was Pete's third murder in less than a year.

Eight

GIMME THE LOOT

PETE'S AMBITIONS FOR SEX MONEY MURDER were leading the crew into the upper echelons of New York's elite. The new face of Ralph Lauren, Tyson Beckford, was one of Pete's friends. They bonded over a passion for motorcycles—the model and the gangster charging around Harlem, Pete on a high-powered Honda CBR600.

A few weeks after Mestre's murder Pipe was tagging behind Beckford, pressing through the crowd at an uptown club. Beckford had taken a shine to the tough little kid Pete always brought around with him. "Tell these bitches you my little brother," Beckford said as they pushed into the club. Pipe couldn't believe his luck: Early in the day he'd passed a giant billboard on the West Side Highway with Beckford's image, and here was the man himself calling Pipe his little brother.

The gangster affiliation gave Beckford status, while their alliance brought Pete closer to emerging players in the worlds of fashion and entertainment who might help him launder drug money in a legitimate business.

Throughout the night a roving spotlight picked out top players, and toward the end of the party, the finger of light fell on an embarrassed, stick-thin seventeen-year-old, half drunk, with a jutting jaw and a subdued air of violence. Pipe mugged in the spotlight. Beckford and Pete roared with laughter.

Sometime before 3:00 a.m. Tyson suggested they go to the Tunnel before it closed at 4:00 a.m. Beckford and his manager led a flotilla of luxury vehicles the wrong way up Twenty-Seventh before coming to a grinding halt on the sidewalk right outside the Tunnel's front door. A couple of black-clad bouncers stormed over. "Get that fucking car outta here!" Tyson stepped out, and the bouncers abruptly changed their demeanor, clearing the way for the model and the Sex Money Murder crew.

After the club closed they all spilled out onto the sidewalk. Twenty minutes later Pipe had a stunning woman he'd just met in the passenger seat of his new Mercedes, on the way to Beckford's apartment in midtown. Drunk from champagne, he squinted as he drove. Once out of the elevator, the entourage entered a vast open-plan apartment. The beautiful girl Pipe had driven up with sidled up to him. "So," she said, "how do you know Tyson?" Before Pipe could answer, Beckford boomed from the other end of the room. "Yo, that's my little brother! He's family." The woman slipped closer.

Pipe savored the moment, realizing he might be enjoying the best night of his life. He padded over to the window and looked out at the lights of New Jersey reflecting on the Hudson River as dawn rose. He looked back at Pete, ensconced on the sofa, draped in diamonds and gold jewelry. Sex Money Murder was thrusting Pipe into a lifestyle he could never have imagined. "You wanna go to the bathroom?" Pipe asked the girl.

"Sure."

✦ ✦ ✦

DESPITE THE high-profile nights out, jealousy and paranoia began to corrode Sex Money Murder. One broiling evening in August 1994, B-Love stood on the block with Pipe. B-Love had just gotten out of prison for shooting a Soundview man and then lying to a jury while pleading guilty, resulting in a sentence of eighteen months to three years, of which he served the minimum. Pipe and B-Love grumbled about how Pete was treating them, B-Love complaining that Pete favored those in the crew who weren't violent and a potential threat to him. He gave Stymie—an older hustler who never picked up a gun—three kilos at a time to sell in Soundview and Bronx River. And yet he only gave Pipe and B-Love one kilo to share. B-Love said Pete was paranoid, afraid he'd be usurped by a young blood looking to make a name. Pete simply thought in terms of ever greater profits, B-Love said, most of which flowed directly back to him, while his hustlers on the street absorbed the risk.

The pop of gunshots curtailed their conversation. They pulled semi-automatic pistols out of the mailboxes at 1710 Randall and headed toward the sound, before they came across the head of the local Netas gang, who said a white car had been prowling near Cozy Corner. Pipe moved up the block to see a white Cadillac, with blacked-out windows cracked an inch, cruising past Pete's grandmother's house at walking pace before abruptly making a U-turn and returning. There were so many beefs going on with Pete's murders that it could be anyone looking to straighten the score.

"You niggas get on point," Pipe said. Every available member of Sex Money Murder left to retrieve weapons. Pipe hastened back to 551, where he retrieved a cut-down AK-47 from a hollowed-out hiding place beneath the rear entrance's stairs. He gave Ro the .357, but his brother wanted the machine gun. They quarreled like kids over a toy before Pipe's rank as older brother won out, and he ambled up the block toward the car with the AK-47 on his shoulder, muzzle pointing backward, finger on the trigger.

Half a dozen Sex Money Murder members surrounded the car. They forced the driver and the passenger out at gunpoint. B-Love cracked the passenger over the head with his pistol. "What the fuck you doing here?" he demanded. They ordered the driver to open the trunk.

As Pipe advanced on the scene, Nut, a junior member of SMM, cycled past him. He wore an oversized white T-shirt and pedaled one-handed, his free hand cradling a .380. Nut pulled up next to the driver, threw his bike to the ground, extended his arm, and, wordlessly, shot the driver in the side of the neck. At first, unsure of where the shot had come from, B-Love and the others panicked. They opened up on the car. Pipe, two car lengths away, discharged the AK-47 in the air. Amid the shooting, the car's passenger took off running though the projects, B-Love firing after him.

When sirens erupted, the crew scattered in different directions. Pipe looked back to see the driver of the car lying prone in the middle of the road, a puddle of blood spreading around his head. Telephones rang across the projects, and residents relayed what they were seeing as the police descended. A rumor circulated that the cops were asking about anyone wearing a white T-shirt. Pipe looked down and clawed his off.

At dusk, with the police still at the scene, crew members drifted out of the buildings and convened at the Pink Circle. One of the gangsters, panicked, said he had dropped his beeper near the driver's body. He called over Smokey Joe, a local crackhead, who took Nut's bicycle and cycled up to find it. He returned empty-handed but confirmed rumors that the police knew the shooter wore a white T-shirt. Nut heard the news and beamed. He still wore his white T-shirt. Now he, too, a junior soldier of little repute, would advance up the ranks in Sex Money Murder. No one in Soundview would risk identifying him as the killer.

A few days afterward posters appeared in the buildings detailing a wake and funeral for the victim, a man named Tony Morton. A story quickly circulated that Morton was merely in the neighborhood trying to find the right house to pick up his daughter.

Nut approached Pipe on the block. He asked if he had heard any more about the shooting, if witnesses had come forward.

Pipe said he hadn't.

"You got rid of that gun, though, right?" said Pipe.

Nut said he had sold it.

"How you sell a gun with a body on it?" admonished Pipe.

Nut said it would be his word against the man who bought it. And, besides, he said no one would dare snitch on anyone in Sex Money Murder.

Pipe was disgusted. Drug dealers were fair game, but regular people picking up children were not.

"He was killed for nothing." Pipe paused. "*For nothing.*"

"Well, what do you want me to do?" Nut said. "There's nothing I could do about him. If he was the wrong one he was the wrong one. I killed him. What do you want me to do? Cry over spilled milk?"

"No," Pipe shot back. "I just wanted you to know that you killed the kid for nothing." Nut shrugged and slouched off.

+ + +

ALTHOUGH PIPE balked at the senseless killing, his pursuit of money inspired an ugly narcissism. One night at a club Pipe tried to seduce a singer from a new group called Total, one of Puff Daddy's signature acts. When she wrinkled her nose at his advances, he threw a fistful of cash in her face to show money meant nothing to him and she was beneath his scorn. "I'm Sex Money Murder, bitch."

The money flowed so thick through Soundview that the boys had to search for ways to spend it. They went south with jet skis on the back of their SUVs, once to Virginia Beach, where they took over the fourth floor of a hotel and the pool area. A few weeks later they drove to Charlotte, North Carolina, for an expo scheduled to feature the Notorious B.I.G. The event was promoted by a Sex Money Murder associate, a cousin of Pete's. Pipe was getting ready to leave with Pete and a few Castle Hill friends, driving Pete's Mercedes, when Bemo, wearing a filthy pair of jeans and T-shirt, demanded to go with them.

"You ain't getting in the car all dirty like that, nigga," said Pipe, wrinkling his nose. Bemo begged to go, saying that he would change. Pipe relented, drumming on the steering wheel while his friend went upstairs. Bemo returned in a crisp, brand-new shirt but still wearing the same filthy jeans. "Oh my lord," said Pipe to the others in the car, "nigga will never learn!" Bemo climbed in, ignoring the taunts at his appearance.

When they arrived in Charlotte they set out to meet Biggie, whose new album, *Ready to Die*, was about to be released. A furious argument had erupted between Biggie, sprawling in a hotel shuttle with the door open, and Pete's cousin. Each blamed the other for a lousy crowd.

Bemo slipped up beside Pipe. "Yo, slip me the .40, Moe," he said, asking for Pipe's .40 caliber pistol as he eyed Biggie's Rolex. Pete, sensing what he was about to do, took them all aside. "What you think, we burglars or stickup niggas?" he said irritably, bristling at the breach of protocol. "Leave it alone. We got Rolexes!" Bemo pouted like a frustrated child. "Yeah? You got a Rolex. I ain't!" Still, he knew better than to ignore the order.

Pete refereed the argument between Biggie and the Soundview promoter and eventually got each side to agree to take a $5,000 loss on the event.

That night they hit the clubs, pretending to be famous rappers, and brought girls back. The scene in the hotel quickly degenerated into a debauched gangsta party. Pipe took one girl to his room, started to have sex with her, and then left when he grew bored and headed downstairs to Pete's room. Pipe's enduring image of the evening was of a fully clothed Pete, the sexual adventurer, still wearing a bulletproof vest, his baseball cap on backward and his fly unzipped, thrusting behind a young woman who was naked and bent over the bed while she gave Stymie a blow job. Pete never used condoms.

✦ ✦ ✦

ON THEIR RETURN to Soundview, Pete focused on the thirty kilos of cocaine, all neatly packaged with gray duct tape, that he still needed to off-load following the murder of Anthony Dunkley. A Soundview connection, called TV Dave due to his large, boxy head, said he knew about lucrative markets in North and South Carolina. In September 1994, Pete and Pipe set out on what would be the first of several business trips.

Dressed in long black trench coats to conceal their guns, they drove a new burgundy Nissan Quest minivan outfitted with stash boxes on hydraulic lifts under the front right seat. They made connections with local dealers, dropped off three to four kilos, and took in around $30,000. In Charlotte, North Carolina, they surveyed some dilapidated houses around West Boulevard that might be useful as crack houses. Pete stopped to buy a Rolex; the store manager was visibly nervous at the sight of the young men in long raincoats.

At some point Pete took a call. Ladu, Pipe's longtime friend from Buffalo, had been killed outside 615 Rosedale two days earlier by two men on a motorcycle. Pipe sensed that Pete took some twisted glee in giving him the news; he seemed to find humor in murders that were a result of someone slipping. Pipe quashed his grief. It wouldn't solve anything, and besides, the killer was allegedly a Sex Money Murder member, and that had to be his first allegiance.

Three weeks later, in October 1994, Pete, Pipe, Codd, and TV Dave drove to North Carolina to pick up payment for the cocaine they'd delivered. Along with guns and and cloned cell phones, Pete packed a copy of *Blow* by Bruce Porter, the story of George Jung, who made $100 million working with the Medellín drug cartel smuggling cocaine into the United States. Pete tossed Pipe $10,000 just to ride along with him. On a hotel floor that night, they counted out $225,000. They stashed the money in the Nissan minivan and set out for Lumberton, North Carolina, the next morning. There they picked up $150,000 from one dealer and continued on to South Carolina, where they collected $60,000. Finally, in Rockingham, they tried to collect a $90,000 drug debt from Covington, a friend of TV Dave's, at a joint he owned. TV Dave and Codd went into the bar to get the money; Covington told them that he didn't have it. He handed over part of his debt in a bid to mollify Pete. But Pete was furious. "You ever wonder why I don't get out of the van?" he said. "Because just in case I got to murder somebody, ain't nobody know what I look like." After some more back-and-forth, Pete consented to give Covington one more day to come up with the money.

They drove to a Comfort Inn, where Pete called Twin. He had connections in the area they could use to off-load their remaining three kilos, and with Covington's nonpayment, Pete had decided to cut him in.

Twin arrived in Lumberton the next day. They followed him out to his grandmother's house deep in the marshes near Wilmington. Pipe, tired of driving, opted to stay with Twin. Pete handed over the cocaine and a gun before setting out to get his money from Covington.

The following day, Twin's cousin drove them around doing errands in a broken-down Mazda as they played Notorious B.I.G.'s *Ready to Die* on repeat. Their first stop was an army-navy store, where they picked up bulletproof vests and another gun. They found some local dealers and undercut their supplier by $2,000 a kilo, thereby making their first sale. Their second day, driving around in a different car, this time with stolen plates, they were pursued by the police. Twin killed his headlights and roared off around the backcountry, eluding the cops by hiding behind a school.

After three weeks the kilos had been sold, and Twin and Pipe returned to New York. But Pete had a serious story to relate.

✛ ✛ ✛

WHEN PETE left Pipe and Twin, he returned to Rockingham to get his money from Covington, who was resisting calls to pay up, at a Quincy's in town. TV Dave was concerned about a setup, so he, Pete, and Codd parked at a Wendy's about half a mile away and walked to Quincy's. TV Dave kept calling Covington, and when he finally got through, out of earshot of Pete, he told him not to come to the meeting—he suspected Pete would murder Covington regardless. When he returned to Pete and the others he played dumb and suggested that Covington was not going to turn up and they should leave.

They left the restaurant, and Codd and TV Dave said that they would leave the van and pick it up early the next morning. They already had $300,000 from all the drug deals, and they didn't want to hang out with that much cash. Besides, Covington owed only $30,000. "No, man, I ain't going for it," said Pete. "Ain't nobody going to live in this world that owe me money."

They returned to the van, where Pete grew increasingly angry. "Dave, man, yo, take me to his house," said Pete, "because I'm going to murder his wife and kids. I ain't playing."

An argument ensued over what to do next while TV Dave tried to placate Pete. Then sheriff's cars swarmed in from every direction. Covington, it turned out, was an informant, and they had all been under surveillance. Dogs barked and pawed at the van, but the stash box escaped notice. Pete and the others were taken to the Richmond County Sheriff's Office, where Pete's and Codd's fake driver's licenses were copied. Saying that he didn't have any evidence to hold them, the sheriff freed them. He said that he would keep the van and that if he found drugs he would come to New York to arrest them.

They left the jail and went to a phone booth, where they called George Wallace, who arranged for a lawyer to call them back. As they waited, two deputies appeared with guns drawn. A Nissan mechanic had found the stash box containing drugs, money and guns. Pete, TV Dave, and Codd were arrested for trafficking and possession of two kilos of cocaine, along with gun charges.

The police said that they had found $250,000 in cash; Codd suspected that he had left at least $450,000 to $470, 000 in the van. According to him, someone had stolen the rest. Bail was set for each at $500,000; the number would increase the following day to $1 million per person.

A lawyer, Kelly Williams, arrived and advised that if TV Dave and Codd could give him $2,500 he could get the bond dropped to around $100,000 and they could get released. They complained about the size of the bond, but Williams returned to jail a second time and said they each needed to come up with $100,000. If they did, and as long as they never returned to Richmond County, the warrants against their pseudonyms would remain but would never be served, he said. Codd and TV Dave heard the sheriff say that the money could be placed into an escrow, or even a bank account. Another lawyer from New York, hired by Pete's uncle, arrived. TV Dave remembers the bond being dropped to $25,000 cash, which Pete's uncle paid on their behalf, and their release took place at midnight. They flew straight back to New York.

At a meeting at Pete's lawyer's office in New York with George Wallace and Codd, it was agreed that TV Dave would take the weight for the case, as he had led everyone down there. He would likely get twenty months when he returned to North Carolina. But a deal could not be struck, and eventually he was told never to return to North Carolina and that his psuedonym would stay on the record, not his real name, as had been agreed. But TV Dave returned to Charlotte to continue to sell drugs just six months later.

✦ ✦ ✦

THE DAY AFTER Christmas, Pipe drove through Manhattan and past Lincoln Center in his Mercedes. Just seventeen, he enjoyed a sense of superiority over the soft, scuttling white Manhattanites. He felt smarter, more resourceful, part of an elite warrior class. He had born with nothing, and here he was with a wad of notes in his pocket at the wheel of a Mercedes running with a group of dangerous outlaws who would kill and die for him.

The crew had planned on a night at the Palladium, where Notorious B.I.G. was playing, but a heavy police presence and several undercovers had deterred Pete. A drug dealer from Queens they knew rolled up in a Range Rover and suggested they go to Sweetwater's instead, a club on West Sixty-Eighth Street and Amsterdam Avenue. He said that he knew the bouncers and could get them all in with weapons.

After entering they spotted another Soundview dealer, Arthur "Frisky" Johnson, a longtime gangster with weapons and drugs charges dating back to the 1980s. He'd shot one of his Castle Hill dealers in the leg when he returned $5 short after a night hustling. Johnson had pioneered the pipeline into North Carolina, sending kilos through TV Dave to Covington long before Pete. Word had come back to Pete that Frisky harbored a grudge against Pete and Sex Money Murder for taking his business. Frisky was dangerous because not only could he pull the trigger personally, but he had funds enough to pay any young shooter in the projects who'd be eager to make a few thousand and a name for himself. He let it be known that he saw them as neighborhood "kids who needed a good spanking." But he had underestimated them. Frisky, it was rumored, had brought a hit man up from North Carolina to kill Pete.

Frisky caught sight of the boys and bounced up nonchalantly, dizzy on champagne, like an old friend. Pipe suspected he was playing nice. Pete smiled back, but he sent the crew to make inquiries. It turned out that Frisky had been seen talking to a heavyset man in a maroon sweatsuit earlier in the evening who told someone he came from North Carolina. "You niggas need to get my nine from the car," Pete said, referring to his 9mm pistol.

Pete and others took up position behind some brass railings, passing out champagne to partiers, Frisky among them. "We gonna rock that nigga to sleep, Moe," Pete whispered to Pipe. At 2:00 a.m. Pipe and Twin stood on one side of Frisky, Pete on the other. Twin pulled out a .38 revolver jammed in the front of his jeans, reached across Pipe, and shot Frisky point-blank in the side of the head. Frisky crumpled to the floor.

The music droned on in refrain: *"Gimme the loot, gimme the loot."*

Pipe looked down at Frisky, kicking his thigh to see if he was alive. "Oh, shit," Pete exclaimed to some girls nearby. "I think someone's been shot." They screamed and charged for the door; the crew was swept along in the stampede to the exits.

Pete picked up his car with Twin, circled the block a few times, and then got out. He wanted to make sure that the job was done, and he also hoped to catch his would-be assailant. He slipped among the crowd with a gun under his jacket. A body bag was lifted out on a gurney, but he saw no trace of the man in the maroon sweatsuit. They all departed for Soundview.

Twin now had his first body. But rumor attributed the killing just as often to Pistol Pete.

Pipe was to learn subsequently that Frisky was his cousin on his father's side. People thought that Pipe's involvement in the murder showed heartlessness. Life was war, he reasoned. Frisky would have killed Pete, and Pipe could never allow that to happen. He hadn't felt much more after the killing than a vague and fleeting sense of relief that he and his crew had survived.

Nine

BLOOD

WORD SPREAD OF A $50,000 CONTRACT on BO Barnes. Ever since Pete had murdered Karlton Hines, almost a year ago, Barnes had been threatening retaliation. Twin had heard one night that Barnes was in a nearby club, so he'd had Pipe drop him off at the front entrance. He intended to gun him down, but Barnes had spotted him and fled through a back door. But now Barnes was extorting Sex Money Murder's main supplier, John Castro. And it was Castro who had set the bounty. Even Suge, two years into his sentence in prison in Massachusetts, heard about it. "Yo, I hear they got fifty stacks on BO's head," he said to Pipe on a call. "I hope he's still around when I get out. I want that money."

In May of 1995, six months after Twin had killed Frisky in the night-club, Dula Martin spotted Barnes, wearing black sweatpants and a green hoodie, a diamond-encrusted gold Rolex on his wrist, standing on the corner of Castle Hill and Powell Avenues with a rap producer. Dula called Twin and then Pete. Both raced to the scene, competing for the privilege of murdering Barnes. Twin reached him first, delivering a shot from a few feet away that slammed into Barnes's skull an inch above his right eyebrow. He fired once more into his chest. The record producer fought Twin for the gun, but Twin shook him off. Pete's phone rang, and he relayed the news to Pipe. "Twin got him."

+ + +

PUFF DADDY had been gradually caving to Pete's pressure to sign Lord Tariq and Peter Gunz since Pete had first suggested it toward the end of

1993 at the meeting in the Tunnel. And through his father's old connections, Pete now had an in with Tupac himself. Pete was in talks to set up a record label with Tyson Beckford. In addition to the glamour inherent in these business moves, Pete saw the potential to churn his drug money through legal businesses and emerge as a mogul with a patina of respectability. He also had his own dream of being a hip-hop impresario. Puff and the others he worked with could not have known that Pete wanted to wash his drug money, or indeed how much of the money he would invest was legitimate and how much was illicit.

Away from the brutal daily business of Sex Money Murder, Pete nurtured a softer side. He paid for the college tuition of his longtime sweetheart, who lived in the Soundview Houses. He had also had a son with another woman, and while he was chasing other girlfriends, and largely abandoned her romantically soon after the child was born, he still contributed to his son's care. He had vowed that their son would find his way out of Soundview through education rather than drug dealing.

But Pete's murderous history on the streets was catching up to him. In June 1995, a kid from the block came running up to say that Pete had made the *Daily News*. Pipe read the notice aloud to everyone. "Most Wanted in the Bronx," said the headline. It went on: "He's armed, he's dangerous and he's wanted for murder." A youthful picture showed Pete at sixteen, dressed in a T-shirt, his hair cut in a tight fade and his head thrown back, glaring into the camera lens. The piece went on to say that Manhattan homicide detectives were searching for him in connection with the murder of Kato during Harlem Week roughly two years earlier.

To Pete the notice wasn't cause for concern; it was cause for celebration. They went to Red Lobster at the Cross County mall—by now a postevent tradition—to celebrate. In the days following, they had T-shirts made with the *Daily News* headline and Pete's image on the front.

Later that year, a Princeton professor, John J. DiLulio Jr., would spark a nationwide focus with "The Coming of the Super-Predators," a piece in the neoconservative *Weekly Standard*, warning of American kids who were impulsive, irredeemably violent, and lacking in remorse. Many saw his assertions as having a racist subtext. Two months after DiLulio's piece, in January 1996, *Time* magazine ran a cover story with the head-line "Now for the Bad News: A Teenage Time Bomb," part of a wave of public sentiment about the youth violence epidemic. Pistol Pete was a poster child for a national paranoia.

But beyond Pete's reputation for machismo on the street, he confided to Pipe in quieter moments how vulnerable he felt after he'd carried out four murders in the space of just two years. Personal security now dominated his life. He told Pipe the story of the Mafia boss Albert Anastasia, who had been gunned down in a barber's chair at the Park Sheraton Hotel in Manhattan. Pete said: "He was caught slippin'."

Pete went to a barbershop in the Bronx with tight security. Patrons were admitted by a video camera/intercom system. Deadbolts protected those inside. Pipe and the others, always armed, went with him. When Pete shot hoops in Soundview Park he brought three or four bodyguards to stand on the sidelines.

"You better keep a low profile, too," Pete told Pipe. "They might snatch you up just to get to me."

But Pete's outsized ego required sustenance. Exactly two years after Kato's murder, he returned to the Harlem Week festival, lured by Twin, who called and told him about the expensive cars, and the women in bikinis and jean shorts parading in Riverside Park. Pete rode down on his motorcycle. He parked in a garage, then jumped in a car with Twin. As they cruised around Pete caught sight of a young woman he knew. "Hold on, let me holler at that shorty," he said.

Pete alighted from the car and ran her down in the shadows of Grant's Tomb. As Pete chatted to the girl, someone recognized the Bronx's "Most Wanted" from the newspaper, and within minutes Pete turned to see two cops moving up on him. He tried to slip away, blending in with the crowd, but they had him pinned. Pete pulled his pistol and tossed it into a huddle of people. Then he stopped and put his hands in the air.

The police handcuffed him. Someone came forward from the crowd holding his discarded gun. Overhead, on the frieze of the monument, are two reclining figures, representing Victory and Peace, framing the words LET US HAVE PEACE.

+ + +

INCARCERATED IN Rikers Island on murder and gun charges, Pete delegated the drug business in Soundview to Pipe, now eighteen years old. Pete relayed the message that he wanted Pipe to stay out of trouble and keep a low profile so that he could safely govern Sex Money Murder until he was out.

His decision to award Pipe responsibility was a clear signal that Pete trusted him over obvious successors such as B-Love. Pipe had learned how to run a drug crew from his time in Buffalo, and he could handle money responsibly. B-Love wasn't the smartest hustler; he often blew his money on women and nights out, and he was slow to pay debts. Pete felt Pipe was loyal and capable. He left Pipe the keys to his apartment in Queens and the keys to his Mercedes. Pipe set about building some connections of his own.

One hot summer evening he piloted the Mercedes into Soundview with a kilo of cocaine in a duffel bag from a new source in Manhattan. In the passenger seat was a young woman. He glided to a stop outside 551 Randall Avenue and stepped out, ready to hand off to an underling. Pipe relaxed, standing on the sidewalk, tapping his feet to the music from the car stereo and enjoying his newly exalted status.

A twenty-two-year-old Jamaican weed seller, Natle Brown, approached. He and another old-time Jamaican had been allowed to sell on the block as long as they limited their business to marijuana. Pipe had bought weed from Natle for the past two years. He asked if Pipe needed any. "Nah, I'm good," Pipe said.

Turning on his heel to check on the woman in the Mercedes, he looked back to find himself staring down the barrel of a gun. "I don't want to do this," stammered Brown, "but give me everything." Pipe winced at the humiliation. Soundview was Sex Money Murder territory, a safe haven and the last place he expected to be robbed.

He made to hand over the duffel bag, thinking that Natle wanted the cocaine. Natle refused—he wanted everything in Pipe's pockets. Pipe reached into his jeans and tried to separate a few bills from the $5,000 knot in his pocket. "Stop playing games!" Natle shouted, slamming the gun butt down on Pipe's head. Pipe staggered and pushed a fistful of money, maybe $4,000, into his assailant's hands. Brown ran off.

With blood oozing into his eyes, Pipe jumped into the car, leaving the bag of coke on the sidewalk, and hit the combination for the stash box. He grasped a 9mm.

The girl became hysterical. "I wanna get out," she screamed.

"What you crying for?" raged Pipe. "He didn't even know you was in here. I got hit, not you!"

He set out in the car for Stymie's apartment. He and Stymie searched the neighborhood, to no avail.

Pipe brooded for days. "That nigga violated," he said to anyone who would listen. The ultimate insult to a gangster, and certainly one who had just been handed the keys of the Sex Money Murder empire, was to be robbed publicly in his own territory. For years, ever since his first shooting, Pipe and the crew had built a reputation that was meant to provide security. For the first time since that day, seven years earlier, he felt he had lost control. Were other crews now going to challenge the authority of Sex Money Murder and try to undermine his new role as boss? Did they think Pete was the only one who shot people? And was Pipe going to end up like ET Larry and his crew, drummed out of the kingdom by a younger and more violent clique, failing Pete while he was in jail?

Pipe told Pete about the robbery on the telephone. "Don't do nuttin' about that," said Pete. "I need you on the street." Pete ordered Stymie to handle it instead. But Pipe knew that he had to act. If he let this pass unpunished, he might as well walk around with a target on his back. He tried to work out the motive for the attack. He was in a store on Cozy Corner one day not long after when an unknown gunman sprayed bullets from a speeding car. Some zinged off a lamppost. The shooter had been aiming at some Jamaicans hustling marijuana on the corner.

Not long after, an old Jamaican known as Scandal approached Pipe. He said that a crew from East 183rd Street was trying to take over the marijuana trade in Soundview and that Natle Brown was playing a dou-

ble game. The Jamaican offered a solution. He would set Brown up for
Pipe to shoot him. The plot would work in both of their interests.

Pipe feigned a willingness to discuss peace with Brown, dispatching
Scandal as his emissary. The robber knew he'd be a marked man until
Pipe was killed or the beef quashed. At around 10:00 a.m. on a muggy
July morning, Pipe was standing outside 551 when Scandal, escorting
Brown, approached. A few terse words were exchanged. Brown ner-
vously offered a can of Heineken from a six-pack. In return Pipe offered
Brown a draw from his blunt. Scandal broke the silence. "He just wanted
to apologize." Pipe nodded.

"My uncle's got a boat down on the water," lied Pipe, suggesting that
they take a stroll through Soundview Park. "We can chill, smoke blunts
and all that." Brown nodded, and they set out.

"Look, that little four grand you took, it ain't nothing," Pipe said
as they walked. "If you needed some paper you shoulda asked me. I'da
hit you off—boom, boom—and we woulda been good, know what I'm
sayin'? But then you bust me upside the head?" Pipe made a theatri-
cal show of a confidence broken. "C'mon, man, that's fucked up! You
ain't need to do that." They walked south past the projects, made a right
down where Lacombe Avenue ended, and pressed up behind the houses
before entering a muddy trail that led into the jungly expanse of Soundview Park. Pipe couldn't quite believe that Natle was following him; the
mention of a boat must have impressed him.

"I know you niggas is getting money," said Brown.

Pipe played along. "Yeah, you seen us come through in the NSX and
the cars like it ain't nothing. I woulda let you hold something. You didn't
need to hit me like that." Brown nodded in contrition. *I'ma rock this
nigga to sleep*, Pipe told himself. *He's slippin'.*

They moved past the spot where Pete had dumped Dunkley's body.
Brown slugged down his Heineken and tossed the empty can in the
bushes. Suddenly he realized that he was walking two or three steps
ahead of Scandal on his right-hand side and that Pipe, who had been on
his left, was behind him. It was too late.

When the two Jamaicans pulled ahead, Pipe unsheathed the .357.

He paused momentarily to get a clear shot at the back of Brown's head. Brown turned. Pipe squeezed off two shots in quick succession. A bullet ripped through Brown's neck and he collapsed. On the ground, Pipe shot twice more at his chest.

Pipe turned to fire at Scandal, not wanting to leave witnesses, and let loose three shots, all he had left, but the Jamaican had disappeared into the bushes. So thick was the cover that he was gone within seconds. Pipe had been half drunk and half stoned, but the surge of adrenaline cleared his mind. Pipe knelt down and saw Brown's eyes rolling up into his head. He felt his pulse. Nothing.

He bought two more six-packs and returned to his position outside 551, where he gulped them down. When he'd carried out his first shooting, at eleven, he didn't care if he hit his targets or not. Now he was killing to stay alive. The shooting was merely what was expected of him.

The next morning, "911" flashed across the screen of his beeper. He raced up to Soundview. "The nigga you shot last night ain't dead!" someone told him.

"Get the fuck out!" Pipe said. "I shot him in the head twice!"

Brown had crawled through the bushes and eventually emerged on Commonwealth Avenue, a small street lined with narrow three-story redbrick houses. He lurched up the steps of number 46 and rang the bell. When the door opened, the startled homeowner saw a bloodied man with a disfigured face who struggled to stand, a gaping wound in the side of his neck. The man called the police.

Brown was taken to Jacobi Hospital. Doctors found a bullet lodged under his left ear, which had damaged his hearing. The other round had passed through the left side of his neck and out the front of the right. The shots Pipe had fired to his chest had missed his vital organs.

Pipe figured that Brown would not cooperate. But six weeks later, on September 1, 1995, Pipe was in a store at Cozy Corner around 6:00 p.m. when a carload of homicide cops drove by. They didn't stop, but he handed his Glock to the store owner's son for safekeeping. He bought a pack of Newports and walked outside, peeling off the cellophane and jamming a cigarette in his mouth as he fumbled for a lighter. He heard a gun cock behind him. Two uniformed cops slapped on handcuffs before marching him to the middle of the horseshoe. One went to get reinforcements while a rookie cop covered him nervously, his gun drawn.

Bear, Pipe's longtime protector, walked up with some young women, who started screaming when they saw Pipe in handcuffs. "Moe, what's good?" said Bear, staring angrily at the police. "Be easy," said Pipe. "It's all good. They got nothing on me. I be out in no time."

At the Forty-Third, Pipe was placed in a room for questioning. The police found $3,000 in his wallet. "Listen, we know who you are," a detective told him. "We've seen you since you were a kid selling crack, running around for drug dealers, and now here you are giving orders out there, a big shot." Pipe said he didn't know what they were talking about. The detective tried to convince him that they knew it was a hit paid for by Scandal. "Just tell us somebody paid you to do a hit and we'll get you five years," said the detective. Pipe refused to rat but made a mental note. The only way they would know that was from Scandal himself.

The detectives pushed a wheelchair in. Brown sat in it, so heavily bandaged he looked like a mummy. "Yup, that's the nigga that shot me," he said.

Pipe exploded. The man had violated the street code. "You fucking cocksucker," screamed Pipe. "You supposed to come back and retaliate! You ain't meant to tell. I should have fuckin' killed you. I didn't tell them when you robbed me, how you now tell on me!" He charged at Brown before the detectives could restrain him.

WITHIN A FEW weeks Pipe found himself in Rikers Island with Pete. They were in opposite ends of the prison, Pipe in Mod 1 while Pete bided his time in C73, an area reserved for the most troublesome inmates. Pipe arrived with $3,000 in cash and wearing a Rolex, which one of the guards tried to pocket when he checked his personal belongings. On the block, men sized Pipe up as an adolescent dealing with his first time on the "island." Pete had put out the word that Pipe was to be taken care of, so they knew that he wasn't easy prey. And they saw the respect that seasoned Soundview gangsters accorded him, particularly when Pipe produced a picture of himself with B-Love and Pete.

But while Pipe went into prison as East Coast gang royalty, he lay in his bunk on the first night, floundering in melancholy. He faced serious time, and now his mother would not be sitting in the visiting room to wait for him anymore. In Spofford, at fourteen, she had come to see him and said that she would never leave him, no matter what happened. There was no girlfriend who cared for Pipe like that—they only came when he had money. Pipe stifled his sobs, folding his arms over his head and curling into a fetal position in the darkness.

The next morning he steeled himself again. He was done with grieving. He tried to get ready for his first visit to Bronx Criminal Court. He'd been charged with attempted murder in the second degree.

The bullpen behind the courts was notoriously dangerous. Young men from warring factions all over New York found themselves confined in close proximity, and Pipe wouldn't have the protection of Sex Money Murder's name among kids from Brooklyn or Queens. Before being led off, he had taken the illegal razor he had been given when he arrived in Rikers, covered it in plastic, smeared the small package in Vaseline, and secreted it up inside his anal cavity. He kept an eye on men who robbed other defendants for their sneakers in the bullpen. It began when they asked others, "What size you wear?" If it was a match, some defendants would later arrive in court bleeding and shoeless.

Pipe's lawyer, paid for by Pete, advised that it was better to take a plea than go to trial. This would be his first felony as an adult, and the court might be more lenient if he admitted his guilt. Moreover, during his explosive confrontation with Brown at the Forty-Third Precinct, Pipe had all but admitted to shooting the man, and that evidence would now be used against him.

B-Love and the others came to visit Pete and Pipe on alternating days so that they could courier messages from one to the other. B-Love told Pipe that Pete was angry. With Pipe gone, the crew had lost its top man in the street. Pipe took the scolding like a little brother and shrugged it off. Further, Pete told him to try to beat the charges at trial rather than taking a plea as the lawyer had suggested. Retaliatory attacks were being carried out against the Jamaicans to warn them off testifying, although it hadn't seemed to make any difference.

The next few days would be crucial. Pete was weighing a big decision for Sex Money Murder. He had grown close with one of New York's legendary gangsters, Omar "OG Mack" Portee, the godfather of the United Blood Nation, formed in 1993. Portee now ran the most powerful prison gang on the East Coast.

He had grown up in the tenements at West 183rd Street and Davidson Avenue, to the west of the Grand Concourse, raised by his grandmother. At seventeen he helped carry out an armed robbery, among other crimes, and was sent to prison. Freed two years later, in 1990, he was sent to California by his mother, who thought he might find another path there. Instead, he learned that his relatives were deeply involved with the Miller Gangster Bloods, a powerful crew in South Central Los Angeles.

Portee admired the Bloods' command structure and their rigorous adherence to the colors. When he returned to New York and his own gang, he told them he had permission (now disputed in gang circles) to convert them to a Blood set. They became the One Eight Trey, the first Bloods in New York City.

Portee was arrested for attempted murder in 1992 and sent back to Rikers Island. As an African American, he was victimized under the boot of the Latin Kings, who targeted blacks. The Latin Kings controlled every aspect of prison life, from the drug trade to recreation areas to the phones. Yellow bandanas were tied to the phones to indicate they were for Kings only; violators could be killed. Some of the guards were Latin Kings or associates. The black street crews were in complete disarray, fighting each other rather than consolidating against the Kings.

In July 1993, Portee reached out to black gang leaders, preaching the philosophy of the Black Panthers and urging them to unify. The first few inmates who agreed became the Nine Trey Gangsters. Within days more gangs joined, including the Valentine Gangsters from the Bronx River projects near Soundview, and a Brooklyn crew led by a savagely violent man named Leonard "Deadeye" McKenzie.

OG Mack crowned himself First Superior, or Godfather, of an organization he called the United Blood Nation, the umbrella name for fourteen sets of Bloods from all of New York's five boroughs. Mack later called his top lieutenants Original Gangsters, or OG for short.

In Rikers he drew up a constitution, a list of thirty-one Blood rules and an orthodoxy for his new group. The first commandment stated: "In our organization we will have no snitches." Anyone who snitched would become "food"—meaning that he would be killed by the Bloods, and those who balked at their duty would themselves become "food." To kill a snitch would immediately give you status in the organization. To keep members under control he formed the "Bloody Bastards," whose role was to hurt or kill members who didn't carry out orders. OG Mack and OG Deadeye developed a mode of attack called the "Buck 50": slashing someone's face with such viciousness it would require 150 stitches. The twenty-eighth commandment was to revere OG Mack. "In our organization we will honor OG Mack the God Father of the re-born United Blood Nation." The twenty-ninth was a command to multiply: "In our organization we will breed with Bloodettes to create Blood Drops."

OG Mack's genius was to harness the fear that marked every disenfranchised kid's life in the street—terror of death, jail, arrest—and then offer a quasi-military hierarchy and the chance to be lieutenants and then generals in a fully functioning, cohesive army, rising in rank from one-star general all the way to five-star.

The Bloods took over cellblocks from the Latin Kings by conducting all-out war, tearing off the yellow bandanas on the phones and replacing them with red ones.

Authorities saw the Bloods' growing threat and dispersed them among various prisons to weaken their power base in Rikers. But this only served to spread the movement like a virus. New recruits had thirty-one days to learn the commandments, often written in code. As the authorities deciphered the codes, OG Mack changed them again, calling a new list Death Notices, and when those were cracked, he came up with the Dirty 100's.

As the violence intensified, OG Mack became an invisible deity in the prison system, a gangster God with disciples to do his bidding. He let the streets know that he might not control every block on the outside, but on the inside—where every dealer could expect to spend some time— you entered his kingdom. If you didn't do the Bloods' bidding in the free world, then when you came to prison you were a marked man.

Within a few weeks of Pete's arrival, OG Mack was courting him to join the Nation. He filled Pete's head with stories about black civil rights leaders and how, by joining, he could become more powerful than he ever imagined within the prison system.

Pete wasn't convinced. Not only was he was a boss already, but his deadly reputation on the street far outstripped OG Mack's. Why would he relinquish control to fall in behind OG Mack, taking rules from some- one who was a lesser gangster to begin with? Pete refused. OG Mack returned two weeks later with a more tempting offer. He offered Pete and Sex Money Murder total autonomy within the United Blood Nation, the only crew to have such distinction. In prison they would have protection and even more power, but on the street Sex Money Murder was free to do what they had always done. They would answer to no one. And Pete would have the power to form subsets of Sex Money Murder.

When B-Love and Stymie visited Pipe, they brought a question from Pete: Would Pipe endorse the transition to Bloods? Pipe had already beaten up a Blood who had interfered with his phone time, so he wasn't wholly impressed with their mettle. However, he said to tell Pete that Sex Money Murder had ascended under his leadership and Pipe wasn't going to question his decision-making now. Deep down Pipe knew that Pete was lonely. He didn't have his crew around him—the fraternal love, deference, and protection—and he was making decisions based on the aching solitude he was experiencing in Rikers. Pipe suspected Pete wasn't serious about the Bloods, that it was just a phase. But if Pete wanted the switch, Pipe would back him.

✦ ✦ ✦

THROUGH A SERIES of hearings in Bronx Criminal Court, Pipe learned that Natle Brown was recovering and prepared to testify against him. Brown wasn't scared of Sex Money Murder without Pete Rollock on the street. The lawyer tried to work a deal with the district attorney, who offered leniency if Pipe pled guilty and waived his right to a grand jury indictment. Despite Pete's insistence that he should go to trial, Pipe had been told by his lawyer that Brown's testimony could result in seven to twenty-one years behind bars. He caved, copping a plea.

In September 1995, Pipe shuffled into Bronx Criminal Court, AP6, for his sentencing. Sitting in the front of the public gallery was a well-dressed Jamaican woman, Natle Brown's mother, and one or two relatives who looked at Pipe with loathing. His victim wasn't there. The judge asked Pipe to admit his guilt. "Yeah, I shot him in the head," said Pipe.

"Did you shoot to kill him?"

"Yeah, I was trying to kill him," said Pipe. "But he lived, and if he hadn't I wouldn't be here."

He was sentenced to three to six years. As he was led out of court he shot a contemptuous smirk at Brown's mother and her family.

On October 16, 1995, after a few weeks in Rikers, he was shipped to Ulster Correctional Facility. He was issued a green uniform, and a prison barber shaved off his cornrows to the nub. Two weeks later he was moved to Washington Correctional Facility, north of Albany. Without the stress of the street, Pipe got healthy again, lifting weights as the dull routine of prison life stretched the passage of time.

About six months into his sentence, a young Blood gang member approached him. "You Pipe?" he asked. Pipe warily said yes. The young man explained that he had a message from Pete. Pipe brightened. "You're 031," said the Blood. Pipe didn't understand. "You're second in command of Sex Money Murder, right?" Pipe nodded. "Pete says he is First Superior, 030, and you are Second Superior, 031." And then Pipe got it. These were Blood codes denoting rank. Pete had flipped Sex Money Murder to a Blood set.

OG Mack and Pete had completed a massive underworld merger, and now they were figureheads in an organization that wielded enormous power in prison and was taking over neighborhoods on the outside. If

Pete wanted something done, he only had to reach out to any of the Blood sets up and down the East Coast.

Sex Money Murder was now officially entered into OG Mack's "Bible," the ledger that contained all the Blood sets and the corresponding ranks of members within them. In a rare breach of protocol, Sex Money Murder had been accepted without having to prove themselves with acts of violence. Their name alone inspired fear.

Pipe knew that the change would be immense. They'd become part of a small army, a national movement that controlled the prisons. But he also nursed serious doubts. Sex Money Murder had been highly lucrative, but he could see nothing about the Bloods that would increase SMM's profitability on the street. The Bloods deal would give them protection in prison, but it was a bonus Pipe felt they didn't need anyway: They were feared already. And the price of Pete's decision was that Pipe had to watch his back more than before—all the Blood feuds and their enemies were now his, too, thanks to Pete. Pipe suppressed his anger. All he wanted was to do his time quietly before getting back on the street to make money.

Still, as the days wore on, his new position conferred a feeling of immeasurable power on the nineteen-year-old. As a Sex Money Murder lieutenant, he was now the highest-ranking Blood in Washington Correctional Facility, leader of 150 gang members in the prison. In the streets, he controlled a few members of Sex Money Murder in the projects; inside, as an OG, he was revered by young men from Brooklyn to Harlem, from Rochester to Albany—many of whom he had never met— who would put their lives on the line for him without a second thought. Moreover, in a prison hierarchy that saw convicted murderers enjoying higher status than attempted shooters like himself, Pipe now controlled serious gangsters with many bodies to their names.

As they marched single file to breakfast, Pipe led his fellow Bloods in a chant.

"Peace to the Almighty!" he yelled like a marine drill instructor.

"Peace Blood!" answered forty men in unison.

"Up top!" shouted Pipe.

"Down low!" they responded.

"Red light, green light."

"Bang! Bang!"

The guards looked on impassively.

"Whose house?" shouted Pipe.

"Blood house!"

Ten

NASTY BOYS

O'MALLEY ARRIVED FOR WORK AT Federal Plaza on February 21, 1995, and took a corner office on a lower floor. The detective from the Bronx found himself surrounded by Ivy League–educated prosecutors, many from wealthy families. On Friday nights they ordered in Lorenzo's pizza and beer and sat in the seventh-floor conference room trading stories about their first gun-collar cases, a rite of passage for new AUSAs— assistant United States attorneys. They were some of the most intelligent young men and women in America, and they wouldn't last ten seconds in the Bronx projects alone, and they knew it. They looked to O'Malley for guidance and protection. O'Malley often acted as translator of gangster slang for the brand-new federal prosecutors. He watched them taking notes and noticed if they stopped writing, puzzled, when a gangster said things like "went for his gat" or pulled "the heat"—both slang for guns—or "got rocked." O'Malley waited until they were on break, or sometimes asked them to step out if they were really confused, before he explained the terms out of earshot of the cooperators so that the prosecutors wouldn't look green in front of them. He made sure the AUSAs never exhibited indecision or a lack of comprehension.

A few months after O'Malley's arrival, in September 1995, prosecutor Liz Glazer founded the Violent Gangs Unit at the Southern District, focusing on street and drug gangs. The FBI, long preoccupied with the Mafia, had no division designated solely for street gangs, something many federal agents considered beneath them and mainly a local problem. Glazer's new section was a pioneering move for federal law enforcement.

By 1995, New York City's gangs had evolved from the street crews of the late 1980s to become part of the framework of national gangs, a trend exemplified by the Almighty Latin King Nation, which had its origins in Chicago. In New York they were led by the motivational Luis "King Blood" Felipe, who had turned victimized Hispanic inmates in a predominantly black prison population into the dominant prison gang, before the war with the Bloods. But they had also begun to assume serious power on the streets. While in prison for shooting his girlfriend, Felipe wrote hundreds of coded letters decreeing that his followers "T.O.S." (terminate on sight) anyone found to be a threat. One man had had his hands and head cut off and his gang tattoos sliced from his body before his corpse was burned in a bathtub.

O'Malley, chief investigator on the case, followed protocol by bringing in the FBI as the lead federal agency. He was impressed with their access to resources. Just to get started, they had a $20,000 account to pay informants. In his days with the NYPD, he had paid subjects $20 out of his own paycheck.

The first order of business was breaking the Latin Kings' codes in letters. O'Malley used connections within New York State corrections intelligence to find cooperators in the prison system, whom he interviewed. They helped him crack the ciphers and in turn start to build a case against King Blood and his gang. O'Malley checked the weapons used in the killings and discovered that chapters of the Kings all over the five boroughs passed the same guns back and forth. He toured the precincts, getting homicide reports to check the murder weapons used, and was able to draw a huge ballistics chart showing how just a few guns were deployed in murders all over the city by gang members. This detail proved that the Kings could be classified as an "enterprise," which meant that the case was eligible for RICO prosecution. Eventually, fifty-one Kings were indicted. O'Malley worked with a young prosecutor, Steve Cohen, who liked to recline on the sofa in his office in worn jeans, reading classics.

The federal system is predicated on the idea that a federal prosecutor should never lose, because the cards are entirely stacked in the government's favor. A prosecutor has huge power in deciding if charges should be brought and, crucially, who can plead and who can't, and who can be offered a deal. Ninety-five percent of all criminal cases are resolved with pleas, and for those who lose at trial in the federal system, judges have little leeway in breaking away from sentencing guidelines. Cohen leveraged his near-invincibility in court when he and O'Malley got Latin Kings to flip. It didn't take more than a few weeks for him to receive a call from a lawyer after they talked them into cooperating. "Welcome to Team America," Cohen said when one agreed to cooperate.

Every time King Blood appeared in court, demonstrations took place outside, with gang members shouting, *"Amor de rey!"* Their chants could be heard inside the US attorney's office. O'Malley spotted men with outstanding warrants and started to pick them off outside court. In time, the demonstrations stopped. Only King Blood went to trial, and he got life plus forty-five years. O'Malley and Cohen had flipped the rest, who either pled guilty or cooperated.

Without a squad and a partner who knew the streets, the work was lonely at first. O'Malley plotted a landscape of crime in the city and incubated cases with detectives who began to turn to him. The doctrine of the streets was entirely different from the logic of American jurisprudence. One young female prosecutor demanded to know why the owner of a bodega in the Bronx could not be subpoenaed to give evidence. When O'Malley resisted, saying he would be killed for testifying, she said, "We'll move him." O'Malley explained that the bodega was his livelihood and that he would lose it if he testified; moreover, the next murder they would be adding to the indictment would be that of the store owner.

O'Malley instructed the prosecutors to go to crime scenes, to get out of the office and see the communities where the crimes took place. He warned them not to react with shock when cooperators admitted their crimes. "Make like you've heard it before, okay?" A violent robber known as Chuck told a story of sending a pretty girl to knock on the door of a drug den and then bursting in with a gun when the door was opened. He said that he had made everyone in the apartment lie on the floor. Still the dealer wouldn't give up his stash. "Normally we torture them, but I saw a baby," said Chuck. "So I put the baby in the microwave." The prosecutor blanched and then looked like he might faint. O'Malley used the story as a teaching moment.

The NYPD got a boost from incoming chief William Bratton, who had a strong mandate from Mayor Rudolph Giuliani to reduce crime. Cops were issued 9mm semiautomatic pistols and could choose between Glock, SIG Sauer, and Ruger instead of the old-fashioned Smith & Wesson .38-caliber revolvers. The three arms of the NYPD were merged, and, as O'Malley saw it, crimefighting gained a more serious focus with the "broken windows" approach.

In 1995, the NYPD launched CompStat, the brainchild of a former transit patrolman, or "cave cop," Jack Maple, known for wearing saddle shoes, three-piece suits, and a homburg. Maple had created "Charts of the Future," fifty-five feet of hand-drawn diagrams of crime hot spots for robbery squads to tackle. When felonies fell by 27 percent, Compstat was taken citywide. Between 1993 and 1995, New York City's annual homicides dropped from 1,946 to 1,170, a decrease many attributed to CompStat.

Coupled with the success of CompStat, Bratton had also heard of the feds' success in taking out street crews. He demanded that all commanders bring him RICO cases. One particular area of Hunts Point, identified after a CompStat meeting, offered an ideal place to build a case.

Sergeant William "Sean" O'Toole, the commander of Bronx Homicide, offered to take Liz Glazer to Hunts Point. A sense of hopelessness pervaded the area. Vacant lots, spiderwebbed with cracks and weeds, and forbidding tenement buildings had proved impervious to law enforcement. On the "hooker stroll," HIV-ravaged women, scarred from beatings by their pimps, offered sex for $20 and blow jobs for $10. They complained to arresting cops that crack addicts were offering sex for so little that their own prices had been forced down to rock bottom. Police rarely arrested them because they were afraid of coming into contact with HIV.

Here murder victims were laid out for hours before the police were called. Three drug crews fought for turf: the Nasty Boys, the Beniquez Organization, and the Bryant Boys. They sold directly opposite each other, competing for customers. Bronx Homicide worked with a narcotics module in conducting undercover buys as they looked for a way to make arrests and stop the killing.

Glazer was looking for a way to get gang members on federal charges. Under state law, gang members faced gun charges so small that they wouldn't even bother to return to court after they'd been charged and bailed. So she pioneered Triggerlock, a federal gun-charges program that mandated four years with no parole.

Meanwhile, one of O'Malley's old partners at Bronx Homicide, Joe Marrero, flipped an enforcer for the leader of the Nasty Boys on Rikers Island, and a major RICO case ensued. In November 1995, thirty-one members of the Bryant Boys and the Nasty Boys were indicted. The arrests transformed the neighborhood; the murder rate in the Forty-First Precinct dropped 51 percent in the first ten months following the arrests.

O'Malley worked some of the proffer sessions. It generally took several meetings for someone to offer up information. During the Bryant Boys' trials, O'Malley sat at the back of the courtroom watching a defense attorney grill one of his cooperators. "You met with the government fifty or sixty hours, right?" The gangster nodded. "And you told them everything, right? Told them all the crimes you'd ever done? And you plead guilty to all those, right?" The gangster gave an effusive yes for the last question. "Did you tell 'em about the time you raped your brother?" O'Malley heard his cooperator gasp. He'd been happy to admit murders to a female prosecutor, but not male rape. They still got the conviction, but O'Malley had learned something. From then on he told his cooperators to admit any sexual aberrations to their lawyers before trial.

O'Malley was gaining experience and adding layers to his work as an investigator. From 1993 to 1996, over three hundred gangsters were charged and convicted of more than 250 homicides in the Southern District of New York. O'Malley garnered a reputation in the tight-knit criminal circles in the MCC. "I wanna talk to O'Malley" became a familiar refrain as gangsters realized that making a deal was the only way out.

Meanwhile, Detective Gil Lugo from Bronx Homicide had learned in interviews with some of the Nasty Boys about another crew who were even more deadly. They called themselves Sex Money Murder, and their leader "hid the bodies" of men he had killed. The information checked out, especially allegations of homicide and drug trafficking over state lines, which could make another RICO case. Lugo and O'Toole passed it to a former Bronx homicide detective they trusted who worked on the inside at the feds. O'Malley, intrigued to hear of an ultraviolent gang from his old neighborhood, began work.

Act III

ULTRAVIOLENCE:
THE
FALL OF
SEX
MONEY
MURDER

Thus he grew to manhood without the slightest conception of right and wrong, with an aversion to honest labor that amounted to actual loathing, and with a keen admiration for the man who was able to get much for nothing. Moreover, his only escape from the misery of his surroundings lay in excitement, and he could imagine no outlets for his turbulent spirit save sex and fighting.

—Herbert Asbury, *The Gangs of New York: An Informal History of the Underworld* (1927)

One

THE FIST

SUGE, TWENTY-TWO YEARS OLD, stepped outside the weathered brick walls of the Old Colony Correctional Center in October 1996. A Department of Corrections bus took him thirty miles north to Boston and then on to Springfield. As he rolled through the green folds of the Massachusetts countryside, he thought only of all the drug money he heard was now flowing through Soundview.

Once back in the Bronx, he embraced Miss Julia, who looked him up and down with a weary welcome. "You stay your ass out of jail," she said with mock severity beneath a wreath of cigarette smoke. She bustled around the kitchen preparing a celebratory dinner for him.

The preparations were still going on when Baby appeared on the threshold an hour later. Suge saw that his old rainmaker wore a gold Rolex on his wrist and a diamond earring in his left ear. He had put on weight. Baby hadn't come to visit Suge in prison because of the superstition that a drug dealer coming to visit would jinx his own operation, but he had paid money into Suge's commissary account.

Baby tried to stuff a wad of bills into Miss Julia's hand as the pair got ready to take off. Suge abandoned the dinner she had prepared for him. She waved him off irritably. The door slammed behind them.

They climbed into a Mitsubishi Eclipse—a beater car Baby used to traffic drugs—circling the horseshoe a few times before heading to City Island. The quaint streets were lined with antique stores and clapboard seafood restaurants. They went into Sammy's Fish Box and slid into a red leather booth.

"I'm bubbling right now," Baby bragged about his flourishing drug business. "You feel me?" Suge was impatient. He'd done his time, put his life on the line, and felt Baby owed him something. Baby talked about a new pipeline he had opened in Roanoke, Virginia, where he was selling kilos for $38,000 to $40,000 each. Baby offered Suge a position hustling and filling in as a gunman for late payers. Suge demurred. He simply wanted money and a good time after his prison stay.

Baby pulled out a roll and peeled off $3,000. "Just hold that for now," he said lavishly. "That's your pocket money." He caught Suge eyeing his Presidential Rolex. Baby took it off his wrist and handed it to him. Suge examined the twinkling diamonds, the weight of the finely tuned mechanism. He'd never held a $25,000 watch. "This is what I want right here," Suge said.

"You focused?" Baby asked Suge. He lectured Suge on smoking weed, reminded him how it dulled him, weakened him as an enforcer. Suge yawned. He wanted a few days to catch up with old friends, to party, and to get laid. They scarfed down some shrimp before Baby dropped Suge back at his grandmother's.

A few days later Pete returned to Soundview, released on two-week bail from prison. He had dodged the murder charge after the witness retracted her statement. Twin's sister had been asked by police to iden-tify Rollock in a lineup. When Twin heard that she was helping the police put his friend away, he threatened to kill her. She pulled out, and the detectives' murder case crumbled. Pete still faced a gun charge for the arrest at Grant's Tomb.

Suge detected a change in his old friend. Back in 1993, when they'd last seen each other, he was customarily brash. Today, he was solicitous and reflective. He asked if Baby was looking out for Suge, suggesting, as he often did, that Baby was exploiting him.

Suge learned that Sex Money Murder had grown in power as Pete and Pipe dealt with legal battles and incarceration. But everything crumbled when Codd was arrested behind the wheel of a speeding Camaro with half a million dollars in cash on August 7, 1996, in Cleveland, Ohio—a major blow for Sex Money Murder. Codd had set up an auto store in the city that sold high-priced rims, audio systems, and, of course, stash boxes. The shop drew all of Cleveland's drug dealers into Codd's orbit, but it also attracted law enforcement.

Pete angrily told Suge that he suspected that with the right pressure, Codd would fold and tell all. He couldn't do hard time. Pete recalled that in North Carolina Codd had given permission for the sheriff to search the van, which had led to the seizure of the money and drugs and ultimately their arrest. Suge guessed that Pete would now have Codd killed if he could.

Pete told Suge that he had turned Sex Money Murder into a Blood set. He pointed to his red Converse sneakers. He'd also developed another name for the crew, Blazin' Billy. He showed Suge the gang sign, arms folded over his chest, index and middle fingers of both hands pointing skyward like pistols.

They laughed, and Suge practiced a couple of times before his attention began to drift. For a while they joked about the women of the projects, and then Pete headed out. The following day, Baby took Suge on a shopping spree at Jew Man. Suge told him that Pete was Blood. Baby had his own confession. He had turned Crip. All the animosities over the years had calcified into Pete and Baby choosing to be natural class enemies. Baby told Suge to keep his affiliation a secret.

Baby bought Suge Pelle Pelle leather jackets, down coats, and a small diamond earring. Afterward, they drove to Sylvia's, a Harlem soul food institution. There Baby elaborated on his plans. "I ain't looking back no more," he said. "I'm going to be a millionaire." He was shifting his efforts from the drug game to the rap business. Baby spent his days at the mixing desk at Chung King Studios in Manhattan. He had a group, Evil Minds. And he'd been heading to LA and claimed something of a relationship with a model/actress who had a small part on *Baywatch*.

They drove to a parking garage at West 121st Street and Frederick Douglass Boulevard, where Baby showed off his fleet of cars: a Mercedes, a black Range Rover, a Yukon Denali, and two Honda Accords. "Yo, Suge, you take this Honda." Suge sneered ungratefully. He wanted the Range Rover. Baby tossed him the keys and the title to the Honda, and

Suge climbed in. Baby showed him the stash box and handed over a cloned cell phone. "Let me know what you wanna do," said Baby.

Suge smiled. "I'ma get me some shorties and some pussy."

He cranked the seat back and drove to Soundview. He ignored Baby's advice to lay off the marijuana and focus on hustling, and bought some weed and linked up with a young woman in the projects, Latoya. He bought her some sneakers and she went to bed with him. For two months he lived like this, drifting around the projects, blowing money, and partying. He heard everywhere about Pete's rise to power, his "bodies," and his new status as a Blood.

Four days after Christmas, Baby called an urgent meeting. Suge drove with B-Love, sharing a blunt as they slowed to a halt outside 551. Baby pulled up behind them. He spilled a garbled story about being robbed for his Rolex. Suge, high from the weed, giggled. "Yo, Suge, stop playing," Baby said. "Harlem niggas stole my shit."

Back in August, Baby and another drug dealer had gone to a party hosted by an entertainment company, Final Four Entertainment, in a Manhattan club. Baby had been showing off, buying everyone champagne. A young woman split off from a group of men and hung on his every word, transfixed by his Rolex. When Baby and his friend left the club, they were jumped in a nearby parking garage by a few of the guys who'd been with the young woman. One of the men pulled out a gun and started shooting. Someone grabbed the Rolex off Baby's wrist and snatched a gold chain from around his neck, making off with both. In the weeks following the attack, Baby had discovered that his assailants were from 140th Street, a crew led by a man called Joseph "Joe Dix" Coppedge. Tonight Dix had been spotted at Jimmy's Cafe on Fordham Road.

As they were talking, Bemo pulled up behind Suge's car in a sky blue 1998 Oldsmobile. He stepped out, bulked up in a large red jacket, and approached Baby with an easy familiarity. For the first time, Suge realized that Bemo had taken his place as Baby's enforcer while he'd been in prison. Baby had solicited Bemo to kill Dix in return for a steady supply of cocaine. For months they'd been looking for an opportunity.

"I'ma go get the guns," declared Baby. "I'ma tell Bemo to put that work in." Suge's jealousy stung like hives. The way he saw it, *he* was Baby's enforcer. He'd just done a three-year bid for Baby. The murder of Joe Dix would be an opportunity for Suge to get paid and to ingratiate himself. "Nah, I got this, Baby," Suge said. Baby had recently cut off Bemo's cocaine supply—he had messed up a couple of consignments. This was an opportunity to win back favor. Bemo pressed for the job.

There was no need. Baby had made up his mind. And after all, Bemo was a proven killer. Suge had yet to "catch a body." Baby offered Bemo $10,000 and half a brick to do the hit. Suge exploded. "Let me do it!" he shouted. "I know you and Bemo do your thing, but I'm your gangster, your man, homes."

Baby waved him off. "You just came home," he said. "Bemo's gonna do it."

They quarreled some more before Suge stomped off to the car to smoke another blunt. Baby left briefly before returning in a black Yukon. Bemo climbed in, and they sped off into the night to kill Dix. They found him standing on the corner of Cedar Avenue and West Fordham, waiting to go into a nightclub. Bemo, armed with a 9mm Glock, calmly walked up and, with a single pop, ended his life.

The murder was all over the TV news and the early-edition newspapers. Baby flaunted his victory, driving up to Harlem and parking his Mercedes on 140th Street. He got out and leaned back against his car, throwing his hands behind his head in a show of power.

On the block in Soundview, Bemo bragged to Suge: "Yo, you see my artwork?"

Suge called Baby. "I'm ready to get paper with you now." He'd decided to stop the partying and get involved.

Baby wasn't convinced. Suge was unstable, pugnacious and nursed a sense of entitlement. He constantly demanded money, cars, and favors. Baby wasn't sure he wanted to be around him that much anymore. He offered Suge a share of the kilo he'd promised Bemo. And he handed Bemo only $1,000—$9,000 less than originally agreed. It was a dangerous move, but as compensation Baby supplied Bemo with more work and gave him another car, and the debt was satisfied.

Suge wanted back in, and refused to be placated. They met in Sound-view, where Suge ended up tossing the keys and the title of the Honda at Baby and storming away.

Two days after the murder, Suge returned to Springfield to sell the cocaine that Baby had given him. The competition had stiffened, and the block swarmed with police. Suge was arrested on New Year's Eve for distribution of cocaine. He was bused back to prison to restart his four-to-seven-year sentence for violating probation.

+ + +

SUGE'S LAWYER worked hard for his release, and he left prison in early October 1997. He returned to Soundview at a pivotal period for the neighborhood. Killing had reached its height in 1993, when Sound-view had sixty-nine murders; toward the end of 1997, that number had been reduced by two-thirds to twenty-two.

More broadly, 1996 saw fewer than a thousand murders across New York City; homicide rates plunged more steeply than other crimes, a milestone not seen since the mid-1960s. Some were claiming that the war on crime in New York had been won.

Many pointed to the decline of the crack epidemic, which had abated significantly. For SMM there were still big markets, but the drug was ebbing, and many of the lower-level dealers had been taken off the street.

Even Pistol Pete was no longer untouchable. He returned to court in New York, where he was convicted on the gun charge and sentenced to two to six years. With good behavior, he'd be out by 1998. But on December 16, 1996, he was served with papers at the Oneida Correctional Facility, in Rome, New York, where he was doing his time. They came from a North Carolina prosecutor, Gretchen Shappert. He had been indicted for conspiracy to distribute cocaine and committing a violent crime while in possession of a gun in relation to drug trafficking stemming from his activities in North Carolina, which, unbeknownst to him, had been investigated. The US Marshals delivered him to a magistrate judge in Charlotte, on January 2, 1997, where he was arraigned before trial on February 6. Peter Rollock would face federal justice and a possible life sentence.

✦ ✦ ✦

SUGE WAS ANGRIER than ever now that Baby was avoiding him. He pressed Baby for money relentlessly. "Where's my paper, J?" he demanded, indignantly. "You ain't letting me hold nuttin'." When Baby gave him some, it was never enough. Suge kept coming, demanding more and more, with veiled threats of violence. He defined himself by money, and when Baby resisted, bitterness gnawed at him; the lack of money hurt his pride. As he saw it, Baby was "violating" him by not giving him any and playing him for a fool. Eventually Baby agreed to pay him as an escort on some drug runs to Roanoke. This time when they counted out money Suge, with a gun in his waistband, throught about robbing him but didn't carry through on the urge.

When he returned to Soundview, Baby avoided him again. B-Love, like a manipulative court adviser, whispered in Suge's ear. "Nigga, he shitting on you," he said, inciting Suge further. "How come he don't snatch you up and yet you always running after him?"

Baby had shunned Bemo, too, after the hit on Joe Dix. A corrosive paranoia spread among all three. "Yo, is Baby trying to get you and me to go against each other?" Bemo asked Suge. He wondered whether Baby was setting them up to kill each other. A few days later a thought crossed Suge's mind when he saw Bemo. "Baby ain't never tell you about rocking me, right, Beam?" asked Suge, circumspectly.

"Nah, he love you, Moe."

Suge had preferred to think of the kids from Soundview as being like marines, guided by loyalty and code; he needed that structure, but what was apparent now was the self-interest, treachery, and mistrust that had always lurked beneath the surface. Bemo and Suge robbed some of Baby's upcoming rappers in the nearby Sack Wern Houses. Suge broke a kid's jaw. The next time, they held them up at gunpoint, going into their pockets to steal their jewelry and money. "Yo, tell Baby to call us," Suge commanded.

Pete had somehow gotten the word that Baby had become a Crip. He ordered that Baby be robbed and killed. He had never liked him, and

Baby's success and importance threatened his own; now, the Crip affiliation added legitimacy to his plan. B-Love would carry out the murder.
Suge was brought in and told about the robbery, but not the murder;
B-Love felt that he would tell Baby. But he had no scruples when it came
to money, and wouldn't balk at a violent robbery, even of his old friend.

They enticed Baby to the block, and Suge, armed with a pistol, jumped
him almost as soon as he stepped out of his Mercedes. Baby took off running through the Soundview Houses. The police arrived and chased both
of them. Suge managed to escape. Baby was arrested; he had $20,000 on
him, and his car had been left on the horseshoe. Under cover of darkness,
Suge broke into the vehicle but was unable to locate the stash box.

A few days later Baby called Suge to threaten him, but Suge wouldn't
hear it. "You violating me. I'm out here and you ain't showing me no
love!" Baby tried to be conciliatory again, offering Suge more cocaine.

Suge began to see that Pete and Sex Money Murder were the true
power brokers in Soundview, and that a switch in allegiance from Baby's
crew would serve his long-term interests better. Besides, to Suge, Sex
Money Murder was glorious, noble, and untouchable.

From prison Pete began to play on Suge's animosity toward Baby,
drawing him closer into Sex Money Murder. Pete called his grandmother's house frequently, sending his uncle down to Cozy Corner to
bring Suge to the phone. He told Suge that he was now automatically
a Blood. Suge took it to mean that he was now officially Sex Money
Murder. He truly belonged. No longer was he Baby's stooge, used and
then discarded.

Suge went back to Jew Man and decked himself out in red clothing
from head to toe. He now felt part of an organization, and he wanted to
wear the uniform. He was made head of security, a broadly defined role
that involved checking who came into the neighborhood, identifying
threats, and then, if necessary, responding. Some even gave him a new
street name: Ugly Man. He answered to Bear and then B-Love, the top
tier of Sex Money Murder.

The neighborhood had come under some heat from the city's Tacti-
cal Narcotics Team, whose officers had been raiding street corners on

Mayor Giuliani's orders. Dealers had been driven into bodegas, where they were less exposed. Sex Money Murder moved their drug trade into Papa Yala's. The owner's son, enamored with the crew, stored their loaded guns behind the potato chips or in the freezer. If any gang member needed a weapon, he just had to approach the Plexiglas window and ask for "ChapStick on Medicaid." The store clerk would get the gun, put it in a paper bag, and hand it through the window.

✦ ✦ ✦

IN THE SUMMER of 1997, Pete had devised from prison a new structure for Sex Money Murder that he called "the Fist." On July 26, he mailed Ro a detailed outline of his vision, in which he conceived of the organization as an "underworld superpower." In his neat, close handwriting he said that the Fist's command structure would be based on the five families. He likely took his inspiration from stories about John Gotti. In 1985, after ordering a successful hit on Gambino boss Paul Castellano at Sparks Steak House in Manhattan, Gotti took over his former boss's empire. Before the killing, Gotti and other disgruntled capos, along with soldier Sammy "the Bull" Gravano, called themselves the Fist.

"the Fist will be divided into three different branches," Pete wrote, specifying it should be spelled with a lowercase *t* and capital *F*. "Each branch will be made up of five dog [Bloods] strong. We will have a superior of the unit, a second in command, a head of security, adviser and counsellor of all situations and an overseer of finance. Each branch will have their own indignity [*sic*], the superior unit will be called 3-0's. 301 the superior of our family. 302 second in command. 303 = head of security. 304 = adviser or counsellor. 305 = overseer of finance."

He outlined three founding sets: Five Deuce, Four Trays, and Three Os. The last would be headed by Pete, who crowned himself Albert Anastasia, after the ruthless Mafia executioner. Pipe, second-in-command, was Carmine "Lilo" Galante, the cigar-smoking head of the Bonanno crime family. "Each member of the Fist will have their own duty and must serve his or her positions thoroughly. Whenever a problem should arise in our family, it will be looked over and discussed by all members of the Fist. Once a decision is made orders will be given and whatever has to be done will immediately be taken care of. There will be no exceptions to this rule."

The Fist would function in three tiers, with the lowest, the street hustlers, giving $25 to the captains above, who would in turn give half of all they collected to those above them, the superiors. Crucially, though, any hustler could work his way up the chain by putting in work: making money from drug sales or killing for the organization.

Pete concluded with a powerful summation of his ambitions: "I hope you can see what I'm trying to prepare for our family. Remember we S.M.M. are like no other set. Once we are fully organized, I will open up many doors for us, that we will have no choice but to be recognized as an underworld superpower. Our hands will be in everything. My plans for our family is on the same level as the early Don's and Godfather of the mafia. If everyone feels as strongly as I do, once we are Together we will never be able to be broken down mentally, not Physically and definitely not financially. Do you Feel me. Five ten. Lock and load like a million men marching." He signed his letter "The Pistol!" and drew a cavalierish Zorro-style slash underneath.

✦ ✦ ✦

PETE BEGAN regularly sending letters that were read aloud at Blood meetings behind the Soundview Houses, where the crew huddled like disciples hearing the word of a new messiah. His epistles demanded that the rules he drew up, the Blood codes, and his directives be followed to the letter. He ordered the establishment of a legal fund and allocated an amount of money for his mother. Suge saw that he incorporated some of the slogans from the skellzies games they played as kids—such as "Hit a killer, be a killer"—into his new Blood doctrine. Now those words, no longer a childish reference to sliding tops, took on a deadly realism.

At one late-night meeting, B-Love stood and read a chilling message to the figures gathered, hoodies pulled up, hanging on every word: "I want the DoubleMint Peter Rolled." A silence descended. Pete wanted his very name to be synonymous with murder. He wanted Twin dead. He went on to explain that Twin was "999," cooperating with the police. He was a "Dusteater." As they dispersed, many were confused, Suge among them.

+ + +

JEALOUSY HAD inspired Pete's wrath. Twin had partnered with Codd when Pete was arrested in 1995. Without Pete, many assumed that Codd's force field was gone and he'd be targeted by the vultures, robbed and shaken down. But with Twin, who had a reputation just as dangerous as Pete's, Codd continued to amass a fortune. Twin had reputedly secured a hundred kilos of cocaine directly from a Colombian cartel and was distributing to crews all over New York City, New Jersey, even Ohio. Without the heat Rollock brought to the operation—his constant thirst for the spotlight and his lust for murder—they were free to make money. Twin felt that he was representing Sex Money Murder in Pete's absence, growing the organization and swelling its coffers with Codd as his partner. He was supplying B-Love, stepping into Pete's role in supplying Soundview with crack. Twin wanted to hand Pete back an organization that was stronger when he got out of prison than when he went in.

After Codd's arrest in 1996, Twin got more sophisticated in laundering his proceeds. He linked up with another man from Castle Hill, Nelson Rios, who drove around the neighborhood in a blue BMW Z3 convertible and convinced Twin that he'd been to Harvard Business School. He used the alias Nelson Ramirez on credit cards and a fake driver's license to open numerous bank accounts to launder money.

He incorporated SMMC Inc. (Sex Money Murder Crew Inc.) in October 1997 with a registered address of 2264 at Powell Avenue in the Bronx. With the official company documents, Rios opened an account with State Bank of Long Island and issued Sex Money Murder soldiers biweekly paychecks that would show parole officers, for example, that they were legitimately employed. Twin was building a drug empire that was a bona fide American corporation, something Rollock could only have dreamed of when he founded the organization.

Despite all this, those close to Pete and Twin saw that Twin retained his modesty, a mark of his upbringing in the Castle Hill projects, in contrast to Pete's more privileged background. He still drove his white Toyota Camry, refusing to get a grander car like other dealers. He gave drugs on consignment to those in need and asked for no recognition for doing so. Pete wanted to be known for every act of generosity, spreading crumbs around to create a sense of obligation among his followers. Twin treated Codd as an equal partner, whereas Pete had exploited him. Twin's goodwill allowed him to broaden his operation, and his reputation as a gunbuster and a savvy businessman was starting to eclipse Pete's.

Pete, impotent behind bars and stressed from the pressure of his cases, began to feel the streets had forgotten him. All he ever heard from Soundview was news of Twin's meteoric rise, Twin's sophistication, Twin's reputation on the street—which was beginning to dwarf his own. He was bitter that most of it had been achieved with his erstwhile business partner Codd. Futhermore, he was angry Twin wasn't contributing money to Pete's mother, Ma Brenda, thereby violating an unspoken rule in Soundview. There were also unsubstantiated rumors that Twin was romantically linked with the mother of Pete's son. It was a dangerous situation.

+ + +

SUGE HAD left the meeting near the basketball courts pondering the letter. Twin's growing reputation on the street as a major drug dealer didn't conform with Pete's rat story. Once or twice Suge had "chopped it up"—chatted—on the block with Twin, and they both said they hoped Pete would be home soon. They missed him. Twin loved Pete as much as Suge did.

A few days after the letter, Suge took a phone call from Pete. "Yo, black ain't no good," said Pete, with slow deliberation, referring to Twin, before continuing his deception that Twin was informing. Finally, Suge fell into line, figuring that if Pete said Twin was a snitch, then he must be. "See, I told you about fucking with that nigga," Suge said. "If you mess with Castle Hill, that's what you get." Pete played on Suge's line of thought, manipulating further: "Yo, this dude violated. He don't want me to come home."

Suge understood that killing Twin could propel him to the top of Sex Money Murder. No longer would he be chasing Baby, or be subservient to B-Love and Ro. He might, he hoped, be awarded his own section of the Fist. For the first time he'd be a boss, not merely an enforcer. "Don't worry about it," said Suge. "I'ma knock his head in. Don't say another word, Moe."

✦ ✦ ✦

ONLY BEAR, serving head of SMM, protected Twin from harm, telling the crew that they were not to kill him. He knew that Pete was finessing the situation and that Twin wasn't a snitch. Twin might as well have been Pete's brother. But in September 1997, Bear was killed in a motorcycle accident.

Bear's mother asked if Pipe could attend the wake. Granted leave by the prison authorities, he arrived outside the R. G. Ortiz funeral home, a bustling funeral parlor that catered to dead gangsters and overdosed drug addicts, in a prison van, shackled and handcuffed. The nervous guards looked out on a sea of red: two hundred Bloods in crimson swarming the street and the funeral home. "Whoa, you're going to be all right out there in that?" one of them asked Pipe.

"Be all right?" Pipe said. "That's my family, my brothers. 'Course I'll be all right." They removed Pipe's handcuffs but left his legs shackled. He slid out of the van and shuffled inside to the wake. Unmarked detective cars were all over the street, Forcelli in one of them, photographing the mourners and license plates along with any gang tags. Inside Pipe met B-Love and some of the others. Pipe took a final look at Bear, resplendent in a red suit, his elaborate casket draped in blood-red bandanas and festooned with red roses.

Forcelli and the other cops trailed the funeral procession down to Saint Raymond's Cemetery in Throgs Neck, a vast expanse of gravestones framed by the Whitestone Bridge, photographing Pipe and the other Bloods. It was the final resting place of Typhoid Mary, Billie Holiday, the mobster Vincent "Mad Dog" Coll, and now Bear.

With Bear gone there was no one to protect Twin.

✛ ✛ ✛

THE SCHEME to kill Twin echoed around the projects. B-Love had squandered a significant amount of drug money he owed Twin, and kept ducking his demands for repayment. Twin hunted for him in Soundview and complained to Suge that B-Love had better pay up or there would be mortal consequences. B-Love's ulterior motive to have Twin eradicated furthered the plot. And Ro, who was looking to make a name for SMM, had returned home from a spell in Elmira—"the Hill," a maximum security prison in upstate New York, where he had been "blooded in" by OG Mack himself—admired and liked Twin but knew that his murder would consolidate his position in the Bloods.

A young Hispanic Sex Money Murder member known as Green Eyes had been a junior player in the crew since the beginning. Gang members called him "Tom Cruise" because of his ivory skin and his ability to bed any woman in the projects. He'd been sleeping with a particular girl and let slip that moves were afoot to do something to Twin. What he didn't realize was that the girl was also sleeping with Twin. Somehow, word got back not only to Twin but also to Bemo, who then relayed the information to B-Love and Ro.

Ro wasted no time in writing to Pete. The SMM leader's solution came quickly. He wrote in Blood code: "Make Green Eyes' 711, he must work around the clock and flip the clip for digging in the stash. Make him prove that he paint the town red."

In other words: Green Eyes should do the murder; he must become a shooter as punishment for informing. Make him show that he loves the Bloods. If not, kill him.

Rollock wanted Green Eyes to play a key part in the murders so that he would be less likely to snitch, a tactic of the Mafia.

Meanwhile, Twin, aware now of the plot to kill him but unsure who was involved, made a preemptive move to demonstrate he wasn't frightened. He and his brother drove into Soundview where Twin alighted outside B-Love's building and made a long, slow walk back to Castle Hill, daring anyone to shoot. News of the bold display spread across

Soundview, reaching Suge. He and one of Pete's cousins, along with Ro, commandeered Pete's grandfather's gold Cadillac. Suge stuffed a gun in his pants and hopped in the back with Green Eyes. They circled the block a few times with the guns on their laps, but Twin was long gone, vanishing somewhere near Holy Cross School. He never caught sight of his would-be assailants.

Ro wrote to his brother to tell the story.

+ + +

PIPE BEGAN to read Ro's letter on his bed in the prison dormitory. His OG status meant life in Cayuga passed easily. Bloods cooked for him and let him use their lockers to store his overflowing commissary. And he had ultimate power to punish anyone who disrespected him. Pipe had recently ordered a Latin King beaten for attempting to stab him, an act his assailant had carried out to get status in the Kings.

Pipe's comfort turned to agitation as he read about the hunt for Twin, and his 999 status. He knew it was a lie. They'd all been in North Carolina together, and if Twin were cooperating, then Pipe would be in Pete's indictment for their drug bust there. Pipe recalled his last phone conversation with Twin in May. "Pipe, my man!" said Twin. "When you get out you don't worry about nothing. When you come home, I got you."

Pipe suspected Twin's success was making Pete jealous. Pipe respected the order of the Mafia; if a leader went to prison, the underbosses kept the organization running smoothly. Pete wanted to emulate the Mafia, but he couldn't live up to the code. Instead, he was scheming to kill his successful underboss out of simple jealousy, an act of fear, even paranoia, which would have been beneath a true godfather. Pipe wrote to Ro telling him to stand down.

+ + +

A FEW days later, Ro read Pipe's letter out loud at a Blood meeting, which sparked a fight. Ro punched B-Love in the face for not giving Pipe his money. But the most crucial part of the letter—Pipe's order not to kill Twin—Ro omitted. He took Pete's word above his own brother's.

One night not long after that, at 11:00 p.m., about twenty members of SMM stood in the dark near the basketball court as B-Love devised the plan to kill Twin at the Thanksgiving Day football game, where he would be unarmed. Suge and Green Eyes would kill Twin. B-Love would go after his brother, Damon. MAC-11 suggested that he lay down covering fire to get the crowd moving so they wouldn't be able to identify the shooters.

Two

THE OFFICE

IN MID-OCTOBER 1997, FORCELLI AND his partner, Benny Tirado, a Puerto Rican detective with a thick mustache and slicked-back black hair flat to the scalp, pulled out of the Forty-Fifth Precinct in a gray Ford Windstar minivan on the way to a secret assignation with Bigga D, one of Pistol Pete's associates.

The NYPD had formed a Gang Task Force in the Bronx that month, bowing to the pressure from New Yorkers panicked that LA-gang-style violence might come to the city, due to a slew of stories in publications such as the *New York Post* and the *Daily News* that were an almost daily drumbeat by November: "6 Bloods Arrested in Gang Rape—Cops." "Bloods Raped Her for Slight, Sez DA." "Bloods Busted in Bid to Bash 101-Year-Old Rev." "Cops: Female Bloods Proud of Cabbie Slay." On Halloween that year hundreds of children stayed home when rumors circulated that the New York City Bloods were going to be randomly slashing people in rites of initiation. Even though crime rates were falling, residents feared the prospect of indiscriminate violence carried out by young men or teens with something to prove to their gang.

Because of Forcelli's detailed inside knowledge of the Soundview and Castle Hill projects, and his successful arrest of Poison and other SMM affiliates, he was selected to lead an investigation into Sex Money Murder, in partnership with O'Malley and the US attorney's office. This was his chance to turn the tide in the projects and to take down the crew that had blighted the neighborhoods he had worked since his days as a rookie.

Liz Glazer saw the takedown of Sex Money Murder as key to her strategy of reclaiming urban neighborhoods from street gangs that had morphed into serious drug-trafficking organizations. Forcelli had met her early on, but she was taking maternity leave and would help in an advisory capacity only. This would be one of the last big cases of the 1990s street crews that had begun with the Cowboys.

The five-man NYPD task force was housed in a former broom closet on an upper floor of the Forty-Fifth Precinct, a graveyard for detectives on the verge of retirement. Resources were nonexistent. One of Forcelli's first jobs was to head to a musty municipal surplus depot to scavenge for new desks. He clawed through hundreds to find four that were still serviceable, carting them back to the precinct in a police van. They were given a laptop by the US attorney's office, but the brass at the NYPD felt that the detectives couldn't be trusted with something as valuable as a computer, so they never saw it.

The case took off when Tirado and Bronx detective Gil Lugo developed a relationship with the investigators from North Carolina who were behind Pete Rollock's federal charges. They met with Sergeant Tom Bevins of the Charlotte Police Department, who had noticed a flood of New Yorkers with their gold chains and distinctive swagger inundating his town and had begun tracking them. Bevins teamed with ATF agent Terry Tadeo as they made arrests and flipped informants. In August 1996, making an undercover buy, they arrested TV Dave, the Soundview dealer who had been with Rollock on those early trips to North Carolina. He flipped quickly, and in an interview room weaved an elaborate story about a drug dealer named Frisky who had been killed in a nightclub over the growing North Carolina drug trade. The detectives saw that Frisky's replacement, Pistol Pete, terrified TV Dave. He told Bevins and Tadeo that Pistol Pete headed a gang called Sex Money Murder, and he believed that they operated in half a dozen states.

TV Dave offered garbled stories about the murder of a basketball star, along with three other homicides he said Rollock had committed personally. And he gave an inside account of their arrest in Rockingham. He revealed how a lawyer had helped broker a deal between the drug dealers and the sheriff. The officers were dumbfounded to learn that Rollock, TV Dave, and the others had been released on bail despite the seizure of two kilos of cocaine, a large sum of cash, and guns.

TV Dave had returned to North Carolina to sell drugs, which were transported to him by female mules dispatched by Pete Rollock in the Bronx. He then sent the profits back in order to pay off the debt Rollock said he had incurred paying the bail for their release. TV Dave said Rollock had ordered him to buy a 9mm pistol for the murder of a witness who was due to pick him out in a lineup on a murder charge.

But Rollock had grown frustrated with the meager sums TV Dave was sending back. He had called him, demanding more money to pay his lawyers. Shortly afterward, Rollock had decided that he wanted TV Dave dead; hence, Dave's telling all to the police on his arrest. He now needed protection.

The investigators left the interview room stunned. A Bronx-born sergeant who worked in the police station heard their story and figured they were onto something big. Their superiors ordered them to work the case full-time. They headed over to Rockingham and interviewed the local sheriff, who produced the confiscated guns. They named their case Tropical Storm.

The pair flew to New York to investigate Rollock's homicides. But the two struggled in the Bronx precincts, where cynical detectives, distrustful of outsiders, offered little help. The game changed when they partnered with Benny Tirado and Gil Lugo. Tirado and Lugo flew south numerous times, once staying for a month. The team concentrated on Codd, who had been transferred to face trial with Rollock on drug trafficking. His lawyer convinced him to cooperate, and soon he was talking to Tirado and Lugo.

In August 1997, Bevins and Tadeo arrested the man who cooked up Rollock's crack, Bigga D, in the Bronx. When he realized the cops were from North Carolina, he shook his head. "I'm screwed, aren't I?" Now they had access to the inner workings of Sex Money Murder. They got in touch with Benny Tirado from Bronx Homicide about the arrest, and he in turn set up the meeting with Forcelli and Bigga D.

✦ ✦ ✦

FORCELLI AND TIRADO drove a van to the southern end of White Plains Road at the tip of the Soundview peninsula. Forcelli didn't like working with confidential informants; they often lied and tried to play their handlers. He slowed to a halt near a new housing development, Riverwalk Harbour Pointe at Shorehaven. A sinewy man with spiky hair, dressed in jeans and a sweatshirt, signaled to Tirado and climbed into the back of the van.

Bigga D had developed a reputation among detectives for being skittish and panicky, an informant who needed to be "babysat" at times, he was so afraid. He wasn't a flinty street guy like Suge or Pipe, and it took a while to set Bigga D at his ease.

As the conversation ebbed and flowed, he told them that Rollock had bragged about his murders of Mestre and Hines. After two hours, he trusted them enough to let them drive him back to the precinct. Once there, Forcelli produced pictures of the key members of Sex Money Murder culled from arrest photos and surveillance. They combed through the set book—a series of mugshots in a photo album—as Bigga D gave them names and background on each. He told them about Crackhead Bemo's son, Bemo Junior, who had boasted about murdering Kiron Little. When they were finished they drove him back to Shorehaven, where he slipped quietly out of the van and melted back into the landscape.

✦ ✦ ✦

AFTER QUESTIONING Bigga D, Forcelli drove downtown to check in with O'Malley at "the Office" to share information on some of the homicides he had unearthed. O'Malley had become a mentor to him. Forcelli grasped John O'Malley's large hand, taking in his steel gray eyes and tall, authoritative presence. "Howyadoin', pal?" said O'Malley, showing Forcelli a chair. Only in his early forties, O'Malley possessed a gravitas that suggested he was much older.

O'Malley took a seat behind a huge desk strewn with documents. Forcelli looked up to see framed plaques that denoted some of the most successful federal prosecutions of gangs in the past few years, which had significantly lowered homicide rates in underprivileged areas of New York City.

Forcelli had first met O'Malley in the summer of 1996 when he was investigating a Co-op City murder that was linked to Wolf Johnson, one of Puff Daddy's bodyguards. But Wolf was murdered outside a nightclub in Atlanta, and Forcelli's participation in the case ended.

As they started laying out a strategy for the case against SMM, O'Malley was intrigued to hear more on how organized and sophisticated the first major Blood set targeted for federal prosecution had become. The Latin Kings had largely been a prison gang, but Sex Money Murder had evolved from a neighborhood crew to become a multimillion-dollar organization with significant resources, a fleet of cars, and tentacles reaching into half a dozen cities, from New York down to North Carolina.

Forcelli learned from O'Malley that no blueprint existed for multi-defendant racketeering cases like the one against Sex Money Murder. They would need a team of law enforcement officers from different divisions who were willing to collaborate, share information, and avoid the kind of competition and resentment that often disrupted such investigations.

O'Malley would be the point man from the US attorney's office, acting as the linchpin for all agencies conducting the prosecution under the aegis of the Organized Crime Drug Enforcement Task Force Program, a program that combined the work of federal agencies into one coordinated attack against large-scale drug-trafficking organizations. The lead federal agency would be the Bureau of Alcohol, Tobacco, and Firearms, led by Rob Berger, who didn't attend this first meeting. The ATF was just beginning to focus on violent criminals and murderous gangs, leaving low-level traffickers and drug dealers to other law enforcement agencies. This would be Berger's first gang case. Forcelli and Tirado were the NYPD component and would be the link to the street, since they knew the machinations of the neighborhood and the players. Meeting with Forcelli and O'Malley today was Lieutenant Sean O'Toole of Bronx Homicide. O'Toole had worked with Glazer on the

Bryant Boys and Nasty Boys cases, and had originally pitched the feds on Sex Money Murder. Alexandra Shapiro would prosecute the case (although she would be replaced a few months later when she moved into the private sector). As is often the case when prosecutors compete for cases that could be tried in different jurisdictions, she'd had a furious argument with North Carolina prosecutor Gretchen Shappert over who would prosecute Rollock for the homicides. In the end, the power of the Southern District of New York won out. Robert Ryan, from the Internal Revenue Service, would handle the financial elements of Sex Money Murder's enterprise.

All of them looked to O'Malley. Forcelli and the others were accustomed to active investigations where they used wiretaps or bought drugs and guns undercover in order to make arrests and build a case. But O'Malley could assemble a historical case, putting together all the pieces in a giant jigsaw with homicides that stretched back decades or more by proffer sessions. He was about to teach Forcelli and Berger how effective he was at getting gangsters to talk.

As far back as June, when the Sex Money Murder case had been mooted by Glazer, O'Malley had heard from Detective Lugo about Bronx guys in North Carolina. In March 1996, he went down and attempted to flip one or two, to get the lay of the land, but came back with nothing. After the arrest of Bigga D, Lugo and the narcotics module started making undercover buys on Cozy Corner. Through low-level dealers they assembled a composite picture of Sex Money Murder: Rollock, the Twins, and, crucially, John Castro, whom Lugo interviewed.

This was easy, as cases go, because Rollock was already being charged as a major interstate drug trafficker between New York, Pittsburgh, and Charlotte—what the feds called the "crack cocaine triangle." They already had most of their work done in proving enterprise under RICO, so the first order of business would be to prove the murders, with Rollock as part of the endgame. The final stage would be the evidence of money laundering, which would fall under the IRS and Robert Ryan.

It was clear they'd use not only RICO but also Violent Crimes in

Aid of Racketeering (VICAR)—known among prosecutors as "1959," for the year it came onto the statute books—which made it a crime for anyone to commit violence for a promise of "pecuniary value" or "for the purpose of gaining entrance to or maintaining or increasing position in an enterprise engaged in racketeering." In RICO indictments, for every offense charge Glazer also had her prosecutors add a stand-alone 1959 to beef up the government's case.

Forcelli briefed O'Malley on what he had heard from Bigga D, who had corroborated some of the street-legend murders attributed to Rollock. He produced diagrams that placed Rollock in the center with links to three of his murders and, erroneously, the murder of Frisky. Also at the top was John Castro; then below him was Rollock and several links to victims. There were also links to suspected criminals in North Carolina. At the bottom was the name Shawn, and a possible connection to the murder of Tony Morton. Beyond that, no one knew anything about Suge.

To begin, O'Malley would track down key members who might be in prison to flip them. He had discovered over the years that he had far greater leverage when his targets were incarcerated than when on the street. Forcelli was impressed with his detailed knowledge of the arcane bureaucracy that governed prisons and his ability to find almost anyone in the system.

Meanwhile, Forcelli and Tirado hit the street looking to corroborate homicides. That would mean visits to precincts to pull homicide files. Shortly after the first meeting with O'Malley at the Southern District, Forcelli was deputized and swore an oath in front of the US Marshal. This gave him the power to make federal arrests in any jurisdiction and any of the half-dozen states in which SMM operated.

Forcelli started his investigation by looking into the murder of Kiron Little, information he had first gotten from Bigga D. He crossreferenced the 9mm Ruger that Bigga D had said Bemo had used with the medical examiner's file. He looked at crime scene footage and went back to the bodega where the murder had taken place to validate what he was hearing from informants. The investigation began to take shape.

The boastful grandstanding by Bemo and Pete about their murders was driving the case forward.

✦ ✦ ✦

O'MALLEY TRACED two of SMM's major suppliers, Codd and Wallace, to prison. O'Malley felt that Codd might give it all up more readily than George Wallace, a known gangster who would stick to the code of silence. So on October 2, 1997, he went to visit him in Ohio, along with Berger and Lugo. Berger and Lugo had had a few beers at the Yankees-Indians game the night before, and they joked about who was in worse shape: the two of them with their hangovers, or O'Malley, who was recovering from a bout of meningitis that had nearly killed him.

At 8:45 a.m. they arrived at the Euclid police station, nestled among a row of redbrick houses in the Cleveland suburb, and were led into a claustrophobic interview room. A few minutes later Codd, dressed in a jumpsuit, came in, eyes downcast. He nodded at Lugo, who knew him well by now. They had developed a bond; Lugo had repeatedly gone down to North Carolina on Rollock's case.

O'Malley spoke first. "Listen, I want you to hear me for ten minutes," he rumbled in his husky Bronx burr. "Ten minutes of your life. That's all I want. I want you to look at me and listen to me." Codd stared ahead impassively. "After that you got some really big decisions to make. You're under arrest. There's no doubt in my mind that you're going to get convicted of those crimes. And you're facing life. So you have some decisions to make. And you can't make decisions until you know all the facts. I'm not asking you to help me. I'm not asking you to flip. I'm not begging you. I don't need you. But I'll tell you right now, if you don't flip, or if you don't talk to me today, tomorrow somebody else from your crew will be right in that chair. It's like musical chairs, see. And you're sitting in that chair right now. But tomorrow I'm going to give another guy from your crew the same opportunity. And then next day, another guy from your crew. And you know what? Somebody is going to talk to me. And I'm going to find out from somebody what you did."

O'Malley paused for effect.

"So it's in your best interest for me to find out what you did from you, because then you get the benefit."

Another pause.

"So if you want to play hardball and you get convicted, and you go away, then in ten or fifteen years' time you will see other guys getting out who cooperated. And you're going to think back to this day when a guy was sitting across from you, and you're gonna say, 'Boy, did I fuck up. I should've listened to that old guy.'"

Codd took in the blank legal pad on the table. Then he switched his gaze to O'Malley. O'Malley threw out some names just to convince him that he knew, among others, John Castro. He was careful not to suggest that Castro had been arrested or that he was cooperating. It was fatal when you bluffed and got caught doing so; it forever ruined the relationship with a potential cooperator. But there was enough insinuation that Castro might be helping, or that he had been identified by O'Malley, for Codd to suspect that they knew everything from one of Sex Money Murder's key suppliers. Codd crumbled.

He described the murder of Karlton Hines. Immediately O'Malley built a picture in his mind of the car bays on Boston Avenue. When Codd described how Rollock had crept in to gun down Hines, O'Malley felt he was telling the truth. O'Malley knew that the murder had taken place in the Forty-Ninth Precinct and that he'd be able to retrieve the medical examiner's report—and through that find the next of kin and the family member who had identified the body.

He tried another of his favored tactics: "What about the next murder?" O'Malley didn't have one in mind, but Codd fell for it. He detailed the murder of Dunkley. This was the mother lode, a senior lieutenant and now cooperator who could take them deep inside the inner workings of Sex Money Murder. The investigation would make a slight pivot back toward Rollock, whose murders Codd had corroborated.

O'Malley was looking for evidence of conspiracy. Codd told him about George Wallace. But what he heard next surprised him. Codd said that Sex Money Murder had recently incorporated in Delaware, setting up bank accounts through which money was laundered by a man named Nelson Rios. He claimed hustlers were actually given pay stubs. All this would have to be investigated. If that was true, O'Malley knew that they had additional proof for a solid RICO case. Codd talked for six hours. O'Malley's hand cramped from writing. "You know sooner or later Pete would have gotten rid of you, too, right?" he asked. O'Malley was shocked that Rollock had left Codd alive. He was a soft businessman rather than a gangster, and after he had witnessed so many murders he was an easy target for law enforcement.

At the end of the interview, O'Malley had to ensure that everything was legally binding. If not, defense lawyers would destroy Codd's information. He even went so far as to write an addendum at the bottom of each page affirming that Codd had given the statement of his free will and could not claim later he'd been under duress. O'Malley made sure Codd initialed every page.

The trio returned to New York victorious. Detective Lugo appeared before the grand jury for several hours. This was another advantage of the federal system: An investigator could testify on behalf of witnesses, lessening the need to identify those worried about retaliation. The jurors came to a decision, and finally the key players of Sex Money Murder would be indicted.

But O'Malley had a sense that the public was not safe despite Rollock being behind bars in North Carolina awaiting trial.

Three

THANKSGIVING

THANKSGIVING MORNING SUGE WOKE AT around 9:00 a.m. in his girlfriend Latoya's bed, at 541 Rosedale Avenue in the back of the projects. He pulled on sweatpants and some new sneakers and went to the store. The street was thronged with kids in football gear, all anticipating the game. He ran into Green Eyes's brother, known as Blue Eyes, who had been tasked with getting Suge bullets. They stopped briefly by Green Eyes's apartment, where Suge used the bathroom. A turtle was finning around in a bucket next to the toilet. "You need to put that shit back in the river," he said to Blue Eyes's mother on his way out. Wild animals gave him the creeps.

Suge and Blue Eyes arrived at a redbrick row house on Lacombe Avenue. Inside, a white man handed them two boxes of bullets, .45-caliber and 9mm. Suge stuffed them into the hand-warmer pocket in the front of his hoodie. Back at Cozy Corner he gave a valedictory fist bump to Blue Eyes and suggested that they meet up in front of 551 Randall later in the day, just before the game.

Suge returned to Latoya's apartment and set two guns on the floor: a Colt 1911 .45 and a 9mm Smith & Wesson semiautomatic. On the back of a chair was a white bulletproof vest with a heavy ballistic plate in front. He removed his hoodie and tugged it on, then cinched it around his torso with Velcro fasteners.

Latoya woke as he was dressing and suggested he should wear her spandex leggings for the football game. "It's cold out there." As he strained to get the spandex on, she sat up. "Omigod," she said, looking at the weapons and bullets on the floor. "What's all that for?"

Suge was dismissive, and she rolled over and went back to sleep. She'd lived in Soundview long enough to know when to stop asking questions. Suge pulled on some football socks and another T-shirt, then pulled the hoodie on again. He liked the way the bulletproof vest fitted him so snugly, undetectable, as he smoothed the folds of his hoodie over it.

He tucked the 9mm into the small of his back and jammed the .45 in the pocket of his hoodie in front. Yesterday he'd sat with Green Eyes in one of the stairwells, sharing a spliff and testing the heft of the .45 in his hand. He put a bullet in the chamber and pulled back the hammer before straining over his shoulder to grab the joint, only to squeeze the trigger by accident. It left a smoking hole about the size of a quarter in his track pants and a lump of masonry on the steps.

He emerged into the kitchen, where Latoya's mother wished him luck in the game. "Make sure you come back here and get turkey afterwards."

Outside, cleats clacked on the street as players in colored jerseys made their way to the field. Some swung helmets in their fists.

Twin arrived at 2:30 p.m., dressed in a white Dallas Cowboys Deion Sanders football jersey and accompanied by his brother. Ro greeted them, watching closely for any sign that they knew about the plan as they walked to the field. Twin smiled. He wanted Ro to initiate him properly into the Bloods. "When you going to bring me home?" he said. "Make it official, you know." Pipe's brother had taken the Blood oath more seriously than anyone else and was now something of a point man for the organization. He said he would do it as soon as he could.

Twin relaxed, safe among the crew he called his own. He joked with a couple of players and moved to the center of the field, loosely throwing the ball to warm up, grinning as he tossed it back and forth with his bodyguard, E-Man.

Suge met with MAC-11 outside 1704. B-Love, architect of the plot and designated killer of the second twin, was nowhere to be found that morning. They'd have to move ahead without him. MAC-11 would go after the other twin instead. They climbed to the top of the building and looked down on Green Eyes and Ro chatting with Twin, rocking him to sleep.

+ + +

FROM HIS CAR Forcelli heard muffled cheering at a touchdown as he cruised around the horseshoe. There were at least a hundred spectators, some families with children. Cars were double-parked all over the horseshoe. A few fans held bottles of rum or drank beer from plastic cups.

Forcelli was looking for B-Love. Sex Money Murder might have become a Blood set now, but no one was stupid enough to wear red gang colors. The top Sex Money Murder lieutenants liked to move incognito. For a detective, the holiday presented an opportunity to see who might be visiting gangsters in the projects—women they were sleeping with, mothers of their children, relatives and friends. There was no one of immediate interest, and he didn't spot the men on the roof of 1704, who ducked their heads, so he kept driving and moved off to get lunch at Jack's Diner on Westchester Square.

+ + +

SUGE BOUNCED out of the apartment building and headed to the field.

It all happened in a haze of quick-moving shapes and gunshots.

Suge went back to Latoya's apartment, peeled off his clothes, slipped on some jeans and unlaced Timberlands, and put on dark glasses. An hour or so later B-Love appeared at the door. He said that Twin's brother had limped to his brother's body and desperately tried to stanch the flow of blood from a femoral artery wound. An ambulance had taken them both to Jacobi Hospital.

Suge gave B-Love the guns, and B-Love went out to get rid of them. He returned after a short period. "It's like they got the motherfuckin' National Guard out there," he said. "Shit, scene is crazy."

+ + +

FORCELLI WAS climbing the steps of the Forty-Fifth Precinct when Tirado and two other detectives burst out of the door clutching radios, shouting about a shooting in Soundview. Forcelli ran upstairs, dumped his lunch, and pulled on a bulletproof vest.

All four jumped into a minivan and took off for Soundview. A mobile phone rang. It was Bigga D. They met him on a side street. He told them Rollock had ordered the execution at a meeting of the crew. He threw out some names: B-Love, Green Eyes, and MAC-11.

The cops at the scene—largely rookies on Thanksgiving—were disorganized. One had been assigned to guard the football, lying in the middle of the field. Bloodied sweatshirts were strewn about, as were bottles of discarded liquor. The crime scene was enormous. The blood trail left by Twin ran for three hundred yards. A victim dressed in Nike cleats and a green hoodie lay dead on the path.

Forcelli learned that five men had been shot, the biggest shooting in Soundview history since Fat Mike's murder. Brass casings covered the ground like confetti after a wedding. Forcelli mingled among the crowd, trying to pick up the names of the shooters. From shards of conversations he learned that all the men who had been shot came from Castle Hill. One of them, Twin, was reputedly still clinging to life in the hospital. Forcelli suspected that an attempt might be made to finish him off in the ER.

The detectives jumped back into the minivan and headed north to Jacobi. They caught sight of a four-door sedan containing four men from Castle Hill, which they pulled over, ordering the occupants out at gunpoint and forcing them to lie on the ground. Forcelli radioed for more units. They demanded and checked IDs but failed to find guns. Other police arrived to take over.

Forcelli wasted no time heading into the ER, where the waiting area was chaos. As overwrought relatives milled around, one man hurled a garbage can across the room. More uniformed police flooded through the doors and attempted to restore calm.

Forcelli hoped that the less injured of the two twins might yield information. The doctors told him that neither brother was in any shape to talk. With the hospital secured by other cops, Forcelli drove back to the Forty-Third.

+ + +

SOMEWHERE IN all this, B-Love, Ro, and another gangster, Xavier "X" Williams, had driven up to the ER doors. X was sent inside to finish the job if he found Twin still alive.

X ran the crack trade in the Bronx River Houses and had met Pete in Rikers. The Sex Money Murder godfather had immediately offered him status, to the chagrin of Suge and everyone else who thought he spent his time "fronting" in an empty show of bravado. But Pete's ambition brooked no mercy. He told Ro in a letter that if X was suspected of bringing any feds into Soundview he was to be killed. Meanwhile, X tried to prove his fealty at every opportunity. Now he would kill Twin if Suge had failed.

He returned a few minutes later to the car to say there was no need: Twin was dead.

+ + +

SUGE CALLED Baby late in the afternoon. "Moe, I don't know if you know what's going on, but I just killed Twin," he said. "I need to get the fuck outta here." Baby said he was in Jersey City but would drive to Soundview to meet him.

Meanwhile, B-Love returned from the hospital with X and confirmed for Suge that Twin was dead. Suge nodded. He went over to Pete's grandmother's house, full of Thanksgiving revelers, and was given a plate of turkey with cranberry sauce.

Before he'd taken a mouthful, he saw that family members were chattering excitedly, handing around the telephone and talking to Pete on the other end. Shortly, it was Suge's turn. Pete already knew about Twin. "Yeah, good looking," said Pete.

"Yo, happy Thanksgiving," replied Suge.

Suge looked around to see that most of the family was of one mind—they were celebrating Twin's death and its implications for Pete. "Petey coming home soon," said one of Pete's cousins, grinning broadly. Suge believed that he had liberated Pete.

But Suge couldn't join them. He resisted conversations, gave quick answers to questions, sat by himself. He couldn't bring himself to feel joy about the killing.

After the shooting, Ro went back to a girlfriend's house and climbed into the shower, where he burst into tears. He had sacrificed a brother for Pete and the Bloods. Like Suge, he had seen the wounded look in Twin's eyes, the look of someone deceived by those he regarded as his blood brothers.

+ + +

PIPE HEADED into the dorms after his workout in the yard at Cayuga. His muscles ached as he marched in with his Blood entourage. Before taking a shower, he moved to the recreation room to tune in to the local TV news from New York.

"Thanksgiving Day massacre ... Soundview ... bloodbath." The newscaster said that two were confirmed dead after a gunman had brazenly opened fire at a football game. Other inmates from Soundview rose to their feet in disbelief. Pipe's thoughts immediately turned to Ro. Had he been killed?

The guards called a head count. After the count, and eschewing a shower, Pipe called everyone he knew at home. Unable to get through to anyone, he went to bed, his mind cartwheeling, with no answers.

+ + +

SUGE MET BABY out on the horseshoe. They quickly climbed into Baby's green sports car and drove slowly around the projects. The police were everywhere. Spotlights threw a blanket of light over the corpse of Twin's bodyguard, E-Man. Crime scene technicians in white coveralls scurried over the football field taking measurements, dropping numbered yellow plastic markers where the casings were. Suge realized that he hadn't seen his own grandmother for Thanksgiving.

Manhattan flashed by the window before they neared a row of dingy motels on the other side of the Holland Tunnel in New Jersey. Baby paid for a room. Suge threw himself on the bed. He rolled on his back, sucked on a spliff, and stared up at the ceiling. His muscles loosened and his head dulled. But still the killing replayed in his head, ending with the image of Twin's reproachful eyes.

Suge called a woman in the projects, Nikki, and persuaded her to come over and see him. He asked Baby to pay her cab fare. She arrived a short time later, breathless with news of Soundview. "They done killed Twin," she said. "It's crazy out there. It's going to be hot out there for weeks now."

She asked why he was in a motel in Jersey, but Suge shrugged the question off. Baby left the two of them alone for a while.

Baby arrived a couple of hours later to find Suge more serene. He gave Nikki money to take a cab home. Alone, the two men filled the room with marijuana smoke. They joked and laughed, slap-boxed, wrestled each other to the ground. Then they did some push-ups together to try to burn off the adrenaline. Spent, they reminisced about their childhood in Soundview. Baby laid out his plans to be a music mogul and leave the drug game behind.

And yet Baby, Suge noticed, kept leading him back to the murder, asking for ever more detailed descriptions. Baby was like a journalist working a source. Suge grew annoyed as he told the story for the eighth time. Finally, Baby let him alone. "I still love you," he said. "It ain't make no difference with us." Baby headed out in the early hours, and Suge slept deeply.

In the morning Baby came by with the paper. "They got MAC-11 on the front page," he said. Suge scanned the article, looking for his name. Already the police knew that Green Eyes was involved. He had escaped to Kingston, Baby said.

Suge was unsettled to see the coverage. He thought that this was just going to be a commonplace projects murder and that as long as he got away, he would escape any retribution. He didn't know that the homicide rate in New York City was plunging. You couldn't just kill anyone anymore and get away with it. Pete had numerous bodies, and Bemo had two, and yet neither of them had ever been convicted of murder. Suge reached the end of the story to read the last line aloud: "Police are looking for another unidentified male."

Baby interjected. "You good . . . just as long as Green Eyes and MAC don't tell on you." Suge brightened, certain that no one in Soundview would talk to the police.

✦ ✦ ✦

FORCELLI REACHED O'Malley at a family Thanksgiving dinner at his sister-in-law's house in Connecticut. He told him the news, and they talked for a few minutes about the common fate of these gangs, the inevitable turning against their own.

Forcelli hung up and got to work in the depths of the Forty-Third. But as night fell, Soundview residents, young and old, appeared in the precinct, demanding to talk to detectives. Forcelli had never experienced this. Not since the murder of Fat Mike had the community come together as one and insisted on justice. With the murder rate in decline and the police winning the war, residents wanted peace in Soundview, and this, the one day set aside for their families to relax and give thanks, had been destroyed by Sex Money Murder. Of course there was overlap between the gangsters and the residents of Soundview, and some mothers encouraged their kids to sell drugs. In some ways, some of the gang's extended family saw that Sex Money Murder's existence had benefited the community. But they had gone too far, violently desecrating their own neighborhood. The killing was affecting everyone now; all in Soundview were at risk. The code of silence that Forcelli and O'Malley had battled against their whole careers seemed to be giving way in one night.

Forcelli directed witnesses like a stationmaster on an overcrowded platform, sending them to interview rooms. Every time he sat down to conduct an interview, he was interrupted by someone else who wanted to talk. They refused to give their names, and the information wasn't crucial, but fragments helped build a larger picture. One person gave detailed descriptions of the shooters, and significantly MAC-11. Information came through on who their families might be.

In the early hours of the morning, a Hispanic girl came in and offered up what she knew. She'd been romantically involved with a number of men in Soundview and knew the inner workings of the plot. She was appalled that they would do this in front of so many people, with children present. She said that the plan was to shoot into the crowd. She was amazed more people weren't hurt.

Forcelli briefed two chiefs, Chief of Detectives Borough Bronx Charles Kammerdener and Chief of Department Louis Anemone, the third-highest officer in the NYPD, in the lieutenant's office. This was followed by some bickering about jurisdictions and who was going to control the case. Finally, Forcelli and his men won. They were going to find the killers.

Two days later, on November 29, news came in that MAC-11 had been collared in the Soundview Houses. Forcelli was needed to verify his identity. He rushed over to find the long-haired twenty-one-year-old being led out of 1686 Randall Avenue in handcuffs. He was taken to the Forty-Third, where a bevy of reporters and photographers camped outside asked if he had anything to say. "Do *you* have anything to say?" he shot back with contempt.

For three days, Forcelli had worked at the precinct following leads. Each day his wife had brought a change of clothes and some food. Finally, he returned home after MAC-11's arrest and sat at the end of the bed almost delirious from lack of sleep, looking down at his shaking hands.

+ + +

SUGE AND BABY drove to Port Authority. Suge was relieved to read that no one had identified him. He began to relax. Baby had given him ten ounces of crack and $3,500. Suge decided to take the bus to Sumter, South Carolina, where he could lie low for a while.

They parked, and both slipped on Ray-Bans and strolled the stores. "We gotta be low," said Baby. "You a hotbox out here." They bought new sneakers and Versace shades, all paid for by Baby. Suge missed his bus, so they smoked a spliff, and then Baby left him, sternly instructing Suge not to contact anyone for a while. Suge made his way into the crowds of the terminal alone.

Explicitly against Baby's advice, he paged B-Love, who called straight back. "They just snatched up MAC-11," he said. "I gotta get up outta here." Suge told him the plan for South Carolina and offered to pay for a cab to the bus station.

B-Love was there within the hour. They divided the crack in the public restrooms, ten grams each, and put it under the insoles of their sneakers. After a seventeen-hour ride they were in Sumter.

The weather there was warm, the air fragrant. Suge made his way over to his aunt's on Broad Street. Quickly his country cousins heard that their New York cousin was in town. Suge had been down a few months before to hustle some of Baby's product and already had a network set up. He handed off the crack to his cousins, who sold it on the street, returning the profits to Suge. This left Suge and B-Love free to smoke weed with his aunt all day. At first they set B-Love up with a trailer out in the country, not far from Suge's aunt's home. But B-Love freaked out. Snakes slithered under the trailer, and at night the chorus of cicadas and the gentle soughing of the wind in the palmetto trees made his skin crawl.

B-Love yearned for the Bronx and a woman he had left behind. Every day he called her, and they fought for hours. She told him that Soundview was virtually under siege: There were cops everywhere. Despite this, after a few days, B-Love decided to return and try to work it out with his girlfriend in person.

✦ ✦ ✦

FORCELLI AND the team were pressing Soundview like never before. B-Love, the leader, was the highest priority. When he returned from South Carolina in early December, a week or two after the shooting, detectives pounced. Forcelli was brought into the squad room, an open-plan floor area where detectives hammered away on typewriters and the iron bars of a cell ran alongside one wall. B-Love was combative: "I ain't have nothing to do with this bullshit." His girlfriend had provided an alibi, saying that she'd had an allergic reaction to shellfish and that B-Love had driven downtown to see her work supervisor to convince him that she was indeed sick. A search of his car revealed no weapons or drugs.

Frustrated, Forcelli had little to hold him on, so he tried another approach. "Can I look in your wallet?" he asked, mildly. He was looking for a stolen credit card, maybe a small amount of cocaine—anything to arrest him and keep him in custody. B-Love offered no resistance. As they talked, Forcelli thumbed through the wallet. He found a neatly folded piece of paper among some cash. On it were phrases written in Blood code, a few of which he could make out: "I want the Doublemint Peter Rolled" and "Blazin' Billy." Another phrase for Sex Money Murder.

Forcelli couldn't believe his eyes. Here was a letter from Pistol Pete himself ordering the murder. Forcelli had just found the holy grail. Detectives wasted no time charging B-Love with murder under state law, part of the ongoing dispute between the agencies over who had jurisdiction. Forcelli, though, was here to take the case federal. He called O'Malley and prosecutor Alexandra Shapiro and told them the news. Shapiro said that the letter was enough to charge B-Love with murder. Moreover, it proved conspiracy and validated the RICO charges they wanted to bring.

They had thirty days to indict him. The race was on to flip B-Love. If the leader of the Blood set cooperated, the investigation would rocket forward.

A few weeks later Forcelli and O'Malley sat opposite B-Love at the Southern District. They told him he was facing racketeering charges and could be eligible for the death penalty.

O'Malley didn't have to press too hard to get B-Love to cooperate. The acting head of Sex Money Murder gave curt, monosyllabic answers. But he began to talk about Rollock's murders. He revealed that Rollock sometimes referred to his killings as "wet T-shirt contests," a reference to the amount of blood that soaked his victims' clothes. Even for the Bronx, Rollock's killings, committed in broad daylight and followed by days of boasting, struck Forcelli as bizarre. B-Love confessed that in Blood code, crews now "Peter Rolled" their victims. The detectives were able to triangulate Codd's information from the proffer sessions with B-Love and then Bigga D. Forcelli disliked Codd intensely; he was slippery and conceited. He avoided the sessions with him. Yet his truthfulness was opening up the investigation, notably the murder of Anthony Dunkley.

Forcelli and Tirado drove out to the precincts and pulled the old unsolved homicide files. Tirado had located the homicide file on a John Doe found in Soundview Park who had later been identified from fingerprints. The crime scene photos showed a severely decomposed corpse, the face entirely eroded by maggots. From Codd they knew the caliber of handgun used in Dunkley's murder, and that the bullets were shot into the back of his head. They cross-referenced this with the medical examiner's report.

Forcelli lugged so many beige homicide files down to the Southern District that they filled a shopping cart. They joined a mountain of others that included files on the murders of Kato Jenkins, Karlton Hines, and Carlos Mestre.

O'Malley presented his evidence to the grand jury. He'd never seen a panel so entranced by the narrative he told.

More cooperators flipped. In April 1998, Dula, tracked to an address in Chesapeake, Virginia, was arrested. He told them about the murder of Barnes, whom Twin had killed. Forcelli pulled the homicide documents on that case, along with Frisky's murder in the club. On that case he discovered that one of the detectives working the homicide had had a relationship with the dead gangster's girlfriend, which led to furious recriminations at the US attorney's office. The cops and the gangsters were often drawn from the same neighborhoods; situations like this were inevitable.

Most nights when they finished, the team ate together at a Chinese restaurant near the courthouse—all but O'Malley, who preferred to spend a few more hours at the office.

Back at the US attorney's office, the proffers with B-Love continued. He admitted to O'Malley everything he had done, and on April 21, 1998, he signed a cooperation agreement. In the process he described to O'Malley a turbulent, wildly unpredictable gunman known as Suge.

+ + +

SUGE THREW himself into gang life in South Carolina with his cousins. One day he was sitting in the car waiting for one of them when the man dragged his half-naked girlfriend outside by her hair, having caught her cheating. A day or so later, they armed themselves and drove to the Waffle House in a strip mall in the early hours to ambush and kill the guy she'd been with. When he didn't show, they drove around for a while, got picked up by the police, and were arrested for illegal gun possession. Suge used a fake ID, and a relative bailed him out for $5,000. He took to the road again soon after. He went to New York first, then up to Springfield, where he blooded in some young men and arguably established the first Blood set in the city. He was restless and edgy, and heard from old contacts that Damon Mullins, the twin who had survived, was coming after him.

Rudderless, he drifted back to New York and into the arms of Latoya. The two went skating in Rockefeller Center, holding hands. He was trying to forget his troubles among New Yorkers and tourists in thick scarves and berets, all of them oblivious to the killer with the gun in his waistband, gingerly making circles among them.

BUT THEN Suge's aunt, panicked and angry, called him from South Carolina. A homicide squad had kicked in her door at dawn in a raid, looking for him. Armed men had told her that her nephew was a highly dangerous gang member wanted for a brutal execution in the Bronx. They turned her place upside down and forced Suge's cousins against the wall at gunpoint.

Suge's aunt told him that the police had information that he was armed and willing to shoot police rather than be captured. Suge knew that the only person who would have known where he had been was B-Love, who was now telling O'Malley everything. Suge's aunt warned him never to come back to South Carolina. Once more, Suge hit the road.

Four

"MAKE IT REIGN"

AT MIDNIGHT, DEEP IN THE prison dormitory sometime in mid-December, Pipe wrote to Pete in Blood code sitting in a pool of light thrown by a lamp clipped to his cot. The shock waves of the Thanksgiving murders were still reverberating through Soundview. The betrayal by Sex Money Murder of their Castle Hill brethren had reignited long-dormant prejudices between the neighboring projects. The Castle Hill gangsters said there would be a "bloodbath" in reprisal against Soundview. Pete and Twin's partnership under the aegis of Sex Money Murder had once united the projects, but now they were at war. A letter appeared in Soundview from Pete that had "Twin RIP" scrawled upside down: a disrespect to show he was pleased at his former partner's murder. Some said that there would be retaliation against Pete's mother, news that reached Pipe in prison. Pipe warned Pete in a letter: "In Deathro is that 550 101 Blazing Billy had thick like quicks flip the clip, so Bear only got one skyline 102 that the word is Dusteater Number #2 is going after Number One." Translation: The word in New York is that the First Superior of Sex Money Murder has put out a hit on the remaining twin because he is going after your family.

Pipe added that he hadn't read Machiavelli's *The Prince* and Sun Tzu's *Art of War* for nothing. He ended his letter with a declaration of loyalty: "I don't give a fuck what we go thru I'll always love you." He signed the letter "VP AKA The Gorgeous Gangsta!" Pipe had had the phrase tattooed across his midriff by a convict who had made a tattoo gun with the motor from a Walkman. He signed off: "Thug life. Always and 4Ever!"

Pipe had begun to sense a sadness and longing in Pete's letters: The Sex Money Murder leader was alone and missed Pipe and his loyal lieutenants. He had always had Bear or Big Ant or one of them around to follow his orders and act as an extension of his ego.

Pete received Pipe's letter with glee. On December 28, 1997, he wrote a reply. It was never sent.

✦ ✦ ✦

FORCELLI TOLD the North Carolina investigators that Peter Rollock was ordering hits by letter. Bevins and Tadeo applied for intercepts to read all Rollock's incoming and outgoing mail.

On December 29, carrying a warrant, they entered the Charlotte-Mecklenburg cells to search Rollock's possessions. They were accompanied by a lone deputy, in case Rollock turned violent. Bevins made sure not to turn his back on Sex Money Murder's twenty-three-year-old leader.

But Rollock, wearing round-rimmed glasses, rose to his feet politely when they arrived. They asked him to step out of his cell where they handcuffed him. Tadeo informed him that any materials concerning his case would be returned but that the rest would be taken. Rollock nodded obligingly.

The officers entered a meticulously neat cell. Under the bed were several transparent plastic bins containing fifty-one letters, most received, some unsent. There were address books and documents—one a fact sheet about STDs—and fifty-three photographs.

One handwritten document was a list of black civil rights leaders, including Booker T. Washington and W. E. B. Du Bois. The officers gleaned that Rollock saw himself not as a murderous drug dealer but as a leader, rising up to claim what was his at the head of a small army bent on economic emancipation.

Bevins pulled out letters from Rollock's father in prison. He told his son to be a strong black male and not to talk to the police. He extolled the power of black culture and told him to "look after black women."

In an unsent letter Rollock had written to his half brother, he urged him not to get involved in the drug game. He also hinted at his high-level entertainment connections. "I don't know if daddy told you before I got locked up me a Tyson Beckford (The model) was going half and half on a record label, I also had Puff Daddy and Biggie Smalls do a few shows for me."

He added: "When I come home I will start all over to build a family business. I want to put something together for all our family that is so tight, none of our loved ones will have to struggle. Again, you are of age now, and can be a big part of this, but you must stay out of jail, don't make the same mistakes me and Daddy made, stay in school and get a profession, knowledge is power. I want you to always remember this no matter how long our father has been away from us, we are blessed, if we stay close to him we will be ahead in life, remember that."

Another, to his girlfriend, scolded her for abandoning him in his hour of need.

And finally there were pages of Rollock's self-mythologizing rap songs that extolled a "ghetto celebrity, young rich and deadly" who "wore enough ice to make the average motherfucker shiver." Rollock railed against snitches: "spending G's on a bitch instead of trine get rich; flip a few bricks, niggers snitch, Sign a plea like a bitch, that's why I keep my circle tight." He went on to rhapsodize about cars—Mercedes-Benz and NSX—and his sexual prowess: "Dick harder than a broom ready to rip a bitches womb."

Bevins and Tadeo were looking for proof of the Sex Money Murder enterprise. They found it in the songs: "Makin moves nigga, you hesitate and you lose, bust my Gun paid my dues, paved the way for my crew. I made move's Nigga you hesitate and your history. I'm a Sex Money Murder Motherfucker till the death of me."

In the letters, Rollock detailed orders for Green Eyes to carry out one of the murders on Thanksgiving, among other key facts. And there was a letter to a gangster called Pipe.

Finally, they started to work through the photographs. Midway through, they found a picture of Rollock flanked by two celebrities. On one side stood Tyson Beckford. On the other, dressed in a red top and blue jeans, with a slender, bare midriff, was the model Tyra Banks.

+ + +

IN JANUARY 1998, O'Malley found the man at the top of one of Forcelli's charts; John Castro, incarcerated at Otisville, in upstate New York. O'Malley had put out a warrant for his arrest, but Castro ended up getting picked up in Florida, in possession of a large amount of drugs, under the pseudonym Orin Johnson.

O'Malley drove to the prison and gave Castro his spiel. After Castro consulted with his lawyer, he flipped, too, confessing to murders in which he had had a hand. At Jimmy's Bar in the Bronx, he had shot a man who helped himself to beers behind the bar. On another occasion he hired a hit man to take out a man selling drugs on a Washington Heights block. Castro drove the hit man to the scene, but when he hopped out of the car to deliver summary justice, he pressed the magazine release on the gun and the magazine went clattering to the sidewalk. Castro leapt in front of him and ended up killing the drug dealer himself. Castro offered a detailed insight into the Sex Money Murder hierarchy and the murder of Barnes, for which he had offered any potential killers a bounty.

By February, O'Malley and Bob Ryan, the dogged financial investigator, also born in the Bronx, were beginning to map out Sex Money Murder's finances. On Ryan's wall in his office was an IRS recruitment poster of Al Capone that declared: "Only an accountant could catch Al Capone."

Ryan knew from Codd that the gang had a bank account and that they had even incorporated. Codd produced a pay stub from which Ryan was able to track down the account. Through that, and with Codd's help, Ryan was able to identify the Castle Hill man and Sex Money Murder associate Nelson Rios. He had been arrested by Secret Service agents, who had found a handgun, and counterfeiting material on various computers, at his house. Rios was out on bail when Ryan and O'Malley arrested him again and took him to the Forty-Fifth Precinct. O'Malley rolled his sleeves up and flipped his chair around in the interview room to face him, while Ryan laid out some of Rios's forged documents on the table. "We know what you did," said O'Malley. "And this man here is an IRS investigator. This is a federal racketeering case. You're in big trouble."

Ryan had never seen anyone flip so quickly. Information poured out—he admitted that money in SMM accounts was laundered drug money—as he tapped his feet and fidgeted. When they left the interview room for a break, O'Malley joked: "We could put a pair of drumsticks in his hands and he'd be beating out a tune for us!"

Rios explained how the gang had incorporated as SMMC Inc. and about the corporate paychecks. Rios had been clever enough to pay in amounts of less than $10,000, known as "structuring." Anything above that and the bank would ask for his Social Security number and job, and the money would automatically trigger a Currency Transaction Report (CTR) to the IRS, inviting scrutiny. Structuring payments to avoid CTRs in this way was a federal crime under the Money Laundering Control Act of 1986. It was a textbook method for cleaning drug money; but Rios's efficiency had merely provided a paper trail for Ryan.

In May 1998, Ryan flew to Pittsburgh, where he learned how the gang had laundered money by overpaying on car leases, part of the scam with Three Rivers Leasing. The dealership had avoided filing IRS 8300 forms reporting cash payments over $10,000 and had also made sure none of the gang members' names appeared on lease paperwork in case they were stopped by police.

Ryan's investigation would deepen, ensnaring more in the Bronx underworld who worked with SMM. Ryan arrested Harry Miranda, a Bronx playboy involved in real estate who secured stash houses for Codd and some of the others in the crew. Shelton "Kooly" Smith ran a clothing and fashion design business in Maryland. He was arrested for buying cocaine and heroin from SMM and opening pipelines in Maryland and also for his involvement with SMM bank accounts. Ryan confiscated his clothing business, a Lincoln Navigator, and a Honda CRX, among other assets. As Ryan plunged into SMM and its network of affiliates, he seized about $2 million in assets.

As more Sex Money Murder members cooperated, Ryan was brought in on the proffer sessions. Introduced as a special agent, he gave his own short spiel and said that lawyers' fees were not covered by attorney-client privilege, and any funds derived from narcotics proceeds or any other illegal activity as defined by the Money Laundering Act of 1986 could be subject to foreiture. The lawyers in the room looked at their shoes.

+ + +

SUGE STOLE back into New York City sometime in January 1998, visited a woman he knew in Queens, then went to a tattoo parlor there to get *SMM* inked on his right pectoral muscle in rounded copperplate. That same month, he learned that Rollock had been convicted at trial of drug trafficking and that Codd, TV Dave, and many others had testified against him. Codd had tried to back out at the last minute, but Detective Lugo and others convinced him to take the stand. Pete would be sentenced in a few months. Finally, Pete's run seemed to be over.

In the Bronx, Suge linked up with Bemo, who told him that everything had changed, that the feds and the police were everywhere. Bemo said he had a solution. They could find a new future in Cleveland, where Suge had been once before. Bemo said that the city had a black mayor and that it was a good place to sell drugs and get rich without too much police harassment.

They decided to make a run. Suge smoked weed the whole way to settle his nerves, but the pair sniped constantly. Both were anxious. They set up a base in an apartment on 116th Street in downtown Cleveland through a connection of Bemo's. In between crack sales they watched movies and picked up women at an after-hours club.

On April 10, 1998, they learned that Pete had been sentenced to forty years for drug trafficking in North Carolina. He would be lucky to get out of prison in his sixties.

Suge broke down in tears. Murdering Twin hadn't freed Pete. It had made no difference. "He did it to himself, man," said Bemo. Pete had gotten greedy. Worse, in Bemo's eyes, the only thing Pete gave him after he killed Kiron was a gun. "Go and rob someone," Pete had told him. "Fuck the Pistol," Bemo said. "He ain't never given me nothing."

With $6,000 in his pocket, Suge decided to return to Springfield. He moved around for a few days and then hooked up with a cousin of his old flame Gina. She took him to an apartment opposite a liquor store in the southeastern part of town. One day Suge tried to call Latoya in her apartment on Rosedale Avenue from the landline in the apartment. There was no answer. He had no way of knowing that ATF agents were standing in her apartment interviewing her and were now writing down the Springfield number that came up on caller ID. The agents called Rob Berger at the Southern District, who traced it.

The next day at around 1:45 p.m., Suge heard dogs barking downstairs. Gina's cousin told him to lie down and ignore it. Suge, worn out from hours of lovemaking, lay back and closed his eyes. Then he heard a knock on the door. Gina's cousin went to answer it.

✦ ✦ ✦

A SMALL team of law enforcement officers, including two US Marshals and ATF agents Jim Markowski and Tom Lyster, had taken positions around the building with rifles drawn. An agent knocked at the door. A young woman he assumed to be around eighteen opened the door a crack. Lyster stuck his foot in the door and demanded to know who was upstairs. When she said that her boyfriend and a friend of his from the Bronx were in the house, Lyster charged through the door past her while officers behind him led her away. At the top of the stairs they found a man wandering around. He was pulled out and handcuffed. Two agents entered the apartment; another agent covered the door. The two men expertly cleared the room before moving to the bedroom.

✦ ✦ ✦

SUGE HEARD a boom as a door crashed open somewhere in the house. "Get the fuck down," he heard from a room next door. Instinctively he remembered the guns in the bedside drawer and, for a split second, considered shooting his way out. He made his way over to the window, saw the twenty-foot drop, and thought about it before he caught sight of armed police outside.

His will to fight evaporated. He gave up and sat with his head against the bed's headboard, arms folded. Agents burst into the room to find a twentyish African American male dressed in a brand-new blue Adidas sweatsuit. "'Sup?" said Suge with mock puzzlement. "What's this all about?" The men tore him out of bed and threw him against the wall, fastening handcuffs that bit into his wrists.

Outside, they demanded his ID. Suge asked them to loosen the cuffs before tugging out his wallet. It contained the fake license that had worked in South Carolina. Handing it over, he said he was up from South Carolina visiting friends. The men looked him up and down. Suge thought he was in with a chance because he hadn't been put in a car yet.

Then one of the marshals put the warrant picture next to Suge's face. "Nah, that's him," he said. "Your run is over." They pulled up his shirt and caught sight of the SMM tattoo on his chest. "Sex Money Murder, huh?" said the marshal.

✦ ✦ ✦

IN JAIL, Suge slept more soundly than he had in years. For cops it's a truism that the guilty sleep after arrest. In some sense Suge was relieved to be off the street, where he wasn't going to be shot or arrested anymore. The following day, he refused to tell a judge his real name, thinking he could still slip out of the noose.

He was remanded without bail. A day later he was transported to a federal prison in New Hampshire.

The austere and highly regimented atmosphere was nothing like the state prisons he had been in before. He asked one of the marshals what was going on. "I'm not going to lie to you," he said. "You're not gonna see the streets anytime soon. A lot of y'all are facing the death penalty." Suge screwed up his face in disbelief.

The following day he was driven to an airstrip where an unmarked plane sat on the tarmac, surrounded by vans with flashing blue lights. Shackled in a "three-piece suit"—leg restraints and a belly chain that his hands were fastened to—Suge was escorted up the steps and into the bowels of the plane. This wasn't the sort of treatment they gave prisoners in the New York State system. Inside, as he was marched to the back, he saw a familiar face. There, in an orange jumpsuit, sat Pete, although much thinner than Suge remembered him. "Yo, what up, Moe!" Pete laughed. Suge felt that there was little to celebrate. "I'll talk to you when we get off the plane, man," he said irritably as he shuffled past.

Rows of inmates were shackled to the floor. In the back, Suge was manacled to a chair armrest and the floor. One of the other convicts muttered something about only the marshals having parachutes if the plane went down. Suge leaned back and went to sleep.

He awoke in New York, where they disembarked and he was placed in a van with Pete. "Yo, what the fuck is up?" asked Suge. "You know B-Love's telling, right?"

Pete was calm. "Ah, man, we gonna find everything out. Don't worry about it." He smiled. "You happy to see me, man?" Pete tried to introduce Suge to some other Bloods in the van. "I'm not not with that shit right now," Suge stormed. "I'm facing some real bullshit here." The Bloods were riled at the disrespect, but Pete placated them.

The van moved along the Brooklyn waterfront and past empty warehouses and cracked asphalt lots. Then the Metropolitan Detention Center loomed into view. Once inside, Suge surrendered himself to paranoia. His progression from kid in the projects to twenty-four-year-old gangster, enemy of the state, was now complete. The processing lasted until the early hours of the morning, prolonged by Suge's furious outbursts and refusal to follow orders. He refused to be fingerprinted. They asked Suge for his federal ID number. Suge said he couldn't remember it. Pete stepped in smoothly and calmed him. "C'm on, Moe, please?" Suge settled down when he discovered that he and Pete were to be housed in the same block.

A few hours later, they had their first court appearance. It was May 7, 1998. Suge went next door to Pete's cell. He was holding everyone up as he primped and fussed, brushing his hair with short, vigorous strokes to make it shine. "A hundred strokes make 'em poke," Pete said with a wink. While Pete preened, MAC-11 approached Suge on the landing outside Pete's cell. Suge hadn't seen him since Thanksgiving Day.

Suge called Pete out of his cell to introduce them. Pete wore a pair of Cazal glasses, just one of the five pairs he had with him, and which he would wear in court to give him a bookish air. Pete greeted them like an emperor giving an audience. "Yo, Pete, this is the one that put that work in," said Suge. Pete embraced MAC-11. "Don't worry about all this," Pete told him. "Together we stand, divided we fall." Suge saw MAC-11 beam, radiant to have met his idol.

They were strip-searched and placed in a van going to the "Mother Court," the Southern District of New York's Daniel P. Moynihan Courthouse on Foley Square. The van drove to the south side of the building on Pearl Street between the courthouse and the Metropolitan Correctional Center. Steel shutters opened electronically, and the van proceeded to an elevator that dropped three stories into the basement. When the doors opened again, the van moved forward into a concrete subterranean enclosure and then onto a large black steel plate. The van revolved 180 degrees on the steel plate before it backed up to a small door. Everything the prisoners did or said was recorded by multiple cameras connected to a bank of twenty or so monitors deep in a darkened room on the fourth floor. All conversations were noted by the marshals.

Suge and Pete bunny-hopped in their chains to general holding cells. There, handcuffed but without leg restraints, they got on another elevator, which took them to the fourteenth floor. They stepped out facing two cages in a small confined area of bleached white stone and reinforced concrete with a speckled floor, known as the bullpen. Herded into one of the cages, Suge took a seat on a gray plastic bench against a wall. A low steel partition offered some modesty for prisoners who wanted to avail themselves of the brushed steel toilet against another wall. Housed in the other cage were Ro, Total Package, and several other members of Sex Money Murder, along with Pete's uncle George Wallace. All had been swept up by the feds.

After a while, the marshals unlocked the prisoners and swung open the six-inch-thick oak door that led into the wood-paneled courtroom.

As the prisoners shuffled in, defense attorneys gathered to watch. Pete led his crew in a flamboyant pimp roll. Their footfalls were deadened by the deep, royal blue carpet. Pete's father had walked into these courtrooms to be convicted under the RICO statutes. Now, a generation later, his son was facing justice in the same courts. There were so many gangsters that they were led to the jury box rather than the defense tables.

The courtroom was full of people from Soundview, women in low-cut tops with freshly painted nails, who greeted the men as if they were rock stars. The prisoners were so unruly that each had two marshals assigned to supervise him. "No talking in the courtroom!" they ordered. Suge looked at a marshal with contempt. "Get the fuck outta here! The judge ain't even here yet." Gone were the impeccable manners of the Mafia dons the marshals had once escorted. Suge and the crew carried on talking while their lawyers came over. Suge was approached by a saturnine man who introduced himself as Martin Siegel. Suge disliked his quiet manner, his detachment.

The court rose as Judge Miriam Goldman Cedarbaum, a diminutive woman with an empathetic expression who had a reputation as a relatively liberal judge, took her seat. She asked the marshals to remove the defendants' handcuffs. Slowly and methodically, she asked each defendant to stand. With conversational warmth, she asked each of them a bit about themselves: jobs they had worked and their level of education. Rollock spoke first but mugged at some young women in the back while he did so. When Suge's turn came, he claimed he had dropped out of school in eleventh grade—even though it was the ninth grade—adding that he had achieved a GED while incarcerated in Massachusetts.

The procedure wound on; Suge barely paid attention until the reality of his fate was confirmed. "As the Court is aware from the previous superseder," said the prosecutor, Alexandra Shapiro, "there are some defendants who are death-eligible, and several of the new defendants are death-eligible as well."

Cedarbaum asked, "Yes, who are those?"

As the prosecutor read off Pete's and Suge's names, there was an audible gasp from the Soundview contingent. A chill spread over Suge's skin.

He looked at Pete, who stared serenely ahead. Pete's charges numbered twenty-eight counts: racketeering, murder, kidnapping, tampering with a witness, and the use of a machine gun in furtherance of some of these crimes. Suge faced eight counts including murder, racketeering, and kidnapping. He couldn't understand why they were thinking about executing him. He'd seen people get murdered his whole life, and nothing much had happened to the killers. Even Fat Mike's killer got life in the state prison, not the death penalty, and that was for three bodies. "Twin got two bodies!" Suge raged at his lawyer. "He a killer. They gonna murder me for rocking him?"

✦ ✦ ✦

WITH THE MAIN Sex Money Murder players in custody, O'Malley and the team widened the net. Tyson Beckford's name kept coming up in proffers as a close associate of Pete's. The detectives couldn't understand how somebody so successful could be caught up in this. They brought him in. Tyson arrived with a lawyer, Eddie Hayes, dressed in a pin-striped Savile Row suit. Hayes had celebrity connections with everyone from Robert De Niro to Anna Wintour. The lawyer had come in alone a few days before and asked what charges his client faced. O'Malley said that there were no charges; they just wanted to talk. Beckford knew they had nothing on him. O'Malley showed him to one of the proffer rooms, where Forcelli, the prosecutor, and Benny Tirado awaited him. Tyson tried to pat down Tirado, who told him in no uncertain terms to keep his hands to himself. Beckford had a tattoo on his neck that seemed to reference Sex Money Murder. O'Malley threw out a few questions. Beckford said that he and Pete shared an interest in motorcycles. When O'Malley mentioned the murder, racketeering, and drug charges against Rollock, Beckford gave a speech about Pete's virtue and his contributions to his community.

O'Malley had no aces to play. Beckford asked, with a wry grin at O'Malley, "Anything else?" The investigators shook their heads.

O'Malley walked him to the elevator but couldn't hold his tongue. "Listen, that was a nice little dog and pony show in there," he said.

"Hopefully me and you will see each other again—maybe next time you'll be here with handcuffs on."

Beckford smiled and looked his questioner directly in the face. "You got the wrong guy, man," he said. "All I do all day is fuck Tyra Banks and lift weights." The elevator door opened, and Beckford and his lawyer vanished.

✦ ✦ ✦

ONE EVENING a few weeks later, Forcelli and Tirado strolled into the Sports Plus Cafe on Castle Hill Avenue like two sheriffs entering a Wild West saloon. They pulled up stools on one side of the bar. On the other were scowling Sex Money Murder members. O'Malley thought Forcelli took a risk sitting at a bar with gangsters who favored sneaking up on their victims and shooting them in the back of the head. But Forcelli wanted to send the message that he was unafraid, that there would be no sanctuary for gangsters. He scorned Rollock as a coward for shooting unarmed men. Forcelli's rolled-up sleeves revealed thick, muscled forearms adorned with ink. Over several years he had added dragons, snakes, a tiger, and St. Michael, the patron saint of police.

Ignoring the sneers across the bar, the detectives laughed about the previous week's arrest at the Bronx courthouse. They had targeted Pete's cousin Cheo White, who was still out on the street, thumbing his nose at the cops. If Forcelli arrested him, it would send a clear message to the neighborhood that the police were coming for all of them. They snatched him on the other side of a metal detector after he'd taken his belt off to go through. Cheo thrust his hands in the air when the cops pounced, only to have his pants drop to his ankles, revealing that he wore no underwear, eliciting ribald laughter from everyone around.

O'Malley and Forcelli had created an extensive list of SMM members, and as information continued to flood out of proffers they were able to cross-reference crimes and hierarchical positions in the group.

More arrests followed. They'd made it a priority to go after the most violent offenders or anyone Rollock could use to kill cooperating witnesses. Pipe's brother Ro was one of the most dangerous and ardent of his followers. When they learned he was being held on a parole violation at the Bronx House of Detention, Forcelli turned up and arrested him on a federal warrant. Ro assumed he was being taken to a precinct to be interviewed, but once they crossed over into Manhattan and started to speed south down the FDR Drive he panicked. "Where you taking me, man?" he demanded. Forcelli told him the case was going federal. At first Ro didn't believe him, but as they neared the Metropolitan Correctional Center and the court complex, he slumped. He knew what federal time meant.

As the detectives talked in the bar, they struggled to hear each other against the rising volume of the bar's sound system. The song "One Life to Live," from the album *Make It Reign* by Soundview rappers Lord Tariq and Peter Gunz, echoed around the bar. The rappers had finally made it big, despite not being signed by Puff Daddy. Their album was an undisguised homage to Pistol Pete, Sex Money Murder, and Soundview. When Pete was arrested, Lord Tariq had made a very public gesture of unclasping his $25,000 Rolex and handing it to Pete's mom as a gift. Now the song's words pounded into the detectives' ears:

You got one life to live, one gun to bust.

The chorus built to the kicker:

It's all about sex, money, life or death.

Five

BANGIN' FOR THEIR RATS

BACK IN THE METROPOLITAN DETENTION CENTER in Brooklyn, Pete and Suge took over the dormitory in Four South. The prison held a maximum of 1,861 inmates. One new inmate called it "snitch central," the last stop before cutting a deal with the feds or trying to beat the government at trial.

Suge got a job buffing the recreation deck's floor and put in a word for Pete, who began cleaning the warden's office. But within weeks Pete was having sex with one staff member and arranging for another to smuggle his letters out.

On darker days Pete seethed about Codd and B-Love's cooperation. "We need to whack their moms, yo," he said. "Send a message." On days like that he talked about a master plan. "We're going out with a bang," he declared. "We're going to run the prisons like we did the streets. We're going out like ghetto celebrities!"

Suge wondered whether Pete had planned all along to get everyone in prison with him so he wouldn't have to face the time alone.

After supper one night, Suge and Pete's conversation turned to Twin. Pete froze when Suge asked about Twin's role as a snitch. Suge said he had thought that by killing Twin they would allow Pete to walk free, but then here they all were. It had made no difference. Pete paused, crossed his legs leisurely, and then pushed his glasses up his nose. "Yeah, that was a bad call."

What the fuck? Suge thought. *A bad call?* He'd thrown his life away for *a bad call*? Pete seemed to be intimating that Twin wasn't a snitch.

Wordlessly, Suge pulled on his headphones, stuck his hands in his sweatpants, and shuffled back to his bunk. Never did they discuss it again.

For days he brooded over how he'd been played, used to kill a man who wasn't a rat. He felt completely trapped. The code was that he be loyal to Sex Money Murder, but the code had failed him, had deceived him. Pete had played him like a pawn.

Suge increasingly gave himself over to gratification from violence. One evening a Jamaican gangster called Ras was using the phone longer than allowed. "You on my time," Suge complained, but Ras ignored him. Suge persisted. "You done, son?" The Jamaican turned to Suge. "Go suck your mother!"

Suge swallowed it and forced himself to think tactically, as Pete had taught him. "Okay, man," he said, and raised his hands in a placatory gesture. "No problem."

Suge stalked back to the dormitory formulating a plan. If he'd had a knife or a shiv he would have buried it deep in Ras's guts. Back at his bunk he spotted his neighbor's combination padlock. He could put it in a sock and use it as a cosh.

Suge tested the weight of the lock in the sock. He tried various lengths to see how it might best swing. He shortened it up so that he could swing fast but with enough slack that the momentum would carry through. Suge stuffed the weapon in the pocket of his sweatpants. Ras strutted past. "Dat pussy ras-clat push me for di phone," he laughed to his bunkmate, climbing into his top bunk.

When the lights went out, Suge crept out of his bunk and moved up beside the Jamaican's. He whirled the lock down on the man's forehead with a crack. Metal on bone. *A perfect one-shot,* thought Suge, *straight-up sniper shit.* The Jamaican jumped to his feet screaming, "Murda! Murda!" Suge swung at his legs trying to hit him again.

Guards ran in. Suge tossed the bloody sock on Ras's bunk before guards knocked him to the floor. Handcuffed, he was made to sit cross-legged as paramedics tried to revive the Jamaican, who was drifting in and out of consciousness. The sheets on his bed were soaked with blood.

The assistant warden entered the fray and asked Ras, who came to groggily, who had hit him. He pointed at Suge. Standing at the back of the dorm, Pete gave Suge a smile. "Good work," he said. Suge found himself in the hole. Pete sent him batteries for his Walkman and again passed on his compliments though a prison officer. "I was told to tell you that Pete said that was a good shot," the officer said.

Suge was charged with assault, which carried another five years, but he no longer cared. He was considered so disruptive, particularly when he was emboldened by consorting with his SMM brothers, that he was moved to the county jail in Passaic, New Jersey. He found the regime there slightly more relaxed, so he took advantage and blooded in a couple of inmates. Sometime during his stay he received a letter from prosecutors saying they would not file a death notice against him and the other defendants in the case. (Suge's charges were death-eligible, but prosecutors had to check with Main Justice in DC before they could file a death notice, normally done just before trial. Prosecutors did, however, receive permission from Main Justice to file the death notice against Pete.)

Suge was soon in trouble again. He talked back to a guard, and a fight broke out. New Bloods jumped in to back him up. Suge was taken to a hospital off-site, where he received twelve stitches in his upper lip. The next day in court, Pete and Ro teased him about his giant lip in the holding cell. They said he looked like a duck. Suge pouted and began shouting so loudly that Forcelli could hear him even in the public gallery on the other side of the heavy oak door. Forcelli was there to monitor the proceedings and to protect the judge, court officials, or anyone in the public gallery if things got out of hand. His street informants had said there were death threats against Judge Cedarbaum and the prosecutors; some were even ordering up Santeria hexes on the detectives.

In court Suge defied the marshals and growled at anyone who spoke to him. He stomped the floor demanding medical attention. At the end of the proceedings when the marshals approached he shouted, "Y'all can go get the motherfuckin' goon squad. I ain't goin' nowhere. Look what they done to my lip, man. I ain't going back to Jersey. Motherfuckin' police tried to kill me in there!" He said he wanted to be in MCC with his codefendants.

Out of habit, O'Malley sat at the back of the courtroom near the door.

It offered a prime vantage point for everything unfolding in court—who attended in the public gallery and who the defendants waved at, which often offered leads. He could also read the faces of the jury. O'Malley took a personal dislike to Suge, with his temper tantrums and his fervent allegiance to Pete and SMM. Marshals were coming in from other courts to deal with him. Suge's lawyer made a request to Judge Cedarbaum that he be moved. Finally, the judge took pity on him and allowed him to be transferred to the Metropolitan Correctional Center attached to the courthouse. As he was led out of court, Suge felt the eyes of the white man in the back lingering on him. Looking at Suge, O'Malley thought to himself: *This one's going down hard, and he's going down all the way.*

✦ ✦ ✦

WITHIN TWO weeks at MCC Suge landed in trouble again. Moved to 11 North, Suge and a Sex Money Murder inmate called Scruff extorted commissary from other inmates with threats of violence. Suge was sent to the hole for a few days.

There he met another old friend. Fresh from testifying in North Carolina, Codd had been placed in the Special Housing Unit for his own protection. Suge had fostered a relationship with a guard who he suspected had Blood affiliation. Many guards were adherents of the anti-snitch rhetoric. "Put me up on L tier," said Suge. "My rat up there."

On Suge's way to a shower, the guard unshackled him and let him wander to Codd's cell. On the other side of some thick Plexiglas, Codd sat on the bed. "What's good?" said Suge, pressing his face up against the glass. Codd looked at him with a hollow gaze. "Come to the door, man," said Suge from the other side. Codd sensed the threat. "It's over," he said in defeat. "There's only one way out of this." Suge shook his head in disgust. Suge was no rat. He knocked on the glass and then, thwarted, made for the shower.

Meanwhile, Suge called his attorney relentlessly. He demanded the lawyer work a plea deal to get him a fifteen- or twenty-five-year sentence. His lawyer explained the federal system of mandatory minimums and said the prosecutors would not budge. "Look," he said. "You still got multiple charges for murder, conspiracy . . . If you commit an act of violence in furtherance of an enterprise—and you still have all these counts here—you're going to jail for thirty years minimum, probably life. And there's no parole in the federal system." Going through discovery submitted by the government, Suge looked at photographs of the bloodied white football jersey Twin had worn when he murdered him. And he saw the blood-caked pants that indicated Suge had hit an artery in his leg. The same images, and worse, would be presented to the jury.

The court appearances came and went. In what had now become routine, Suge was led through multiple doors in the MCC to the basement, where he was passed from prison staff to federal marshals. They hopped, clanked, and stutter-stepped through a long tunnel some forty feet below Pearl Street, under the footsteps of commuters on their way to work on Wall Street. Officers in distant surveillance stations watched through cameras and opened and closed the doors remotely. At the end of the corridor was an elevator that took them to the courthouse cells.

But while Suge was steadfast in his support of Pete, the godfather of Sex Money Murder was cutting a lonelier figure at each court appearance. The jury box began to empty around him. An absent seat meant an erstwhile stalwart had decided to cooperate. One day it was TP. A few weeks later in the bullpen, just before court, George Wallace confided in his nephew that he was terrified and couldn't do any jail time. "Hey, Petey," he whispered, looking around at MAC-11 and the others. "I don't know these kids. You gotta get me up outta this, man. I got nothing to do with this stuff with you and these guys." Rollock stared at him blankly. "I told you to kill Codd," persisted Wallace. "If you'd have done what I said we wouldn't be here." He paused. "I will make sure your son is a millionaire and I'll take care of your lawyers. Just keep me off this."

Pete looked his uncle up and down. "I ain't going to do the government's job for them."

The next court appearance saw another empty seat in the jury box. Wallace was cooperating. Suge began to see the silver-haired detective O'Malley as a specter who snatched his brothers away.

Suge and Ro ran their tier like OGs. They controlled the phones, stole gold chains from other inmates, and responded to any challenge with violence, Suge slashing one inmate with a shard from a razor blade. They were mentored by the six-foot-seven gangster Clarence "the Preacher" Heatley, also under federal indictment with his Preacher Crew. "You two are real gangsters," he said. "I like that."

Both the young men were familiar with the legend of the Preacher on the streets of the Bronx. So called because of his oratorical powers, the Preacher was known in the Harlem and Bronx communities he controlled as "the Black Hand of Death" after at least thirteen murders, largely drug dealers who defaulted on "rent" he demanded to sell in his territory. Once he took two drug dealers to the basement of an apartment building at 2075 Grand Concourse, the crew's headquarters, held a mock trial, and had them both strangled to death. The killings were carried out and supervised by a housing cop, John Cuff, who helped to dismember the victims with a circular saw.

Preacher told Suge the story of how in April 1993 he kidnapped the singer Bobby Brown, husband to Whitney Houston. As Houston's star was rising, Brown had sunk into cocaine addiction and owed $25,000 to a dealer in New Jersey. Preacher bought the debt and had his men feed Brown top-quality cocaine in a New York nightclub before luring him to a Bronx apartment. There he was knocked out and awoke "naked and hog tied." The Preacher beat him until he called his famous wife demanding that she bring $400,000 in cash to settle the debt. According to the newspapers, disguised in a wig and dark glasses she brought the money the next day.

As the Violent Crimes Unit continued to lacerate gangs in New York City and more members found themselves in the MCC, former foes united over one common enemy: cooperators. The Latin Kings approached Rollock and offered a trade-off: They'd attack and try to kill Sex Money Murder's rats, and SMM would do the same for them. Some Latin Kings were onto Green Eyes as a snitch. Pete surprised his acolytes with his stance. "We stand on our own, man. We grew up from the sandbox together," he stated. "Ain't nobody touch no Sex Money Murder rats."

Suge and Ro heard that the Kings were going to get Green Eyes sometime during recreation in the open-air, steel-cage-enclosed basketball
court on top of the MCC. In preparation Suge, Ro, and Preacher went
to the roof with hidden razors to protect him.

All prisoners were handcuffed as a matter of course; as they reached
the deck, they had to put their hands through a slot, where a guard
uncuffed them. The Kings had fallen in with a Hispanic guard, sympa-
thetic to the gang, who may have been in on the plot. He began to uncuff
them first, giving them the advantage. Preacher saw what was about to
go down and jumped in front of the still-handcuffed Suge and Ro. He
faced down the Kings, who were now walking over ready to fight. "Any
one of you come in front of me and I'll kick ya fuckin' head off," Preacher
said. Uncuffed, they attempted to throw punches. Ro tried to razor one
of them before the guards rushed in. Preacher stood on the sideline holding back any Kings who wanted to exploit the situation. "I dare any of
y'all motherfuckers to move," he warned.

Afterward Sex Money Murder got a reputation in the prison for loyalty. "Sex Money bangin' for their rats!" went the cry on the cellblocks.

Codd demanded help after hearing Bloods next to his cell in the hole
speaking in code. "Shit, they scheming on me, man," he complained to
Ro. When Ro asked Suge what he should do, Suge told him. "Give him
the codes so he can be on point," he said. "He from the 'hood. He one
of ours."

Following the assault on the Kings, Suge spent twenty-three hours a
day in lockdown in March 1999. One evening a ghostly, disembodied
voice echoed around the cell. Maybe he was hearing things? It seemed
to float up from the toilet in the corner of his cell. He knelt down to get
closer. The voice belonged to Green Eyes, now cooperating with the feds.

A quirk of the plumbing offered a toilet-style phone system between
inmates on different floors. Suge was overjoyed to speak to his friend.
The two spoke long into the night. Suge confided in Green Eyes. "I
wanna go home, Moe," he said. "I'm done with this shit."

"You can go home," said the voice out of the toilet bowl. "Bring Baby
in. Give them that." Suge refused. He loved Baby like a brother. Green

Eyes persisted. "Ain't no one gonna take care of your kids like you." Suge
slumped. He had a five-year-old son in Springfield.

"You know Twin wasn't telling," whispered Green Eyes. Suge sat
upright. He knew from talking to Pete that it had been a bad call and
Twin likely wasn't a snitch. Suge bade him good night and retreated
to his bunk, where he brooded all night. Suge had been willing to give
thirty years, or more, for Pete. But everything was disintegrating. Even
Ro had disappeared a month earlier, presumably becoming a cooperator.

Suge thought back to a day on the roof when they'd made a pact to
help each other, depending on who got down to cooperate first. Even the
Preacher had suggested Suge turn. "You and Ro like my sons," he said
one day. "Fuck, Pete, get yourself up outta this shit. The *Titanic*'s going
down, grab a life jacket. They stopped me at third base, but you can do
it." The Preacher had tried to cooperate with Liz Glazer, but they'd shut
him down: too many murders, and besides, they knew he had fathered a
child by his own daughter. They could never put him in front of a jury.

The next morning Suge called up to Green Eyes. "You think they'll
talk to me?" Green Eyes said there was an older white guy everyone
trusted. "Ask to talk to O'Malley," he said. "He'll look out for you."

✛   ✛   ✛

O'MALLEY DIDN'T believe at first that the Thanksgiving Day shooter,
the lunatic who had been shouting and screaming in court, wanted to
come and talk. Some of the higher-ups in the office were reluctant on
moral grounds to sign up killers as cooperators. Also prosecutors sometimes had a tendency to "overbuy" the number of cooperators, including
those with serious charges—in order to get the inside track on a conspiracy and to make the case impregnable.

Rollock's lawyers thought that he had a winnable case. He wasn't at
the scene of the shootings on Thanksgiving. To get the actual shooter
would be beneficial to Nicole LaBarbera, who had taken over as prosecutor from Alexandra Shapiro. And there'd been some problems with the
current witnesses. Codd had written to a friend outside the MCC that
when he got out he was going to do it right next time and not get caught.

The letter had been intercepted. Rollock's defense lawyers would use his boasts as a way to damage his credibility on the stand.

A former English major at Princeton, the thirty-one-year-old LaBarbera, whose good looks often made gangsters shy, came from a sheltered childhood in suburban Long Island.

LaBarbera earned her law degree at Fordham Law School and then later signed on as a clerk to Judge John F. Keenan in the Southern District of New York. Long after everyone had left the office she pored over Keenan's trial transcripts and crime scene photographs. The trial narratives reminded her of the Sam Shepard plays she'd loved as an undergraduate. She saw the work of a federal prosecutor as honorable, representing and pursuing the truth while protecting the public. Defense laywers, she felt, sometimes didn't have the same obligation to the truth and merely advanced the causes of their clients.

She immediately felt at home in Liz Glazer's Violent Gangs Unit, which offered a uniquely investigative and aggressive crimefighting mandate. She found common cause with O'Malley, and she saw that when he worked with cooperators he expressed exactly what he was thinking. It wasn't a game to him, and he didn't fool people into trusting him.

The experience of her first trial against a Harlem drug dealer had been unnerving despite securing a conviction. Over time LaBarbera discovered she much preferred the behind-the-scenes investigative work, solving cases with detectives and investigators and building a rapport with cooperators, to the grand theater of court that other, more extroverted prosecutors thrived on.

But nothing could prepare her for the challenge of Sex Money Murder, a vast and sprawling multidefendant case. On her first day in court she faced a jury box full of gangsters who shot her poisonous looks. LaBarbera had been driven into Soundview in a blacked-out federal cruiser, and even before they hit the block the crews knew they were coming. LaBarbera felt someone might try to shoot them. She was struck by how many feral dogs roamed the neighborhood. Soundview could have been a sanctuary on the banks of the river, she felt, were it not a failed social experiment. LaBarbera saw a role for herself in fighting for a community oppressed by fear.

Suge seemed to be one of the gang's worst, veering near her table menacingly when he came into court. She wondered how a jury would react if a killer like Suge were given a break in return for his testimony for the government. She had serious misgivings about using him and was doubtful he would even be honest. After all, Rollock had never been offered the chance to cooperate, because he'd have to plead to all his murders and then give up someone bigger than himself. The feds don't sign up the whale to get the minnows.

They decided to move ahead with the meeting with Suge. But O'Malley took no chances. He insisted upon extra marshals and Forcelli as backup in the proffer room. They called Suge's lawyer to set it up.

✛   ✛   ✛

SUGE'S LAWYER was as baffled as anyone else that his client would consider cooperating. Suge said that he was just mulling it, nothing definite. Some lawyers were anti-rat, too, and disliked cooperators because it cut into the fees they could earn from a trial. Others didn't think anyone should cooperate as a matter of principle, and hated opening up their cooperating clients to the prosecution's questions. "You my mouthpiece, right?" Suge said to his lawyer. "Then get down there and let me see what they have to say."

That night Suge settled uneasily into the bottom bunk, alone in his cell, weighing his decision.

A bridge ran from the MCC to the old courthouse and then to the US attorney's office. Suge was moved across it to a small holding cell. He was left to wait and wonder whether he was making a mistake, whether he could handle becoming the kind of rat he had always hated. He had come to doubt the loyalty that had drawn him into Sex Money Murder, the faith that his brothers would always protect each other. But his faith in the family was still hard to surrender entirely.

A tall, imposing man in an open-necked shirt whom he knew as O'Malley appeared at the door with a burly, swaggering cop. The prison handcuffs were removed, and the white-haired man fastened his own set of cuffs around Suge's wrists. They led him out. The man towered over him, gripping his biceps with a strong hand. They began to walk over from the old courthouse to the US attorney's office, a metaphorical passage to the world of the cooperating witness. Sunlight fell through big, dusty windows on his right, warming Suge's face as they walked. By just crossing the bridge he was closer to the outside world again; all he had to do on the other side was talk. But every footstep was one step closer to upending his universe.

The room where they took their seats was hot and airless, choked with mismatched chairs, some high-backed leather, some wooden, laid out around three tables. On the far wall someone had set up a whiteboard.

Suge sat next to Martin Siegel, his lawyer. He found himself blushing at LaBarbera's beauty, in spite of his urge to frown at the seriousness of the situation. Reflexively he thought he'd have an easier time with her, that she'd be more lenient than a man and he could charm and manipulate her. Forcelli sat next to LaBarbera. O'Malley took a seat at Suge's right elbow and stared at him.

O'Malley told Suge that this would be the most important ten minutes of his life. He didn't want him to say a word, just to listen. "I never thought you'd come down here," he said. "I never liked you and I didn't like what you did in court." Suge hadn't expected this to start on such a negative note. He had thought they'd want to hear what he had to say. O'Malley chewed on the earpiece of his glasses, contemplating Suge with indifference.

"We're not promising you anything," O'Malley said. "A lot of your guys are going away for a long time. Some won't be able to do that time. Those who can't want to sit in that chair you are sitting in right now. You are already in that chair, so you're ahead of the game. Once you leave that chair, you can't get back in again, because you've been replaced. In the past, guys like you have gone away and watched their buddies testify, and they say, 'I should have listened to that old guy.'"

LaBarbera followed O'Malley's lead. "I know this isn't your thing, Suge," she said. "We'll be honest with you, but you have to be honest with us." Suge leered at her as she talked.

O'Malley told him that he would have to describe every crime, from stealing out of his grandmother's purse to what happened on Thanksgiving. "I want the whole loaf," he declared. "Not just slices." Suge nodded. "Ninety percent of everything we already know," said LaBarbera. "What you think we don't know even now, we know. We don't need you to make this case." Suge was unsettled now. He thought he'd be here laying down his conditions, and yet it was the other way around. He grew enraged, not knowing whether he could trust them.

O'Malley asked him a few questions to test him, and Suge offered what he thought was his trump card. "I killed Twin." The words hovered over the table.

"We know that already," LaBarbera said.

Suge struggled to give them something. "Pete ordered it."

LaBarbera said, "We know that, too."

They knew everything. This was a sealed deal. There was no way he would have won in court. Anxiety washed over him. The guys who had gotten to O'Malley and LaBarbera before him had given it all up. He had nothing to offer. O'Malley asked about the guns used on Thanksgiving Day and where they were. Suge didn't know. He felt humiliated and stupid. He got angry and defiant again. And then, abruptly, it was over. Back at the MCC he was strip-searched. After previous proffers, marshals had caught prisoners with pens, paper clips, even a foot-long Subway sandwich tucked inside the front of someone's underwear. (The attorney whose sandwich it was said he'd lost his appetite when the marshals offered to return it to him.)

Once in his cell, Suge turned the encounter over in his mind and felt it had gone badly. Nothing happened for a week.

O'MALLEY AND LaBarbera read the situation differently and felt the meeting had gone well, and that Suge had told the truth under pressure. He had been honest right from the get-go. They always spoke about the crime the defendant was charged with first as a test of probity. He might have thought of playing games, like they all did, but he hadn't. O'Malley told LaBarbera that he thought Suge would be an excellent witness. He suggested they bring him back.

At the second meeting they all had pizza together. O'Malley felt breaking bread in these situations solidified the deal. He explained that Suge might be offered a cooperation agreement, but that he would have to plead guilty to everything he had ever done. After that, LaBarbera would write a 5K letter—so called because of section 5K1.1 of the US Sentencing Guidelines—on his behalf. It was a request for leniency from the judge for his "substantial assistance" to the prosecution. And that was it. No promises. "If you fuck us, we're going to fuck you back so bad you'll never get over it," O'Malley said. "I catch you lying, we're going to tear that agreement up. You'll have pled guilty, but you'll be on your own."

"Okay," said Suge. "What do you wanna know?"

The proffer sessions went on for hours at a time. LaBarbera thought that Suge resembled a hyperactive cartoon character. He described acts of violence cinematically, with frenzied onomatopoeia and a boyish sense of pride. She'd never encountered anyone quite so raw. He went from volatile to sanguine in seconds, and back again. Sometimes he spoke fast, offering dense color and detail, providing atmosphere, without adding to a factual sequence of events. He wanted to show that he was a tough guy, and he seemed interested in saving face. Other Sex Money Murder cooperators often just gave up the facts in a natural and unguarded fashion. Suge's posturing got in the way.

At the next session, O'Malley walked in with a slim file. "What do you know about Baby Jay?" Suge's heart rose in his throat. He'd been dreading giving up Baby and had obfuscated every time his name was mentioned. O'Malley opened the file for Suge. Inside lay a single picture of Baby. As the investigator pressed for details, Suge lost his temper when they implied that he was lying. He slammed the table, kicked his chair back, and raged. He looked as if he were about to hurt someone, and for the first time, LaBarbera felt physically threatened by a cooperator. She was relieved when O'Malley and Forcelli put the handcuffs on and he was restrained. The marshals took him back and LaBarbera gratefully returned to her office just around the corner.

The next day they asked again. And on it went, with Suge often fudging and holding back or shading the truth. LaBarbera realized that Suge saw no moral value in turning down a drug deal over taking one, or resisting violence versus enforcing it. He didn't understand the distinction. And for that reason she felt little hope he might ever be redeemed. All the while, they were probing the limits of his knowledge and his truthfulness—throwing in the odd question they knew the answer to.

Suge didn't want to give up Baby. O'Malley demanded answers. It was all or nothing. His agreement would be void if he held anything back. Slowly and reluctantly, Suge shared what he knew about his old friend. Over several sessions, O'Malley's file grew fatter, with more papers and information. Next they pressed about Bemo. Suge squirmed, deeply uncomfortable. He had no choice but to talk about the murders of Kiron and Joe Dix.

When they were done, Forcelli escorted Suge back over the bridge. They chatted about the neighborhood. The conversation turned to the murder of Fat Mike ten years earlier. Forcelli said he had been called to the scene. Suge pushed him for details of Fat Mike's death. Forcelli volunteered one or two pieces of information, which took Suge by surprise. Forcelli asked how Suge's family was holding up. No one had ever asked Suge how he was doing before; he was taken aback.

O'Malley and Forcelli had warned Suge that his cellmates would be suspicious. If anyone discovered he was ratting, they'd kill him. O'Malley always made sure that no one saw him coming down with them, and he offered Suge excuses to take back to the block. "Say the motherfuckers just hit you with more charges."

The more O'Malley worked with LaBarbera on the case, the more his view of cooperators changed. He always tried to buck his cynicism when Glazer talked about Weed and Seed—the federal program to remove gangs from neighborhoods and inject funds for renewal—and he avoided all meetings with social workers and community do-gooders. His job was to seek out the truth and to lock the bad guys up—to stop the killing. But LaBarbera brought out the humanity in some of these young men from Soundview. At first men like Ro tested her with vulgar language or stories of their sexual conquests designed to shock, but in a few months she'd picked up their jargon and now threw back their own street slang to disarm them. When prosecutors adopted the argot of the street, O'Malley smiled inwardly because it signified to him that his mentorship had been successful. Over time, many of the young SMM men came to respect her and didn't want to let her down. It was extraordinary.

O'Malley, by contrast, had trouble getting past the lack of remorse in these killers. It was the one part of the process that never figured for him. Killing was a job, or an obligation; a duty, or the outlet for their rage. But he struggled with how little they seemed to notice or mourn for the humanity of those they'd killed. Suge was charming at times, but he had no remorse. He was more preoccupied with Pete's betrayal than he was with taking a life.

Suge grew more comfortable as more sessions passed. He mistakenly read O'Malley as the steel gauntlet, LaBarbera as the velvet glove. And O'Malley had never met a young gangster quite so charismatic and funny. "I'm as cool as a fan, yo," he'd say when they asked how he was before they started. He joked sometimes, when the going got tough, flashing that incomparable charm. "Yo, Nicky," he'd say, winking at Nicole. "Let me holler at you off the record on that one." They'd enjoy the levity for a bit, but LaBarbera would circle back and press him as hard as O'Malley. "Look, you're lying," she'd say. "There's no point carrying on with this anymore." Suge bristled angrily, held back, flourished his pride. He fought the urge to call her a bitch.

He went back to the cells each time thinking he was making a big mistake. He knew he could be killed for what he was doing. But over half a dozen meetings, he found his confessions liberating. O'Malley just listened. He never judged. He never acted shocked. You could tell him anything.

For months, one question sat on his mind: Was Twin a snitch? Weeks into the meetings, he asked them directly. "No," said LaBarbera. "He probably would have been on this indictment if he was alive." Suge pushed his chair back furiously. He was going to give Pete thirty years of his life for a lie? After the session, Forcelli took him back to the cell. The detective saw the anger and frustration brimming over. "I loved Pete," said Suge to the detective. "I still do. But he ain't love me." He found it easier to give up Sex Money Murder after that.

"Listen, Suge," O'Malley said. "If I ever find you withholding something, you and I are going to have a serious problem." He sensed that Suge was still holding back on Bemo and Baby Jay. "How many bodies you got in Springfield?" None, Suge said. He might have shot at a few people, but he'd missed. "Right," said O'Malley. "That's attempted murder." Suge pressed on, but he began to hate the sessions.

Back in MCC, he reined in the violent urges, but he couldn't stay completely out of trouble. He got into fistfights. One day, settling into his chair in the proffer session, grinning at LaBarbera and ready to start work, he was caught off guard when O'Malley lunged across the table. "What the fuck is your problem, Suge? You're not a Sex Money Murder gangster anymore. You're a cooperating witness now. You cannot knock people around!" Suge sat in his seat, humbled. O'Malley pressed on. "I got your balls in my hand, Suge."

Sometime in early 1999, Suge went to court with Pete and his remaining codefendants. In the bullpen with his old friend, Suge finally confided. "Something gotta give, Moe," Suge said. "I ain't feelin' this no more." Pete offered his usual knowing calm. "Be all right," he said. He didn't realize that Suge had just said good-bye.

Finally, after an extended period of doubt, Suge gave himself over entirely to O'Malley and LaBarbera. They weren't friends, that was clear, but there was respect. O'Malley, with Suge's permission, called Suge's grandmother to tell her that he was cooperating and that he might have a chance to turn his life around. "It don't matter," she barked. She never came to visit. And in time Suge's baby mother stopped coming, too.

LaBarbera and O'Malley wrote a detailed memo about Suge and all his criminal acts. It stated what Suge would plead guilty to if he went before a judge and, crucially, what he would be able to do for the prosecution if he was formally signed up as a cooperator. The memo went to two deputy chiefs in the Criminal Division, who signed off on it, satisfied that Suge could provide invaluable support to the prosecution.

On April 29, 1999, Suge was led into Judge Cedarbaum's courtroom to admit his crimes. Alone, without his codefendants, he stood behind the defendants' table with Martin Siegel. He caught sight of O'Malley. Their eyes met. Suge knew what he had to do. He admitted all of it: racketeering, murder, distribution of narcotics . . . It was over quickly. Afterward, he signed a formal cooperation agreement. His fate would now rest entirely in the hands of the judge, who might be swayed by LaBarbera—who he hoped would write a strong 5K letter.

Afterward, Suge was taken back to the hole for his safety. His plea was sealed so that it couldn't be seen by his codefendants or their attorneys. For O'Malley, the days after a defendant pled guilty were fraught. Other inmates might suspect that an inmate was cooperating, but when they pled out, there was no doubt. In complex multidefendant gang cases, O'Malley did his best to keep everyone separate. After a plea, the hole was the only place cooperators were safe.

LaBarbera suggested that Suge think about going into the federal witness protection program, known as WITSEC. They'd heard from other cooperators that Suge was now "food," in the language of the Bloods. Gang members had a duty to try to kill him for his treason, and anyone who passed up the chance could be targeted for failing to live up to Blood protocol.

Suge decided to enter the program. He took a polygraph test. An examiner asked if he harbored any ill will toward other cooperators, the judge, or the prosecutors. Some prisoners tried to get into WITSEC segregation units just to be able to kill codefendants on their cases. Suge passed and was moved to a specially constructed third-floor unit of the MCC, a prison within a prison, with its own security entrance.

He was given an alias as soon as he arrived. Only the warden of the prison knew the real names of the inmates. Visitors had to stand in front of a two-way mirror so that cooperators could first see who came to see them before they were granted access. A prison guard selected random trays of food from the mess hall for the WITSEC unit to prevent poisoning.

Life in WITSEC took on a far more benign aspect. Cooperators could relax among their own. The deeply etched alliances based on race or gang affiliation that were crucial in the general population were erased in the unit. Italian mobsters mixed with Jamaican gangsters, and Aryan Brotherhood members mixed with black Bronx street crew members like Suge. But Suge struggled with his bland surroundings and asked to be moved to a different prison. LaBarbera found him a place in Arizona. There an Aryan Brotherhood turncoat whom Suge befriended called him a nigger while they were playing cards. Suge punched him in the mouth and opened a wound that would need five stitches. He wound up back in the MCC.

He joined Alcoholics Anonymous, because they taught public speaking and he wanted to excel on the stand. He told O'Malley and LaBarbera that he would stare Pete down for his betrayal. But LaBarbera worried about Suge on the stand. She felt that jurors wouldn't find him at all likable, and his easily provoked temper would offer a soft target for a defense lawyer. Meanwhile, Suge readied for a showdown with his old friend.

Six

MYTH'S END

IN MAY 1999, PIPE WAS CALLED TO a meeting with senior prison staff in Cayuga. He suspected it was due to his rising reputation for violence after he had recently ordered an attack against some "food"—an inmate who had assaulted a Blood. He was slashed so severely with a razor that he needed a hundred stitches and staples to put his face back together. Prison staff wondered if Pipe wanted to be moved into protective custody. "Why would I want to do that?" They told him that his brother might be cooperating and that therefore Pipe could be targeted. "Do you know who the fuck I am?" Pipe responded. "I'm the fuckin' OG. I ain't need no protection. Motherfuckers need to be protected from me, yo."

Pipe left the meeting puzzled: His brother cooperating? He didn't have much time to dwell on the news before the guards returned and found an ice pick Pipe had secreted in one of the boxes of rice he also used to hide contraband. One of the Bloods had snitched on him for having the weapon. Pipe was sent to the Special Housing Unit (SHU) in the Auburn Correctional Facility, a maximum security prison. Alone, he ruminated. News of his brother's betrayal began to corrode his thoughts. How could Ro have turned, particularly on Pete, who was family? Someone must have gotten to him.

Pipe got his answer a few weeks later, when an investigator with the Southern District showed up. Pipe was led into an interview room, where he encountered a tall, graying man in a sport coat. Pipe was offered a chair, and after sitting down immediately pushed it back onto its two rear legs to show sullen contempt. O'Malley started in on his pitch.

✦ ✦ ✦

O'MALLEY THOUGHT that he might be able to bluff Pipe. He wouldn't flip right away, but he might respond to the realization that he was being watched, and that he would one day be apprehended. O'Malley wanted to get inside his head. After the meeting they'd monitor his calls and see if that opened fresh leads.

O'Malley said that guys were being arrested every day and that he knew the whole story, because Ro was cooperating. Pipe could help himself by telling what he knew. "If you don't," said O'Malley, "I'm going to get you anyway. So it doesn't make much difference."

Pipe sprang forward in his chair. "Let me explain something to you, Mr. John O'Malley, or whatever the fuck your name is. If you had any type of information on me you wouldn't be up in here talking to me, cocksucker. You'd be here to lock me up." O'Malley sat still and blank-faced. "So go get some more information, man. And don't come here no more trying to see me, right? My brother? He's a grown man and I'm pretty sure he knew the consequences behind what he was doing. So you go tell him to cooperate. I ain't telling him shit. Now get the fuck outta here."

O'Malley stood up, looming over Pipe. "Once we finish decoding those letters and we find out you gave the okay to have David Mullins killed, we're going to come and get you." A pause, and a face-off. The investigator concluded, "Remember what I told you." Pipe smirked.

O'Malley handed Pipe a business card. The gangster looked at it, tore it up, and threw it back. "Whatever the fuck you say," he said. The guards came to take him away.

But Pipe was deeply rattled. In the exercise yard that day he burned every one of Pete's letters and watched the smoke drift away over the wire.

✦ ✦ ✦

A FEW MONTHS later, in October 1999, Pipe was released from prison on twenty-two months of parole. On Halloween, dressed all in black—black hoodie, black Levi's, and black suede Timberland boots—he arrived in Soundview.

After a quick tour of the neighborhood, he made his way to his sister's new apartment on East 182nd and Walton, just west of the Bronx Zoo. A banner across the living room proclaimed: WELCOME HOME BIG BROTHER! There were cheers, music, and libations for the new head of Sex Money Murder. Twenty-two-year-old Pipe surveyed the room and the homies who looked at him now with the same reverence they had given to Pistol Pete. The feds had arrested the entire first generation of the gang. The new generation would have to live up to the reputation of the founding fathers. None had done murders with Pipe, and developed that communion from bloodshed. In the swim of callow faces at the party, Pipe tried to remember all the street names: Strong, Ghost, Gorgeous Indian, Venom and his brother Baby Face Gangsta . . . He was apprehensive about the new breed.

Worse, Pipe had left prison broke. B-Love had been holding most of his money, but with his arrest those funds became unavailable. And Twin, the man who was going to set him up back in the drug game, had been murdered on Pete's orders. Finally, Sex Money Murder had been dismantled as a moneymaking machine—the contacts and distribution networks all destroyed by the feds. Pipe would have to build the gang from scratch. He'd need a serious gunman, others who were good with money, and hardworking hustlers on the lower tier.

For most of his sentence Pipe had had a picture of Jonelle in her bikini up on the wall, and it was understood by both that they would resume their relationship when he got out. She snuggled up to him as the party wound down in the early morning hours. There'd once been an ugly scene in the prison visiting room when Pipe's sister, who'd brought Jonelle up one day, told him that his girlfriend had been sleeping with another man in the projects. But they had mostly smoothed it over, and after everyone left they had their reunion amid the streamers and empty champagne bottles.

✦ ✦ ✦

PIPE SAW Pete in person—the first time since 1995—at One Foley Square when Pete was produced for an appeal of his North Carolina conviction. Pipe arrived at the courthouse, handed over his ID to the marshal at the door, and took a seat in the public gallery. Pete, at the table with his lawyer, caught sight of Pipe and gave a wide grin and then a flatline from his heart. Pipe returned the salute.

But the smiles evaporated when Pipe caught sight of O'Malley standing discreetly to one side, back to the wall. He'd seen the tributes the men had offered each other. The next time Pipe went to meet his parole officer, he briefly caught sight of O'Malley at the office. The officer relayed the news that Pipe would be reassigned from regular parole to a more draconian and restrictive regime reserved for gang members. When Pipe asked why, he was told that he'd been seen associating with a known felon, Peter Rollock. Pipe now realized why O'Malley had been there to visit his parole officer.

In the parole office Pipe was shown some of the evidence the feds had against him. A chart described links between the Sex Money Murder Bloods, with a picture of Pipe at the top. Below were his three top-tier leaders. O'Malley was refocusing his attack from Pistol Pete and the original crew to the new OG of Sex Money Murder.

Out on the street, cops were harassing everyone. Pipe and some of the others were playing dice in the lobby of 551 when the police descended. One of the Bloods protested they were disrupting a friendly game. They were all charged with trespassing and bused to the Forty-Third Precinct's holding cells. A summons received while on supervised release could get Pipe thrown back into prison. Some of the policemen came down to the cells and tried to instigate a fight. "You Blood guys think you're tough, but you're just a bunch of pussies," said one. Another attempted to get Pipe to swing at him. "So you're the new OG, huh? Come on, take a shot! Let's see how tough you are." Pipe controlled his temper. The Bloods were booked and released.

Back on the block, the next couple of weeks passed in a blur of parties. Women from all over the projects tried to get close to Pipe. He was broke, but as OG of Sex Money Murder they knew he wielded power that he'd eventually turn into cash.

One night, Chantal, a smart and lovable single mother five years Pipe's senior, with two sons he had known for years, offered to cook for him.

She made him rice and beans and then made her play, suggesting that he move in with her and help the family out financially. In return she could offer him a base right in the heart of the neighborhood. A dim promise of a romantic liaison formed part of the pitch, but for the most part she was proposing a practical arrangement. Chantal had grown up in Soundview and remembered her mother being terrified of even going to the store. Living with the new OG of Sex Money Murder would bestow safety on her family.

At first Pipe resisted. "I ain't down like that," he said. But in a day or two, he fell under her spell. He moved into her seventh-floor apartment at 1669 Randall Avenue and dumped Jonelle. As the winter gloom descended, he discovered that Soundview could be more dangerous than when Pete was on the street. The dissolution of Sex Money Murder after the federal onslaught had left a vacuum. Young guns were looking to make a name. The first indication came when Pipe caught sight of Bemo pushing himself up the block in a wheelchair. A few weeks before, Bemo had been waiting for the elevator in his building when he was confronted by a young gangster brandishing a gun. He was shot nine times in the legs. Avoiding the hospital because he didn't want to risk being questioned by the police, he was nursed back to health by B-Love's mother. Rumors circulated that the shooting was payback for Thanksgiving Day, which everyone assumed Bemo had been involved in because he was so tight with SMM. Bemo returned to Kingston, where he was robbed in his wheelchair. The thieves even took his sneakers. When he was picked up by Kingston cops on a drug-dealing warrant, he bemoaned the lack of respect among the new generation of gangsters. "These kids are wilding out," he complained.

On the block Pipe struggled to control the small, rambunctious, and ill-disciplined army that was Sex Money Murder. It seemed every male of fighting age in the neighborhood wanted to fly under the banner of the United Blood Nation. Back in the day, when SMM was an operation of maybe twelve members, there was authentic loyalty. When Pete killed Kato for Twin, or Twin killed Barnes for Pete, it was seen as a demonstration of selflessness and a dedication to the "family." The Thanksgiving murder had torn that myth apart, exposing the brute selfishness and jealousy at the heart of the organization. If the top leaders like Pete could betray and murder their own, who was truly safe? And now Pipe controlled forty or more Bloods, far bigger than the original team, but most of them just restive kids. No one really knew who was who. Cab-drivers were robbed and pistol-whipped; gold chains were snatched from residents. They had ongoing feuds with each other, shooting up one another's houses, but a will to take on those who disrespected Sex Money Murder was absent.

Pipe was driving past the White Castle when he spotted a rival young gun from Bronxdale. A few months earlier, while Pipe was in prison, the man had bicycled into Soundview and shot at three Bloods before riding home. Pipe knew the man; he approached him, and the two embraced. "I got respect for you and Pete," said the man by way of apology. They exchanged friendly words before Pipe headed back to Soundview, where he found the Bloods the man had shot at. Pipe had been "rocking him to sleep" and only drew him into a hug to see if he was "strapped." He told the Bloods he had located the culprit, and further, he was in the White Castle unarmed. It was a perfect opportunity for revenge. But the Bloods were all too scared to do anything. Disgusted with how weak they made SMM look, Pipe thought about shooting the man himself. They talked him out of it. "If you get knocked, we lost the OG," they complained. Disgusted, Pipe gave up on the whole thing.

In Pipe's absence, Soundview's distrust of the police had reached a new low: On February 4, 1999, twenty-two-year-old Amadou Diallo had been shot nineteen times by four NYPD officers from the elite Street Crimes Unit as he stood in the doorway of his apartment on Wheeler Avenue, reaching for his wallet. Charged with second-degree murder and reckless endangerment, officers Kenneth Boss, Sean Carroll, Edward McMellon and Richard Murphy were all eventually acquitted. Soundview hit the front pages once more.

For Sex Money Murder, the rancor over the Thanksgiving shootings continued nearly unabated after two years. Pipe stood on the block one day to see the remaining twin, Damon Mullins, drive around a corner and head toward him. In the weeks after the murder, news had spread that Damon was going to retaliate and therefore should be shot on sight. But nobody followed the order. Everyone had loved his brother. As Damon drove up, Pipe eased back on the hammer of the gun in his pocket. The window rolled down. "You okay?" said Damon. Pipe nodded. Damon drifted off. A few weeks later Damon left the neighborhood and moved down south.

✛ ✛ ✛

MEANWHILE, PIPE had set about establishing a fledgling drug empire on his own by ordering a local hustler, Midnight—selling in breach of SMM regulations—to give him half his profits within a few days of his return to Soundview. After about two months, Pipe had amassed $10,000 from the arrangement, and he simply ordered Midnight to leave the block. Now Pipe had enough to get started. He selected three men to be his lieutenants: his cousin Scruff; Bear's younger brother CB; and Fat Daddy, a short, overweight hustler who was something of a homebody but had an aptitude for cooking up crack.

Pipe devised a way to keep his hands clean, so as not to breach his probation, but to still have the profits rolling back to him. He suggested that each of them put in $3,000, for a total of $12,000, for half a kilo. Fat Daddy and a young gangster named GI bought the cocaine. They hooked up with a crackhead, offering him free product in exchange for the use of his apartment in Academy Gardens, where Fat Daddy did the cooking. And then they bagged it up for the fifteen or so hustlers who would sell on the street. Carefully, Pipe annotated every detail of inflow and outflow, both cash and product, in a spiral-bound notebook, using code in case the police ever got hold of it. A thousand dollars' worth of crack was detailed as one white T-shirt. He knew who was given how many "white T-shirts" to hustle, and what their returns were. Pipe took a 70 percent profit from every batch.

Within five months, things were up and running. Every morning, he went to the store for coffee and checked his hustlers. Then he retired to Chantal's apartment, where each night he stashed his money and a .45-

caliber Ruger in a charcoal-colored safe hidden in the bedroom closet. After a good day on the block, he might sink into a bubble bath Chantal had run for him and sip Hennessy. For the first time since he'd been a teenager, he eschewed marijuana. He needed to be on point.

There was little time to relax, though. The neighborhood was now deemed a "federal block"—under surveillance by the feds. Rumors circulated that even the sidewalks were bugged, so the crew spoke mostly in Blood code. For years they'd operated in defiance of the police, but everyone was truly scared of the feds. And it was clear that there were rats in their midst. Those in the neighborhood knew that Codd had betrayed Pete, and Pipe wasn't surprised by it. George Wallace had always told Pete to eliminate him, and now Codd's weakness had been Pete's downfall. But if a top lieutenant could be so weak, it meant anyone could be an informant. Pipe himself didn't trust anyone, even family.

Things got worse when Pipe was given handwritten documents that detailed statements B-Love had made to federal prosecutors, among them a claim fingering Nut as having shot a Puerto Rican kid on the block—meaning Tony Morton. MAC-11, facing federal charges and in prison, had obtained the documents and passed them on to his brother, who immediately turned them over to Pipe. An emergency meeting was held to try to deal with the new threat that federal prosecutors would come after them for more murders. "He's sitting on me," complained Nut fearfully, meaning that B-Love could testify against him in court.

B-Love was going to be a devastating witness against Pete in his upcoming trial. One of Pete's lawyers, Avraham Moskowitz, a former Southern District prosecutor, called Pipe and asked him to come to his office on Seventh Avenue in Manhattan to talk about undermining B-Love's credibility on the stand. If they could catch him in a lie and unearth crimes he had committed that he had not told the investigators about, they could destroy him in court.

At the meeting, Pipe was advised to think carefully about helping Pete; his participation could easily draw him into the dragnet. If he was called to testify, there was a good chance that his involvement in the North Carolina drug operation would be revealed. "I don't care," said

Pipe. "That's my man." Pete's legal team passed Pipe a message: "Pete says he loves you. Tells you to keep your head up."

A few weeks later, Pipe met the lawyers again. This time they produced an old letter from Pete. Pipe had had no reply to the last letter he'd sent Pete from Cayuga, but in fact Pete had responded. His response had been seized in the jailhouse and was never sent. In code, it began by stating how much Pete loved Pipe. It went on to complain about the feds and their work to take down SMM. Pete wondered if information from Codd had implicated Pipe: "Wack is on some triple nine shit and has skylined them females about the Madhatter (101) and the rest of the fam." He went on: "So keep reading because I don't know if he skyline about the mad hatter passing off drop Top with Carmine 'Lilo' Galante [meaning Pipe] or what."

Pete seemed panicked about the seriousness of the situation. "So far they are trying to charge the mad hatter with five peter rolls and they are saying had real rights flip the clip on Thanksgiving day." Pete was being charged with five murders along with the shootings on Thanksgiving. He claimed—falsely—that a new indictment would involve as many as seventy-four members of Sex Money Murder. Pete sent word to the neighborhood that everyone was to be armed at all times. "It's time for everybody to play their positions. If it's going down let's make a whole lot of noise and take care of all of them. Take out orders. Everyone of them triple nine's flintstones are shining stars so put the word out." That is: If Sex Money Murder is going down, they need to go out with a bang. Be advised that all the cooperators' children are to be killed.

Pete had finally lost his mind. There had been rumors of gangsters killing the families of their enemies, but no one had done it. Pipe wasn't falling for it. It looked to Pipe as if Pete wanted to bring everyone into prison with him.

When Pipe had finished translating the letter for the lawyers, there was silence. One of the lawyers said that Pipe was lucky not to have received it.

An investigator hired by the defense couriered messages between Pete and the executive OG. He told Pipe that Pete said there were at least twenty-three confidential informants operating between Castle Hill and Soundview. Pete's mother reiterated the message a few weeks later. "The block's hot," she warned Pipe. "Be careful."

+ + +

PIPE TOOK some solace from the comforts of his home with Chantal, and from a rampaging sex life elsewhere. He became a surrogate father to Chantal's two boys, six and seven, lavishing attention on them and taking them to City Island and Rockaway Beach for Sunday lunches. He dropped them off at school in the morning, enjoying his fatherly role. In between drug work his driver delivered mistresses to him from all over the projects. Women sensed the cash he might spoil them with; one answered the door to him naked, and once some young women even came up from Brooklyn to meet him. Pipe took the women he favored to a motel on Boston Road. Then he returned to the block and checked on the day's drug sales before spending the afternoon with Chantal and picking the children up from school. In the evenings he often arranged more trysts at the motel.

About $10,000 a week flowed in and was deposited in the safe, which was as large as a nightstand. Only he, Chantal, and two others had the combination. Chantal needed to be able to access cash in case Pipe needed bail money.

+ + +

NICOLE LABARBERA prepped a cooperator for trial at a remote prison in Pennsylvania. She had moved him there because there were threats against him in New York for cooperating against Pistol Pete. He was terrified, trapped between two frightening worlds: the severity of federal justice and now potential fatal retaliation for becoming a snitch among his own. She hoped that he might relax a little, away from the chaos at MCC. Yet the sounds of animals in the woods and owls at night beyond the high fences spooked him. When the cooperator turned twenty-one, LaBarbera ordered him a cupcake from the commissary.

She felt despair that a man this young was leaving his childhood behind in a federal prison and all she could do was bring him a cupcake. When she was alone with him and he stopped projecting menace and power, drawing from the pack instinct of being with his co-defendants, she saw that he now wanted a different life. Arduous proffer sessions were, for some, like being a penitent at confession, and she could see that there was a glimmer of atonement in the process as these violent young men confided in her and O'Malley. LaBarbera hoped that the contact with her could show these young men that there were people in the world who could be counted on to say and do truthful things. She was saddened that the cooperator lived in a world where he was unable to form emotional attachments which were viewed as a vulnerability. His story, and how young some of these men in SMM were, weighed on her. It was a feeling she expressed to her husband, prosecutor David Kelley, chief of the Organized Crime and Terrorism Unit, who had prosecuted major cases such as that of Ramzi Yousef, who bombed the World Trade center in 1993. Some of the violence she heard about in the proffers or saw in photographs, like the one of Keenyon Jenkins's baseball hat filled with blood as he lay on the sidewalk, had become lodged in her mind. She couldn't shake them, unlike her husband and O'Malley, who could compartmentalize their work and move on.

One evening after another meeting with the cooperator, she returned to her motel near the prison and got a surprise phone call from US attorney Mary Jo White. White informed her that she had received a call from Peter Rollock's lawyers. With just a few days before his trial was due to start, Rollock wanted to plead guilty, on the condition that the government drop its request for the death penalty. Over the next few weeks, a deal was hammered out. LaBarbera felt that Pete should be allowed to plead, but on the condition that he spend the first eighteen months of his sentence in solitary confinement so that he could no longer order hits from jail. After that, the rules of his confinement would be reviewed by the court and the Bureau of Prisons. His lawyers agreed to the stipulation, which surprised LaBarbera.

On January 4, 2000, Peter Rollock entered Judge Cedarbaum's court just after 3:00 p.m., dressed soberly in glasses and a suit and tie. Affecting a studious air, he referred to Cedarbaum as "ma'am," and his lawyers made much of his politeness, his likability as a client, and how he had had no infractions since he had been in prison. But now the road had ended, and he would have to confess to who he really was.

He rose at the defense table alone. All of his closest lieutenants had deserted him. Judge Cedarbaum demanded answers. The prosecution team was taken aback at his candor in discussing the murders. Judge Cedarbaum asked about his first murder—of Kato. "Did you kill Keenyon Jenkins in order to promote the purposes of Sex Money Murder?"

Rollock replied, "No, for the . . . to protect ourselves."

He claimed that he had been threatened. And he made the same assertions concerning Karlton Hines. Questioned about the murder of Anthony Dunkley, he replied that Wallace had told him to kill the Jamaican because he feared that Dunkley would be arrested and flip, informing on them.

Rollock revealed how Twin had killed Frisky. And finally, he maintained that B-Love told him that Twin was going to testify against him. "I was told—I was told by others that he was supposed to be a witness cooperating. I don't know to what extent." He said that the only person he had asked to carry out the hit on Twin was B-Love. Furthermore, he said that he had not directed the attempts on Twin's brother or the other man killed on Thanksgiving, Ephraim "E-Man" Solar.

LaBarbera was mildly surprised at how forthright Rollock had been about what he had done. There was no sign of remorse, but Rollock did at least admit guilt.

The judge asked him about the formation of Sex Money Murder.

"What made you the leader?"

Pete answered quickly. "It was respect."

✚   ✚   ✚

ON THE BLOCK, Pipe listened with sorrow as Pete's mother broke the news that he had pled guilty. Pipe had put money in Pete's commissary and given his mother as much as $1,000 every few weeks for herself. Ma Brenda had become increasingly fearful as the investigation wore on.

She thought that federal agents had bugged her house and asked to meet with Pipe secretly in his car. She told him that she was going to be named in the indictment for accepting $40 in drug money from B-Love, information B-Love had given to federal prosecutors. She said that Pete had only pled guilty to avoid her being named in an indictment. The rumor spread through Soundview: Pete had only pled guilty to save his mother. "They used me to kill my son," she told Pipe.

In fact, Peter Rollock's mother was never looked at in any way for prosecution.

In May 2000, Pipe's parole officer told him that O'Malley wanted to talk to Pipe directly, though he reminded Pipe that he was under no obligation to agree. Pipe decided that he might be able to get some information from the feds, so a week later he took his seat in a bland conference room on the first floor of the US attorney's office.

"You saw what happened to your brother and Pete, right?" O'Malley began. Pipe said nothing. "We know you're the leader now. You and Pete are close. But don't think Pete can't have something done to you to send a message to your brother." Pipe said he would kill anyone who tried to get to him first. Inside, though, he was certain Pete would never kill him and O'Malley was wrong.

Next to O'Malley sat a young, soft-spoken redheaded man who Pipe thought looked like Richie Cunningham on *Happy Days*. O'Malley introduced him as Dave Burroughs and said that he was an FBI agent. Straight out of college, he worked security investigations at a local bank, and from there he applied for the FBI and was transferred to New York in the middle of the crime epidemic in the late 1980s. He distinguished himself and was offered a post in C-30, the Violent Gang Squad. O'Malley had brought in the FBI again not only for the greater resources the agency offered but also because of Burroughs's skill and low-key demeanor.

O'Malley had told Burroughs that he thought the young OG could be flipped. He told him about Pipe's crazy and violent younger brother Ro for background. Burroughs would be using the RICO laws, along with conspiracy to distribute, to bring down the gang. He made his pitch gently to Pipe, appealing to his sense of reason. He was looking for confidential informants who wouldn't have to testify but would just feed him information now and then. He made it clear that he wasn't offering a get-out-of-jail-free card. Even if Pipe agreed, he would have to stay absolutely clean while working as an informant. In return, he would be paid a few hundred a month. "If you decide not to help, that's fine," said Burroughs. "But I'm carrying on with my investigation anyway. It won't change that." Pipe signaled that he understood.

"Think about it," Burroughs said. He saw in Pipe an intelligent man who probably would have been a success in any other career had he been raised in a different place.

+ + +

PIPE NOTED how Burroughs kept eye contact throughout. The man seemed honest. Pipe slept badly that night, turning the idea over in his mind. He knew that Sex Money Murder was moribund, and that sooner or later the feds would come for them. But he made thousands a week, and they expected him to roll over for a few hundred? The thought of it infuriated him, and he was rattled to find himself even considering the offer. Perhaps if he worked with them he could extract information on the twenty-three informants in the neighborhood that Pete had told him about. Then he could turn the tables to plot against the feds, or at least buy some time to figure out how to save himself.

A few days later Pipe discussed the scenario with Chantal. If she wanted to leave, he would understand. To be uncovered as a snitch would be dangerous for all of them. But Chantal was happy where she was; she liked the money he brought in and believed that Pipe was above suspicion as the OG.

A few weeks after their meeting, Pipe signed the agreement with O'Malley.

Burroughs gave Pipe a beeper and arranged covert meetings every few weeks. The first time they met, Pipe pulled up behind Burroughs's federal car in a red Honda on Compton Avenue, a secluded backstreet that pushed up against the southeast corner of Pugsley Creek Park. Pipe checked that the coast was clear and jumped in with the FBI agent. To show good faith, Pipe told Burroughs there was a gun stashed in an old car parked in the back of the Met Foods supermarket. Within half an hour police units swept in and recovered it, hoping to link it to homicides. Pipe was shocked at how quickly the police moved on his call.

In the early weeks, Pipe felt like a mastermind, playing both sides and seeking to protect his own. He started to probe Burroughs for information on informants in the area. Burroughs had expected this all along. He knew that informants usually had their own reasons for signing up. For some it was purely financial; for others, revenge. Still, he told him the truth. "We probably only have one other informant out here." Pipe had compromised himself for nothing. The few hundred dollars he got from the feds he tossed to Chantal to buy groceries.

As time wore on he continued to feed Burroughs tidbits of information. When a shooting over some petty beef was about to go down, he gave the feds information to enable them to stop it. And on it went, a slow cat-and-mouse game with diminishing returns for Pipe.

+ + +

PIPE AND Nut set to work penning a song called "Living Life Is Like a Suicide," a paean to Pistol Pete, who awaited sentencing in November. They recorded the track in a basement studio on Commonwealth Avenue. The track focused on "hugging the chrome" and "blue steel" and in part on Ma Brenda's pain and the legend of Pistol Pete:

> *I seen the world through the Pistol's Eyes*
> *Tell me why they want to see my homie die, and sit back and watch*
>   *his mother cry*
> *To see the news and they speak in many lies, on the streets we just*
>   *bangin' to survive*
> *To stop us they use our mom's to behead us.*

Nut, who came to the recording studio with two underage prostitutes he pimped out at Hunts Point, reserved his greatest contempt for Forcelli and Tirado, who were now pressing Sex Money Murder every day. Tirado, dressed in a black leather trench coat, frequently stopped Pipe on the block and threw him up against his car. "For fuck's sake, Benny," said Pipe under his breath. "You're making me hot." When Pipe ran into Tirado at the US attorney's office, Tirado told him that he was just trying to help with Pipe's cover, but Pipe didn't believe him. Nut penned the song's chorus: "Fuck Benny Tirado, murder's a sport!"

The song got some play for a while in clubs in the Bronx. Pipe even performed at a showcase on the advice of a record label talent scout under the rap name Mastermind, a sly conceit, and an allusion to his new roles on both sides of the law. A representative from the company wanted to sign him, but they didn't want Nut. Pipe refused the deal out of loyalty, a decision he would come to regret. He and Nut sold CDs for $5 at the Bronx Festival and in some of the stores on Fordham Road, along with T-shirts with Pete's image and the legend CERTIFIED GANGSTA. On the back it read THE VIEW over an image of a Glock with a suppressor.

Pipe took a copy of the CD to the US attorney's office and left it for Tirado and Forcelli. Tirado was furious when he heard it, but O'Malley calmed him by saying that a shout-out like that meant he was doing his job well and getting under their skin. The song was played in the Violent Gangs Unit offices. Burroughs caught himself humming it on the way home from work.

On Pipe's twenty-third birthday, he sat on the gum-encrusted sidewalk outside Met Foods on Cozy Corner, listening to the music pounding out of the open doors of his Honda nearby. He mixed cognac and vodka in a giant tumbler. He looked out on the corner, his eyes glazed. This was the place where his whole life had unfolded: his mother's kidnapping, the drive-by shooting, his first arrest that led to prison, and all the other dramas in between. He lay back on the sidewalk. Pete was gone, despite his efforts, and all the original crew were in prison, most of them snitches. Was there anyone he could trust now? Was he making the right calls? The slightest error and he'd be dead. He never would have been caught slipping like this—drunk and lollygagging on the sidewalk—if Pete were still around. But today he just didn't care. He passed out blissfully.

An hour or so later he woke up, clambered back into his car, and drove home, veering all over the road. When he came close to Chantal's apartment he saw that two cars had parked on opposite sides of the road leading in, leaving a very narrow passage between them. He floored the car for a straight shot, pushed through, then tumbled out and shuffled upstairs to bed. The next morning he couldn't remember how one side of his car got twisted, until it slowly came back.

✦ ✦ ✦

WHEN BURROUGHS couldn't make his meetings with Pipe, O'Malley showed up instead. Pipe much preferred Burroughs. He hadn't forgotten his first meeting with O'Malley up north, and he disliked O'Malley and Tirado equally.

The relationship thawed when O'Malley offered him the chance to meet with Ro at the US attorney's office. The brothers saw each other for the first time in seven years. Ro had bulked up with prison weights and had a scythe-shaped scar on the left side of his face, the result of a prison slashing. They pounded each other on the back, grinning. They spoke about home, family, and what they were facing. Pipe's soul lifted. O'Malley had given him a gift.

One day in Soundview, O'Malley pulled up in his sleek black federal car behind PS 69, directly across the road from his old alma mater, the place where he'd sold Christmas trees all those years ago. The bank where he'd seen the robbery was now a funeral home, the place doing a brisk trade in one of the most troubled areas of the Bronx. Pipe, dressed in a red leather Avirex jacket, dived into the backseat and lay flat on the floor. O'Malley piloted the car down to Clason Point.

He pointed out his old school to Pipe. The gangster couldn't get his mind around it; it seemed impossible that a white cop working for the feds had grown up in Soundview. As they headed down White Plains Road, O'Malley pointed out the simple house he had lived in as a boy; Pipe sat up to look. The oak tree O'Malley's father had planted was now a colossus. Spreading over their little house, it stood witness to the passage of time. Some of his friends had ended up in jail; others became electricians, firefighters, or cops. It was hard to predict where life would take anyone. But today, O'Malley had the OG of one of America's most dangerous gangs in the backseat of his car, a son of Soundview like himself.

He nosed the car down toward a narrow, rutted backstreet lined with fishermen's cottages near the tip of the Soundview peninsula. Pipe moved to the front seat. O'Malley worried about Pipe's safety. Every time they met, he asked Pipe if it was safe to talk here. "What the fuck you mean?" said Pipe. "This is white-boy territory. We fine." O'Malley's concern touched him. O'Malley updated him about his brother and passed on a couple of messages.

Their relationship had changed—while they were not friends, they weren't exactly enemies. To Pipe, the police had always represented the corrupt and repressive hand of the state. Ever since he could remember they had torn his family apart. Some in the neighborhood felt that the poverty, the violence, the drugs—all of it was the result of the white man's efforts to keep them down, to quarantine them in squalor and deprivation. Some asserted crack had been brought to the neighborhood by the CIA and the government so that young black men would kill each other off or be sent to giant prisons run by white men. By rights O'Malley and Pipe should be at war forever.

But O'Malley started to assume a different aspect for Pipe. He knew the streets, he could read the currents, a knowledge Pipe thought a white man could never possess. O'Malley seemed to care about the neighborhood. For example, anytime someone here got shot or stabbed, Pipe's phone would go off within five minutes. Somehow O'Malley knew.

They discussed a recent shooting as they sat looking out of the car. "There could have been a kid or an old person there who got hit," said O'Malley. "I'm not going to lie to you, Pipe. Some of those guys out there are dirtbags, and some of them probably deserve what they get. But I never take joy from hearing that someone has been shot up. Never. It's not for me to judge how men have to survive in the street. You all have mothers, sisters, kids, daughters . . . We all have someone that cares about us."

Pipe thought about his sisters, whom he had moved out of Soundview for their own protection. "I feel you, JO," he said, using a nickname he had come up with for the investigator. "My family don't live in the 'hood no more, so nothing ain't going to happen to them that could affect me. As long as I move the right way, I'll be fine."

O'Malley nodded. He knew that if they ever found out that Pipe was informing, they would kill him. They turned to work. O'Malley needed Pipe to ID a couple of players from some photographs. When they finished, O'Malley shifted gears. "Wow, did you see that Tiger Woods the other day? He killed it at the Open."

"JO," said Pipe with a weary frown. "Do I look like the type of motherfucker to you that watches Tiger Woods?"

The detective laughed, started the car, and drove Pipe back to the block. Pipe alighted from the car to see Scruff lumbering past, staring at them. The hair on his scalp tightened. On the block Scruff probed, suspicious at what he'd seen.

Pipe told Scruff that the man was his parole officer. "They got me on this gang parole shit, but this time he come to the 'hood and didn't have time to go to the office." Scruff knew better than to contradict the OG and left it alone.

+ + +

FORCELLI WAS determined to bring down the remaining elements of the crew. He found Rollock's decision to plead anticlimactic, preferring a trial, when all the work with the cooperators could come to fruition. There would have been great satisfaction in seeing the cooperators and the evidence in court, but at least the man was off the street.

Forcelli had been trailing the gangster X—the man who had gone into the hospital to confirm that Twin was dead—for some time. Bob Ryan had traced his wire transfers from Pittsburgh to his relatives in the Bronx. Forcelli checked the addresses, but there was no sign of him. Then Ryan ran all the parking tickets for X around the Bronx River Houses. He found him at 1609 East 174th Street.

Strapping on a Glock, Ryan waited outside until he saw X's Nissan in the parking lot at around 9:00 a.m. He called Forcelli and other detectives for backup. When X went to leave, they blocked in his car and pounced. In the back of an unmarked car, Forcelli read him his Miranda rights and asked if they could search his car and apartment. "Go ahead, you won't find anything," X said. They found a gun in the car, the one used to murder Barnes, and a Santeria candle in the trunk, with text on the side reading: "To keep away law enforcement." Ryan couldn't resist. He turned to X, standing on the sidewalk in handcuffs. "You know why this didn't work, don'tcha?"

The gangster shook his head.

"Because you didn't fucking light it."

Forcelli then went after Bemo. He had last been seen pitching crack on Webster Avenue and returning to a tenement building behind the Grand Concourse. Burroughs had tapped the phones. They waited for a suitable time to hit the apartment to make the arrest.

Forcelli and Tirado were returning from a court date in October when Sean O'Toole, head of Bronx Homicide, called to say that Bemo was in the apartment and that they should hit it now. They had no time to plan or summon a SWAT team. When they arrived at the address, a heavily armed FBI entry team was nearby on another job. Forcelli asked them to step in; they expected Bemo to shoot back when they came for him. The leader of the squad made an excuse and said his team didn't have approval to make an entry. Forcelli quelled an urge to snap at him.

In shirtsleeves, without bulletproof vests, the two detectives unsheathed their guns and proceeded in. Moving up a stairwell, they kicked in the door of apartment 17. Bemo burst toward them. Forcelli wrestled him to the ground, and they tumbled a few stairs to a landing. Bemo continued to struggle, but Forcelli had him cuffed in seconds.

Finally, the killer who had signaled Sex Money Murder's ascendancy with the murder of Kiron Little was in custody. A search of the railroad apartment revealed a handgun in a drawer.

Within weeks Bemo was in the Metropolitan Correctional Center, where he ran into his old friend Suge, who asked for news of the neighborhood. "Pipe's moving funny," said Bemo. "Nigga ain't moving like the old Pipe. He don't want to kill nothing no more."

✛ ✛ ✛

ON NOVEMBER 8, 2000, Peter Rollock was sentenced. Karlton Hines's mother put on a crisp dress, lightly applied some makeup, and made the journey from the Melrose projects downtown to Manhattan to face her son's killer. It had been almost six years since Karlton's murder. She kept all the newspaper cuttings about his death in an overflowing blue scrapbook. In court she took her place alongside two other families whose sons had been killed. All of them were there at O'Malley's request.

O'Malley had come to rely on his relationships with relatives to support the prosecutions. When they asked about the investigations, he couldn't reveal anything, so he said they'd have to trust him, but once his work was over they could ask him anything they wanted. Many were involved in the drug game themselves. Some victims' families asked him how much money or drugs had been recovered and if any might be coming their way.

During the case, O'Malley had picked up Damon Mullins, the surviving twin, sometime after he'd been released from the hospital. Stopped at a light on the way to a court hearing, Mullins bounded out of O'Malley's car and ran down the street. It took two weeks to lure him back though an aunt who worked in the Manhattan DA's office.

O'Malley had to explain to the aunt, who had taken on representing the family, that to put Rollock away they had to make a deal with her nephew's murderer, Suge. It was a difficult and uneasy situation, he understood that, but it was the only way to ensure that Rollock would be convicted. Ordinary people would be too scared to testify, and the only way to have eyewitness testimony was to get those inside the gang to flip. Many were deeply uneasy with the reality that Suge could cut a deal. This was the unfortunate moral dilemma: To put away someone far more dangerous, Peter Rollock, and to stop the murders of more young men, the feds had to offer the possibility of a deal to a killer like Suge. The family took the news unhappily, but on balance knew they had no choice.

Mike Dunkley, Anthony's brother, was delighted that Rollock had been caught. He put O'Malley in touch with his twin sisters, who in time introduced him to Dunkley's mother. She came to the US attorney's office to meet O'Malley and LaBarbera, embarrassed that her son had gotten involved in drugs. O'Malley warned her that she might hear hurtful things at trial. She took the advice graciously, but the family came to the pretrial conferences and kept in touch by phone.

✛   ✛   ✛

THE PROCEEDINGS opened with Rollock's lawyers protesting a section in the presentence report that said he had conspired to murder the cooperating witnesses against him, an allegation that might later have a negative effect on his being freed from solitary confinement. A request to serve his sentence in the New York area was rejected. Next, Rollock addressed the court. Defendants often made a performance of this speech, pitching an emotional case to the judge that they were the products of their environment. Conversely, Rollock was laconic and direct. "I would like to apologize to my family, the community, everybody who was affected by my actions, for whatever it's worth, and I hope that the government steps up and takes a stand to bring the victims' families, their loved ones, to the attention of the other people who was involved in this case, as far as who plotted, who was there, who turned into government witnesses, the same thing, take it upon them to look at us all as the same in dealing with this case and give them a chance to speak as they are doing here. That's it."

And then the victims had their chance. LaBarbera introduced Keenyon Jenkins's mother to the court. "I don't have no way of consoling my son and raising my son," said Mrs. Jenkins. "He took his life. I will never see him again. He will never breathe again . . . My family members and me will suffer for the rest of our lives because my son is not here. Every time I pass his room, I go through something. Every time I look through the window and see his friends on the corner I got to go through something. I just ask God to bear with me and ease the pain . . . If I may, I would request him to be placed in a special housing unit called a SHU where he be locked down twenty-three hours a day and let out only one hour a day."

Next, Mrs. Hines made her way to the front of the court. She'd thought about this moment for a long time, even chosen proverbs from the Bible to read out, but in the moment just decided to speak candidly. "I know Mr. Rollock," she said, speaking softly and deliberately. "I grew up with him. His father, his grandmother knew me when I was a little girl, when I had all my kids. I am so sorry for him, but he needs this penalty. He needs to go far away where his family have to spend lots of money to travel. He needs it." She continued, "He needs to be in a coffin, just to feel where my son Karlton is. I had to bury him. I have to see his children grow up. His children are suffering, Your Honor.

"You do need it, Mr. Rollock. I feel so sorry for you, but you are going to feel what it feel like but you're not going to be dead. But you should be placed in a coffin for a bed. You should not get out, Mr. Rollock. You should not have the privilege to be with your children." She spoke about Karlton's plans as a basketball player. She concluded: "And I hope, I hope, Mr. Rollock, when you go to sleep that you visualize all the bodies that you murdered, that they come to you at night. That's your penalty, they come to you at night, they haunt you."

Judge Cedarbaum looked at Pistol Pete and pronounced the sentence: life plus 105 years, to run consecutively. The first eighteen months of his sentence would be spent in solitary confinement. Entry into the general prison population would be decided later. Rollock was forbidden from any communication with codefendants, Sex Money Murder members, or Bloods and ordered to pay the families of the victims $25,400.

He was twenty-six years old.

"Mr. Rollock, you have done terrible, terrible things, vile things, in your young life, things that have destroyed others totally," said Judge Cedarbaum. "I hope that you will spend your time in prison reflecting on how you have both wasted and destroyed your own life and caused terrible, terrible harm to many other people, both to your followers and your victims. Some of your victims, of course, have been your followers. You are still a very young man." She summed up. "And I do hope that everyone in the courtroom will carry the word back to your neighborhood that the path that you have followed leads to life in prison, without any prospect of ever being released."

✦ ✦ ✦

PETE'S SENTENCING echoed around the underworld. Mrs. Hines was ushered out of court through a back door. Outside, a reporter asked if she wasn't scared speaking her mind to Pistol Pete. She held her head erect and shooed the man away. A few weeks later, a copy of *Don Diva* magazine circulated on the block with Pete's picture on the cover and the legend SEX MONEY AND MURDER INC. Rollock's mother had given a full interview. She said: "I'm sorry for those women but their sons weren't angels, some of them had murder charges too. I'm sorry that the other mothers lost their children but it's not my son's fault that he was quicker. Anyone of them would have killed him first had they gotten the chance."

Pipe was devastated. He'd never see his old friend ever again. He now saw posters pasted all over the neighborhood by officers in the Forty-Third Precinct. It was part of Glazer's plan to show what happened when the feds got you.

LIFE WITHOUT PAROLE
PETER ROLLOCK a/k/a PISTOL PETE
FORMER OCCUPATION:
LEADER—SEX, MONEY, MURDER GANG
FORMER TURF: SOUNDVIEW/CASTLE HILL
CURRENT TURF: THE FEDERAL PENITENTIARY
DON'T BE NEXT!

The poster showed Pete in a white T-shirt staring out impassively with a sleepy expression. In some way, Pete had gotten the fame he wanted. Just like his Mafia idols. For days after his sentencing, boys on the block noted that "Pete got more time than John Gotti." Pipe tore the posters down whenever he saw them.

By December, Pipe had gotten word that Pete had been moved to the ADX, a maximum security prison in Florence, Colorado, known as "the

Alcatraz of the Rockies." America's worst were bused in, or flown in by Black Hawk, to the squat, sprawling complex, surrounded by a dozen guard towers all lying on a dusty plain framed by snow-capped mountains. Pete would see the Rocky Mountains for the first and last time on his way in. He joined the 1993 World Trade Center attacker Ramzi Yousef; the Unabomber, Theodore Kaczynski; and Larry Hoover, kingpin of the Gangster Disciples.

Pete was led to a concrete cell where all his meals would be received through a small hatch in the door. His entire world consisted of a concrete bed rising from the floor, with a thin mattress and a sheet for comfort. A concrete stool was affixed to the floor near a small foldout table. A toilet sat in the corner.

For just one hour a day he would be shackled and led past hundreds of cameras and sliding doors into a small cage, slightly bigger than his cell, where he could look up to the sky, his only view. And his only human contact would be close family members and lawyers. Solitude for a man like Pete was a dark, brutal fate.

Back in Soundview, his sentence was seen by many in the underworld subculture as martyrdom. He had sworn to be a gangster and taken the oath to uphold the code of the street, for which he had accepted life plus 105. To counteract the posters put up by the feds, someone put up posters of their own. Pipe read one: "Fuck Da Feds Fuck Janet Reno Fuck Da 43rd Most Of All Fuck Dat Bitch Judge Miriam Goldman." (The author had gotten Judge Cedarbaum's name wrong.) At the end was one final rejoinder: "Fuck All Snitches."

Seven

DROPPING THE FLAG

IN THE FALL OF 2000, PIPE DISCOVERED that the outgoing drugs he was detailing in his logbook did not match the money coming back to him, leading to a $4,000 shortfall. When he confronted the crew, GI and Fat Daddy confessed that a hustler called J-Money was always coming up short, giving crack to his girlfriend free of charge. They hadn't told Pipe because they didn't want him to hurt J-Money, with whom Pipe had served time up north. Pipe cornered him in Soundview on the horseshoe: "Treat me like a crab-ass nigga?" J-Money could keep what he had taken, but he was banished from Soundview.

Pipe soon cut the rest of his crew loose. Pocketing $20,000 from the stash, he decided that he would buy his own product and let the old team buy from him, then sell it on their own. He was tiring of his Blood affiliation, too. OG Mack had been released from prison in June of 1999, five months before Pipe, and established his street kingdom on 183rd Street in the Bronx, helping to run an interstate prostitution ring from Hunts Point, directing robberies of parking lots, and establishing a credit card fraud and identity theft ring, along with a steady business drug trafficking and extorting drug dealers. But a political rift had been rending the United Blood Nation since Pipe first heard rumors during his prison bid that godfather OG Mack was a snitch himself—the very man who had labeled snitches "food." (Back in 1989, OG Mack had falsely testified in court that a defendant had murdered someone—putting him away for twenty-two and a half years to life—in exchange for a deal on the substantial time he was facing on his own case.) With that embarrassing revelation many Bloods "dropped their flags."

Still, Pipe pressed on with the business of the street, dealing, robbing, kidnapping. In December 2000, he gave his blessing for GI to rob Queen Bee, a portly female drug dealer working out of Academy Gardens. GI crashed into Queen Bee's apartment and took $16,000 in cash, her drug stash, and a .38 revolver. He passed half of the money and a portion of the cocaine to Pipe. Retaliation came swiftly. Queen Bee kidnapped GI's brother Ghost before Pipe negotiated his release. But then Ghost and another young gangster, Baby Ange, robbed Queen Bee and took her heroin.

On New Year's Eve, just before the clock signaled the start of 2001, Queen Bee's crew kidnapped Baby Ange's mother. Pipe and the others tried to find her, but when they came up empty, Pipe turned his attention to the New Year's party. He filled his car's trunk with Belvedere vodka and Hennessy and drove up to Cozy Corner, ready to hand drinks to anyone he found there, displaying his benevolence as OG.

But he arrived to find a black sedan surrounded by his crew, guns drawn. Before Pipe could fully register what was happening, the rear door of his car was opened and a woman, blindfolded with a red bandana over her eyes, was tossed in the backseat. Pipe recognized her as Martha—she sometimes drove for Queen Bee. Baby Ange climbed in after her, jabbing the barrel of a gun at her temple. "Bitch knows where my moms is at," he shouted to Pipe.

Ange wanted Pipe to drive them to get his mother. If Pipe refused, the crew would question his loyalty to Sex Money Murder. If he participated in the kidnapping, he would be breaching the terms of his agreement with O'Malley and Burroughs. He paused only a moment before driving off.

When they arrived at 1665 Randall Avenue, Pipe made a pretense of staying behind to keep watch while Baby Ange and a few others dragged their hostage inside. About two hours later, Pipe stood alone in the darkness. The New Year's Eve fireworks had long fizzled out as the cold swept in from the river. He wondered what the crew had done to Martha. He decided to find out. Inside the apartment he saw her strapped to a chair while Baby Ange and another gangster beat her with the butt of a shotgun. Pipe tried to figure out his next move.

They wanted to kill her. Pipe interceded. "Listen, man, you can't kill her, otherwise I'm going down for murder as the OG of Sex Money. That's conspiracy." He looked at Martha's bloodied, swollen features. "You gotta let her go. She don't know nothing."

Their decision was made for them when more of Pipe's crew burst through the door to tell him that Martha's boyfriend had alerted the police that a man driving a white Honda—Pipe's car—had kidnapped his girlfriend. They brought her down, blindfolded, hands bound, and pushed her into another car. Leaving the Honda behind, Pipe borrowed a different vehicle and drove off alone. The car with Martha inside had driven only to the end of the horseshoe when police lights burst out of the darkness.

The gangsters removed the captive's blindfold and unbound her hands. The police moved in. Pipe watched the cops examining his white Honda from the safety of his backup car, then drove off in the other direction.

The next morning, January 2, Pipe called Burroughs to report what had happened. The FBI agent felt that Pipe was downplaying his participation. Worse, his involvement in a serious felony would end their relationship. Under the rules of their agreement, Pipe could not commit a crime. Burroughs had no choice under FBI guidelines. He could not interfere, and he had to take a backseat and let a police investigation take its course. If Pipe was guilty, he had to suffer his fate.

Later in the day, Pipe and a few others were in a female Blood's apartment when the phone rang with a number they recognized as Baby Ange's. Pipe and the crew armed themselves and went over, expecting to find Queen Bee. When they pushed through the door, they saw Baby Ange's mother blindfolded and tied to a chair. Meanwhile, afraid her son would be murdered or would kill someone else, she called the police on him. He was arrested and locked up at the Horizon Juvenile Center for his own safety.

The next day Martha ran into Pete's cousin Missy, who had confronted her friend when she heard she might testify against Pipe. Martha agreed to leave the case alone if Pipe could retrieve a gold chain that Baby Ange had stolen during the kidnapping. Pipe ordered Baby Ange to return the chain. At Pipe's meeting with his parole officer a day or so later, Burroughs urged Pipe to turn himself in. After protesting for a while, Pipe let Burroughs drive him to the Forty-Third. The police asked to see his white Honda and fingerprinted it. They called Martha to inform her that one of the kidnappers had turned himself in and asked if she could come down and identify him. But because Pipe had returned her gold chain, she was true to her word and refused.

Pipe was released and, in discussing the incident with Burroughs, told the FBI agent that he had an upcoming meeting scheduled with the crew to try to establish some order. A half-dozen squabbles like the Queen Bee episode were brewing, any of which could end in murder. Burroughs suggested that he record the meeting. Since the kidnapping there was an added urgency to their investigation, although Burroughs and O'Malley nursed concern because they knew it would be dangerous for Pipe, despite his authority figure status in the group. Pipe understood that if he wore a wire he could well be called into court as a witness. Burroughs offered him money, promising that the feds would relocate him and his family should they ever have to appear in court.

At 5:10 p.m. on January 17, 2001, Burroughs and Pipe parked a few blocks from Soundview. The agent handed Pipe a beeper with a secret internal recording device. They set up a phrase Pipe would use in the event he was discovered: "I'm going to Hawaii."

Not far from the meeting site, Burroughs listened through a headset. Pipe appeared nonchalant, playing Jon B.'s "Are U Still Down" on his car stereo with the windows lowered He parked and entered a top-floor apartment on Rosedale where a few gangsters lounged in a living room—Nut, MAC-11's brother, and Jessica 730, the crew's first female member, who was admitted on the condition that she have sex with the members she liked. They waited for a while for Silk, but when he didn't show up Pipe pressed on with business, addressing the minor agenda

items for a while before turning his attention to the freelance violence
and kidnappings that had lately disturbed the crew. He scolded them
for Martha's kidnapping, reminding them that under RICO laws they
could all be prosecuted collectively for any individual's crime.

He lectured them on the risk of informants. He drew their attention
to the fact that many among them might turn. "All you need is three
niggas in the system to say something about you and they coming for
you," he said. "It ain't even gotta be true. You know what I'm sayin'?
That's why a lot of times when shit happens and niggas do shit I'll be
doing like—I'm saying, Moe, you bugging out—boom boom—and
you say play, niggas tell me." Pipe ended: "I'm not ready to do fifty years
because you want to do stupid, you know what I'm sayin'?"

Burroughs struggled to hear the conversation over the sounds of gangsta rap in the room. The conversation waxed and waned. Pipe ordered
everyone to stop carrying on in "renegade mode." He addressed rumors
that some Bloods were going to kill Ro for cooperating. "Listen, if you
feel any sort of way about my brother I'm letting dudes know now that
if anybody plans on doing something to him, I'ma kill you and I'ma kill
your family. So if you feel some sort of way you gotta let me know now."
Burroughs let his head fall into his hands. The last thing he wanted was
a cooperating witness making threats to kill. After the tirade, a silence
fell. Only one gangster spoke. "I ain't got no problems out of respect for
you," he said. "But everyone else telling, like Suge, I got a problem with."

Concern was raised over the number of Bloods now selling on Cozy
Corner in competition with each other. "This shit is real, Moe," said one.
"Niggas gone get knocked on the block, yo. They come to the block they
see forty niggas, Moe, with seven different types of work." The decision
was made to move all the sales into Papa Yala's to avoid the police. When
Sex Money Murder was under pressure, they always moved all their sales
into the store, but inevitably one or two drifted back out to Cozy Corner
to sell because it was easier and customers were more plentiful.

The meeting, originally scheduled to take a few minutes, went on for
hours. And then a sudden high-pitched shriek emanated from Pipe's
beeper. Everyone looked at him quizzically. Pipe's blood turned to ice.

Would they suspect? He looked to see who might have a gun he could grab. Hurriedly he called the meeting to a close and scurried away.

"What the fuck, Dave?" said Pipe, exasperated, when he got back to the car. Because the meeting had gone on so long the battery had died, emitting the sound. Pipe drank a bottle of cognac that night to settle his nerves.

✦ ✦ ✦

AFTER THE RECORDING revealed the gang's plans to focus more on selling out of Papa Yala's, Forcelli approached the owners about the possibility of placing clandestine surveillance cameras there. The owner's son immediately relayed the intelligence to Pipe. He shifted plans and told the crew to hustle out of the liquor store next door. But Burroughs and Forcelli, already suspecting that their intentions had been revealed, placed cameras there. The owners were terrified of the crew and had refused to cooperate, but the FBI had applied for a warrant and did the installation regardless. Crucially, Burroughs didn't tell Pipe.

Forcelli had the unenviable task of watching endless hours of crack sales on surveillance footage. One corner of the store offered a secluded spot out of sight of the camera. Tirado installed a large potted plant to force the hustlers to move to the center of the store to make their transactions. Forcelli knew every hustler on sight, often just by the way they shuffled, moved their hands, or held their head. They sometimes kept the crack secreted in their anal cavity. Every so often they'd fish it out from the back of their underpants and hand it to the clientele.

Sometimes Forcelli had Burroughs take over. He'd watch the tape up in his office, praying he would never see footage of Pipe, with whom he'd grown close. But eventually, he came to footage from February 7, 2001, which clearly showed Pipe, at 5:35 p.m., selling to a disheveled-looking man and then to a woman who put the crack in her bra before handing Pipe money. The FBI agent cursed under his breath and hurriedly rewound the tape to watch it again. Burroughs felt sorrow for Pipe. He'd come to like the young man, but he'd have to face his fate with the rest of his crew now.

And that made Burroughs look bad as Pipe's handler. Any defense lawyer could exploit the fact of a cooperating witness using federal money to buy and sell crack to undermine a prosecution. He called O'Malley, who wasn't surprised. There was some dispute in the office as to how to handle Pipe. Many felt that his agreement should be torn up. But in the meantime he would be targeted, just like any other dealer, in the federal sweep of mass arrests of Sex Money Murder that was about to move through Soundview.

✦ ✦ ✦

ON THE day he was caught on camera, Pipe grinned when he saw Crackhead Bemo come into the liquor store. The old-timer was legendary in Soundview history and, in some sense, the personification of the neighborhood; his twinkling eyes and easy laughter always made Pipe feel at home. Crackhead Bemo's rap sheet ran to thirty pages and fifty-four arrests. He'd been in and out of prison five times himself. Out of respect for the OG, and for a few grams of crack, he made sure no one broke into Pipe's cars. This loose arrangement didn't mean that Bemo wouldn't steal from other cars, but he was so beloved that most people left him alone. His victims turned a blind eye, some from fear, others out of loyalty to one of their own.

Pipe slipped Bemo a couple of dimes of crack in the liquor store, completely unaware that he was being recorded. In an ironic twist, Crackhead Bemo had been Pipe's first mentor in the drug game, and now he would end Pipe's drug-dealing career.

Three months later, in early May—as the feds laid plans to pounce in Soundview—Pipe was slumbering in his apartment when the phone rang. Crackhead Bemo had been breaking into a car for a stereo when a part-time school bus driver, Victor Vicenty, aimed a .22-caliber rifle from his apartment window and shot him in the head, killing him instantly. Within hours, death threats poured in against Vicenty, who faced charges of second-degree murder. He and his family were hustled out of the neighborhood under police protection.

Pipe wandered up to Cozy Corner, where two dozen votive candles and some flowers littered the sidewalk. The owner of the pizza shop where Pipe had first hustled with Crackhead Bemo told a reporter from the *New York Post* that he had probably given the old-timer two thousand free pieces of pizza in his lifetime. "I miss him already," he lamented, in a story headlined "Urban Legend Fell Victim to His Own Myth." Kids in the neighborhood went door-to-door collecting for his funeral. Forcelli and his partner Pat Kelly mourned his loss. They'd both helped Bemo out when he'd been beaten up for selling breadcrumbs as crack or was down on his luck and had no food. They bought him lunch and gave him a few dollars on occasion.

His body was embalmed at R. G. Ortiz on Soundview Avenue, the same funeral parlor onetime SMM OG Bear had also passed through. Within a few days he was laid in a casket, dressed in a tuxedo, hands folded over his chest. A public defender who had come to know and love Bemo gave a beautiful eulogy at the packed funeral.

Crackhead Bemo's demise—the abrupt, violent death of Soundview's soothsayer—marked a metaphorical denouement in the crack epidemic. The term "crackhead" now had such a negative connotation in the neighborhoods across New York that it repulsed youths who might be the new generation of addicts. The market for crack had dwindled significantly; these days, kids smoked blunts and drank 40-ounce bottles of malt liquor. As they put Bemo to rest, no one in the new generation could aspire to be like him.

Pipe brooded at the symbolism of Crackhead Bemo's death while he and others stood on Cozy Corner and offered libations to the dead man, splashing Hennessy on the sidewalk. Pipe felt that Soundview should have been safe for Crackhead Bemo. His death caused Pipe to wonder if everyone had something to fear.

✦ ✦ ✦

THE FEDS planned to execute their takedown on May 31, 2001, about three weeks after Crackhead Bemo's murder. Burroughs and LaBarbera went to the grand jury and secured indictments. They wanted Nut, who had murdered Tony Morton. Normally, arrests by a squadron of granite-faced FBI agents in dark blue raid jackets would follow a federal indict-ment, but Forcelli convinced Burroughs that as soon word leaked out that the feds were on the block, the neighborhood would empty out. They'd be lucky to make two arrests. Instead, he proposed sending in plainclothes housing cops, the same ones the gangsters greeted with weary disdain every day. To Forcelli's surprise, Burroughs agreed.

Forcelli prepared for Operation Cozy Corner with something of a heavy heart. After the operation, he'd be moving on from the NYPD. The work of fighting gangs through the federal operation had given him the idea of applying to the ATF, and he was starting June 4. Sorry as he was to leave the NYPD, he couldn't go back now to the revolving-door convictions, the dealers and killers back on the street soon after their arrest, the poisonous relationship between the DA and the police. This would be Forcelli's swan song, the final takedown of a crew that had hovered over his whole career in the Bronx.

He'd wanted to make arrests personally; only he could identify all the Sex Money Murder suspects for the arrest teams. Instead, to his chagrin, he'd be parked in the surveillance van a few blocks away from Papa Yala's as a forward observer pointing out targets. At the morning briefing, a dozen pictures of Sex Money Murder gang members were circulated to three teams of six plainclothes officers. In all police operations, a "color of the day" was worn on the wrist to mark officers on the team. If they had to open fire, the band would reveal that they were police, so that no one would be shot in the confusion. Today it was green. In reality most cops lost the bands and it became a formality. Sergeant Paul Marren of the Scorpio One arrest team bantered with his counterpart in Scorpio Two, Lieutenant George Duquette. "We're gonna get more than you," they said, laying bets. "We're going to crush you guys!"

Forcelli had made a decision to go out with a celebratory buffet. He went to Joe's Deli on Tremont Avenue, where he bought a container of seasoned mozzarella, a tub of stuffed cherry peppers, and a three-foot-long hero. At around 1:00 p.m., he climbed into the surveillance van and, for the last time in his NYPD career, drove into Soundview.

He parked two blocks from the liquor store, pulled down a folding counter, and laid out his food. As he looked out, he reminisced on the countless arrests made here. They had barely dented the crime rate in the neighborhood. And then he'd linked up with O'Malley.

At around 2:30 p.m. Forcelli spotted the first hustler through a periscope that provided a 360-degree view of the street. He called it in over the radio, and an arrest team moved in. They told the perp that they were arresting him over an outstanding warrant, rather than sounding the alarm by announcing the federal operation.

+ + +

PLAINCLOTHES OFFICERS pounced on Pipe, his cousin Scruff, and another man in Papa Yala's. Pipe glared from beneath the brim of a red New York Yankees cap. A third man with Pipe, a music agent, protested, saying that he was here with his artist, indicating Pipe. The detectives let Pipe go but took his cousin away in handcuffs. When they left, Pipe sprinted to his baby mother's apartment, passing Forcelli's van on the way. Forcelli had told the arrest team not to take the guy in the red Yankees hat, because if the OG got snatched from the block early in the morning, the game would be up.

+ + +

PIPE RETURNED to the block later that afternoon to watch as detectives grabbed the brothers Venom and Baby Faced Gangsta. He called GI, who said that an undercover police car was parked outside his building. Something big was going down.

Pipe drove away from the neighborhood without a plan. As he headed up Lacombe to the intersection of Commonwealth behind the projects, a tinted-out Crown Victoria, unmistakably a federal car, sat in the middle of the street. Pipe took a hard left down the block only to see more unmarked policemen coming toward him. He jumped a stop sign before slamming to a halt outside his apartment and running upstairs.

"The police are chasing me," he told Chantal when he came inside. "I'm going to run." Chantal broke down in tears. She said they had been unable to find Scruff at the Forty-Third.

"Don't leave," she screamed. Pipe brushed her off. Outside, an old friend sat idling in his car on the block. Pipe asked the friend if he could drive him to pick up his Acura at a local car shop. They ducked down some streets and then pulled up on an apron of concrete in front. The place was closed. Suddenly, from behind, Pipe caught sight of a team of FBI agents with AR-15 assault rifles trained on him. "Bronx Homicide Task Force!" Another: "FBI!"

Pipe emerged from the car with his hands up. "What's your name?" barked one of the men. Pipe responded. The men mumbled something about a parole violation. Pipe lost his temper. "Ain't no way in hell I got a parole warrant," he countered. Pipe knew that FBI teams didn't make armed arrests for parole violations.

This, he knew, was the beginning of the end.

✛ ✛ ✛

EARLY IN the day, Forcelli had caught sight of two black men in their fifties sitting in lawn chairs outside the liquor store, drinking from brown paper bags. Every time a Sex Money Murder gangster was arrested, they laughed. Forcelli panicked, fearing that they would alert the neighborhood to the cops. But when he called in yet another arrest, they did the unthinkable. They raised their bottles to the van in celebration. So in the last hours of his last watch, as another raised beer can went up to him on another arrest, he chose to see that the people of Soundview were thanking him.

✛ ✛ ✛

PIPE WAS taken to the Forty-Eighth Precinct. In the cramped chaos he passed Scruff being led out of an interrogation room. His cousin shook his head, offering just two words: "Big boy." The case was federal. After booking, Pipe was taken to a back room, where he came face-to-face with his friend Burroughs. Pipe knew, somehow, that the agent had found out about the dealing he had done. "I already know what you're going to say, Dave," he said sheepishly. "I know you gotta do what you gotta do. I'm really sorry, man." Burroughs knew how this would play out for Pipe.

He'd be charged the same as the rest of them, despite his confidential informant status.

Pipe was pushed into a holding cell with the rest of the crew. A police radio crackled long into the night with the news of more arrests. At around 10:00 p.m., police descended on an address on Gun Hill Road where they caught Nut naked in bed with a young woman. "Suspect is unclothed," said the police radio. Pipe snickered. An hour or so later, Nut entered the holding cell. "Niggas bust in the crib and I'm butt naked," he raged. "What the fuck is this bullshit, anyway?"

At around eleven, Burroughs went to McDonald's and bought twenty Quarter Pounders out of his own pocket for the gangsters, which they devoured. The following morning, after a session in front of the magistrate, they were all driven south to the Metropolitan Detention Center in Brooklyn.

There Pipe met Baby Jay, who complained that Suge, his former lieutenant, had confessed everything to O'Malley and caused his downfall.

By the time he got picked up, Baby had almost crossed over into legitimacy. He'd moved to a middle-class housing development in the Rockland County town of Nanuet, New York, and taken out a mortgage on a half-million-dollar home. Five months earlier, O'Malley had surveilled the house for several days before swooping in and searching—to no avail. He and his partners couldn't find Baby. O'Malley nonetheless suspected that he was in the house somewhere. "That's it," shouted O'Malley, standing in the sumptuous living room. "Send in the dogs. They'll tear his ass up!" He winked at one of the cops. They had no dogs. But from deep within a crawl space came rustling and then a muffled shout. "Okay! Okay!" Baby Jay emerged.

In the days ahead, Pipe and twelve other members of Sex Money Murder stood in Judge Thomas Griesa's courtroom, on the twenty-sixth floor of the Foley Square Courthouse, one of the grandest courts in the building, with views north to the Empire State Building and beyond. Pipe was assigned the veteran defense lawyer John Jacobs and his junior assistant Stefanie Plaumann, straight out of Brooklyn Law School. She hadn't yet received her bar results. As she and Pipe got to know each other, he had to explain to her what the term "OG" meant.

+ + +

IN JUNE 2001, in the same spot on Cozy Corner where Robert Moses had sat for the groundbreaking ceremony of the Soundview Houses, another ceremony began. Forcelli, LaBarbera, Bob Ryan, and US attorney Mary Jo White sat amid lines of folding chairs facing a wooden rostrum with a placard that read: Now Entering a Weed and Seed Community.

In the wake of the "weeding" of Sex Money Murder, federal grant money had been siphoned to the Bronx DA, who in turn had set up a safe haven for children for after-school homework mentoring and some gardening and computer classes. Police officers had volunteered to teach kids karate and basketball. Thinking that the neighborhood was now safe, one woman had called the police about some gangsters who hustled near the front of her house. The following night a dead rat was thrown at her door.

Before the ceremony, O'Malley arranged for a heavy police presence. He liked the idea of Weed and Seed, but he suspected that the neighborhood would go back to its old ways—within weeks, if not days or hours.

Weed and Seed organizers sensed the danger that neighborhood residents would face if they painted over the SMM graffiti at Cozy Corner, wiping out the names of dead gangsters. So they bused in federal prisoners on probation from other boroughs to do the job. Students from IS 131 painted a vibrant jungle scene and an image of some visitors looking at paintings in an art gallery. A grocer on Cozy Corner gave the kids free drinks and sandwiches for their efforts. As they worked, a drug dealer in a glossy black car slowed alongside. Two suspected Bloods walked past and made threats. And then, three weeks before the Weed and Seed ceremony, the mural was splashed with pink paint. When they repaired the damage it was defaced again. Finally, members of the National Guard were called in to paint.

As the ceremony got under way, Mary Jo White unveiled the mural. "Where the violent Sex, Money and Murder gang once imposed its will and blatantly marked its territory, students of nearby 131 have now made their own proud and positive statement," she said. "This latest indictment, together with the spirit represented by the wonderful murals, hopefully signals the end of the SMM gang and a new bright beginning for the neighborhood."

O'Malley and Forcelli looked out on the neighborhood. Behind the Soundview Houses was Clason Point Gardens, a well-tended collection of two-story row houses, each with a small garden. O'Malley's grandmother had lived there, and he'd played in their shadow growing up. Clason Point Gardens and Soundview both had low-income residents, but Forcelli had rarely been called to Clason Point during his career. In 1969, the city planner and architect Oscar Newman redesigned the area, giving residents a greater personal stake in their homes. After his improvements, the overall crime rate in Clason Point Gardens dropped 54 percent in the first year. Looking up at the Soundview Houses around him, Forcelli wondered if, given those same housing opportunities, the lives of people here could be improved.

Toward the end of the Weed and Seed ceremony, several key members of the community expressed their gratitude to the prosecution team, who were handed awards for their work. One man approached Forcelli in tears. His children were now safe to take the bus to school, he said.

In the weeks following, the mural would be defaced yet again. A reporter with the *Daily News* tracked down one man who refused to be named but explained why he preferred the old mural. "It had the names of guys who were significant to the neighborhood. This [stuff] don't mean anything to us."

✦ ✦ ✦

ON JULY 31, 2001, guards came to the cell at Brooklyn's Metropolitan Detention Center that Pipe shared with one of his codefendants, GI.

But this time they only called GI for a court appearance. In the MDC, defendants who weren't called to court with their codefendants inspired suspicion. Yet Pipe had not made a deal.

In court, Chantal waited to catch a glimpse of Pipe. She did her hair and nails before every court appearance and bustled around among the other girlfriends and mothers, offering help and counsel to those who hadn't been there before. Today, Chantal sat jammed in with other Soundview relatives and friends on polished wooden benches in the public gallery as the crew was led out by the marshals. But this time Pipe wasn't among them.

Chantal craned her neck, astonished. Quickly, she sensed a rising discomfort from the other families around her. People shot her looks. Chantal stared ahead. Then people began to gather their things to move to the other side of the courtroom. Within a few minutes, Chantal was alone. At the end of the session the marshals noted the commotion in the public gallery and escorted Chantal out.

Back on the cellblock, Pipe's cellmate returned and told him word was out that he was cooperating. Pipe caught dirty looks from Peter and Carmine Agnello, John Gotti's son and son-in-law. The Italians periodically sent out flunkies to engage other inmates in conversation, or do them favors, while trawling for information. Pipe had honed his disposition in prison. He walked with a stiff back and swiveled his eyes around any area he entered to let others know that he was aware of their presence. Sometimes he might throw out a smirk to suggest that he knew something he didn't. He kept to himself, stayed out of the mix, and observed. In time, he learned that the officers had left him out of the hearing because of an administrative error, but the damage was done.

A month or so later, ostensibly called out for a bail hearing, he found himself in one of the proffer rooms at the US attorney's office, face-to-face with O'Malley once more. LaBarbera was there, and Pipe was joined by his lawyer Stefanie Plaumann. "I told you I would see you again," O'Malley said. Pipe sneered, but everything that O'Malley had predicted when they'd first met in Cayuga had come true. Pipe had few cards left to play.

The two men stared at each other. Pipe had lied and used deceit as a way to make his living for years. He'd risen to OG and managed to play the feds and his crew. One slip and he easily could have been found behind the projects with a bullet in the back of his head, his body all but forgotten like Anthony Dunkley's. But he had survived at the top. For his part, O'Malley had flipped hundreds of men since he'd started at the US attorney's office in 1995.

Despite Pipe's double-dealing, LaBarbera had fought to give him a chance. The office remained sharply divided between those who believed he should never be trusted again and those who argued for a second chance. LaBarbera had forged a good relationship with Pipe's brother, knew a lot about the family, and sensed that Pipe would not only be useful but might be capable of redemption. She knew about Pipe's parents and how they had struggled to raise the family. But she felt that he would be a more sophisticated and dangerous person than Ro.

At first they all made small talk. LaBarbera wanted to know how he had gotten his nickname. O'Malley joked that it was because "he lays a lot of pipe" and made a sexually suggestive gesture with his hands. They all laughed. Pipe was grateful for the levity before the session began.

They wanted to know about Nut, the only one of the crew accused of murder in the indictment—for the killing of Tony Morton. Pipe said that he might help but that they needed to move Chantal out of Soundview, something that had been promised when he assisted as a confidential informant. And he told them, irritably, to always bring him out to court with his codefendants. "You made me hot," he complained.

O'Malley pushed Pipe to admit that he was an eyewitness to Morton's murder. Pipe began to weave a lie. He said that he had seen Nut bicycle up to the scene but that when the shots went off his vision had been obscured. The investigators stopped writing. O'Malley's unyielding, cold blue eyes bored into him. He'd seen this a hundred times: the low voice, lack of eye contact, and fidgeting. Everything would have to be turned over to the defense. A lie like this, if consigned to paper, would destroy Pipe's credibility in front of a jury.

"You're lying," rumbled O'Malley. "You're fuckin' lying. You saw exactly what happened." Pipe stared ahead. O'Malley could visualize the crime scene in his mind—saw Pipe walking up the flat expanse of Rosedale Avenue and knew, from what he had described before, that Pipe had watched Nut murder Morton. Proffers were the ultimate chess match. Abruptly, the session ended. O'Malley stood up and unlocked Pipe's handcuffs.

He told Plaumann to explain to her client the seriousness of proffers. And then in seconds Pipe found his wrists handcuffed again. O'Malley led him out of the room, heading for the MDC. As they started across the overpass, the two were alone. The bridge between the free world and prison was the best place to talk sense into a potential cooperator. Up ahead was a reinforced door that led to federal incarceration. Here, out of earshot of attorneys, O'Malley could talk frankly. This time, knowing Pipe as he did after their conversations on the Clason Point waterfront, he scolded him viciously. No one had ever spoken to Pipe this way. O'Malley told him that he'd lose the opportunity to get a cooperation agreement by bullshitting like that. Worse, he was jeopardizing everything with blatant lies. There was no laughing now. "You protecting someone, huh, Pipe?"

✦ ✦ ✦

PIPE RETURNED to the cell and turned it all over in his mind. His bravura won out. He felt he could win at trial. The feds had little on him besides the drug dealing. But a few days later, his lawyer received a call from LaBarbera. They were going to release to the other defendants' lawyers the secret recording Pipe had made with the wire. It would be part of the so-called 3500 material—the prior statements of government witnesses. Pipe's lawyers raced over to the MDC the next day. Neither of them knew anything about a recording. John Jacobs was an old-school lawyer who disliked rats as much as the gangsters did. He was astonished to hear that Pipe had made a recording for the feds. Pipe complained that he'd been "bamboozled," that the feds had told him it would never be released.

As Pipe was reassessing O'Malley's offer to cooperate, a letter from someone inside the MDC arrived in his cell. If inmates wanted to send each other notes, they would write a return address on an envelope in the top left-hand corner—which would actually be the inmate they wanted a letter to reach—while purposefully omitting a real addressee. The mailroom clerk would assume a mistake had been made and return the letter to the sender. Pipe read a corrosive letter from a gangster in the Monroe Houses that cursed him for snitching. The gangster said that he knew where the safe in Pipe's house was, and that his crew was going to break into the apartment. If they found Chantal and the children there, they'd be at enormous risk. Pipe called to warn her. The only other person he could think of who who knew about the safe was Nut.

A few days later, a codefendant meeting was held. Formally, these were occasions to discuss the case, but they were also social gatherings. Pipe approached Nut. "You know the only person who could hurt you in all this is me and B-Love, right?" he said. Nut nodded. "So if you snake me, Moe, you know what that is." Nut signaled that he understood. Pipe continued. "So you know nothing about some kid going in my crib?"

"Nah, Moe," Nut said. "Word to Bear." Swearing on the deceased gangster Bear was the ultimate oath. "Okay," Pipe said, pounding Nut on the back just before they left to return to the cells, giving no indication he knew he had lied.

Afterward, he broke away and sidled up to Plaumann out of earshot of the others. "Call Nicole and them," he said. "I want to talk."

Finally, after years of living the street life, lying, deceiving, protecting the guilty, Pipe had had enough. He'd protected Nut for the murder of an innocent man; he'd bailed him out with $2,500 when he got caught in November 2000 pimping underage prostitutes—one under fourteen—in Hunts Point. The supposed loyalty among Sex Money Murder and the Bloods was a complete farce. Pipe wasn't going to give up his life for a bunch of young Bloods who weren't even part of the original crew. Pete had already gone down, so he wouldn't have to testify against him in court. But his crew were just kids in the neighborhood who'd fuck him if given the chance. Pipe was going to protect himself first.

The next time he sat down with O'Malley, he agreed to take the biggest step of his life, something that went against everything he stood for. He would talk.

As the sessions began, they teased out Pipe's entire criminal history. He found it grueling. He felt like a total sucker, not only for informing but for having to confess his own crimes—in effect, informing on himself. He spoke about hustling on Cozy Corner and shooting the kids outside the Lafayette towers at the age of eleven. As he spoke, Plaumann was the only one in the room who registered discomfort, particularly when Pipe owned up to playing Russian roulette with one of the crackheads after pistol-whipping him, an episode even Pistol Pete had found disconcerting. O'Malley listened, never judging and never shocked. Pipe detailed murders, drug deals, the inner workings of Sex Money Murder from its inception. Pipe's confession lasted for days.

When he returned to his cell after the sessions, he felt wrung out and vulnerable. As he lay staring up at the ceiling he wondered if O'Malley would screw him. But now he had no choice.

O'Malley had warned Pipe that he would become a target. Word of his cooperation reached the street quickly when Chantal was spotted at the US attorney's office in the process of being relocated out of Soundview. Pipe was now "food."

But after half a dozen sessions stretching over weeks, Pipe found that the confessions lifted a weight. "I like you, Pipe," said O'Malley. "Tell the truth and you and I will be fine." Pipe nodded. "You know that if we hadn't interceded you'd probably more likely be dead by now." Pipe knew that O'Malley was right, but he also knew that the detective could never fully understand his limited choices growing up. "I just played the hand I was dealt in life, JO," he said.

Outside, Chantal bore the brunt of it. She went from being the respected and wealthy consort of the OG to being a struggling outcast. Threats came every day, sometimes directed at her children. A trip to the store became a nerve-racking expedition. When she put the garbage out, she looked both ways. At night, people kicked her door when they walked past. Female friends she'd gone to get her hair done with, women with whom she'd swapped stories and advice about raising children, suddenly abandoned her. Her two boys walked to school terrified.

Chantal's father worked for Con Edison, and her brother worked as a police officer in North Carolina. They disapproved of her life with Pipe and felt, in some sense, that this was just deserts. The mother of one of the gangsters Pipe would testify against destroyed his red GTI, smashing all the windows, stripping the car, and puncturing the tires. As Chantal ran out of money, she ran up his credit cards and sold his jewelry. She pawned the diamond-encusted THE WORLD IS YOURS globe that Pete had given him when SMM was at their zenith. She got $800 for it at a pawnshop on Third Avenue in the Bronx. Still, she put $200 a week into Pipe's commissary account and got a couple of new tattoos. On her way to visit him one day, changing trains at Atlantic Avenue in Brooklyn, she heard a woman shouting at her: "I know what shit your boyfriend's in. He's a snitch." Chantal had never seen the woman before.

Sometimes she brought the two boys, who jumped up into Pipe's lap and asked when he'd be coming home. By sometime in 2002, the US attorney's office had put Chantal and the boys in a hotel. None of them felt safe anywhere in the open. They jumped at shadows. Pipe told her to leave him, that he was done for, but she persisted. They got permission to be married in the MDC. Eventually, however, after a second relocation, this time to a housing project in Manhattan, they drifted apart. Even there, rumors soon circulated that her husband was a rat.

+ + +

ON FEBRUARY 28, 2003, Pipe walked into Judge Griesa's courtroom. O'Malley betrayed no emotion as Pipe caught his eye. Had Pipe been wrong to trust him? He realized he'd admitted everything and yet nothing had been promised in return.

After the preliminaries, Judge Griesa looked down at Pipe through his glasses. Pipe focused on a red-and-green tapestry behind the judge as he spoke quietly and deliberately, admitting his role as OG of Sex Money Murder. He confessed to racketeering, violent crime with a machine gun, and selling drugs, along with the unlawful transport of firearms. The charge of kidnapping had been dropped. Baby Ange, the instigator of the plot, had been killed on the block.

And then it was over. Immediately on his return he was moved to the Special Housing Unit for his own safety. All contact with his codefendants was severed.

The MDC was full of men trying to stay alive while pretending they weren't snitches. Despite his new status as cooperator, Pipe still had social capital, which only increased when a magazine mentioned Pipe and the original Sex Money Murder crew. "I didn't know you was that strong in the street," said an inmate who had read the story. He boasted about his crew on Long Island and how much money he would make on his release, but Pipe knew that he, too, was cooperating. He asked if Pipe had concerns about cooperating against the Bloods. "I wasn't loyal to no Bloods," snapped Pipe. Even OG Mack, the Blood founder, had been revealed as a snitch. "I was loyal to the Pistol," Pipe said, although Pete had already been sentenced by the time Pipe cooperated and he wouldn't have to "sit on him" in court. "That's who I grew up with, started a gang with, and that's who my loyalty is to. As far as people on my case, I don't know these dudes, man." Pipe paused. "I got a clean conscience. Any of them Blood dudes try to hurt me or jump out the window to hurt any of mines, then they gonna have a problem."

O'Malley and LaBarbera offered him the protective custody program, telling him that several others had taken advantage of it. Pipe refused. "I may be a cooperator," he said, "but I'm still a gangster. I ain't running and hiding from no one."

Eight

5K

IN THE MIDDLE OF THEIR PINOCHLE GAME, Sammy Gravano laid down his cards to offer Suge some advice. The old-time Mafia hit man had sent nineteen men to the grave. Now he was shriveled and pink, with limpid saucer eyes, the result of plastic surgery to evade the $2 million contract on his head after putting John Gotti, the boss of bosses, and numerous other mobsters, away. Suge thought he looked like an alien.

The two had grown close while incarcerated in the MCC; they worked out together and shared books. Gravano had served only five years for his murders but had now been convicted of selling Ecstasy and awaited sentencing. Suge had confided to him his deep unease at becoming a snitch. "No matter what you do in this world," Sammy said, "if you can get up and look at yourself in the mirror and tell yourself you love you, that's all that matters."

On May 14, 2003, Suge was led into the Honorable John Martin's courtroom, where he stole a glance at his old friend Bemo, sitting in a sober gray suit. Both he and Bemo, as Pete had done, were wearing glasses, although neither of them had problems with their eyesight. Between the defense lawyers sat federal marshals in suits, no badges or guns, nothing to suggest to the jury that the accused was dangerous. Suge had fought to hold out for Bemo, but the lies had crumbled in the face of O'Malley and LaBarbera's questioning. He looked across the packed courtroom and saw O'Malley toward the back of the public gallery, checking him out. Up until now all his confessions had been in private with O'Malley and LaBarbera, but as soon as he opened his mouth in court his new status as a cooperator would be public. He felt exposed and lonely. He turned to O'Malley standing in relief against the wood paneling, but the investigator just stared ahead placidly.

The prosecutor took Suge through his crimes in Springfield, the shootouts against ET Larry, and the eventual murder of Kiron Little. Suge told the story of his kidnapping and pistol-whipping. He looked at the jury, believing that he could elicit their sympathy if he told the story well. If there was one incident that made him as violent as he was, he would say it was being held in an elevator in the projects at gunpoint, blood leaking down his face, convinced he was going to die. Suge's eyes kept drifting toward an Asian woman on the jury who regarded his testimony dispassionately, which unsettled him. He admitted killing Twin on Rollock's orders, explained the conversation he had had with Bemo about the murder of a kid named Joe Dix.

A defense lawyer, Larry Krantz, noted that Suge had lied to federal agents, and that after he had signed documents saying he would commit no more crimes while on probation, he had murdered Twin. The lawyer pressed him on his motives for cooperating. "Did you decide at that point to become a cooperating witness because you had a change of heart, seen the error of your ways and wanted to unburden yourself for what you had done?"

"No," said Suge.

Throughout, no matter how uncomfortable it got, Suge was direct and honest, often when it wasn't in his own best interest. O'Malley was impressed.

✦ ✦ ✦

PIPE FOLLOWED Suge a day later. He'd heard rumors that Baby Jay, now also cooperating as the star witness in Bemo's trial, had offered to pay for Bemo's appeal. When Pipe reached the stand, Bemo smiled slightly and shook his head. Pipe assumed that he was intimating that he knew how the federal game was played. He thought that Bemo understood that he was just taking a shot at freedom, as Bemo might have done in his position.

The prosecutor described Pipe's double-dealing with the FBI, then ran through his crimes. "We played by the rules of Sex Money Murder," said Pipe. As he continued to offer testimony, he caught sight of a Sex Money Murder member from Castle Hill in the back of the courtroom alongside a well-dressed man in a white suit. The SMM man kept standing up, shooting caustic glances at Pipe as he testified. Just before recess for lunch, O'Malley, sitting in the back, saw the SMM gangster, tapped him on the shoulder, and asked to speak to him outside. There he discovered that he was on parole and in violation by being in court to consort with felons. O'Malley got him locked up shortly thereafter.

Meanwhile, Pipe was returned to a special holding cell for cooperators. It was a comfortless place, without even a window so that no one could see in. After lunch, a marshal opened the cage and Pipe went up in the elevator. But there'd been a mix-up. As the elevator door slid open, Pipe came face-to-face with Bemo. Fearing that the two men would try to kill each other, the marshals jumped between them. "What you doing?" Bemo said to one of the marshals. "That's my man." Pipe added, "'Sup, Moe!" They pounded each other on the back "I see you inside," said Bemo. "I love you, nigga."

✦ ✦ ✦

GIVING TESTIMONY on the stand was a lonely experience. The defense lawyer, Larry Krantz, goaded Pipe, and he barely resisted an urge to jump up and punch him in the face. "I told you in opening that you would see a parade of criminals the likes of which are almost unbelievable," said Krantz in summing up, "and I submit that is exactly what you saw here. A parade of individuals with no moral center, no moral compass whatsoever; a parade of individuals who probably, based on what you heard on the witness stand, could be labeled pathological liars, sociopaths." He continued: "These are murderers, liars, con artists. These are people who have devoted their life to lying and criminality. They are trying to spare their own life. Without cooperation they will die in prison."

When the jury took a second day to deliberate, O'Malley fretted that SMM had gotten to one of the jurors. But the jury finally returned a guilty verdict on the most serious of the charges. In September 2003, Bemo was sentenced to fifty years with no parole. As the jury filed out, they all avoided eye contact with Bemo. After any guilty verdict, the marshals moved prisoners swiftly out of the courthouse because the transfer after sentencing would be the most likely moment for an escape attempt.

News of Bemo's conviction spread throughout the MDC and the MCC with startling speed, and O'Malley knew that more potential cooperators would be coming in the next few days. Bemo's conviction would send a strong message. He waited for attorney phone calls on Monday, and they came.

✦ ✦ ✦

BY MAY 2003, Chantal had stopped coming to see Pipe, and he was now completely alone. In August, when Nut stood trial for killing Tony Morton, Pipe was again called to the stand. LaBarbera had left on maternity leave; a new prosecutor, Helen Cantwell, a Harvard graduate, stepped in. She approached cooperators with exactitude and little warmth. For Pipe, her approach and LaBarbera's contrasted sharply. She found Pipe particularly arrogant. "I'm not here to be your buddy," she said. Pipe dreaded the sessions with her because if he was caught leaving anything out, even unintentionally, she'd rip up his agreement and he'd be left with his guilty pleas and a life sentence.

In court, Cantwell initiated the government's case with the testimony from a couple Nut had robbed in the projects. The following day Pipe testified, along with B-Love and several others. On his way to court he crossed paths with Nut himself. "You a fuckin' rat," Nut said. "You're going to get your head popped off. And your fiancée, she's going to get her head popped off too. The government can't protect you forever." Nut was now claiming to be the new OG of Sex Money Murder. "You can be the new OG," said Pipe with a shrug. "I'm happy for you."

On August 16, 2003, the jury found Nut guilty of RICO conspiracy and murder. He was sentenced to life plus five years.

+ + +

THE DANGER of retribution for snitching was now omnipresent. Some saw cooperators as traitors who deserved a summary death sentence. On a Tuesday in June 2004, Pipe was trying to relax in his cell on the ninth floor of the SHU in the MDC, where he'd been moved for a violation. A familiar figure kicked his cell door. Pipe hadn't seen MAC-11 for ten years or more. He had a tattoo of Sex Money Murder on his arm, and he wore a red doo-rag to signify his Blood membership. Pipe remembered him as a boy who used to run errands to the store for him and other senior members of SMM to win favor, all before he helped Suge and the others murder Twin and E-Man. MAC-11 had never relinquished the gangster creed and refused to cooperate. He eventually pleaded guilty a few weeks after Pete and was sentenced to thirty years for his role in the Thanksgiving Day shootings. He'd returned to the cellblock after being sentenced and set fire to the mattress in his cell and assaulted the guards who came rushing in to douse the flames.

Pipe and Mac chatted briefly.

The following day MAC-11 asked Pipe to join him for recreation, which he did. Normally gang members, particularly those cooperating against one another, were segregated, but as the two men weren't on each other's case the guard had no instructions to keep them apart. MAC-11 explained that if he didn't attack Pipe as "food" for snitching against Nut, he himself would become "food" for the Bloods. He was only going to stay his hand, he said, because Pipe had the feds behind him. The two drifted apart.

Back in his cell, MAC-11 slammed his fist into his palm and made choking gestures as he retold the story of his meeting with Pipe to his cellmate, Albert Burgos, a member of the Westchester Avenue Crew in the Bronx. Burgos suggested a quid pro quo: MAC-11 would attack the cooperator on Burgos's case, while Burgos would attack Pipe in return.

A couple of days later a guard led Pipe to the cage containing MAC-11 and three other men. Pipe pulled back, sensing a setup. "What?" sneered the guard. "I thought you was a gangster and you scared?"

Pipe told the guard to to put him in. MAC-11 greeted him with a smile. The guard asked Pipe to walk backward and to feed his hands through the slot. As he did so, Pipe saw a flash from the other side of the cage. Frantically, he tried to free his hands from the guard's grip, but it was too late. Burgos's right hand crashed into his jaw, breaking it in several places.

The guard let go of Pipe's hands, unlocked the door, and dragged him out. "Uncuff me and put me back in there," Pipe screamed. He snarled at Burgos. "I'ma gonna see you! Do you know who I am? You ain't going nowhere in this building now. You a dead man."

Pipe was taken back to his cell. The guards ignored his requests for medical attention and instead tossed him some Tylenol. The pain worsened. At mealtime he couldn't open his jaw to eat. Over the next few days he sucked on potato chips until they were soggy, the salt stinging his mouth, before swallowing. In the end he took milk through a straw.

Pipe suspected that the guard had a Blood affiliation or had been paid. He advanced this theory when MAC-11 was moved up to his tier in the SHU. Pipe heard him shout to Burgos, "What up, son! It is what it is!" MAC-11's deep laughs reverberated down the corridor. "Yeah, you know!"

The pain grew worse as infection set in. Eventually he was allowed a hospital visit, where a surgeon fixed his jaw with a titanium plate and screws, then wired it shut. Although the prison medical team removed the wires after four weeks, almost two more months went by before they took Pipe back to the oral surgeon to remove some braces. By that time, his jaw had healed out of alignment so that his mouth couldn't open straight, and the surgeon told him that to fix it would require rebreaking and resetting his jaw.

+ + +

X WENT TO TRIAL in June 2005. Suge had taken a personal dislike to X and resented his rapid rise through SMM. Suge deplored having to testify against Bemo, a childhood friend, but X was another matter.

The prosecutor asked Suge why he was cooperating. He said he didn't want to spend the rest of his life in jail, then added: "Another reason was that I started to see there was no loyalty and trust in the organization that I was in, too many lies, people deceiving one another."

Though he'd had Pete in mind when he said it, he declared his love for his leader only a few minutes later in testimony. "He was a good friend of mine, and he's the one that always had my back growing up. He was always there for me, any problem I had, any fights. We grew up together, fighting, jumping people. So I could always count on him to be there for me. I was the same way with him."

After a three-week trial, X was convicted on July 8, 2005, of attempted murder and racketeering. He later received a life sentence, along with Elijah Williams, his brother, and Michael Torres, Williams's son.

+ + +

AS PIPE'S sentencing approached, he spiraled into depression and loneliness, doing as many as fifteen hundred push-ups a day to ease the boredom while facing a future tarred as a cooperator. Meanwhile, on the outside Pete was being deified. In 2002 Nas released *God's Son*, and in the first line of the opening song, "Get Down," he referred to "New York streets where killers will walk like Pistol Pete."

On January 25, 2005, Pipe stood once more in Judge Griesa's court, the last case of the day. The familiar figure of O'Malley stood witness once more to another defining point in Pipe's life. Stefanie Plaumann stood at Pipe's side. The pair had grown close and, in a sense, become like a brother and sister. Plaumann had come to respect him, quite unlike the business-only relationship she had with her other clients. She sensed his humanity, despite his acts. And unlike other clients, he never made her feel threatened or blamed her for not helping him. He took it all upon himself.

LaBarbera had written a stunning 5K letter because she believed that if given the chance, Pipe could begin a new life. O'Malley was familiar by now with the subtleties, the inconsistencies, and sometimes the unfairness of the cooperating agreements and knew that not everyone received favor from the judge for their assistance.

Plaumann was hoping that LaBarbera's 5K letter about Pipe's cooperation, which had put twenty people away, would push the judge
toward leniency. Pipe looked out of the court's twenty-sixth-floor windows; it was like peering out of an airplane window at the city below.
He stood up and admitted he wasn't happy about his crimes. He was
young when he started. He had two addicts for parents; one of them
languished in prison for most of his childhood. "This was the only life
I knew," he said. "I thought it was the best way to take care of my wife
and my family. I realize now it wasn't the right way to do things." The
judge nodded impassively. Pipe panicked inside but pressed on. "I want
to apologize to anyone and their families that I hurt, and I want to
apologize for anyone I was affiliated with. I wouldn't wish it on anyone
to lose a loved one."

Time in the courtroom slowed as Pipe clung to the judge's response.
"I really like your speech," Judge Griesa said. "I'm going to hold you to
everything you said. I'm letting you go to make the changes in your life
you want to make." The judge reminded him that if he appeared in court
again, "there won't be any mercy."

Judge Griesa freed Pipe with time served. Pipe didn't understand
what had happened at first. He looked at Plaumann. She grinned. Then
he understood. He subdued the urge to sweep her up in his arms. She
suppressed the impulse to hug him.

Sometime in the early evening, he stood on the swirling and noisy
Lower Manhattan street outside the court, looking out at the fast-
moving city, office workers surging past him on their way home. Pipe
wore the MDC SHU uniform of tight blue pants, a form-fitting jailhouse shirt, and black kung fu slippers. Plaumann asked him where he
planned to go. He said he'd go to Chantal's apartment in Manhattan.
"Are you out of your mind?" she said. "There's a price tag on your head
now!" Pipe shrugged it off, just pleased to be free.

An FBI agent escorted him to a hotel, where they could begin to
plan his transition to the outside world. Before they checked in, the FBI
agent suggested that they stop at Duane Reade to get a toothbrush and
some other essentials. At the counter Pipe asked for a packet of Newport

menthols. Outside on the bustling sidewalk near Madison Square Garden, the noise of rush-hour traffic filling his senses, he ripped off the packaging, tugged a cigarette out of the box, lit it, and took a deep drag. He was swept up in dizziness. He staggered happily down the sidewalk, bracing himself now and then on a street sign.

Nine

EXILE

PIPE'S FALTERING STEPS IN THE FREE WORLD took him to a cheap and modest room in Queens. He had never held a job. He applied for cleaning positions, doing maintenance, using the skills he had learned in prison. Each time he reported his criminal and felony record, he got rejected. Frustrated, he applied for a job as a janitor at the Reebok Sports Club gym on Columbus and Sixty-Seventh in Manhattan, this time leaving the criminal history line blank. He got the job. For $8.50 an hour from 11:00 p.m. to 5:00 a.m., the OG scoured the floors and wiped yuppie sweat off the walls of the gym. He made $207 a week, enough to pay for a day's worth of cognac in his old life.

In the early hours of Saturday morning, people were just leaving the clubs. At the end of his shift as he trudged home he caught sight of one or two gangsters still in the game—dawn's watery light hitting the chrome rims on a Mercedes while they drove one-handed, ball caps cocked to the side, bass pounding from inside their leather-lined cabin—as they swept past him on his lone walk to the subway.

After a few months he moved in to share his elder sister Annette's apartment. Pipe's street legend still flourished. Smoking a cigarette outside one day, he ran into two Bloods. "'Sup, five, where you from?" one of the men asked, indicating that he and his friend suspected he might be Blood by the way he carried himself; the "five" was a reference to the five-pointed star and crown of the Bloods. "Soundview," Pipe answered. The man went on to brag about the night he had spent in the company of the Sex Money Murder crew, including "Leadpipe hisself." Pipe nodded along with fake humility. They were lying. He thought, *These chumps don't even know who I am.*

In August 2005, Pipe got a call from a friend telling him to search YouTube for a song called "Tattle Teller," by Tony Yayo, a rapper with 50 Cent's G-Unit. The song began with a seventies soul funk vibe and then the lines: "Pipe on death row, they told on Pete / They the reason that pistol ain't on the street." Pipe's gorge rose. He had never cooperated against Pete. He had remained loyal to his friend. These rappers had no idea about any of this. They had no idea how Sex Money Murder had deteriorated, how all around him loyalties had crumbled, and how Pete had allowed his jealousy to dictate his orders. The betrayal was Pete's, and the whole crew had turned against one another when Pete went down. Moreover, Pipe had cooperated a year or so after Pete had been convicted and wasn't even on his old friend's case.

The anti-snitch message had gone wide in inner-city communities across the country. A 108-minute video entitled *Stop Fucking Snitching Vol. 1,* produced by the Tree Top Piru Bloods in Baltimore, became a national sensation. STOP FUCKING SNITCHING T-shirts were made up.

✦ ✦ ✦

EVERY FEW weeks O'Malley called to see how Pipe was doing. He wanted Pipe to succeed, and above all he wanted him to know that he wasn't alone. Lost as he was, Pipe latched onto O'Malley and drew on their relationship for reassurance as he faced his new life.

Pipe once again turned to Chantal. They took up where they'd left off, and soon Chantal was pregnant with his son. The news startled him, and he was forced to consider how he could support a child on his minimum wage. One possible solution came when he ran into a couple of Bloods who lived in the apartment below his sister, one of whom was making a fortune selling Ecstasy. The Blood said he could offer Pipe the chance of buying pills at $2 to $3. He was selling them in clubs in Virginia Beach for $40 each. With a small investment of $1,000, Pipe could make as much as $20,000. Or, if he could wholesale the pills in Virginia Beach to a major player for $15 or so, he could off-load all the risk. Pipe said he would think about it. "For you, big homie, I give an even bigger discount," the Blood promised him.

That night Pipe lay in bed turning the proposition over in his mind. The deal would liberate him from scrubbing floors, put him back in a decent car and perhaps offer a route out of poverty. Flipping the first load of Ecstasy would be enough to make a down payment on a kilo of cocaine or heroin. But then, at some point, he knew, the violence would start. He'd have to kill someone, or at least attempt it, to take over a block and show he could not be robbed. And he'd never stop until he was caught or dead. Then Pipe switched focus, letting in a new sensation: a tenderness for his unborn son. He recalled what it was like growing up with an absent father in prison. He thought of O'Malley, how afraid he was to let the old man down. The next morning, he told the Blood he wasn't interested.

Life continued to pulse at a low ebb. His relationship with Chantal disintegrated despite impending fatherhood. Pipe wasn't sure what he felt anymore. He wrestled with his emotions. Sometimes he hated Chantal and other times he loved her. He resented how she had abandoned him in prison when his fate was unclear. They'd been through too much, their relationship born out of the chaos of Soundview.

When his relationship with Chantal finally ended, Pipe took up with another woman, Erica, a friend of his sister's he had met in New York. In 2005, he quit his gym job and moved into the Virginia home she shared with her baby and her baby's father, who was in the US Navy. The sailor lived in the spare room, often supporting Pipe and Erica financially. But when that support dried up, Pipe had no choice but to pawn the last two remnants of his life as OG, two cherished $800 Avirex leather jackets given to him by the rapper Lord Tariq. He got $60 for each, and what he had lost in status and prestige hit home. The money lasted only a few days, after which Erica and Pipe were panhandling for spare change outside the Big K supermarket.

Then the couple had a fight at the house, and the sailor got involved, threatening Pipe with a kitchen knife. Pipe phoned O'Malley, saying he was afraid he was going to hurt the man. O'Malley called the police, who sent two officers and got Pipe out of harm's way; then O'Malley booked him a plane ticket back to New York.

✦ ✦ ✦

NO ONE held out much hope for leniency at Suge's sentencing with Judge Cedarbaum, scheduled for January 31, 2006. Despite Suge's substantial cooperation, O'Malley expected twenty years minimum for the murder of Twin.

Suge had met with the WITSEC staff a few days earlier. Although it was unlikely that he would be freed with time served, they discussed phase two of the witness protection program—life on the outside after release. In these cases, the marshal whisked the free man away to an unknown location, where he was given a new name and Social Security number; he was not permitted contact with any family members or friends, or even the investigator with whom he had worked—in Suge's case, O'Malley. A violation of any of these conditions brought immediate explusion from the program.

At the hearing, Judge Cedarbaum credited Suge for cooperating with the government. "I really hope that it does signify that you have a new outlook on life," she said. Suge replied that he had learned from his mistakes. "And hopefully I'll be able to fit back into society," he said. "And I hope I can give back to others."

Cedarbaum asked him for thoughts on his future. "It's like I was in a coma," said Suge, "and now I'm out of a coma and I have a new life."

Cedarbaum's remarks suggested that she saw Suge's problems as a result of a blind loyalty to bad characters. She advised him to "stay away from bad companions."

"Of course," Suge said. "I learned in my career planning class that the company you keep determines your outlook on things, your decision-making."

"Well, it really shouldn't as you become a man," she replied, "but it certainly doesn't help to be surrounded by people who have different aims than yours. And in your case in particular, when you were influenced by a group, it's very important that you stay away from such groups."

The judge gave him time served—almost eight years at that point—and five years of supervised release. She ordered that he make good on financial compensation to his victims. "I heard some of those victims in this courtroom, the mothers of young men who were killed," Cedarbaum said, "and it was pretty chilling."

Suge almost broke down in tears. O'Malley made his way up to Suge at the defense tables. "I'm bugged out, JO," Suge said. "I'm leaving today? Oh, shit!" But when he learned that he'd have to spend an extra thirty days in WITSEC as things were prepared before his release into phase two, he instantly opted out of the program. Now that he had been freed, he didn't want to spend a second longer than he had to in jail. He was told that once he made the decision to leave the program, he would not be allowed back in. But Suge, true to his nature, didn't think about any of that. He thought about getting laid and smoking a joint. Life was lived by the minute, his decisions guided by what made the most sense in the moment.

O'Malley called him to his office and said that it would be better for everyone if he left New York. Suge suggested Springfield. The office arranged for his supervised release to be handled in Worcester, Massachusetts. O'Malley had some parting words. "I don't want to see you kill anyone," he said. "Or for anyone to put a bullet in you. And I don't want to see you get caught selling drugs again." Suge swore he was going to start anew. O'Malley worried about his cooperators and the death sentence they lived under when they were released. Any Blood looking to make a reputation could make a murder attempt on a cooperator, now "food," for instant status.

That night Suge went directly to Queens, where he spent the night with an old flame. The following day, he broke his promise to O'Malley and caught a cab to Soundview. He wanted to feel Soundview soil under his feet just once more. He hadn't seen his grandmother for years. He slipped into his old building and knocked on his door. Miss Julia, now eighty-one, looked frail but welcomed him. They sat in the living room, making small talk. Suge settled into the old feeling of belonging. After a while Miss Julia's tone turned solemn and reflective. "There ain't nothing but trouble over here," she rasped. "Stay away from Soundview."

After a couple of hours Suge said good-bye and climbed into a taxi outside. He asked the driver to make a detour through Cozy Corner. It looked altogether cleaner than he remembered. The young hustlers there didn't recognize him, nor he them. He passed through quickly. He was a rat now and no longer welcome. He ordered the cabdriver to take him away.

Suge made it north to Springfield, where he still had the remnants of a family. The mother of his son took him in, and Suge saw his child for the first time since age four, when Suge had gone into prison, and now a teenager at thirteen. For a few weeks Suge tried to be a father. He drove his son to his basketball games at middle school. But over time he drifted back to old friends, some of whom still had one foot in the drug game. One of them ran a car lot and got him a battered Lincoln. Suge began making short trips to New York and took up with the woman in Queens.

He learned how to use Facebook, which allowed him to track what people in Soundview were saying about the rats. Many said that Suge should have shared Pete's fate—that he shouldn't have been released with such a light sentence when Pete was locked away for good. He felt himself receding into the purgatorial margins of society, all his rank and power gone. Suge felt it was unfair, and recalled others who had cooperated with prosecutors against the killers of Fat Mike, for example, but who had been welcomed back into the fold of Sex Money Murder. In the complex swirl of emotions he supressed some vague sense of survivor's self-reproach. Eventually, on a drive down to New York, Suge took a call from Pipe. They complained bitterly about one particularly critical Facebook comment. Suge decided to set the record straight. In Queens he picked up his girlfriend and her brother. The brother brought a gun and volunteered to take the charge if they were caught. Suge was on supervised release, and any infraction could send him back to prison. He drove them all into Soundview under cover of night. They circled the horseshoe a few times before they spotted the man. "Yo, let me see the hammer," said Suge to the girl's brother in the backseat. He passed the gun forward out of the darkness. Suge rolled up beside the man on the sidewalk. "Yo," Suge shouted, rolling down the window as he slowed the car. "Let me talk to you real quick." The man moved to the driver's side window. "Oh, you Suge, ain't you?" he asked before recoiling in horror at the gun nestling in Suge's lap in the murky interior of the car.

"Let me ask you something, man," Suge said. "You got a problem with Pipe?" The guy backed off. Suge pressed him. "Don't have me come out of my character, man, and have to come over here." When he saw the man understood, Suge drove off. Pipe called Suge as he neared Springfield a couple of hours later. Everyone in Soundview was talking about his appearance.

Suge returned to Soundview again a few months later to avenge more disrespects. He made threats and left, but this time just as he was leaving his cell phone rang. It was John O'Malley. "I don't want you guys down there," he growled. "You don't have anything to prove. Just stay away." Suge was startled at how close O'Malley was to the street.

Suge took up with Gina, his ex-girlfriend in Springfield, who gave him a home and offered to help him make a fresh start, driving him to meetings with his parole officer in Worcester. He briefly got a job selling vacuum cleaners. But he spent his evenings at a strip club, blowing money and returning home at 5:00 a.m., smelling of cheap vanilla perfume. By August his relationship had crumbled when his cheating was revealed and a woman called Gina at 5:00 a.m. saying she could keep him.

Miss Julia passed away in September 2006. Suge tattooed JULIA RIP on his neck and MOMMA FORGIVE ME on his left arm. Whatever strength he had in rehabilitation deserted him. In November he got caught by the police in a stolen Buick Skylark. When police officers tried to cuff him, he twisted free and sprinted off. Scaling a fence, he mule-kicked a policeman before being dragged off and handcuffed. Once more Suge, now thirty-two, was locked up.

Suge's and Pipe's narratives began to diverge sharply. Pipe had been the opportunist who had sought financial gain through gang life. But Suge, who had structured his whole identity around the code of the crew, couldn't let go of the street. They bickered. Suge derided Pipe for wearing a wire. Pipe criticized Suge for telling on Pete.

In February 2006, Pipe held Chantal's hand as she delivered their son by cesarean section. Their relationship had collapsed, but childbirth brought them momentarily closer. Pipe experienced the first stirrings of parental love and responsibility. Despite living with another woman, he lavished care on his firstborn and tried to make sure he wanted for nothing.

✛ ✛ ✛

IN JUNE 2006, in breach of his unique confinement conditions, Pistol Pete put out a self-published book, *Trigga*. He had started a manuscript in the Charlotte jail in 1997 and written the book in longhand in the ADX. The protagonist of his bildungsroman, Tyvon, a young hustler from Soundview, has an ambitious dream: "New York would be introduced to one of the youngest, most feared Drug King Pins in the city's history," he wrote. He referenced the hustler's dream of untold riches and told how Tyvon attended parties with P. Diddy, Tyra Banks, and Tupac and Biggie Smalls. Pete's murders were thinly disguised, as was the pleasure he had taken in killing:

> Without any hesitation, Tyvon squeezed off five shots from his 45 . . . He walked down the steps and stood directly over Slims body, and fired two more shots at point blank range into Slims head killing him instantly. At that moment an instant feeling of satisfaction and security flowed threw his veins. The adrenalin rush that he heard others talk about feeling after taking a life was now his own boost of energy and just like Shamle, Kane and everybody else like them, Ty enjoyed what he felt. Just like a person inhaling the powerful gray smoke out of a crack pipe for the first time, little did he know, he was already addicted to the feel of the kill.

In the end, Tyvon, head of Money & Murder, makes the top of the FBI's Most Wanted list, chased by an agent, McNally, only to be double-crossed by "one of the biggest rats in New York City history," a member of his own crew; "the damage that this one man would be responsible for would affect families for generations." Tyvon dies in a blaze of bullets, a martyr to the cause of drug dealing, increasing "money stacks," luxury cars and staying true to the game. Pete's book concluded: "In death, the legend of Tyvon Riley had been solidified. Books and magazine articles were written about him and straight to DVD movies were made. He had been immortalized in rap songs, and people who had never been in the same room with him now proudly wave shirts with his likeness printed on them. Gangsters and Hustlers everywhere, both young and old, reverently tell stories about his life."

+ + +

SUGE HEARD about the book but never read it. Although he still venerated Pete and the gangster life he described in his book, the reality of "catching his first body" had created infinitely more problems for Suge than it solved, and was far from glamorous. It was a bitter paradox that he'd murdered to prove his fealty, in the same way that as a boy he had fought for acceptance and a greater sense of belonging in the neighborhood. But now, with this ultimate act of allegiance, he had been exiled from Soundview, more lonely and isolated than ever.

In April 2007, police were called to a dispute Suge was having with a girlfriend in Springfield. He'd been standing outside the apartment, according to a witness, shouting at the woman inside: "You better get the fuck out of here cuz I'm gonna start fuckin' shootin'." The witness said that Suge had acted as if he had a gun concealed under his hoodie. Although no gun was recovered, he was charged with possession of a firearm without a license, assault with a dangerous weapon, and domestic assault. The arrest report detailed the twenty street aliases he used. Suge was taken into custody by the US Marshals and returned to the Southern District of New York for breach of his supervised release.

After only eighteen months, Suge appeared in court once again in front of Judge Cedarbaum. In court once again for Suge, O'Malley's severe expression needed no translation. He felt that Suge had spat in the face of everyone who'd tried to help him. LaBarbera, who knew Suge had never really understood why he might need to change, was deeply upset he had squandered his chance. Cedarbaum went through some formal motions and then, to everyone's disbelief, let Suge go free without charge. Further, she waived the terms of his supervised release. O'Malley surmised that Cedarbaum had become exasperated and just wanted to forgo any responsibility for him. Suge gave O'Malley a fuck-you sneer and skipped out of court. He'd beaten the feds once more. He felt invincible.

He was subsequently arrested on a domestic assault in Vermont, followed by a DUI. Now unwelcome in yet another state, he returned to Springfield, where he was arrested again on a September evening in 2008. At around 8:30 p.m., police officers heard gunshots and stopped a Camry that had been shot at several times by a man on a bicycle. Suge was found in the car, with a pitbull on the backseat and eleven bags of heroin packaged with rice to keep it fresh before it was sold. Pleading guilty, he skipped again with time served. He was the luckiest felon O'Malley knew, somehow always able to use guile, a quick mouth, and a lifetime spent learning how to manipulate the system to get back on the street.

He wandered back to New York, where he linked up with Pipe, then living with Annette. Pipe knew enough about Suge to know he was a danger to her, but she was soon pregnant with Suge's second son. He moved in with her and managed to land a job at MTV in shipping and receiving. He liked the steady money but grew bored. So he left and went on welfare, smoking weed most days to ease his agitation.

Suge was a lost soul, a soldier without a general to take orders from or an army to fight for. He was still prone to violence, and was arrested for assaulting Annette. When arguments erupted she called him a rat publicly, even though O'Malley had told her not to use that phrase in the housing projects—it was too dangerous. They moved around the city. O'Malley worried that Suge would draw Pipe back into the old life. He told Pipe to stay away, but Pipe was now trying to convince Suge to go straight. "When you cooperated, all that gangster shit was finished," Pipe said. "The code's over. You got a new code now. You ain't a gangster no more." But Sugar Shaft had no interest in becoming Shawn again.

+ + +

REDEMPTION WASN'T easy for Pipe. He posted his résumé on Craigslist. A man contacted him, saying he needed someone to mail out electronics in prepaid packages. It seemed like a sinecure, and Pipe signed on. GPS devices for airplanes and other items arrived at his apartment with prepaid packaging. Pipe mailed them out to assigned addresses. Within a few weeks, his parole officer, flanked by a heavily armed detachment of Connecticut State Police and gang squad detectives, burst into his apartment. Pipe had unwittingly gotten himself involved in fencing stolen goods.

After an investigation, he was vindicated. Once more he went in search of work. He and Erica decided to get married. They said their vows in jeans and T-shirts at a church in the Bronx, with Ro as best man. When Pipe thought out loud that he might return to the streets, Erica held firm. "I didn't marry a street person," she said.

Through Erica's uncle, Pipe managed to land a job at a hospital in Queens doing maintenance work for $15 an hour. When Erica gave birth to a daughter, Pipe's attraction to the streets vanished. He doted on her and vowed he would never return to prison and leave her without a father to protect her. Yet his status as a cooperator affected his children even years later. Sometimes his son and Chantal went back to visit his grandparents in Soundview. The kids teased him that his father was a rat. People continued to threaten Pipe over social media.

In the summer of 2013, the hospital laid him off. The electricity in their home was shut off. Pipe's car was repossessed, and he had to pay several hundred dollars to get it back before it was repossessed yet again.

Then, toward the end of that summer, he received a call from the ironworkers union offering him an apprenticeship. A while back he'd filled out some forms and been rejected but told his application would stay on file. The man on the phone warned him that the work would be challenging and that he would have to attend night school three times a week after working a full day. He explained the hourly wage and how it would rise each year. Pipe spun the numbers in his head just as he had with cocaine consignments. He might be able to to buy a home—his dream—within five years.

He awoke at 3:45 a.m. and walked a hilly mile and a half in a New England city to the train station. He worked a full day. "I love money," he told his coworkers. Pipe then went to night school after work. Sometimes he got only three hours of sleep.

Trudging through knee-deep snow, he thought of Pistol Pete, his whole world a concrete cell without a window. He missed his old friend, still loved him. Sometimes when Pipe heard Tupac now he was transported back to playing basketball in Soundview Park on a sweet summer's night, Pete always with that joyous grin, as he dribbled and made jump shots—even though he wondered if Pete might have killed him, too, if the feds hadn't intervened. Pipe contemplated what they would say if they saw each other again.

Word reached the street that Pete had been nearly a model prisoner in the ADX. In his first two years in solitary, he took closed-circuit TV courses in philosophy, political theory, and economics. By 2006, he had racked up numerous hours of Classical Mythology, the Joy of Science, and the History of Ancient Rome. He'd completed an anger management course. His lawyers argued that he was well on the way to rehabilitation and ready to enter the general population. The original eighteen-month review of his solitary confinement conditions had long expired, but still he was kept isolated.

✦ ✦ ✦

THE GOVERNMENT continues to argue that Rollock is a danger, notably because of the reverence he inspires among East Coast Bloods, many of whom may do his bidding unquestioningly. Sometime in his sentencing, he was restricted from contacting his father. "We have concerns that he may enlist his father to have his father's associates do harm to the witnesses and/or their families," wrote a prosecutor.

On the Bronx streets, Pistol Pete's legend still persists, even though the other Bronx crews of his era are long forgotten. Around 2004, Forcelli returned to the Bronx to visit his wife's family. His mother-in-law showed him a T-shirt she'd bought in a neighbhood store for her grandson. It read: FREE PISTOL PETE.

Rollock's viral legacy spread down the eastern seaboard. The first generation of Sex Money Murder was nearly eradicated, but permutations of it survive to this day. In May 2014, three SMM members broke into a Decatur, Georgia, home and shot three women and a nine-month-old boy taking cover in the bathtub. Tanyika Smith tried to protect her son, KenDarious Edwards Jr., as nine bullets tore into her. He was killed, while she and another woman survived. Their killing had been ordered by OG Kenneth Jackson, incarcerated in Autry State Prison, in retaliation for their brother Oslushsla's unauthorized killing of a fellow SMM member he believed was a snitch. Investigators discovered that Jackson had looked for guidance to MAC-11, who had become an exalted ranking Blood leader in the prison system. Jackson, three other gang members, and a female accomplice were indicted by a grand jury in May 2016 and face trial.

Similar scenes play out in the Sex Money Murder's new strongholds in Kingston, New York, and Newark, New Jersey, where SMM's influence and ideology have spread. Younger members use the term "Peter Roll" as shorthand for murder, although they don't know the provenance of the phrase.

+ + +

ON A SULTRY day in the summer of 2016, Pipe stood on the thirty-second floor of 3 World Trade Center, a soaring, thousand-foot monolith under construction. He had completed three years of night school and an apprenticeship to become a journeyman with a rigging supervisor qualification. He had saved up enough to take out a mortgage on a house and sent his daughter to a private school so she could have a different life than his. He hung suspended, swinging back and forth like Spider-Man from the soaring battleship gray supports that surged toward the sky, high above the dizzying drop to the city below. He was profiled against the two cascading waterfalls that marked where the old towers were before 9/11. He had a thick black beard now, and his forearms were corded with muscle. He'd given up hard drinking and weed; his skin and his eyes were clear. For most of the day he manned "the crab," a powerful hoist that lifted 3,500-pound, specially reinforced windows up several stories to be fixed into position. The eighty-story skyscraper glistened in the sunlight, a powerful metaphor for New York City's resilience in the face of adversity. After his crew pulled in the window and he dropped the hoist down, he stole a moment to gaze north up the shores of a city that had become strangely peaceful since the dystopia of the 1990s.

+ + +

EVERY CHRISTMAS, Father's Day, and Thanksgiving, O'Malley gets up from his capacious, faded and worn armchair to answer calls from cooperators who want to thank him. "I'm glad you chose law enforcement," SMM cooperator Dula texted him. "Not because it was for a paycheck, because we both know the money wasn't life-changing money, but because you wanted to make a difference. Very glad I met you. You saved my life." One of those calls always comes from Pipe. He figured that O'Malley had given more young men an alternative to an early grave or a lifetime of incarceration, ensuring that more children could have fathers and flourish for generations, than anyone else he knew.

From the moment of his first shooting, at the age of eleven, Pipe had been trying to gain some control, some sense of purpose and power. Sex Money Murder had looked like his best chance. But that proved illusory. Now, finally, he had a real chance to establish a safe place and a stable life without guilt or fear, but with promise.

Epilogue

"THE STREETS DON'T LOVE YOU"

IN DECEMBER 2012, I WALKED INTO one of the proffer rooms at the US attorney's office to meet John O'Malley. We sat and waited for Suge. A few months before, O'Malley had called me to say that he had two gang members who wanted to tell their story. "It's not bullshit stuff," said O'Malley. "These guys are the real deal."

After twenty minutes a tightly coiled figure dressed all in black, a woolen hat pulled low over his eyes, entered the room. One gold tooth glinted in the front of his mouth. "What's good, JO?" Suge said before turning to me and shaking my hand forcefully with his long, slender fingers. A recently inked tattoo on the back of his right hand read BLAZIN' BILLY, another name for Sex Money Murder. On his right was the five-pointed star of the Bloods. He took a seat at the head of the table.

O'Malley told Suge to be himself and to say what was on his mind. A garbled story tumbled out, full of non sequiturs and unfamiliar names. "Niggas don't even know Pete and they sayin' all this bullshit," he said. "They sayin' they be with him and did this and that." He had particular scorn for a documentary in which a Blood claimed to have been with the original Sex Money Murder crew; no one remembered him. And he was tired of the snitch label; people didn't understand why he had done what he'd done.

O'Malley sat back and watched our interaction, chewing on the earpiece of his glasses. "I've been asked to tell my story already by a lot of people," Suge told me, alluding to a gangster-run documentary company.

"That's bullshit, Suge," O'Malley said. "You sure they're not trying to set you up to get you to go down there so they can put a bullet in your head?"

Suge shook his head vigorously to reject the idea.

He wanted to be made a millionaire for telling his story. He wanted to move to Canada or England and start a new life. "If I ain't getting shit, why would I do it?" he fumed. O'Malley cut in again. "Look, if you're not serious, why don't you let Jonathan go on his way and stop taking up everyone's time?"

"Listen, I'm happy to hear what you have to say," I said. "But I make you no promises. Either you want to tell me about your life or you don't. That's it."

Finally, a smile broke across Suge's face. It seemed I'd passed the first test. "I like this guy," he said to O'Malley, clapping me on the back. O'Malley told us in no uncertain terms to be careful about how we proceeded. "Don't worry," said Suge. "I'd take a bullet for you." I later understood that if Suge felt you could better his life he would, conditionally, go all out for you, but that much of what he said was guided by bravado and self-interest.

He said there was a former OG of Sex Money Murder who also wanted to meet me but didn't want to reveal himself until he got a feel for who I was. Suge would report back, and if all was good, we'd meet at an undisclosed location outside New York City.

So it was that on a bleak January midmorning in 2013, sleet lashed the hood of my old Jeep as I drove around looking for a safe haven— somewhere we wouldn't be recognized. Suge was in the backseat talking a mile a minute, his vigorous frame bouncing from one side to the other. "If we go to Soundview, we have to take guns," he said. "And we probably shouldn't let JO know." He paused for a rare moment of introspection. "Oh, wait, JO said no guns anymore." I told Suge it wasn't necessary. "Okay," he said. "Whatever you need to do to write this book. We can wear bulletproof vests at least, JO says." He laughed. "I'm Gucci, yo." We pulled into a steakhouse off I-95 in Connecticut and sat down with Pipe to talk.

Hunkered around a table, we laid out the story of Sex Money Murder. They scrutinized my every move, my clothing, reading whatever signs they could. "Look at those boots, Skip," said Suge, pointing out my battered desert boots to Pipe. "He got some swag." We had taken a booth out of earshot of other customers. Pipe analyzed me as Suge chattered. Pipe was laconic, unsmiling. He rolled up his sleeves to reveal beefy, heavily inked forearms.

When the men discovered that my wife was Jamaican and from Brooklyn, Pipe almost choked on his food. "What?" His voice rose an octave. "Yo, Suge, he married to a black chick! He likes a little color, Moe."

We spoke in broad terms about the organization, and Suge and Pipe sketched it out on the back of a napkin. They argued about who was a founding member and who wasn't. I asked where everyone was now. Pipe filled me in on a few gang members and said matter-of-factly, "Twin, he's dead. He killed him."

I didn't understand.

"He killed him," Pipe repeated, nodding at Suge. Suge smiled, mock-sheepish. Pipe drew a small diagram with unfamiliar names. "Me and Pipe, we here," he said, indicating where they were on the list of Sex Money Murder leaders. Suge pointed to Pipe. "He's a rat bastard. And the infamous Peter Rollock: life plus a hundred twenty-five years." Suge continued with a soliloquy on how Pete hated bullies and always stood against them. He looked at me. "And his composure is even ten times smoother than yours." Suge was paying me an offhand compliment, at the same time indicating how silent and deadly Pete could be.

He told the story of hunting for Twin in a gold Cadillac, claiming 50 Cent had immortalized the scene in his song "I'll Whip Ya Head Boy." Suge, grinning, went to his phone and showed me a YouTube video, nodding his head in time with the plangent chords: "Two niggaz in the front, two niggaz in the back / That's four niggaz ridin' strapped in grandpa's Cadillac."

Both detailed their shootings—Suge laughing when someone got "rocked"—before telling the story of the murder Twin committed in Sweetwater's. "It's faking left, going right 'cause we gonna kill you regardless," said Suge. "When we rock you to sleep it's like we trying to put you to sleep."

"Make you feel comfortable," added Pipe.

Later in the coversation, though, I could see that Pipe wasn't as enamored of gangster life as Suge. When I asked why he wanted to tell his story, he replied flatly: "People need to understand that we're not animals. Yes, we sold crack and we killed people, but I only played the hand I was dealt. I had moms, sisters who I loved. I want people to know that anyone caught up in gang life is a human being." A silence followed.

Suge followed Pipe's lead. "We want people to know that the streets don't love you. They never did. If people get that message from telling our story, then that's what we want."

We agreed that it was preferable to meet on neutral ground, away from where they lived. A white man visiting Suge in the projects on a regular basis would bring suspicion. And John O'Malley had one rule of his own for me: "You're never to have them in your house." O'Malley didn't fully trust either of them and told me several times to be careful.

The next meeting, a month later, we learned more about each other. Suge had nicknamed me JG. But this time he was agitated as we stood in a restaurant parking lot while he and Pete smoked. He and his girlfriend, Pipe's sister, were fighting. She'd called him a rat. "Our women are representations of who we are and our lives," said Suge. Inside the restaurant, Suge pulled up Twin's picture from a Facebook page on my iPhone. "That look he has in the picture is the same look he gave me when I killed him," he said. A few weeks earlier, Twin's brother had written to Suge on Facebook asking for a meeting. Suge was thinking about consenting. Pipe talked him out of it. "You crazy, man," he said. "He's setting you up."

We talked for seven hours. "You sure you can handle the story of Sex Money Murder, JG?" said Pipe. "It ain't no joke." I pulled out a *New York Times* piece about the Thanksgiving Day shooting. Suge read it while I talked with Pipe. "Yo, look at Yolanda tellin'!" blurted Suge, pointing to one of the sources in the piece. Suge expected no one to talk in Soundview.

We ended the meeting, and Pipe and Suge asked to be dropped at the bodega on the corner to get some loosies. As I parked, I saw two Bloods coming our way. Pipe had seen them before I had. He didn't miss a beat as they marched up and threw down the Blood handshake, pulling their hands back to form the *B*. Pipe threw his forefingers in the air, the sign of the Sex Money Murder set. They spoke awhile before Suge and Pipe got back in the car, laughing. "Homeboy say they busting their joints over here at night in little beefs," Pipe said "Niggas will never learn." They were "food" for the Bloods, and yet here they were greeted warmly and unharmed. Suge and Pipe didn't explain why; the code was baroque and inconsistent.

We dropped Suge off at the Metro-North train station. From a thronging commuter train, Suge leaned out of the closing doors, his jeans drooping below his buttocks and his baseball cap with its oversized brim at a rakish angle. "I love you, JG!" he yelled at me. The few commuters pretended not to notice.

As I started my research, word leaked out that Suge and Pipe were working with a journalist on a book. I got a threatening email from Codd in March 2013. "All I ask you to do is be 2+2=4 before you go any further with this," he wrote.

But in the ensuing months, I came to respect both Suge and Pipe for their willingness to tell this story publicly, beyond most concerns for their own safety, so that the truth could be told. Pistol Pete had in some way devastated both their lives. Suge wanted it known that Pete had betrayed him. He felt no compunction about selling him out in return for his own benefit. And Pipe wanted people to know that he had never turned on Pete, despite everything that had happened. Both men say they still love him.

To tell the full story, I needed O'Malley and Forcelli as well. Forcelli agreed and offered support. O'Malley at first demurred. He hated the limelight and went out of his way to avoid it. When a documentary was made about Pistol Pete, producers approached O'Malley, and he declined to cooperate. "I don't like kicking a man when he is down," he said. "Look, I just wanted to help Suge and Pipe by connecting them with you. They wanted to tell their story. This isn't about John O'Malley."

I told him that I needed to explore the complexities of a serious racketeering case and the process of flipping cooperators. He knew that there was value in revealing the benefits of the federal system, in terms of both reducing crime and offering those who cooperate a fresh start. The revolving door of the state system increases gang membership because inmates are compelled to join gangs to survive in prison, but those who cooperate federally are alienated from their neighborhoods and have to start anew once they're released. O'Malley wanted the same system they'd used at the Southern District—federal intervention and the flipping of cooperators by former detectives from the neighborhoods—to be implemented in Chicago, Baltimore, and other cities, where the murders of young black men had skyrocketed. He agreed to be interviewed.

✦ ✦ ✦

ALL NEW YORKERS know the small one-paragraph mentions of murders that are a regular diet of the daily newspapers, the latest violent death of a young black kid—sometimes an abstraction to readers in Manhattan and elsewhere. May as well be happening in another country. But just north of my Manhattan apartment was a world as dangerous and ruthless as any I had experienced as a journalist reporting in the favelas of Brazil, the garrisons of Kingston, Jamaica, or the killing fields of Colombia.

In working on this book, I was surprised to find how many of those daily murders in the newspapers were connected. I sat for hours in the Bronx DA's office and watched murder scene footage and recognized the same names over and over: Sex Money Murder members or associates. I was shocked, too, to realize that my own life had brushed up against so much of the territory of this story. A family friend, a federal agent, had, it turned out, arrested Suge.

In the begining I had a sense that Suge and Pipe had been molded by their environment. But after the first two meetings and then scores of phone calls late into the night, it became obvious that the two were markedly different, and in many ways unrepresentative of Soundview.

In the summer of 2013, Suge and I began a voyage into his past, starting in Springfield. In a restaurant we ran into one of his old friends, recently out of the federal penitentiary. With expensive gold fronts and his arms etched in ink, he took one look at me at the bar and pulled back, asking to speak to Suge privately. When, after a long, playful exchange on their own, they came back to join me, the other man asked, "You sure you're not a cop?" He looked into my face as if peering through a dusty window. I shook my head. "Man, you need to get at least a tattoo or something. You're way too clean-cut. How you going to roll with my boy Sugar if you look like the 5-0?" When I said I hadn't found anything I liked enough to mark my body with permanently, he screwed up his face in surprise at my English accent. "Shit, nigga sounds like Hugh Grant. What the fuck?"

A few days later my wife dropped into the café where Suge and I were talking. She brought along our newborn son. Suge blushed deeply. "Why didn't you tell me your wife was coming, JG?" He picked at his black hoodie and jeans. "I'm dressed like a street thug, like I'm about to do somethin'. If I'd have known I woulda dressed nice." Suge fussed over our son. When my wife started to put the car seat on the ground temporarily to remove her coat, he jumped out of his seat. "You can't put li'l JG on the floor!" He picked up the baby, clearing a space at the table.

I began to see a radical disconnect between how he viewed people and how they viewed him. When we went to a bodega in the north end of Springfield, he wanted the owner to tell me stories about his old exploits on the block. A small man with a mustache stood behind the counter, chatting pleasantly to one of his customers. When he caught sight of Suge standing in the doorway, a look of pure terror crossed his face. He ducked behind the counter and seemed to be reaching for a weapon. Suge had expected a warm reception. He couldn't understand the man's fear. After we interviewed Gina, his former girlfriend, who told me about buying several of each outfit in case Suge tore one up in jealousy, we took a break in Robinson State Park. "I never knew she did that, JG," he said sorrowfully, in a moment of introspection. "I feel bad." We sat looking out at the river, and Suge seemed disappointed with himself. Within minutes he was on his cell phone, shouting at his son, who was caught up in gang life. Regret was fleeting.

+ + +

AS I GOT to know Suge, I experienced the darker and more unpredictable side of his personality. Even after our second meeting, his temper rose; he pulled out of the project before agreeing to it again, a situation that recurred often over the five years it took to report this book. Sometimes he threatened me on the phone. O'Malley told me that he suspected Suge suffered from a bipolar disorder.

I called Pipe to see what was up. "Listen, JG," he said. "Suge's out of line. We never carried ourselves like that in the street, and we don't carry ourselves like that now. Suge needs to fall back into line or I'll have to straighten him out." Pipe reminded me of an old Mafia godfather, the old-fashioned outliers who held out against narcotics trafficking.

When Suge stepped off a bus in November 2013—after shouting at me on the phone from New York—he gave me a firm hug, joking and slapping me on the back. Reluctantly, I smiled. "Yo, you and Pipe is close," he said somewhat suspiciously. "Thank you for letting me express myself." That was Suge. His mood could turn on a dime, from deadly rage to sappy warmth.

Meanwhile, Pipe mentored me in the code of the street. He taught me how to spot liars, to read when someone was faking moves, and, crucially, how to move in the neighborhoods. Pipe and I slipped into Soundview several times from late 2013 onward, driving through Cozy Corner to see how the neighborhood had changed. It became second nature for me to roll the seat back so that my head was protected by the door post and to drive hunched over the wheel, a baseball cap tipped low. Pipe told me not to pull directly alongside a car with tinted windows and flashy rims, to hang back a few feet so our heads were not level with its doors. When he caught me reading Machiavelli once, he said, "That shit'll help you understand Suge."

I asked Pipe if he felt he might get Suge a job at the hospital. I knew how hard it was to land work as a felon. "Are you joking, JG?" he said.

"Boy would lose his temper within the first two days or smoke himself stupid with the first paycheck and not go back. I ain't puttin' my job on the line."

We spoke about their relationship. "One thing with Suge," said Pipe, "is that he would ride it out with you no matter what. He is loyal to the end. If I ever have a problem, I'm not going to call JO, I'm going to call Suge and I'm going to call Ro." But as Pipe drifted further from his old life, he realized that Suge would only do so with an incentive, that his allegiance was fierce but strictly conditional on how it would benefit himself. I realized at some point that Pipe had never told Suge where he lived.

✦   ✦   ✦

AFTER A YEAR or so, Pipe trusted me enough to introduce me to Ro and his ailing father. In an apartment jammed with pit bulls and a blasting television, Ro, his body sculpted by the weight bench, broke down the tragedy of Twin's murder. Suspicious of me at first, he eventually told me that he had cried after they killed him. Pipe's father spoke about his own years as a gangster and a loan shark, his struggle with heroin addiction, and his time in prison.

As Suge's and Pipe's narratives diverged, I wondered what it was about Suge—who had it easier than Pipe, by some stretch—that prevented him from settling into a straight civilian life. "As long as I don't kill no one, I'm good," he always answered me. "No one's perfect. My life ain't no fairy tale."

Suge lead a progressively itinerant and rootless life, surviving on craftiness and animal instinct. He made friends quickly, and burned them just as fast. Every few weeks he would change cell numbers and I'd get calls from different area codes: Vermont, Florida, various parts of New York, and other places. He might find a job but last no more than eight weeks before drifting away, drawn back to the dissolute life of the street. He lived a life on the run, a man on self-destruct who obscured his past and yet reveled in it, existing on charity and some he knew in the gang life who put him up before he moved on after a falling-out, or a fresh arrest.

In the early summer of 2014, Pipe called to say that Suge had gotten caught up with a crew and was hustling in Harlem, and that it wasn't safe for me to meet with him anymore. "I just don't want Suge to get hurt in the streets," Pipe said. "He plays too close to the edge."

I pulled back for a few months, and Pipe did, too. It was a familiar pattern by now.

✚ ✚ ✚

WHEN I started this book, I hoped to interview members of the Soundview community, but most attempts to reach ordinary residents met with defeat. I called those who had been at the Weed and Seed ceremony. No one returned my calls. I emailed; no one answered. I called the Catholic church. No one called back. I met with prominent local activists who derided my attempts to write about the neighborhood as "poverty porn." Promises of help never materialized.

✚ ✚ ✚

THE SILENCE was broken by Mike Dunkley, who met me in a Brooklyn Starbucks, and later Mrs. Hines, who welcomed me into her home in the Melrose projects and relived the murder of her son. Her eldest son had just died of leukemia, having spent his last months in her apartment. She kept a big box of Karlton's letters from the Maine Institute, and letters from colleges that had invited him to come play basketball, Syracuse among them. There was a scrapbook of local newspaper clippings about his basketball games. She pulled out a picture of him in a long fur coat, standing with Carlos Mestre, also murdered by Rollock. "That's the hustler's fur," she said. "When you making money."

By the time we met she had come to terms with Karlton's passing, and even offered forgiveness to Rollock. "I pray for him," she said. "But he still has to do the time."

As I got to know Pipe and he began to turn his life around, he had been coming to a different realization. "I don't know about Pete sometimes," he said, half joking, as we sat in a fast food restaurant in October 2014. "Maybe he would have killed me, too?"

Pipe and I continued our meetings into 2015 and beyond as he drifted further from the life. We drove to the Bronx and met with Chantal and one of Pipe's sons. As we sat in the car, a couple of gangbangers walked past with their pants drooping down, exposing their boxer shorts. "Look at those little motherfuckers with their pants on the ground," said Pipe derisively, implying as he always did that nothing matched Sex Money Murder's professionalism in violence. "We ain't rockin' that pants-on-the-ground shit back in the day. I wore my burner in my belt, yo. How the fuck you wear a gun when you can't even tuck it into your pants? Shit."

O'Malley emailed me every few weeks to stay in touch. He had revised his assessment of Pipe. He felt his rehabilitation was genuine.

PIPE EXPLAINED the appeal of his old life: "You become addicted. You become addicted to the money. You become addicted to the celebrity status. You become addicted to all the fame and attention you get from these bitches, know what I'm saying? So the power you get, even the love that you get from your dudes—know what I mean?"

In the summer of 2015, I returned to Soundview Park, which had been made over. The view from the roof where Suge had planned the Thanksgiving murder was now obscured by a waterfront condominium complex. The Friends of Soundview Park, who had cleaned up the park and the Bronx River, had turned a place once choked with weeds and garbage into a lawn where local cricket teams in brightly colored uniforms hit sixes with a soft thwock over the emerald green. The Army Corps of Engineers was reclaiming the salt marshes with clumps of cordgrass. Children played around coolers while parents lounged in beach chairs, the grass glistening from a recent microburst of rain.

O'Malley and I took a final drive around the Bronx. We drove to Soundview, where $400,000 condos dotted his old neighborhood. And in the Fortieth Precinct, a war zone, where the C & C crew and the hit man Justice had once roamed the streets, we saw millennials in skinny jeans and oversized Ray-Ban aviators heading into loft apartments.

Developers called it the Piano District. "No one invests in an area where bullets are flying," said O'Malley, thrilled to see the progress.

But the Soundview Houses were impervious to change. A man was shot and killed outside 1725 Randall Avenue, Suge's old building, a few days after we drove through.

Over the course of writing *Sex Money Murder*, I did several tours with the police in the area. A couple of cops took me on a vertical patrol in the houses. The stairwells still smelled of urine; there was a broken toilet seat in one and some syringes in another. Blood graffiti marked the walls. On Cozy Corner, knots of youths looked at me venomously, eyeing my camera. "It's fed TV," they said, sidling off into the night. I did a four-to-midnight tour with a patrol car in the Forty-Third. On the walls of the muster room were the faces of the new gangs controlling the area: a new Crips set, the Stratford Avenue Crew, rubbed up against territory dominated by the Morrison Avenue Boys, a Blood set. The angry faces reminded me of Suge and Pipe, and of the constant churning of young lives lost to gang culture. A young homicide detective from the Forty-Third told me: "We arrest gangbangers and they talk about Pistol Pete like he's some fuckin' Robin Hood. I'm like, 'He didn't give anything to you or your family—why's he Robin Hood to you?' Then they look at me like I'm the one who's nuts. All it would take is another drug like crack, and all this will go up again."

+ + +

O'MALLEY RETIRED in 2015. With the feds he'd solved well over four hundred homicides and put away some of New York's most dangerous men. Sex Money Murder was one of the last big crews that had had a long run—almost ten years from inception. When O'Malley left the Southern District, street crews like Sex Money Murder were generally in handcuffs within a year or two, certainly after the first couple of homicides.

Crime dropped in New York City from 1990 to 2000 twice as much as in any other major American city; it became known as "the New York miracle." The biggest decrease in homicides in all boroughs was in the Bronx, partially attributed by some to the work of O'Malley and Glazer.

O'Malley declined a big farewell function, but Liz Glazer held a private party to celebrate his career. They presented him with an inscribed mug. It read:

> *John O'Malley*
> *Slayer of Kings*
> *Master of Preachers*
> *Bleeder of Bloods*
> *And Our Guiding Light*
> *For 20 Years and Forever*
> *USAO SDNY 1994–2015*

The head of the FBI, James Comey, had gotten to know O'Malley while working as a Southern District prosecutor, and they had both been involved in Bemo's conviction. He called to offer his regards.

✦ ✦ ✦

EARLIER THAT year O'Malley had watched his son receive the gold shield as a newly minted detective for his service on the police force and a SWAT team. He'd be the third-generation O'Malley family detective.

O'Malley's house buzzed with excitement. The family would drive in a small procession to the town hall. John thought back to Danny in his "detective suit" at church when he was eight years old, and all those times the phone would ring with Justice on the other end. He regretted that Annie's father, a legendary Bronx detective, wasn't around to see his grandson receive the gold shield. As the family got ready to climb into their cars, the TV blared in the corner of the house: Fox News was broadcasting a wave of protests aimed at police treatment of African Americans. In some ways, O'Malley felt relief that his father-in-law wasn't around to witness the backlash, and eventual murders of policemen, after the deaths of Michael Brown and Eric Garner.

In the course of his career O'Malley had seen 800 to 1,000 dead bodies—all beyond the glare of TV cameras or social activists who had never been inside a New York City housing project controlled by a gang.

He wished that people could walk in his shoes for one day: make an arrest of a violent felon like Justice, explain to grieving mothers in the projects about their slaughtered loved ones, all the while being treated with scorn as they attempted to find the killer.

O'Malley switched off the news. Just before they left, his cell phone rang. It was Suge, calling about his own son. He had been arrested with a loaded .380 handgun while out on bail on another gun charge.

"Can I get your advice?" Suge asked O'Malley.

Suge, forty and a grandfather, was still the indestructible gunslinger, the wily criminal who could read the streets. He was still Sex Money Murder royalty. But he didn't want his son to go to jail—didn't want to lose his boy to the same cycle of violence. O'Malley and Suge were dealing with sons who had chosen the same paths as their fathers, but on opposite ends of the law. It seemed the cycle would never end.

And then came the call from O'Malley that I knew someday would come. Suge himself had been arrested in Florida on multiple charges, including possession of a firearm as a felon and domestic abuse. "I think I said that Suge would be in jail or dead by the time you finished your book," O'Malley said. "I'm sad to say I was right."

After my phone went quiet for five months, I received a call from a Florida number. "Yo, it's Sugar," came that husky and resilient voice. "I beat the case. Nothing like a little incarceration to focus your mind."

POSTSCRIPT

In the summer of 2017, shortly after I completed this book, Pipe was arrested at his home on a charge filed by his wife, with whom he had been having marital issues over a potential divorce and custody of their child. Pipe is being held in jail, but how these charges will play out is anybody's guess. Suge was arrested in Brooklyn after he was caught fleeing from police and charged with possession of a gun. Detectives were unable to prove that his DNA was on the loaded weapon they recovered, and he was released from custody in December 2017.

Pete Forcelli won a battle with the lung cancer he contracted as a result of his role as a first responder at 911, and he is now a special agent in charge of the Miami Field Division of the ATF. He was a whistle-blower in the Fast and Furious case and testified before Congress about lazy police work and the US attorney's office's reluctance to prosecute straw purchasers buying guns for Mexican drug cartels. Both Pete Forcelli and John O'Malley have gone on to provide crucial evidence and testimony in freeing the wrongfully convicted, including five people from Soundview who were sentenced to twenty-five years to life for the murder of a cabdriver in September 1997. One of them, Eric Glisson, wrote to the Southern District asking for help. His letter was passed on to O'Malley in June 2012. O'Malley and Forcelli knew it was Sex Money Murder who had carried out the killing; two members had admitted shooting a cabdriver in Soundview, although at the time no victim had been recorded at the Forty-Third. O'Malley and Forcelli got the Bronx DA to reopen the case, and eighteen years after they first went into prison, Eric Glisson and the four others were released.

O'Malley and Forcelli continue to work on other innocence cases.

Acknowledgments

John O'Malley offered me his unstinting support over the five years it has taken to produce this book. He has saved countless lives in his work, and I'm deeply honored he let me tell his remarkable story. I am forever in your debt, my friend.

Pipe has been my guide and mentor into the world of Sex Money Murder, and without him none of this would have come to fruition. Men like Pipe don't give their trust easily, and I'm grateful to him for his equanimity and kindness. When the going got tough I'd hear, "I got you, JG!" Maximum respect, Pipe, for the man you've become when the deck was stacked against you.

Pete Forcelli was instrumental in helping me understand the perilous world of a Bronx housing cop in the 1990s and exactly what it took him, and other brave men like him, to take down a major crew like Sex Money Murder to make New York safer.

My wife and young family endured my long absences from home and the nights I was locked in my office on the phone. They have lived with the characters in this book as much as I have, and they are the reason I do everything I do. As ever, I owe my thanks to my father, Anthony Green, always my first reader, who researched statistics and always provided inspiration and love.

Writing a nonfiction book is an adventure. But even before I had a book idea, my friend and agent, Deborah Grosvenor, believed in me. She offered encouragement when I needed it most, a rigorous opinion that has saved me more than once, and unwavering support at every step, and always with grace and wisdom.

Special thanks to John Glusman, editor in chief at Norton, and his assistant, Lydia Brents, who understood what I hoped to achieve with this book when it was merely at the proposal stage, and passionately shared my vision as it developed. John has championed this book at every step of the process, and improved the manuscript immeasurably with a highly skilled and painstaking edit.

Liz Glazer, a crusader, and her incredible team at the Southern District of New York were selfless with their time and connections, enabling me to get to more angles of the story. Nicole LaBarbera helped me even when she didn't want to relive the Sex Money Murder trials, out of selflessness and simply because I asked. Many other prosecutors and sources helped but chose to remain anonymous, and I am in their debt. Bob Ryan filled me with enthusiasm for the Bronx. Dave Burroughs of the FBI exemplifies the high caliber of the team. And thanks to Helen Cantwell for the court transcripts and the help in understanding some of her cases.

Suge, thanks for your quick wit, although I think we'd both agree ours was a tough working relationship, full of ups and downs, as I sought to discover the truth. Now you know the road to publication is a long and difficult one, and while I hope you agree that what is on the page is true, you understand that is all I ever sought to show.

Pipe's lawyer, Stefanie "SP" Plaumann, took me into her confidence and offered a deep understanding of the work of a defense lawyer. Aime Ely, a former AUSA at the Southern District of New York, helped me get legal aspects correct. I am grateful to my connections in Massachusetts: Liz Dineen and Stephen E. Spelman, former drug and crimes prosecutor in the Hampden County District Attorney's office. Thanks to private detective and former state trooper Mike Chapdelaine and former ATF special agent Jim Markowski (know that Fifth Avenue always says thank you!).

I'm blessed with some great friends in the NYPD. My buddy Lt.

Paul "Pablito" Marren escorted me around the Bronx projects on interviews and made connections on my behalf. Onward! Inspector Mike C. Phipps, commanding officer of Housing Borough Bronx/Queens, guided me around Soundview and helped with historical details. And a thank you to Stanley Schiffman, who first connected me with John O'Malley and whose stream of jokes brightens the darkest day. And my particular gratitude to Lt. Sean O'Toole at Bronx Homicide, who donated valuable expertise and time over several visits.

Thanks also to Professor Daniel Richman, Gil Lugo, James Palumbo, Walter Arsenault, Tom Bevins, Terry Tadeo, Rob Berger, Eric Van Allen, Bob Addolorato, and Joe Marrero, who all gave me valuable insight into how a major racketeering case goes. US Marshal Michael Greco gave me a tour of MCC. Rafael Curbelo at the Bronx DA's office patiently answered all my FOIAs and let me view murder scene footage.

I'm blessed to have some richly supportive colleagues, like some of those found in the writing community at Goucher's MFA in Creative Nonfiction program. My gratitude to Dick Todd, Jacob Levenson, Leslie Rubinowski, and fellow writers Theo Emery and Sam Starnes, who both read the manuscript and offered sage advice.

My friend Todd Pitock made shrewd suggestions on how to improve the manuscript and, as ever, was always there to offer his astute support. Sam Douglas helped improve the work hugely.

The dialogue and detail in this book would not have reached the level they have without the work of my longtime friend Jamie Pastor Bolnick, who has transcribed my interviews for years, and pushed on through hundreds of hours of interviews with Suge and Pipe, transcribing them with meticulous attention to nuance. And a salute to Ian Astbury of The Cult, an icon who became a friend and inspiration. My singular appreciation to Mary Gilliatt, who first showed a direction-seeking eighteen-year-old from rural England the dizzying wonder of New York City, a magical place where all might be possible, and suggested that a career in writing might offer some excitement.

And thanks to Professor Ric Curtis, David Brotherton, Tim Lavin,

Matt Postal, Matthew Deighton at Ancestry.com, Sarah Church, Kristen Sherborn, Laura Tsoi at the Bronx Historical Society, Sheila Lowe, Professor Michael Newman, Brendan Koerner, and Paige Williams. And to anyone I have omitted or those countless dozens who didn't want to be named but helped me—thank you.

Select Bibliography

Endnotes for Sex Money Murder *can be found at* jonathangreenonline.com.

Books

Adler, William M. *Land of Opportunity: One Family's Quest for the American Dream in the Age of Crack*. New York: Atlantic Monthly Press, 1995.

Anderson, Elijah. *Code of the Street: Decency, Violence, and the Moral Life of the Inner City*. New York: W. W. Norton, 1999.

Black, Timothy. *When a Heart Turns Rock Solid: The Lives of Three Puerto Rican Brothers on and off the Streets*. New York: Vintage, 2009.

Bourgois, Philippe. *In Search of Respect: Selling Crack in El Barrio*. Cambridge: Cambridge University Press, 1995.

Brown, Ethan. *Queens Reigns Supreme: Fat Cat, 50 Cent, and the Rise of the Hip-Hop Hustler*. New York: Anchor, 2005.

———. *Snitch: Informants, Cooperators, and the Corruption of Justice*. New York: PublicAffairs, 2007.

Butterfield, Fox. *All God's Children: The Bosket Family and the American Tradition of Violence*. New York: Knopf, 1995.

Caro, Robert A. *The Power Broker: Robert Moses and the Fall of New York*. New York: Vintage, 1974.

Century, Douglas. *Street Kingdom: Five Years Inside the Franklin Avenue Posse*. New York: Warner Books, 2000.

Chang, Jeff. *Can't Stop Won't Stop: A History of the Hip-Hop Generation*. New York: Picador, 2005.

Conlon, Edward. *Blue Blood*. New York: Penguin, 2004.

DeVillo, Stephen Paul. *The Bronx River in History and Folklore*. Charleston, SC: History Press, 2013.

Diaz, Louis, and Neal Hirschfeld. *Dancing with the Devil: Confessions of an Undercover Agent.* New York: Pocket Star Books, 2010.

Dumanovsky, Tamara. "Crime in Poor Places: Examining the Neighborhood Context of NYC's Public Housing Projects." Ph.D. diss., New York University, Graduate School of Arts and Science, 1999.

Dyson, Michael Eric. *Holler If You Hear Me: Searching for Tupac Shakur.* New York: Basic Books, 2003.

Earley, Pete, and Gerald Shur. *WITSEC: Inside the Federal Witness Protection Program.* New York: Bantam Books, 2002.

English, T. J. *The Savage City: Race, Murder, and a Generation on the Edge.* New York: William Morrow, 2011.

Faison, Azie, with Agyei Tyehimba. *Game Over: The Rise and Transformation of a Harlem Hustler.* New York: Atria Books, 2007.

Feige, David. *Indefensible: One Lawyer's Journey into the Inferno of American Justice.* New York: Little Brown, 2006.

Goffman, Alice. *On the Run: Fugitive Life in an American City.* Chicago: University of Chicago Press: 2014.

Jonnes, Jill. *South Bronx Rising: The Rise, Fall, and Resurrection of an American City.* 2nd ed. New York: Fordham University Press, 2002.

Kennedy, Dave M. *Don't Shoot: One Man, a Street Fellowship, and the End of Violence in Inner-City America.* New York: Bloomsbury, 2011.

Kozol, Jonathan. *Amazing Grace: The Lives of Children and the Conscience of a Nation.* New York: Random House, 1995.

Leovy, Jill. *Ghettoside: A True Story of Murder in America.* New York: Random House, 2015.

Levenson, Jacob. *The Secret Epidemic: The Story of AIDS and Black America.* New York: Pantheon, 2004.

McAlary, Mike. *Cop Shot: The True Story of a Murder That Shocked the Nation.* New York: Jove Books, 1992.

McDonald, Brian. *My Father's Gun: One Family, Three Badges, One Hundred Years in the NYPD.* New York: Plume, 2000.

Raab, Selwyn. *Five Families: The Rise, Decline, and Resurgence of America's Most Powerful Empires.* New York: Thomas Dunne Books/St. Martin's Press, 2005.

Reinaman, Craig, and Harry G. Levine. *Crack in America: Demon Drugs and Social Justice*. Berkeley and Los Angeles: University of California Press, 1997.

Rollock, Team. *Trigga*. Montgomery, Alabama: E-BookTime LLC, 2006.

Shalhoup, Mara. *BMF: The Rise and Fall of Big Meech and the Black Mafia Family*. New York: St. Martin's Press, 2010.

Thomas, Piri. *Down These Mean Streets*. New York: Vintage Books, 1997.

Umbach, Fritz. *The Last Neighborhood Cops: The Rise and Fall of Community Policing in New York Public Housing*. New Brunswick, NJ: Rutgers University Press, 2011.

Walker, Tom. *Fort Apache, Bronx, NY: Life at the 41st*. Longwood, FL: JBL Publications, 1976.

Waters, Luke. *NYPD Green: A Memoir*. New York: Touchstone, 2015.

Williams, Terry. *The Cocaine Kids: The Inside Story of a Teenage Drug Ring*. New York: Da Capo Press, 1989.

———. *Crackhouse: Notes from the End of the Line*. New York: Penguin, 1992.

Zirin, James D. *The Mother Court: Tales of Cases That Mattered in America's Greatest Trial Court*. New York: American Bar Association Publishing, 2014.

Index

Note: Street names or pseudonyms are used for many individuals.